COLLECTED ESSAYS IN LAW

Living Law

Collected Essays in Law Series

General Editor: Tom D. Campbell

Legal Rules and Legal Reasoning

Larry Alexander

ISBN: 978 0 7546 2004 4

Dispute Processing and Conflict Resolution

Carrie Menkel-Meadow

ISBN: 978 0 7546 2305 2

Objectivity in Ethics and Law

Michael Moore

ISBN: 978 0 7546 2329 8

Crime, Compliance and Control

Doreen McBarnet

ISBN: 978 0 7546 2349 6

Democracy Through Law

Johan Steyn

ISBN: 978 0 7546 2404 2

Legal Reasoning, Legal Theory and Rights

Martin P. Golding

ISBN: 978 0 7546 2669 5

Meaning, Mind and Law

Dennis Patterson

ISBN: 978 0 7546 2749 4

Living Law
Studies in Legal and Social Theory

Roger Cotterrell

ISBN: 978 0 7546 2710 4

Roger Cotterrell

Living Law

Studies in Legal and Social Theory

ASHGATE

Published by
Dartmouth Publishing Company Limited
Gower House
Croft Road
Aldershot
Hampshire GU11 3HR
England

Ashgate Publishing Company
Suite 420
101 Cherry Street
Burlington, VT 05401-4405
USA

Ashgate website: http://www.ashgate.com

British Library Cataloguing in Publication Data
Cotterrell, Roger (Roger B. M.)
    Living law : Studies in legal and social theory. -
    (Collected essays in law)
    1. Sociological jurisprudence 2. Law - Philosophy
    I. Title
    340.1'15

Library of Congress Control Number: 2007941043

ISBN: 978 0 7546 2710 4

Printed in Great Britain by TJ International Ltd, Padstow, Cornwall

Contents

Acknowledgements

Grateful acknowledgement is made to the following for their kind permission to reprint essays included in this volume: Association Droit et Société (Chapter 6); Blackwell Publishing Ltd. (Chapters 1, 7 and 12); Boom Juridische Uitgevers (Chapter 19); Cambridge University Press (Chapter 20); Edwin Mellen Press (Chapter 18); NoFo (No Foundations) Journal, Helsinki (Chapter 2); Oñati International Institute for the Sociology of Law (Chapter 10); Oxford University Press (Chapters 3, 14 and 16); Rowman & Littlefield Publishers Inc. (Chapter 5); Sacher Institute of Comparative Law, Hebrew University of Jerusalem (Chapter 13); Sage Publications Ltd (Chapter 8); Springer Science and Business Media (Chapter 17); Student Bar Association, National Law School of India University (Chapter 21); Taylor & Francis Group (Chapter 4).

Roger Cotterrell is Anniversary Professor of Legal Theory at Queen Mary and Westfield College, University of London, and a Fellow of the British Academy. He was Acting Head and Head of the College's Department of Law (1989–91), Dean of the Faculty of Laws (1993–6) and Professor of Legal Theory (1990–2005). He studied law as an undergraduate and postgraduate at University College London, and sociology and politics as a postgraduate at London University's Birkbeck College, and began his academic career at the University of Leicester (1969–73). He has been a Trustee of the Law and Society Association [USA] and has held visiting academic postitions in Belgium, Hong Kong, Spain, Sweden and the United States.

Series Editor's Preface

Collected Essays in Law makes available some of the most important work of scholars who have made a major contribution to the study of law. Each volume brings together a selection of writings by a leading authority on a particular subject. The series gives authors an opportunity to present and comment on what they regard as their most important work in a specific area. Within their chosen subject area, the collections aim to give a comprehensive coverage of the authors' research. Care is taken to include essays and articles which are less readily accessible and to give the reader a picture of the development of the authors' work and an indication of research in progress.

For Ann

---

and in memory of

Walter Leslie Cotterrell (1897–1977)

and

Hilda Margaret Randle Cotterrell (1910–1970)

Introduction

The contents of this volume have been chosen to avoid including any material already published in two earlier collections of my essays. One of these, *Law, Culture and Society* (2006), focused on comparative law, the relations of law and culture, and general problems of developing sociological interpretations of legal ideas. The other, *Law's Community* (1995), contained essays on legal theory from the 1980s and 1990s. The present volume, much broader in scope than either of those previous books, emphasises recent work but also draws on research from the whole of my career. It aims to show how law – especially juristic ideas and lawyers' ways of reasoning – can be studied consistently from a sociological perspective, in the light of the social theory that I think is an essential aid to understanding it.

Legal Theory and Social Theory

The subject matter covered in the book is diverse but the underlying aim in all the chapters is constant: to develop legal theory as a kind of social theory. In other words, I have tried to treat the study of legal ideas and practices as a window on the social world and to find ways to make it possible to see law as 'a great anthropological document' – to quote the resounding phrase of Justice Oliver Wendell Holmes (1899: 444). I am not sure how far Holmes, the pragmatic American lawyer and Supreme Court judge, treated his words seriously. Taken at face value, however, this image of law as an anthropological document is powerful. It suggests that, if law is studied imaginatively with the aid of the social sciences and history, it can be seen as much more than a set of technical or rhetorical resources for lawyers to harness to their clients' interests. In one of its important aspects law is certainly that, but it is also a crystallisation or sedimentation of widely-felt moral and political aspirations and collective social experience.

It has even been claimed that if 'we know the law of any society, we have an excellent outline of the nature of the social system as a whole' (Fletcher 1981: 33). But this is not usually true if law is taken to be the law of the state and the ways of knowing it are restricted to lawyers' ways. Lawyers often think they know about social life because they know the legal rules that state institutions have laid down to govern it. But social scientists have shown that such confidence is misplaced. Knowing law as lawyers know it does not equate to knowing about social life, or even about the effective regulation and operative rules of social life. This was one of the most important lessons taught by the primary founder of sociology of law, Eugen Ehrlich (1936), whose work is addressed in detail in several essays in this book.

Law, treated as a structure of ideas, does not reveal in lawyers' typical juristic interpretations all the social knowledge embedded and reflected in it. Nor are lawyers necessarily interested in exploring all of this knowledge. A wide range of methods is needed to reveal the social meaning of legal ideas, and hence the significance of law in social life. Law expresses and shapes social experience in certain ways. Often this is, most directly, the experience of practising lawyers, judges, legislators and administrators, who create, interpret and apply the rules of law recognised by state institutions. But law would not have the social significance typically ascribed to it if all it reflected were the ideas and practices of legal officials and professionals. It reaches out into society in a broader sense because legal understandings are often widespread and profound social understandings, even if these are sometimes presented in law in distorted or oblique ways. It is part of the task of legal study to reveal the place of the legal in the social, and to interpret law as an important aspect of social experience. In this way legal study can, indeed, treat law as a great anthropological document.

To see the field of legal inquiry in this way is, however, only one way of seeing it. Law, as lawyers often approach it, is a matter of useful techniques: a way of solving immediate problems – making deals, resolving conflicts, winning benefits, defusing or making threats, achieving reform, organising co-operation, preventing action, neutralising opposition, harnessing power, pursuing claims and seeking justice. Law is the authoritative practical ideas that lawyers, legislators, administrators and judges shape and use to guide and order social (including economic and political) relations as these arise, develop, change and dissolve, endlessly mutating into new forms and manifestations.

Can the claim be made that social theory is necessary to aid these practical legal techniques? I think that this theory is needed to put law as a practice into a broader perspective than that of particular participants (and their advisers) in the everyday transactions, events and accidents with which law is concerned. In this broader perspective the possibilities and limits of legal strategies may be seen more clearly. Legal practices can be put into a context of wider experience, so that lessons can be learned from systematic knowledge of the effects of legal interventions in the past or in other comparable situations. More social scientific knowledge is still needed to clarify what kind of regulatory or governmental technique law is and, in the jurist Roscoe Pound's (1917) term from a century ago, 'the limits of effective legal action'. It is still necessary today to ask what 'effective' means (effective for whom, for what, in what circumstances, with what results?).

There might, however, be dissatisfaction (as I think there should be) with the idea of law as an instrument – in particular, the idea of law as a neutral means to achieve whatever purposes government chooses. If law is seen as a moral phenomenon – a complex embodiment of many different traditions, aspirations, beliefs, values and allegiances – then it should also be accepted that social research is needed to examine the moral conditions in which law exists. Legal philosophy often has much to say about what it tends to treat as universal or timeless moral dilemmas surrounding law, but it rarely shows much interest in systematic empirical study of moral conditions. By this I mean study of the ways in which people actually experience moral choices and moral problems, what parameters of moral decision they see themselves as operating within, and what moral values they recognise as appropriate to govern their actions in particular circumstances. When legal and moral philosophy consider moral issues they generally do so without much reference to what sociologists call social variation (cf Cotterrell and Selznick 2004: 296) – that is, the contrasting social experience of different categories of people in particular times and places. Often philosophers do not know how, or how far, moral considerations are significant in people's lives. But philosophers' speculations about the relations of law and morality may be of little value if they fail systematically to address this variability of social experience, or to consider how far philosophical analyses are relevant to people trying to solve moral dilemmas as *they* (rather than the philosophers) understand these.

Much philosophy, seeking the universal and the timeless, sees the details of empirical social variation as philosophically uninteresting.[1] But social theory, and legal theory if it is treated as part of social theory, must address problems in the historical and social contexts in which these problems arise, generalising only in so far as empirical evidence of these contexts seems to justify it. This does not mean that legal theory is powerless to address moral issues about law; this is surely one of its most important tasks, and many essays in this book are concerned with such issues. But when legal theory addresses moral issues it should see these as arising in particular types of community in particular historical conditions. So, the possibilities for legal theory to give convincing universal answers to questions about law and morality will be limited. But it can and should provide insight into the social conditions in which particular

---

1 Or as requiring such vast labour to consider systematically that an 'army' of researchers, 'lifetime-consuming empirical studies' and 'a mountain of data' would be required (Dworkin 2006: 166–7). The assumption here seems to be that to study *any* variation entails studying *all* variation – an impossible task. See also Green 2005: 574 (suggesting legal philosophers avoid issues about power 'as too particular and too empirical').

moral issues have (or do not have) practical meaning for citizens, and the parameters within which they find it worthwhile to discuss them.

Such theory can explain why debates about, for example, abortion, ecology, polygamy, democracy, slavery, liberty, honour, or obedience to law seem very important in some times and places but not others, or to some social groups but not others. It can consider what social conditions are likely to make debate on such matters seem meaningful, intractable or irrelevant; or to make answers seem obvious, at least to some people in the light of their experience. It can show why moral questions take entirely different forms in different contexts. Legal theory, as envisaged in this book, cannot tell people what to think on moral questions related to law; it cannot relieve individuals from making moral judgments for themselves. But it can make their judgments better informed. It can and should clarify legal and social contexts in which issues are presented and so help in understanding the moral conditions in which law exists and the range of practical moral choices available.

Law, Sociology and Legal Philosophy

The concept of law adopted here is not limited to the law recognised by lawyers and by state institutions and officials. A pluralist concept of law, such as I adopt, accepts that legal doctrine is produced, interpreted and applied not only by 'official' institutions of the nation state but also by other institutions (for example, by international regulatory agencies, corporations, religious institutions, commercial networks and community organisations). Nevertheless, state law, in many societies, is the most intricately and deliberately developed law; it is often the law expounded, interpreted and enforced most generally and publicly – at least it is widely seen to have these characteristics, associated with the doctrine of the rule of law. That does not make it necessarily the most important or effective social regulation in these societies but usually gives it a certain prominence that legal theory recognises. Perhaps the law of the nation state is beginning to lose this prominence as transnational and intranational regulation, not tied to state institutions, become more significant. Here as elsewhere, legal theory must be alert to processes of change. As noted earlier, what distinguishes sociologically-informed legal theory (legal theory as part of social theory) from much contemporary legal philosophy is its constant focus on social (including legal) variation and its distrust of purportedly timeless philosophical knowledge.

These ideas about law are not typical among legal scholars. In rejecting the universalising approaches of much current legal philosophy, sociologically-informed legal theory adopts a critical or distanced view of this philosophy – and so of much of the literature that lawyers tend to turn to when they look for general legal theory. In recent years I have focused on the idea of different types of community as settings for law; thus, in this approach, law is always seen as rooted in diverse networks of social relations. The consequence is not just that law operates differently in different social settings but that the nature of law is determined by the variety of social conditions it expresses. The study of law's conceptual structures has to be rooted in sociology's systematic empirical understandings of social life. The very meanings that we give to the concept of law for purposes of study have to be similarly rooted.

On the other hand, the ideas about law reflected in this book are also far removed from those of most social scientists. Social scientists generally study legal phenomena in behavioural terms – in terms of the actions of, for example, lawyers, administrators, police or citizens – but my aim has been mainly to study law as patterns of ideas. So, despite the consistent commitment to developing sociological perspectives that runs throughout this book and all my work, I am very interested in a juristic outlook on law – that is, one that stresses the logics of interpretation, elaboration and development of legal ideas. Law as a 'great anthropological document' is, at least to a large extent, a document made up of legal doctrine – that is, rules, principles, concepts and values and the techniques or reasoning by which they are interpreted and given meaning.

However, law is as much a matter of practices as of ideas, so it is not just doctrine that is to be considered but *institutionalised* doctrine – ideas created, developed, interpreted and applied by specific agencies and institutions existing for this purpose. Furthermore, in a legal pluralist view it must not be assumed that the institutionalised doctrine that makes up law is restricted to that of the state legal system, recognised as legal by lawyers. Legal doctrine is not always institutionalised by the agencies of the state. It can, for example, be created (in a legal pluralist view) by religious bodies, disciplinary tribunals, trade or community associations, international agencies and organisations, and many other bodies. Lawyers will often not want to call some of the rules so produced 'law', but a sociologically-informed legal theory might often find it useful to do so for particular explanatory purposes. In any case, the focus remains on institutionalised doctrine. I started my career as a lawyer and I have remained throughout it a legal academic teaching legal doctrine to law students, so it is perhaps inevitable that my own research has tended always to return to the study of legal *ideas* in their practical settings, however fascinating I have found sociological behavioural studies to be.

Consequently, putting these essays together in this volume, I find myself in a strange position. I am a legal theorist committed to sociology but relatively unconcerned with some aspects of contemporary legal philosophy. Yet as a sociologist of law I am very interested in analytical jurisprudence and the study of legal concepts and other legal ideas. The essays reprinted here should be taken as an affirmation of an outlook that seeks to wed traditional juristic approaches and wider sociological approaches to legal study and attaches great value to both. I have found it necessary to study in depth the theories of law developed by legal philosophers, but the writers who mean most to me in this tradition are Anglo-American and Continental jurists, from the time of Jeremy Bentham and John Austin to the present day, who have tried to develop general conceptions of the nature of law that reflect lawyers' experience. In general I have not been influenced by philosophers seeking to solve problems set from within philosophy as a discipline. But I have found the efforts of analytical, historical and sociological jurists to make sense in general terms of law as a practice and as a system of ideas deeply interesting, despite what might be seen as the narrowness of many lawyers' perspectives on the social world. What is important is not to be satisfied with these jurists' accounts of law but to see them as valuable professional participant views that need to be relocated within broader social perspectives on the phenomena they address.

As regards sociology, I have tried to immerse myself in its theoretical literature perhaps more than many contemporary legal scholars have done. The aim has not been to develop a sociological jurisprudence – that is, to import social scientific ideas into legal thinking to help to solve problems of lawyers' practice and to improve judicial decision-making. I turned to sociology specifically to try to understand law better; to find ways of developing a kind of legal theory that would locate law as an aspect or field of social experience. If sociology can help to improve law, that is all to the good, but it has not been my overriding concern to help to bring that about. Sociological perspectives on law, for me, are important simply as a means of reading better Holmes' 'great anthropological document' and so learning from law about the nature of social life.

This is not, however, just a matter of using the study of law as a means to the end of acquiring sociological knowledge. As indicated earlier, to understand law as a social phenomenon in sociological terms is, amongst other things, to develop a broader, better informed perspective on lawyers' experience. The study of law – for law students no less than for social scientists – should not be just a study of useful rules. It should be a study of law's ideas, problems, origins, historical development and social consequences viewed as part of wider human experience. The great French sociologist Georges Gurvitch (1947) saw sociology of law as a part of a wider 'sociology of the human spirit'. This term sounds strange today but Gurvitch, committed both to juristic concerns and to sociology, at least captures the idea that the study of law as ideas in action should not be narrow and limited to practical problem-solving. It should reveal law as expressing more than transient and material concerns.

I am ambivalent about the literature of social science. There is much dull scholarship, especially using quantitative methods, that seems to cling to bloodless textbook stereotypes of scientific method. In this literature it is often hard to get a sense of the sweep of history, or the teeming detail of social life and the richness of social experience. Studies frequently report flat, small, cautious findings dwarfed by elaborate statistical analysis. I was lucky enough, when first systematically studying sociology, to be led to some of its best types of scholarship – including the hugely ambitious, wise and rich writings of the classic social theorists, especially Max Weber and Emile Durkheim, who saw so much about their own times, and about the history (and even the future) of Western societies. Not only did they offer the broadest perspectives available on these societies, but they also had sharp eyes for detail and offered insights on many special social problems and phenomena. Crucially, also, they had deep interests in law and saw it as centrally important for sociological study – an outlook which most of their sociological successors did not share and largely ignored. When I first studied the major social theorists systematically, I realised what immense (and at that time relatively undeveloped) potential this literature had for legal studies. It presented theory vast in scope but informed by empirical detail; and it was that combination – imaginative interpretive range and precise observation of social life – that made it powerful.

Good sociological work, however, is not just 'grand theory'. It includes sensitive, theoretically informed accounts of the life of particular neighbour-hoods, social groups or organisations – offering readers a window into different social worlds, portrayed in detail and thoughtfully interpreted. Early in my studies of sociology I encountered some of these accounts – ones that now have classic status in the sociological literature. Among the most memorable are the famous ethnographic, interview-based or participant observation studies of Chicago life in the early decades of the twentieth century (for example, the hobos, taxi-dancers, ghetto-dwellers, rich 'Gold Coast' residents, and the poor of 'Little Hell') produced under the guidance of the University of Chicago sociologists Robert Park and Ernest Burgess.[2] Evocative 'thick descriptions' (cf. Geertz 1973: ch. 1) of social life such as these eventually become documents of social history – thought-provoking lessons about social variation.

Such accounts are still produced, but more often by anthropologists (with their enduring tradition of ethnographic methods and less commitment to either social theory or statistical analysis) than by sociologists. Perhaps a descriptive sociology full of the sights, sounds and smells of social life is harder to achieve now when the pressure for methodological and theoretical rigour and disciplinary scientific respectability sometimes seems to chill the sociological

---

2   See e.g. Anderson 1923; Wirth 1928; Zorbaugh 1929; Cressey 1932; and, generally, Bulmer 1984.

imagination. Indeed, much graphic, illuminating social reporting is now the work of journalists. For them, the story is vitally important but, under pressure of deadlines and copy space, the care in its telling may not reach the standards of good empirical social research. It has been legal anthropologists and other scholars influenced by their methods who, in recent years, have contributed most to the detailed empirical study of variation in legal experience as an aspect of social experience in contemporary Western societies.

Background and Context

The approach to legal theory followed in this book reflects a personal journey and an evolution of ideas in which one case of indecision and two deliberate decisions have played a key part. The case of indecision occurred when I had to choose a subject to study at university. My father suggested practice as a solicitor as a good career. Lacking any better ideas of my own I went along with this and studied law, deciding in the second year of undergraduate legal studies (when I at last began to think seriously about the matter) that a life as a practising lawyer did not appeal. I was interested in ideas and not in any of the practical tasks that solicitors seemed to undertake. And at that time I did not think that studying law could contribute to what I thought of as knowledge. I saw law only as lawyers' practical 'know-how'. A compulsory course on 'Jurisprudence and Legal Theory' in the final undergraduate year suggested for the first time, however, that legal study could be more satisfying. Legal realism (in both its American and Scandinavian varieties) and sociological and historical jurisprudence seemed most attractive. At this stage I made the first conscious decision that shaped my career, deciding to become a university teacher. I thought that as an academic it would be possible to aim for a life of scholarship and to study law in ways that escaped the immediate practical requirements of the legal professions and would allow for more enduring theoretical inquiries.

Things turned out not to be so simple. As a lecturer, from the beginning of the 1970s, I felt that much of what I taught, even in jurisprudence courses, did not extend beyond lawyers' typical professional outlook. I thought of this outlook as narrow because it looked at the world only through the insights that lawyers gained in interpreting legal rules. It looked 'inwards' to the traditions and preconceptions of professional legal and judicial practice, rather than outwards towards social inquiry, and what I thought of as real knowledge. I became fixated on the idea that lawyers' knowledge of valid law was not knowledge at all, because its status could be altered arbitrarily (even sometimes accidentally) by a new court decision or legislative provision. As a result it could cease to be useful legal knowledge through the stroke of a pen or the word of a judge. Surely the study of law must be able to produce a kind of understanding more enduring, more amenable to cumulative development? I started to look enviously towards the social sciences with their professional curiosity about the social world.

Hence a second fundamental decision I made, in the mid-1970s, was to undertake formal part-time studies in sociology as a postgraduate student while continuing to teach in a university law school. But, far from solving the intellectual problems I had encountered with law, this made them more complex. It was easy to see how a field called sociology of law could exist, focused on the behavioural study of lawyers, administrative and enforcement agencies, legislative processes, police, courts and trials, citizens' complaints, access to justice and unmet legal needs, etc. But it was much harder to see how sociology might be used to reshape the study of legal ideas. I remained very interested in juristic legal theory – and in the material I taught in my jurisprudence courses – but I wanted to find ways of grounding it in the social theory that I had now studied.

This personal history is mentioned here partly to illustrate the kind of general dissatisfactions that led many legal scholars of my generation to social science (see also Chapters 1 and 2), but also to indicate particular factors that may help to explain the outlook of the essays in this book. First, unlike many others attracted to sociolegal studies, I did not reject or want to marginalise the traditions of juristic legal theory and especially of analytical jurisprudence and conceptual studies of law. The study of this juristic theory was what made it necessary for me to explore sociology and it has shaped my interests in and aspirations for sociological study of law. Secondly, again unlike many others, I was not pushed in these directions by primarily political concerns. I share the broadly left-wing attitudes typical of sociolegal scholars of my generation, but the impetus for developing my work has been primarily an intellectual and a moral one. Initially, I simply wanted the study of law to be more satisfying, more intellectually rich and more promising as a field of theoretical inquiries. Gradually, however, I became increasingly concerned to identify and study the moral foundations of law in ways that avoided universalistic speculation as much as possible, and were instead grounded in the particularities of social variation that social science can reveal.

This kind of sociological concern with morality and law leads naturally to a focus on relations of law and culture. If culture is (as I think it should be) taken to be a mix of traditions and established common practices, beliefs and ultimate values, shared feelings and allegiances, and projects that link people in networks of interaction, law relates in many different and often contradictory ways to culture. The moral requirements of different kinds of social relations that are expressions of culture will also be diverse and sometimes conflicting.

So morality is not uniform or consistent throughout the different regions of culture. It means different things and makes different demands in different cultural contexts. Since law relates to morality in many important ways, this moral variation is a pressing problem for legal study and legal practice. Several essays in this book (as well as others in *Law, Culture and Society*) address the relations of law and culture and can be seen as the most recent expression of my longstanding concern with sociological study of the relations of law and morals.

Morality is produced in and derives its precepts from social relations of community of diverse types, and the moral meanings of law (as Durkheim well understood) come from the same source. With such an emphasis on 'community', sociolegal theory begins to show its political face. The idea that people can live in society purely as individuals without more than transient connections to other individuals is a neo-liberal fantasy. All social life is lived in communal relations of various kinds. And all law is an expression of these relations. Failure to recognise the importance and consequences of this leads not to free, independent individuals but to pathological forms of community such as youth gangs, unlimited work commitment to employer organisations, and organised crime. This failure impoverishes culture because it tends to reduce culture to instrumental (often economic) relations of community alone – the weakest form of community. And it reduces morality to the morality of instrumental social relations. Ultimately it impoverishes and distorts law too – changing it in practice from a communal resource to a private one, harnessed by organisations and citizens to pursue their aims without regard to any wider public purposes for which law exists.

The mere invocation of words like 'community' or 'morality' – and even 'legal responsibility' (if thought of as something more than a matter of transaction costs) – may, in the current fashion of the times, at least in Britain, produce wry smiles and accusations of utopianism. I think this indicates how far ideas of community in practice now focus (under the influence of neo-liberal thought and a variety of scepticisms) on instrumental, especially economic social relations, and not on other types of communal relations based in what I call 'tradition', 'belief or values' and 'affect' (see Chapter 2). This severely instrumentalist outlook is, however, ultimately unstable, if only because instrumental social relations of community need the support of the other types of community. Without it they may, at worst, atrophy into an egoism that can undermine social relations of any kind. Law, too, must reflect and support the whole spectrum of communal life. My research has gradually led me to a perspective that can be summarised in the claims that (i) law cannot satisfactorily be analysed or interpreted except in terms of a sociologically-informed concept of community and (ii) all law has to find its meaning and significance as an expression and guarantee of social relations of community. These claims are elaborated and explained in the essays here.

Part 1: The Scope of Legal Inquiry

The four parts of the book indicate the main divisions of the work I have done in legal and social theory. Part 1 examines what the theoretical study of law can encompass and what resources are appropriate for it. Chapter 1 originated in a plenary address at a conference of the UK Socio-Legal Studies Association and is intended as a kind of stocktaking of the past hopes for and current possibilities of sociolegal inquiry, as viewed from the standpoint of an academic lawyer and legal theorist working in the context of legal education in Britain. Chapter 4 is, in some respects, a companion piece. The main part of my teaching of undergraduate law students has always centred on courses in jurisprudence. As a taught subject in the Anglophone university world, jurisprudence is typically a compendium of theoretical ideas developed by jurists and unified only by its strategic position in the law degree. It is a pedagogical package, not a research field like legal theory, legal philosophy or legal sociology. I see it as a constructively subversive element in legal education – a means of giving law students some hint of the scope of Holmes' 'great anthropological document' as they race through their busy undergraduate programme. The aim should be to do this in a way that challenges lawyers' professional certainties, conveying the idea that knowledge of law can be broader and deeper than the received wisdom of judges and legal practitioners.

Chapter 3 is also concerned with broadening juristic perspectives, but here the emphasis is on examining the nature of sociology as a resource for legal study. Sociology as an academic discipline fascinates me for its inherent intellectual ambition and its potential subversiveness when it confronts other organised academic knowledge-fields (such as law), but also for its instructive, continually recurring failures of disciplinary self-confidence (Cotterrell 1995: ch. 3). This chapter considers what lessons for legal theory as an enterprise can be learned from the condition of sociology as a professionalised disciplinary field, but also as an enterprise of pursuing knowledge of the social world beyond the arbitrary constraints of any academic discipline. It is this latter, *transdisciplinary* form of sociology that underpins much social theory today and is a primary resource on which the juristic study of law can draw. So it is not necessary to become a professional sociologist to interpret law sociologically. Given a sustained sociological imagination and curiosity and a commitment to systematic empirical observation and interpretation of the social, it is possible to draw materials for this purpose from many research traditions. No particular academic discipline owns access to social theory, or can police its relation to the study of law.

Chapter 2 appears in this section primarily to introduce the law-and-community approach to legal studies which is reflected in much of my work. The chapter links this approach to dissatisfactions with aspects of legal philosophy and sociology that were touched on above. The approach is to be distinguished from communitarianism (discussed in Chapter 5) and is presented as an analytical framework devised specifically for the purposes of legal theory. The chapters in Part 4 are also, in the main, focused on explaining and illustrating this approach, but it underpins more or less explicitly most of my writings over the past ten years.

Part 2: Sociolegal Theory and Theorists

Part 2 profiles the work of particular legal theorists. For those readers who see legal theory as within the province of legal philosophy it may seem odd that there are no chapters here devoted to the writings of leading recent legal philosophers. Instead the focus is on the contribution of legal theorists who have been central in the enterprise of explaining the nature of law sociologically. The social theorists Max Weber, Emile Durkheim and Jürgen Habermas are discussed in Chapter 10 and the work of the primary juristic founder of modern sociology of law, Eugen Ehrlich, is considered in Chapters 5 and 10.

Chapter 10 is based on a plenary lecture given at a conference planned to highlight specifically European traditions and issues in sociolegal research. So its orientation is on sociolegal theorists' understandings of the nature and identity of Europe as a focus of regulation. The discussions in this chapter and in Chapter 5 of Ehrlich's work are certainly intended to celebrate this great pioneer. His achievement should be an inspiration for lawyers who wish to transcend the limits of orthodoxy in their professional vision and see law in wider context as an aspect of social experience. But his failings as a theorist and the obstacles that arose in his way are also thought-provoking. They provide important lessons about the difficulties as well as the intellectual rewards of trying to develop sociologically-informed legal theory that takes full account of lawyers' views of law.

Other chapters in Part 2 consider the work of lesser-known scholars who have taken on this challenge. The French jurists Emmanuel Lévy (Chapter 6) and Paul Huvelin (Chapter 7) were members of Durkheim's tight-knit group of research collaborators, and highly imaginative scholars who tried to translate Durkheimian sociology directly into a legal theory that would relate strongly to lawyers' experience. Lévy tried to fuse Durkheim's insights about law and social solidarity with socialist currents of thought in his era. By this means he produced a genuinely radical legal theory that prefigured aspects of modern critical legal studies. His friend and colleague, Huvelin, tried to adapt Durkheim's sociology of law to emphasise law's independent power as a regulatory technique. At the same time, Huvelin's striking speculations on magic and the ancient origins of private rights open our eyes to the diversity of elements that may have created modern ideas of law over long ages of social development.[3] These two essays are products of an ongoing project on the legal theory of Durkheim and his juristic followers.

The German jurist Franz Neumann, also important for his associations, is remembered particularly as a member of the Frankfurt School of critical theory but it is his powerful scholarship on the rule of law that is the focus of Chapter 8. Neumann's work here offers a good example of how sociologically-informed legal theory confronts philosophical abstractions (here the ideals of the rule of law doctrine) with the specificity of historical conditions and social variation. The transition from what Neumann calls competitive society to corporate society is almost unnoticed in most discussions of the rule of law but Neumann's insight into changing historical conditions provides a sociological input that demands a rethinking of juristic ideas and a revaluation of their significance.

The remaining chapter in Part 2 (Chapter 9) is a critique of autopoiesis theory as recently developed in the work of Niklas Luhmann and Gunther Teubner. This theory purports to explain processes by which, it claims, modern law tends to become an autonomous, self-sustaining discourse or system of communication. If law is self-sustaining in the way autopoiesis theory proposes this would invalidate attempts, such as mine, to present legal experience as an aspect of social experience, and to show law's complex relation to morality and its character as an expression and support of social relations of community. For Luhmann and Teubner, autopoietic law is a discourse that interprets social experience entirely in its own terms, and responds according to its own system imperatives to the social environment it observes. But I argue that autopoiesis theory reifies narrow juristic assumptions about law's autonomy. Ultimately it assumes without justification the self-sustaining character of law. It treats this as a given – a theoretical postulate – and so makes empirical inquiries about law's social effects and conditions of existence impossible.

---

3   Huvelin's work on magical elements in Roman law is still cited with respect a century after he wrote: see Rives 2002. His radical suggestion (as a Durkheimian) of abandoning the key concept of organic solidarity has been echoed in some later Durkheimian literature (see Pope and Johnson 1983).

Part 3: Interpreting Legal Ideas Sociologically

While much of my research has focused on general theoretical inquiries about the nature of law as a social phenomenon, I have also tried to test or refine theoretical ideas by applying them to problems in particular fields of legal doctrine. Part 3 reprints essays illustrating these efforts. At various times I have taught contract law, public law, property law and especially the law of trusts. As I tried to work out ways of interpreting legal ideas sociologically it seemed interesting to see what might be achieved using such methods in these fields.

Chapter 13 deals with a highly technical problem of English trusts law (the validity of private purpose trusts) and sets out to explain in sociological terms both why this strange problem arose and why it has seemed so intractable juristically. The issue could be considered parochial because in many foreign jurisdictions it is solved by legislation or judicial interpretation without much difficulty. But, viewed sociologically, it reveals important things about the entire context of the development of trusts law and especially about the changing moral assumptions that have underpinned this law. The evolving character of trusts law is analysed also in Chapter 14 in the light of sociological literature on trusting relationships. The discussion here looks partly towards the technicalities of trusts law and the striking changes that have occurred over time in the principles that inform legal doctrine in this field. But it also looks to social theory by exploring the nature of mutual interpersonal trust as a moral basis of social relations. So it links directly to the wider concerns of other chapters in this book that focus on the connections between law, morality and community.

Other essays use different methods for different ends. Chapters 11 and 12 (on contract and property law, respectively) are earlier efforts at sociological interpretation of legal ideas. The former, my first attempt at this kind of interpretation, was written for the British Sociological Association's 1979 conference on 'Law and Society', a hugely important event in signalling the scale of activity in sociolegal studies in the United Kingdom at the time and in building the collective confidence of those British academics who were then committing themselves to social scientific studies of law. In the late 1970s it seemed important to challenge Marxist reductionist analyses of law, while keeping the valuable critical orientation they offered and building on their popularisation of the concept of ideology. Thus, in the chapter, a discussion of these themes precedes a schematic attempt to apply Weber's writings on contract to issues about capitalist development. Here contract law is used as a focus for arguing for a sociological approach to legal ideas. The essay on property law (Chapter 12) also contains general exploratory discussion about approaches to the study of legal ideas. It was written for a book considering the relation of legal theory to particular areas of law and it asks how legal theory can broaden perspectives on legal doctrine to enrich and also transcend lawyers' views.

Chapter 15 looks at aspects of law's symbolic power, here focusing on the nature of constitutional symbols and their different content in the United Kingdom and the United States. A study of symbolic aspects of legal doctrine puts in the forefront of attention the ambiguities of legal ideas and the social uses to which this ambiguity can be put. The chapter argues that symbolism is important in the processes by which constitutions secure and provide authority. The different bases of authority of the US and UK constitutions are reflected in the different kinds of authority these constitutions provide for government.

Finally in this section, Chapter 16 examines recent appeals to ideas of legal culture in comparative law. The discussion is sceptical about the assumptions of some comparative legal scholars about the relations of law and culture. But it recognises important reasons why these relations are now emphasised. Here, a sociological interpretation of juristic debates (especially about European harmonisation of law) identifies major political and moral concerns underlying juristic uses of ideas about legal culture. As in the other chapters in this section, the aim is to see more in the development of legal ideas than lawyers often recognise.

Part 4: Law, Morality, Community

The first three chapters in Part 4 all focus on the relations of law to morality, addressing this topic in terms of the sociologically-informed law-and-community approach outlined earlier in Chapter 2. Chapter 17 is based on a 1998 lecture in Finland to an international audience of theologians and ethicists, drawn mainly from Continental European civil law countries. I had been asked to speak on common law approaches to the law-morality relationship, so the chapter explains common law's inductive methods and its approaches to doctrinal systematisation and ways of developing legal principle, as well as the role of the common law judge and the impact of legal positivism. But the main concern is with how law can and does take account of morality. Durkheim's ideas are invoked to clarify the problem of reconciling moral particularity and legal universality and this is further analysed in terms of distinctions between different types of social relations of community that produce contrasting moral requirements. The fourfold typology of community discussed here appears in many chapters in this book. One of the types, instrumental community, is described in this chapter as almost without moral dimensions. In more recent writings, however, I have emphasised that every type of community, even instrumental community as the weakest, requires moral foundations.

Chapters 18 and 19 arise from interventions in recent Dutch debates, one of these being about the nature and effects of legislation, the other about the relevance of ideals as a focus of legal and political studies. Chapter 18 focuses on two views of legislation: as a more or less successful infusion of rules into social environments, or as a more diffuse form of moral communication. The conference in Groningen at which the original paper was given was organised as a good-humoured confrontation between advocates of these two approaches, but my invited comment on the debate tries to take elements from both sides in true Dutch consensus-building style. Arguing for the relevance here of the law-and-community approach, it stresses problems of moral distance affecting all forms of state law, as well as important differences between common law and civil law views of the nature of legislation.

Chapter 19 arises from another occasion in which, as an outsider, I was invited to comment on Dutch discussions. As in the legislation debate, I felt close to those claiming that moral ideas are law's concern and should certainly be a concern for legal studies. But these ideas must be considered in a sociological perspective that emphasises their variability with historical and social context. Chapter 19 considers law's relation to ultimate values, the most abstract region of moral thought and surely one of the most intractable topics for analysis. The analyses here of the (often convenient) vagueness of ideals and values relate closely to the discussions of constitutional symbolism in Chapter 15 and legislative communication in Chapter 18.

As Chapter 19 attempts to make clear, my ideas about law's practical relation to ultimate values are close to those of pragmatism in so far as pragmatism emphasises values as arising from or gaining their meaning from social experience in its specific time and place. Pragmatism tries to resist the search for philosophical universals and focuses on ideas in practice; ideas validated in the specific contexts of their use. It remains, however, for the most part, an approach within philosophy rather than social theory (but cf. Selznick 1992). As such, it lacks the kind of permanent commitment to systematic empirical inquiry about variation in the social contexts of practice that I think is needed in studying law in its relation to morality.

Part 4 concludes with two chapters that briefly summarise ideas about the study of law and culture that I am now working with, using the law-and-community approach. Chapter 20 is based on a paper delivered in Bangalore at a conference on ideas of culture in legal education. It represents an effort to communicate across cultures using an analytical framework sufficiently abstract for this purpose but also sufficiently concrete to address problems of legal studies of clear concern in such different multicultural societies as India and Britain. Chapter 21 is a brief companion piece. When I attended the Bangalore conference I also had the privilege of addressing the students of the

National Law School of India University in the city – some of the new elite of Indian law students learning to meet legal challenges of globalisation in their great, rapidly changing country. Afterwards they asked me to write a piece for their journal. The article is included because it is addressed specifically to students and because it links with issues about legal education raised in Part 1 of this book.

My ideas, like those of most scholars, have been developed partly in the process of teaching students and partly in interaction with other researchers. Among the latter, it is impossible here to thank all who have been important influences but the citations in these chapters give some indications. Since, however, this book is a compilation from my whole career it seems appropriate, finally, to recall three University of London professors no longer living but whom I shall not forget: George Keeton, Roger Crane and Paul Hirst. Very different characters, they helped me to act on the key decisions (to become an academic and to explore sociology's utility for legal studies) that set the direction of my career. Closer to home, the constant support of my wife Ann has made possible all the work reflected in these pages.

References

Anderson, N. (1923), *The Hobo: The Sociology of the Homeless Man*. Chicago: University of Chicago Press.

Bulmer, M. (1984), *The Chicago School of Sociology: Institutionalization, Diversity and the Rise of Sociological Research*. Chicago: University of Chicago Press.

Cotterrell, R. (1995), *Law's Community: Legal Theory in Sociological Perspective*. Oxford: Clarendon Press.

Cotterrell, R. (2006), *Law, Culture and Society: Legal Ideas in the Mirror of Social Theory*. Aldershot: Ashgate.

Cotterrell, R. and P. Selznick (2004), 'Selznick Interviewed: Philip Selznick in Conversation with Roger Cotterrell' **31** *Journal of Law and Society* 291–317.

Cressey, P.G. (1932), *The Taxi-Dance Hall: A Sociological Study in Commercialized Recreation and City Life*. Montclair, NJ: Patterson Smith reprint, 1969.

Dworkin, R. (2006), *Justice in Robes*. Cambridge, MA: Harvard University Press.

Ehrlich, E. (1936), *Fundamental Principles of the Sociology of Law*, transl. W. L. Moll. New Brunswick: Transaction reprint, 2002.

Fletcher, R. (1981), *Sociology: The Study of Social Systems*. London: Batsford.

Geertz, C. (1973), *The Interpretation of Cultures*. New York: Basic Books.

Green, L. (2005), 'General Jurisprudence: A 25th Anniversary Essay' **25** *Oxford Journal of Legal Studies* 565–80.

Gurvitch, G. (1947), *Sociology of Law*. London: Routledge and Kegan Paul.

Holmes, O.W. (1899), 'Law in Science and Science in Law', **12** *Harvard Law Review* 443–63.

Pope, W. and Johnson, B.D. (1983), 'Inside Organic Solidarity', **48** *American Sociological Review* 681–92.

Pound, R. (1917), 'The Limits of Effective Legal Action', **27** *International Journal of Ethics* 150–67.

Rives, J.B. (2002), 'Magic in the XII Tables Revisited', **52** *Classical Quarterly* 270–90.

Selznick, P. (1992), *The Moral Commonwealth: Social Theory and the Promise of Community*. Berkeley: University of California Press.

Wirth, L. (1928), *The Ghetto*. Chicago: University of Chicago Press.

Zorbaugh, H.W. (1929), *The Gold Coast and the Slum: A Sociological Study of Chicago's Near North Side*. Chicago: University of Chicago Press.

Part One

The Scope of Legal Inquiry

[1]
Subverting Orthodoxy, Making Law Central: A View of Sociolegal Studies

The promise of sociolegal research varies for different constituencies. For some legal scholars it has been a promise of sustained commitment to moral and political critique of law and to theoretical and empirical analysis of law's social consequences and origins. To continue to deliver on that promise today, sociolegal studies should develop theory in new forms emphasizing the variety of forms of regulation and the moral foundations on which that regulation ultimately depends. It should demonstrate and explore law's roles in the routine structuring of all aspects of social life and its changing character as it faces the challenge of regulating relations of community not bounded solely by the jurisdictional reach of nation states.

INTRODUCTION

What directions should sociolegal studies in Britain take today? To accept an invitation to debate this issue is to risk the possibility that one's choice of priorities will seem bizarre or just irrelevant to others whose involvement with the field is different. Everyone seriously concerned with sociolegal scholarship has a view of its potential, a view coloured by ambitions or dissatisfactions that first led to involvement with sociolegal work. Institutional work location also affects the nature of each person's ongoing involvement. An important reason for the vitality of the sociolegal community in Britain, as of the law and society community in the United States of America, has surely been its rich, almost anarchic heterogeneity and its consistent openness to many different aims, outlooks, and disciplinary backgrounds.[1] Perhaps it is undesirable to argue that such a field should tilt in any particular direction. At the very least, anyone expressing general views about the sociolegal enterprise should surely reveal the conditioning background factors that provide a context and perhaps a partial explanation for those views.

Here, briefly, are some of those factors. With many other legal academics, what this writer initially sought from sociolegal work was a set of new perspectives on law to allow a breakout from the claustrophobic world of legal scholarship and education, as previously encountered. Most legal study, in my experience as a law undergraduate and postgraduate at the end of the 1960s, seemed to focus on technicality as an end in itself and was unconcerned with fundamental questions about law's nature, sources, and consequences as a social phenomenon or about its moral groundings. Value-judgements pervading legal studies cried out for theoretical examination but were routinely treated as obviously correct or simply unrecognized. Policy argument, the 'unruly horse'[2] that judges were sometimes forced to ride, was not considered to be 'real' legal reasoning and so not given serious attention in the law school, legal study being seen as confined to interpreting rules and analysing their logical or plausible interrelations. Moral argument was to be disposed of quickly so that sophisticated legal thinking could begin. Legislation, an unfortunate necessity, was often presented as a salutary warning about the results of amateur (non-lawyers') dabbling in lawmaking. To draw seriously on knowledge-fields beyond the contents of the law reports was suspect and the fortress walls of law-as-discipline were well guarded, perhaps because of mute suspicions about their ultimate fragility and law's still unsure intellectual place in the academy. The common law judge was the intellectual centre of the legal world; and thinking like a lawyer meant, as it seemed, being condemned to a professional state of intellectual tunnel-vision and moral and political impotence.

In those conditions, social science was a flag to nail to the mast, something to proclaim adherence to in trying to navigate an intellectually credible route beyond the world of orthodox doctrinal legal commentary and debate. The effort especially to apply sociological perspectives to law was not a matter of swearing adherence to sociology as a distinct discipline but of rejecting the boundary claims of academic disciplines, including those of law and sociology. It seemed important to approach legal study as an empirical, systematic study of a field of social experience. That did not necessarily demand that every legal academic must conduct empirical research on behaviour in legal contexts but it

---

1 P. Thomas, 'Sociolegal Studies: The Case of Disappearing Fleas and Bustards' in *Sociolegal Studies*, ed. P.A. Thomas (1997) 2–3; F. Levine, 'Goose Bumps and "The Search for Signs of Intelligent Life" in Sociolegal Studies: After Twenty-Five Years' (1990) 24 *Law and Society Rev.* 7–33, at 9 ff.

2 See *Richardson* v. *Mellish* (1824) 2 Bing. 229, at 242 (*per* Burrough J).

demanded that as a legal scholar one should become well informed about such research being done and about the resources social science could offer legal studies. It involved finding how best to incorporate social scientific insights and perspectives into one's own legal scholarship, and supporting and co-operating with sociolegal empirical research initiatives.

Though sociology appeared initially as a special, relatively distinct intellectual field, miraculously provided to save legal scholarship from itself, it later seemed more appropriate to view it as a compendium of methods, approaches, traditions, and aspirations which could be contributed to by many of the so-called separate academic disciplines and by work not easily fitted into any of them.[3] Using these resources one could gain distance from doctrinal legal scholarship and so develop different perspectives on it but one could also hope to participate in this scholarship in new ways, bringing a fresh outlook to bear on old problems.

Because legal theory had long had an indefinite licence to range beyond lawyers' immediate practical concerns with legal doctrine, it always seemed potentially to be a vehicle for developing an understanding of important general aspects of law that traditional legal study ignored. But this depended on jurisprudence as a taught law school subject and legal theory as a research field being infused with social scientific insight. Although sociolegal scholarship had a vital role in studying the social effects of behaviour in legal contexts, understandings of legal doctrine and reasoning also needed altering. On this view, the theoretical study of legal ideas should not be left to legal philosophers but pursued as an empirical inquiry about the conditions, significance, consequences, and potential of those ideas in particular historical conditions. So the fields of speculation that legal philosophy had monopolized, as the theoretical self-awareness of lawyers, should also be a central concern of sociolegal research. In this way sociolegal studies would not merely be juxtaposed with traditional legal scholarship but would invade it and begin to reshape it in ways that renewed its vital engagement with the currents of change in society that social scientists studied.

It would be dishonest to pretend that the ideas expressed above were fully developed from the time sociolegal studies first began to seem important to this particular academic lawyer in company with many others. But they indicate long-held convictions about what sociolegal scholarship could offer, and they colour all the suggestions to be made in the rest of this paper about directions in which it might be desirable for the sociolegal field to tilt to some degree.

---

3 Stjepan Mestrovic, in his *Anthony Giddens: The Last Modernist* (1998) 209–11, sees sociology as having been traditionally a 'wild discipline', diverse, vast, contributed to by scholars of any discipline or none and taking 'what it needed from the humanities, natural sciences, and the other social sciences ... to make sense of the social world.' This was precisely the basis of its appeal as a rich resource for some legal scholars.

THE USES OF THEORY

Phil Thomas has recently written that sociolegal studies should not be ennobled with the title of 'discipline' because to do so risks marginalizing sociolegal scholarship in the legal academy and defusing its 'growing challenges to orthodox legal pedagogy, traditional research areas and methods'[4] by setting it apart. The temptation to seek status by building disciplinary walls is strong, particularly for new fields of scholarly practice unsure of their identity and overshadowed by powerful, competing knowledge-fields. But the instinct to avoid disciplinary demarcations is likely to be felt strongly by those who took up sociolegal studies as a tool to break open the claustrophobic discipline of law. As sociolegal perspectives seep into virtually all areas of legal scholarship many researchers have stopped worrying about the intellectual criteria of law-as-discipline. Legal scholarship is not weakened by this lack of concern but strengthened and enriched. The same is true for sociolegal studies as they extend their reach, drawing new insights about the legal from whatever intellectual sources seem appropriate.

These views imply no lack of interest in the integrity of the sociolegal field. Strengthening that integrity depends on both an increased sensitivity to its intellectual foundations in classic writings and a sustained effort to develop new sociolegal theory. Sensitivity to intellectual traditions lends perspective to the research culture but the classic sociolegal theorists are still too little valued in the sociolegal enterprise and considered too arbitrarily and marginally. Weber, Marx, and Durkheim receive habitual acknowledgement in current sociolegal scholarship but Georges Gurvitch, Leon Petrazycki, Eugen Ehrlich, Marcel Mauss, Emmanuel Lévy[5] and other important contributors are not celebrated as sources of intellectual tradition in the way that, for example, Kelsen, Bentham or Austin are in legal philosophy. If sociolegal scholarship is to transform the legal academy, its scholarly traditions need to be strongly present in the pantheon of markers of the progress of thought about law. 'Who reads Ehrlich, now?' an American leader of the law-and-economics movement once asked me rhetorically, not concealing his low opinion of other social scientific approaches to law. One might similarly ask, 'Who reads Austin or Bentham?' but, in the case of those writers, scholarly effort strongly maintains their place in a recognized intellectual tradition which in turn shapes a certain outlook on law. As students of cultural studies well know, altering or disrupting the classical canon is a powerful way to reorient an intellectual field.

---

4 Thomas, op. cit. n. 1, pp. 18–19.
5 G. Gurvitch, *Sociology of Law* (1947); L. Petrazycki, *Law and Morality*, tr. H.W. Babb (1955); E. Ehrlich, *Fundamental Principles of the Sociology of Law*, tr. W.L. Moll (1936); M. Mauss, *The Gift: The Form and Reason for Exchange in Archaic Societies*, tr. W.D. Halls (1990); E. Lévy, *Les fondements du droit* (1933).

Beyond a sense of tradition, sociolegal scholarship needs more theory addressing the nature of contemporary law. It needs theory to map and organize the sociolegal realm. Again, a comparison with legal philosophy is instructive. Legal philosophy has not obviously contributed directly to the disciplinary self-consciousness of legal practice but it has elaborated lawyers' perspectives on law and ordered and legitimized general concerns that legal scholars take up. It has reinforced and clarified ideas about the nature of law that lawyers often assume. If sociolegal scholarship is properly unconcerned with disciplinary status it cannot be unconcerned with clarifying its object of study, described conventionally (but, I shall suggest, inadequately) as 'law and society' or 'law in society'. Sociolegal scholarship needs theories appropriate to this task but legal philosophy has not usually produced ideas about the nature of law that take serious account of and are designed to facilitate empirical research on law as a social phenomenon. Indeed, the idea of 'the social' and its empirical variability has been largely absent from legal philosophy but it is this idea that needs most centrality in sociolegal theory. Sociolegal theory has the job of bringing the social as an object of rigorous inquiry into the study of law.[6]

Many people argue for less theory, not more, in legal and sociolegal scholarship and some reasons for this are understandable. 'Grand narratives'[7] of classic sociolegal theories – their broadest agendas and central unifying themes – seem exhausted. For example, Marx's and Engels's vision of a trajectory of world history culminating in the withering away of law and the state no longer seems credible. The concept of formal legal rationality, the primary legal expression of Weber's great thesis of the rationalization of the modern world, seems unable now to capture the vast diversity of regulatory practices of contemporary law and governance,[8] evoking instead a (partly mythical) modern age of 'pure' legal formality that has passed. And few accept solidarity as a master concept to characterize the structure of societies in the optimistic way Durkheim proposed. If postmodernist and post-structuralist writing has been too uninterested in the projects of empirical sociolegal research,[9] it has nevertheless performed an important service in linking together many scattered, accumulating doubts about

6 R. Cotterrell, 'Law and Community: A New Relationship?' (1998) 51 *Current Legal Problems* 367–91.
7 Compare J.-F. Lyotard, *The Postmodern Condition: A Report on Knowledge*, tr. G. Bennington and B. Massumi (1984) 37 ff.
8 For a rich overview of some of this diversity, see the papers in 'Special Issue: New Directions in Regulatory Theory', eds. S. Picciotto and D. Campbell (2002) 29(1) *J. of Law and Society*.
9 For a telling critique of this lack of interest (especially in Jacques Derrida's work) see G. Teubner, 'The King's Many Bodies: The Self-Deconstruction of Law's Hierarchy' (1997) 31 *Law and Society Rev.* 763–87. See, also, A. Norrie, 'From Critical to Sociolegal Studies: Three Dialectics in Search of a Subject' (2000) 9 *Social and Legal Studies* 85–113.

modern approaches to social explanation. Emphasizing the indeterminacy, complexity, fragmentation, and fluidity of social life, postmodernists have shown that across the whole sweep of social theory the main traditions of ambitious schematization of social change no longer resonate with contemporary experience.

This does not remove the need for theory, or for the centrality of social theory in sociolegal studies. Theory provides perspective in a complex, diverse field. But distrust of grand narratives leads to a more modest view of what can be asked of social theory. For example, recent literature on governmentality,[10] inspired by Foucault's work, offers no general theory of the social. But it promises new ways of conceptualizing the diversity of regulation in some contemporary societies. It addresses the complex inter-relations between, on the one hand, actions of state agencies at many levels as legal-administrative regulators and, on the other, the 'quasi-governmental' and 'private' disciplinary strategies and normalizing practices that pervade social life. In reconceptualizing regulation, it avoids the increasingly implausible public/private dichotomy in social and legal thought.[11] Theory focused on the diversity of contemporary regulation also allows an escape from legal philosophy's 'What is law?' conundrums and potentially highlights regulation's fluidity, ubiquity, and varied consequences, making it possible to locate whatever we choose to designate as law in a continuum, network or web[12] of regulatory practices and techniques.

Sociolegal theory needs to specify a realm of the legal but not necessarily in categorical fashion. Identifying the legal merely means enabling sociolegal scholarship to determine its own scope rather than to have that scope given by policy-makers. As many sociolegal scholars recognize, legal pluralist writings provide a partial means to this end.[13] In a sense they are a core of the sociolegal theoretical tradition, contributed to by Ehrlich, Petrazycki, and Gurvitch in still

10 See, for example, *The Foucault Effect: Studies in Governmentality*, eds. G. Burchell, C. Gordon, and P. Miller (1991); M. Dean, *Governmentality: Power and Rule in Modern Society* (1999); P O'Malley, L. Weir and C. Shearing, 'Governmentality, Criticism, Politics' (1997) 26 *Economy and Society* 501–17; *Governable Places: Readings on Governmentality and Crime Control*, ed. R. Smandych (1999); N. Rose and M. Valverde, 'Governed by Law?' (1998) 7 *Social and Legal Studies* 541–51; N. Rose, *Powers of Freedom: Reframing Political Thought* (1999).

11 J. Morison, 'The Government-Voluntary Sector Compacts: Governance, Govern-mentality, and Civil Society' (2000) 27 *J. of Law and Society* 98-132. Sharp dichotomies between formal law and informal regulation are also challenged: see R. Van Krieken, 'Legal Informalism, Power and Liberal Governance' (2001) 10 *Social and Legal Studies* 5–22.

12 Compare S. Picciotto and J. Haines, 'Regulating Global Financial Markets' (1999) 26 *J. of Law and Society* 351–68, at 361, describing 'the new global financial.system' as generating 'multiple layers of regulation ... loosely co-ordinated through horizontal and vertical networks, to form a regulatory web.'

13 For a recent survey see J. Dalberg-Larsen, *The Unity of Law: An Illusion? On Legal Pluralism in Theory and Practice* (2000).

illuminating ways. Leaving aside legal anthropology's work on colonial and post-colonial societies, modern sociolegal scholarship has still not fully explored the potential and problems of legal pluralist theory, perhaps because the pressure to treat as law whatever lawyers and policy makers recognize as such has been almost overwhelming. Yet a legal pluralist approach does not usually entail denying lawyers' or policy makers' views of law but more often supplementing, expanding, interpreting, and explaining them in a broader social scientific context.

A legal pluralist approach does not, for example, force us to say that rules of clubs, schools, factories, and hospitals are law, though it might be interesting to think of them in that way for some analytical purposes. But it enables us to look for phenomena sufficiently like state law in some respects to make comparison illuminating. It also highlights the possibility that some types of regulation whose formal origins or primary bases of practical authority do not lie in the state are becoming so important that to ignore their interpenetration with or consequences for state law is impermissible. Most importantly, a legal pluralist approach raises the question of where law's ultimate authority resides and whether simple positivist tests adequately explain legal validity. Law's authority might depend on how far it corresponds with, or meets, felt needs for regulation of social relations. If social sources of law, located in different kinds of community life, are diverse, law itself will be diverse in meaning or effect, coloured by the varied moral expectations and responsibilities attached to it.

LAW AS ROUTINE STRUCTURING

In another area, theory in sociolegal studies may have a crucial task to perform. Nearly a century ago, Ehrlich complained[14] that lawyers overemphasize disputes and conflicts, the pathology of social life, and so distort the social significance of law. Still today, law is probably often thought of in popular consciousness mainly as criminal law (state action against social disorder) or litigation (private conflict pursued through courts). Lawyers have been criticized for seeing international law as a response to crisis rather than 'issues of structural justice that underpin everyday life'.[15] And where legal education is strongly oriented to case-law it mainly presents law as a product of dispute and disorder.

A major role of law is to repress disorder and to process disputes, but to present it entirely in these terms is to present law and lawyers' work as essentially parasitic on social pathology, the breakdown of social relations of community. Some sociolegal writing reinforces this image: Donald

14 Ehrlich, op. cit. n. 5.
15 H. Charlesworth, 'International Law: A Discipline of Crisis' (2002) 65 *Modern Law Rev.* 377–92, at 391.

Black declares bluntly that law flourishes as community declines.[16] Yet, much sociolegal scholarship, operating in research settings far removed from courts (in lawyers' offices, administrative and regulatory agencies, corporate legal departments, neighbourhoods, organizations, and so on) tells a different story: of law used (with varying degrees of success and failure) to guide and structure social relations, engineer deals and understandings, define lines of authority, make provision for future contingencies, facilitate projects, distribute resources, promote security, limit risks, and encourage trust. Images (whether or not empirically-based) of common law adversarial processes as ritual tournaments, of the excesses of rights culture and of 'litigation explosions'[17] reinforce a view of law and lawyers as part of social pathology. Sociolegal scholarship gives a more balanced view through studies of law's contributions to the routine structuring of social relations, as well as its responses to social breakdown.

This is not an invitation to complacency because sociolegal research often shows how poorly law succeeds in that routine structuring, and this critique is among its most important contributions. But countering the image of law as purely a response to social pathology is part of a wider project of showing law's social centrality and hence the centrality of the sociolegal enterprise. In the image of law as routine structuring, law appears ubiquitous, not socially marginal.[18] The strength of Foucault's work for legal scholarship has been to emphasize the ubiquity of power and its necessity in structuring social relations. As Foucault revolutionized views of power, sociolegal scholarship should revolutionize views of law: from an image of exceptionality and pathology to one of normality and pervasiveness. Law, like power, should be seen as a resource operating routinely in innumerable social sites and settings. Work on law as constitutive of social institutions, practices, ideas, and identities, on law's ideological significance and rootedness in culture, on legal consciousness and on images of law in everyday life all point in this direction.[19]

16 D. Black, 'The Social Organization of Arrest' (1971) 23 *Stanford Law Rev.* 1087–111, at 1108: 'Law seems to bespeak an absence of community, and law grows ever more prominent as the dissolution of community proceeds.'
17 See, for example, M. Galanter, 'Law Abounding: Legalisation Around the North Atlantic' (1992) 55 *Modern Law Rev.* 1–24; M. Galanter, 'Reading the Landscape of Disputes: What We Know and Don't Know (and Think We Know) About Our Allegedly Contentious and Litigious Society' (1983) 31 *University of California at Los Angeles Law Rev.* 4–71. On the adversarial system, see, for example, D. Luban (ed.), *The Good Lawyer: Lawyers' Roles and Lawyers' Ethics* (1984) part 2.
18 Compare B. Yngvesson, *Virtuous Citizens, Disruptive Subjects: Order and Complaint in a New England Town* (1993), claiming that law was 'central as nothing else is' (p. 119) among the citizens she studied, whether or not they took any of their problems to court.
19 For a sample of recent literature relating to these various approaches see J. Brigham, *The Constitution of Interests: Beyond the Politics of Rights* (1996); *After Identity: A Reader in Law and Culture*, eds. D. Danielsen and K. Engle (1995); *Adapting Legal Cultures*, eds. D. Nelken and J. Feest (2001); S.E. Merry, *Getting Justice and Getting*

This is a very different outlook from that of some older sociolegal approaches treating law purely as a policy-instrument acting on society. A view of law as an aspect of social experience makes redundant sociolegal efforts to trace causal relations between law and society, as if law existed as an asocial instrument or technique, external to social life. Instead, law itself, rather than law's effects or conditioning causes, becomes the centre of sociolegal attention: law as normative ideas embedded in social practices. In a legal pluralist perspective, this entails social inquiry about more than state law. The pervasiveness of regulation in social life is highlighted whether the name 'law', in the lawyer's sense of the term, is given to that regulation or not. Thus the study of law as part of a wider field of regulation is not set apart from other social studies but made fundamental to them.

LEGAL AUTHORITY AND TRANSNATIONAL LAW

The significance of these ideas lies in two directions. One is towards recovering a concern in sociolegal studies and legal scholarship more generally with moral foundations of law. Durkheim stressed law's rootedness in the diverse moral milieux of social life, but he did not follow the matter far enough and made obviously unjustifiable assumptions about the moral cohesion of modern societies. He made law central as a concern for social science by stressing its necessary moral resonance (its rootedness in everyday values and understandings of social relations) and its corresponding emptiness if that moral resonance were absent. From a Durkheimian standpoint, a contemporary task of legal scholarship guided by sociolegal perspectives is to rediscover this moral resonance of law, reinterpreting it in terms of the diversity and fluidity of social relations in contemporary society.[20] Crucially, the old Durkheimian 'grand narrative' of an overarching solidarity of modern society needs to be replaced with more modest talk of diverse types of community life and their legal needs and expressions.

Durkheim's linking of law and morality is not taken very seriously today because Durkheimian morality (as distinct from personal or group ethics) is usually thought of as a unifying normative framework of society. Many critics doubt whether such a framework exists and, if it does, whether law has much to do with it. And can law be criticized at all if it necessarily expresses society's moral code? But these doubts about a sociology of law and morals might be largely dispelled if morality were understood not as a society-wide structure but as the varied normative conditions of solidarity in many

Even: Legal Consciousness Among Working-Class Americans (1990); P. Ewick and S.S. Silbey, *The Common Place of Law: Stories from Everyday Life* (1998).

20 For an interesting study along these lines, interpreting Swedish insolvency law practice in Durkheimian terms, see B. Carlsson and D. Hoff, 'Dealing with Insolvency and Indebted Individuals in Respect to Law and Morality' (2000) 9 *Social and Legal Studies* 293–317.

different relations of community which compete, co-exist, conflict, and overlap, continually forming and reforming with often multiple and fluid memberships.[21] Conflicts between different regulatory demands to support relations of community produce conflicts about the substance of law. Sociolegal identification of law's failures in representing and reconciling these conflicting demands provides a basis for powerful moral critique of law.

A view of law as a structuring of social relations of community also points in a second direction. This is towards new perspectives on the familiar claim that the state monopoly of the making, interpreting, and enforcing of law is slowly ending. The best way to conceptualize this matter sociolegally is in terms of changes in the social. If any coherent meaning can be given to rhetoric about the 'death of the social'[22] it is that the identity and boundaries of social life, for the purposes of regulation, cannot be understood as sociology has often understood them in the past.[23] In particular it is now widely recognized that 'society', taken to mean the realm of the social marked by the boundaries of the nation-state, can no longer be treated sociologically as a self-contained totality. Social relations of many kinds (for example, commercial or financial links and interdependencies, bonds of religious, ethnic or ideological solidarity, kinship and friendship ties, security alliances, and political movements) now routinely escape limitation by the political boundaries of states.

If relations of community operate extensively on transnational bases as well as reflecting the fluidity of social relations in nation states, it should be unsurprising that new regulatory forms are being shaped to frame these kinds of relations. Sociolegal scholarship is already extensively mapping and analysing these new forms of regulation[24] in environmental, commercial, human rights, information technology, and many other fields. But much legal scholarship and legal education still implies that nation state law and traditional international law, focused on relations between states, define the essential nature of the legal. Sociolegal studies can help to redraw the legal map, emphasizing how and why the changing character of the social in transnational and intranational contexts forces change in structures of regulation; change which will eventually demand from legal theory entirely

---

21 I have tried to develop this approach in *Émile Durkheim: Law in a Moral Domain* (1999) 219–27; 'A Legal Concept of Community' (1997) 12 *Cnd. J. of Law and Society* 75–91; 'Is There a Logic of Legal Transplants?' in Nelken and Feest, op. cit. n. 19; and 'Seeking Similarity, Appreciating Difference' in *Comparative Law in the 21st Century*, eds. A. Harding and E. Örücü (2002).

22 J. Baudrillaud, *In the Shadow of the Silent Majorities ... or The End of the Social and Other Essays* (1983).

23 N. Rose, 'The Death of the Social?: Re-Figuring the Territory of Government' (1996) 25 *Economy and Society* 327–56.

24 Among the most theoretically powerful contributions are: Y. Dezalay and B. Garth, *Dealing in Virtue: International Commercial Arbitration and the Construction of Transnational Legal Order* (1996); *Global Law Without a State*, ed. G. Teubner (1997); and B. De S. Santos, *Towards a New Common Sense: Law, Science and Politics in the Paradigmatic Transition* (2002, 2nd edn).

new conceptions of law. I think that sociolegal scholarship also has the urgent task of examining where new transnational legal forms can find sources of moral authority – in other words, how law can relate productively to needs for solidarity in networks of transnational social relations. That involves not just asking how law expresses relations of community beyond nation state boundaries but also how legal demands inevitably conflict as relations of community develop in tension with each other and what mechanisms can be developed to address these conflicts.

At present much transnational regulation exists in a kind of limbo. Its legal force and validity are usually assumed to depend on political sources: the acts of national political authorities or international agencies ultimately given legitimacy by the consent of states. This narrow positivist view ignores possible needs for a stronger moral authority for transnational regulation. Sociolegal studies' explorations of law's roots in community become specially urgent in transnational contexts if 'global law without a state',[25] created by agencies often existing at great moral distance from those affected by the law, is ever to become capable of holding its own as stable normative regulation against the play of unregulated coercive power exercised by states that dominate the international arena. The issue becomes ever more urgent with increased interaction and interdependence in and between transnational relations of community.

A consequence of all the developments discussed above is that both limbs of 'law and society' – the traditional object of sociolegal scholarship – are now deeply problematic. On the one hand, the social is no longer merely 'society' as classical sociology defined it: co-existent with the territorial reach of the nation state. On the other hand, 'law' now must be rethought as a diversity of regulatory strategies and forms, evolving from many different social sources in and beyond nation states. Sociolegal scholarship, I suggest, should lead legal studies forward by providing new frameworks for understanding these fundamental developments which make many older views of law and society redundant.

LAW, POWER, COMMUNITY

If, as suggested earlier, social science was a flag to fly in trying to escape the unsatisfactory character of traditional legal education and scholarship, what has been achieved through empirical sociolegal scholarship in Britain in the past thirty years suggests that the flag was a good one to adopt. But we need to take care to ensure that what has been so liberating about the sociolegal enterprise and has given it its potential to subvert and transform the complacency of much legal scholarship is retained and extended, particularly because much more subverting and transforming remains to be done.

25 Compare Teubner, op. cit. n. 24.

The heart of the enterprise in this sense has surely been its consistent focus on power. No concept is more important for sociolegal studies. Most sociolegal work explores the power of law: how it is structured and organized, its consequences and sources, and the way people and organizations seek to harness it, have differential access to it or find themselves differentially affected by it. Traditional legal scholarship has often largely ignored these aspects of the power of law. Instead, where it has considered power, it has typically seen it as external and opposed to law. Law has usually been seen as a control of power, above all of the directive and police power of the state; generally less attention has been paid to law's relation to economic power. The very idea of law as a control of state power indicates the incoherence and naivety of traditional legal scholarship's view of power: law being seen bizarrely as created by the state with the object of controlling the state. Sociolegal scholarship, by contrast, has shown how law as institutionalized doctrine formalizes and channels power rather than controlling it, often making its effects more predictable and precise and its exercise more orderly.

Whatever directions sociolegal scholarship takes in future, surely this emphasis on power should remain. Foucault showed power as a resource but nothing in his work seems to prevent recognition that the resource is distributed unevenly throughout the social and is often heavily concentrated. Law and power often run together as they pervade social life. Yet, despite the decreasing analytical usefulness of any public/private dichotomy, perhaps it is important somehow to keep a firm attachment to the idea of law as a *communal* rather than individual or private resource for channelling power. Law addresses stable social relations of all kinds, which can be thought of as relations of community. Indeed, viewed in this way, law has no valid reason for existence except as an expression and support of community. Major traditions of sociolegal writing stretching back to the beginnings of modern sociology of law in Eugen Ehrlich's work seem to take this view of law, emphasizing its social roots in a way that traditional legal scholarship has invariably failed to do.

But, if such a view is taken, certain consequences follow. To see law as an expression of community is to value it as a shared resource before asking how far and in what ways it fails as such an expression. Such an approach bases critique of actual law on a celebration of the idea of law as a communal resource, a vital part of the definition of communal solidarity. What sociolegal theory requires law to be according to this view, provides a measure of how far law fails in particular contexts. For example, to the extent that symbolic commitments to communal solidarity across the whole range of the social governed by law are weak in some respects[26] or hard to identify, leaving the idea of law itself as the strongest expression of those

26 On the relative strength of different types of social relations of community see Cotterrell, op. cit. (2001), n. 21, at pp. 80–9.

commitments, law in practice may tend to be devalued and debased by private appropriation or reduced to repression: law as a communal resource becomes little more than an object of struggle between individuals or organizations trying to harness it for their own gain or protection,[27] and lawyers themselves engineer or elaborate disputes and claims for similar reasons.[28] Then law is redefined in practice as no more than a private weapon or an engine of profit. Small wonder that, in these circumstances, it becomes often an object of derision or, at best, seen as an unfortunate necessity, a marker of social pathology.

My suggestion for tilting the sociolegal field is thus to reassert links between law and morality, viewing morality sociologically as the varied normative conditions of solidarity necessary to the diverse kinds of relations of community that comprise the social. Relations of community and relations between networks of community are power relations but power, like law, pervades social life. It is not to be regretted but analysed, shaped, and channelled. In transnational relations of community the place of law in channelling power remains problematic and uncertain because of the uncertainty of transnational law's bases of authority. In this context as in others, sociolegal research needs to consider law as part of a spectrum of regulation, defining the legal field in a way that facilitates the study of this spectrum as a whole. We may hope that, from positions such as these, sociolegal scholarship will be able to show how central its researches are for the whole range of legal studies and in addressing many of social science's most fundamental concerns.

27 Compare A. Kronman, *The Lost Lawyer: Falling Ideals of the Legal Profession* (1993), criticizing the incidence of purely instrumental attitudes to law. See, also, M.A. Glendon, *A Nation Under Lawyers: How the Crisis in the Legal Profession is Transforming American Society* (1994). But this is surely not just an American phenomenon.
28 See, for example, M.H. Trotter, *Profit and the Practice of Law: What's Happened to the Legal Profession* (1997) arguing that some large United States law firms grossly inflate client costs and pursue unnecessarily conflictual practice.

[2]
Community as a Legal Concept? Some Uses of a Law-and-Community Approach in Legal Theory[*]

Introduction

I have been asked to speak about my work in legal theory and, for nearly a decade, that has focused especially on an attempt to make 'community' a useful concept in legal inquiry. So this lecture will attempt to explain why I have gone back to community – a very old idea in social science – and tried to develop it into a new idea for sociolegal theory (though one that owes a great deal to the inspiration of Max Weber's sociology).

It is important to stress that what follows is not related to, or even necessarily sympathetic to, communitarian ideas in political and legal philosophy. They have become prominent for different reasons from those that drive my work. The law-and-community approach I want to talk about is not a philosophical approach, arguing, for example, like communitarianism, that communities are more fundamental in ontological terms than individuals. Nor is it a prescriptive approach suggesting that our societies would be better morally, and we would be better people ethically, if we thought about communities more, and individuals less. It is rather a methodological approach. As such, it tries to respond to what I see as defects in both legal philosophy (at least in the forms that are dominant in English-speaking countries) and sociology of law. These are defects in the capacity of both legal philosophy and legal sociology to understand the experienced reality of law.

* The revised text of a lecture at the University of Helsinki, January 20th 2006. I am grateful to the members of the Extreme Legal Positivism group for inviting me to Helsinki; to Professor Kaarlo Tuori for thoughtful consideration of my ideas in an accompanying lecture; and to Professor Martti Koskenniemi for specific comments. A version of this text was published in the electronic journal No Foundations: Journal of Extreme Legal Positivism <http://www.helsinki.fi/nofo/>, vol 2 (November 2006) 11–26.

A law-and-community approach tries to offer a framework for studying law that recognises the deep embeddedness of legal ideas, practices and problems in social experience. It recognises also that social experience is very varied and must be understood in all its variety. Legal philosophy in its dominant contemporary forms is not very interested in the empirical variety of law's social settings: what we can call 'the social' – the world of social experience of which law is an aspect or field. But, equally, modern legal sociology has not devoted enough attention to studying law as legal doctrine – by which is meant here rules, principles, concepts and values and the modes of interpreting and reasoning with these that are central to juristic practice and other legal experience.

The sociologists have failed to study law as a world of *ideas* and as subjective understanding of those ideas in action. The philosophers have failed to study law as a diverse, varied *social and historical experience*; in other words, as legal ideas and practices that do not exist in abstraction but are encountered, interpreted, understood, invoked in different social settings, by lawyers and citizens with diverse personal aims, expectations, projects, emotional attachments, traditions, beliefs and values.

An Engagement with Law

These briefly stated ideas give some pointers to the general themes of this talk. I can best begin to be more concrete by saying something of my own experience. As an undergraduate student of law at London University in the 1960s I found it hard to link legal ideas with important social issues. Legal doctrine in some way reflected a social world 'outside' law but it seemed relatively unimportant to know exactly how law did this, since as doctrine it could be analysed without empirical knowledge of the social world. All that was needed was a general, conservative common sense. The gulf seemed striking between the technicalities of legal reasoning, on the one hand, and large moral and political issues about law, on the other. Legal reasoning and broad moral-political discourses seemed to inhabit different worlds, and the latter clearly posed a threat to the professional maintenance of the former, unless they could be largely excluded from consideration within it.

A compulsory final year undergraduate course ('Jurisprudence and Legal Theory') seemed at first to promise to bridge the divide between legal analysis and moral and political theory. But I quickly felt dissatisfied with the non-empirical approach of most legal philosophy[1] – the lack of concern to ask what

---

1   Legal realism in its Scandinavian and American varieties seemed to offer a refreshing partial exception. Both kinds of legal realism seemed to take psychological dimensions of law seriously, even if this rarely extended as far as requiring empirical research.

people actually experience in relation to law, and how that experience varies for different parts of a population.

To take familiar examples, John Austin, founder of modern English legal theory, sees the social only in terms of the 'bulk of the population' in a 'habit of obedience' to a sovereign; for Austin, the only salient social fact for legal theory is mass submission to authority. In legal theory, the population can be ignored as long as it stays quiet. Again, H.L.A. Hart's contrasting of 'internal' and 'external' aspects of legal rules, and of 'officials' and citizens, hardly seeks to address the complexity of the social or of legal experience. Officials are apparently what the legal system designates as such, yet their 'internal' recognition of certain rules is crucial for the legal system to exist. This circularity remains because of a failure to ask sociological questions about officials and, in particular, to study (as Max Weber did) the historical emergence of legal elites. Again, Ronald Dworkin's work, postulating a political community as notional author of its law, devotes no attention to the idea that there might be *many* communities, competing and conflicting in their interpretation of the same law. Dworkin does not recognise that, to understand the possibilities of relating these communities, we might need to explore (especially in today's multicultural societies) the social conditions and cultural environments that inform differences in outlooks on law.[2]

Problems such as these (which I sensed at the time, rather than understood) led me to begin to read myself into sociology of law from around 1970. In the mid-1970s I studied sociology formally as a postgraduate student in London, while teaching law. Fortunately, my sociology teachers emphasised the great classical sociological theorists (especially Max Weber, Emile Durkheim and Karl Marx), who devoted much attention to law. Perhaps this gave me a particularly rosy view of sociology as an open, imaginative enterprise, relatively unconcerned with disciplinary boundaries. Especially in Weber's and Durkheim's work the ambition to make sense of the social in all its variety and historical complexity seemed immense, almost breathtaking. I felt that beside such giants, most legal philosophers I had read were pygmies, because they seemed to ignore vast social worlds – and the possibilities for understanding these systematically – that the classical sociologists opened up.

Almost paradoxically, sociology's great attraction and value for the legal scholar – its intellectual openness, theoretical ambition and rich variety – seemed to be a consequence of its disciplinary weakness. It is still unclear whether Weber should be labelled as a legal historian, economic historian, economist or sociologist. Marx fits no disciplinary label. Durkheim saw himself

---

2 See e.g. D.E. Roberts, 'Why Culture Matters to Law: The Difference Politics Makes' in A. Sarat and T.R. Kearns eds, *Cultural Pluralism, Identity Politics and the Law* (2001).

as definitely a sociologist – but, for him, sociology is an umbrella discipline that embraces all social studies, including the study of law. I relished this intellectual unboundedness – the huge vistas that sociology opened up for legal inquiry.

Sociology has its problems, however. Its disciplinary weakness has, at least in Britain, often made it a relatively open club, but efforts to professionalise it (most successful in the United States) have worked against the possibilities for using its resources in legal theory. These efforts have encouraged a privileging of quantitative (rather than qualitative) research methods, an emphasis on the importance of hypothesis-testing (rather than more philosophically-oriented inquiries), and a positivistic, value-free stance (with a corresponding lack of overt concern with social criticism or evaluation). These developments are valuable in many respects and have been reflected in 'much good empirical research in modern sociology of law. But they tend to drive sociological inquiry away from the juristic world – and, more generally, the world of legal ideas – and towards the study of measurable, observable behaviour in legal contexts.

This is in sharp contrast to the strong focus on legal and moral ideas that one finds in Durkheim's writing, or on legal reasoning in Weber's. It is also very different from the focus of much early sociology of law, such as the work of Eugen Ehrlich, Leon Petrazycki and Georges Gurvitch on legal experience as a form of social or cultural experience. A focus on legal discourse is important in Niklas Luhmann's recent sociology, and a concern with legal values (especially the value of legality) centrally informs Philip Selznick's sociology of law. But these are exceptions. My strongest intellectual allegiance is to sociology of law, but I gradually felt dissatisfied with the lack of concern of much legal sociology with any need to engage with legal philosophy – to debate with the jurists the nature of law as institutionalised doctrine, as ideas embedded in social practices.

Legal Theory and its Discontents

In general, legal philosophy lacks serious interest in social variation. It has few resources for studying analytically differences within and between legal systems in terms that are meaningful to citizens of those systems. In its dominant (positivist) forms it has little serious interest in ethics or morals: an interest in the former atrophied with natural law theory; an interest in the latter as a social support of law seems weak at best. It also has little interest in history – including the comparative history of legal and moral ideas (for which we might recall here the tradition of Westermarck). It has, indeed, little interest in citizens as such: its focus is overwhelmingly on lawyers' thought and juristic (rather than popular) images of law. It is little concerned with law that is not jurisdictionally bounded by the nation state – i.e. with such phenomena as legal pluralism, and the nature of transnational legal regimes and contemporary international law.

It has yet to come to grips with multiculturalism as a phenomenon raising new issues about legal pluralism in various forms.[3] What of sociology of law? It is seen (even by many of its practitioners) as concerned with behaviour in legal contexts rather than with legal ideas as such, and so as 'external' to juristic discourse. It tends to observe rather than interpret law (yet Weber provided a model of *verstehen* and a method of ideal or pure types to facilitate the sociological study of legal ideas and subjective social experience). Just as Weber emphasised the need for both observation and empathetic understanding of social phenomena, it should be possible to study legal communities from both the 'inside' (as experienced by their members) and the 'outside' (as they appear to a non-member observer). Again, legal sociology is insufficiently concerned with legal values (with notable exceptions, such as Selznick) or with morality as a component of or normative support for law. Yet Durkheim saw a sociology of morals as a vital partner of (and hardly separable from) a sociology of law.

Most fundamentally, modern sociology of law has been mainly *instrumental* in orientation. Historically its concern has often been to address policy-makers.[4] It has been funded especially to be useful to legal and political reformers. Its pragmatist temper has in some degree (especially in the United States) been inherited from legal realism. Sociology has often been understood as inspired historically by a need to confront the Hobbesian 'problem of order'[5] (what makes society or social integration possible) and by problems of capitalism (the poor, the marginalised, the urban proletariat). Sociology of law, like sociology, has often been in the business of helping to *engineer* the social, to shape or steer it. It has been less concerned to *appreciate* the social (and the legal within it), exploring it in its diversity. The dominant focus has been on planned change and reform. It is, indeed, striking how little concern there has been with custom and tradition (and, more generally, with sources of cultural stability and organic social change) in sociology of law.

Because of this pervasive instrumentalism, sociology of law has long been caught up in 'gap' questions.[6] How far does law constitute the social? (i.e. how far is the social shaped by law?) How far does law 'mirror' the social? (i.e. how far is law shaped by the social?) What is the relationship between law

---

3   See e.g. P. Shah, *Legal Pluralism in Conflict: Coping with Cultural Diversity in Law* (2005); N.V. Demleitner, 'Combating Legal Ethnocentrism: Comparative Law Sets Boundaries' (1999) 31 *Arizona State L J* 737.

4   A. Sarat and S.S. Silbey, 'The Pull of the Policy Audience' (1988) 10 *Law and Policy* 97.

5   See, generally, T. Parsons, *The Structure of Social Action*, vol. 1 (1968).

6   D. Nelken, 'The "Gap problem" in the Sociology of Law: A Theoretical Review' (1981) 1 *Windsor Yearbook of Access to Justice* 35.

and social reality? How much of a 'gap' or failure of 'fit' is there between law and the social? All of these questions are, I think, misguided. Law is an aspect or field of the social. What is in issue is not law's relation to something *apart from itself* (the social); the issue is how a certain side or part of the social *takes the form of law*. If we understand the social in terms of social relations we can see how law provides a form or structure of social relations. Any 'gap' or lack of 'fit' is not between law and the social, but between types of social relations (and their law) that may be in conflict with each other.

In some respects, orientations of modern legal sociology parallel dominant trends in Anglophone legal philosophy. Thus, a predominantly positivist orientation tends to marginalise moral issues about law, and to obscure intimate relations between law and morals. A dominant assumption is that law is the unified law of the nation state, supervised by centralised state institutions supported by a monopoly of coercive power. There is an absence of reflexiveness (a sociology and a socio-political history of legal sociology are needed, as they are also for legal philosophy). Most strangely of all, legal sociology's most rigorous recent theory, Luhmann's autopoiesis theory,[7] parallels legal philosophy's tendency to see law as a relatively self-contained discourse. It does so, however, with no greater warrant from empirical studies than legal philosophy claims.

Law and Community

A law-and-community approach seeks to respond to many of these criticisms of legal philosophy and sociology of law, and to transcend the divide between these research fields. What then is the essence of this approach? Here it is only possible to set out, schematically, ideas developed much more fully elsewhere.[8]

Firstly, the unit of study is social relations; all law is a regulation of social relations. The aim is to understand the general conditions and problems of regulating social relations through law. And law is taken here to be doctrine – rules, principles, etc, and modes of interpreting them – institutionalised in the sense that distinct agencies or practices are associated with creating, interpreting or enforcing doctrine, but not necessarily with all three functions. This is a pluralistic view of law – law is not limited to the law created by centralised state agencies (it could be created, for example, by churches or localities), though state law will usually be especially significant. Where social

---

7 N. Luhmann, *Law as a Social System* (2004).
8 R. Cotterrell, *Law, Culture and Society: Legal Ideas in the Mirror of Social Theory* (2006).

relations have a degree of stability, duration and trust, they can be thought of as relations of *community*. Law's role is to protect community and to express or support conditions for it.

All jurists know that legal analysis must use abstractions; it cannot deal individually with every distinct social relation in its uniqueness. The same is true for sociolegal inquiry. As Weber taught, social analysis can make no progress unless it abstracts from the infinity of circumstances in social life by using a limited number of logically formulated types or categories (which he calls ideal types). On this basis, social relations of community can be analysed in terms of just four ideal types that underpin all the different kinds of social bonds that link people in relations of community.[9] In combination they exhaust all the possible forms in which social relations of community can exist.

The types are instrumental community, traditional community, affective community and community of belief or values. Instrumental community arises where people share a common project (often, but not necessarily, economic) or have convergent projects in which they co-operate. Traditional community arises from mere co-existence in the same shared environment – the same locality, language group, traditions, historical experience, etc. Affective community is founded purely on affection. It can be a matter of emotional attachments (love, friendship) but it can be defined also by shared dislikes or hatreds (of 'outsiders' of the community). Finally, community of belief or values is founded on shared fundamental beliefs (for example, religious beliefs) or ultimate values (accepted for their own sake and not for instrumental reasons). These types of community rarely, if ever exist in pure form in actual social reality. They combine and interact in complex ways as networks of community. Separating them out, however, makes it possible to examine the different logical characteristics and consequences of each.

On other occasions I have discussed these four types of community in detail.[10] Here the main concern is with what they can be used for in the light of the criticisms, made earlier, of legal theory in its philosophical sociological forms. A law-and-community approach unites aspects of legal philosophy and legal sociology in a common enterprise of identifying different kinds of general *regulatory problems* that arise when law is seen as the regulatory aspect of the

---

9 They are, themselves, derived from Weber's own four ideal types of social action – instrumentally rational (*zweckrational*), value-rational (*wertrational*), affectual and traditional – which, he claims, are combined in an infinity of ways in actual social life. For Weber, all social phenomena can be understood in terms of patterns or combinations of these four types. See M. Weber, *Economy and Society* (1968) 24-25.

10 R. Cotterrell, 'A Legal Concept of Community' (1997) 12 *Canadian J Law & Soc* 75, reprinted in adapted form with later relevant papers in *Law, Culture and Society, op. cit.*

social. A map or agenda of legal theory's essential regulatory concerns can be sketched by speculating on general characteristics of the types of community. For example, when people are linked solely by common involvement in a project, the scope and limits of this *instrumental* social relation are usually relatively clear. The relation focuses on *that* project (e.g. as contract, deal, association or enterprise) and lasts until it is completed. The relation links people on only one relatively narrow plane of common and perhaps transient interest. But because of this clarity of scope and aims, legally regulating instrumental community may be relatively easy and effective. Contract and commercial law, for example, are typically sophisticated, well developed kinds of law. As comparative lawyers know, they often 'travel well', making strong juridical sense across and between jurisdictions.[11] Instrumental community may often be limited or attenuated community, but with strong law.

Traditional community is similar in some respects. Merely happening to be in the same environment of co-existence does not necessarily make for any strong or deep social bonds. But this mere co-existence can be guaranteed by strong, well-understood law: for example basic tort (delict) or criminal law; law that aims at preventing friction in everyday interactions. But if the focus is on environments of co-existence, the crucial complicating factor for regulation is that the meaning of 'environment' varies and constantly changes. Which environments are most important, most deserving of protection? New forms of environmental risk arise (relating, for example, to public health, climate change, security and ecology). Protection of one environment may be at the expense of another. What is to be taken as the essential *arena* of co-existence for regulatory purposes? (the local neighbourhood, the city, the nation, the world?) The law of traditional community is basic in one sense (in governing everyday interpersonal contacts), but very complex in others (in assessing often poorly understood risks and trying to balance them).

What of community of *belief or values*? A community based on shared fundamental beliefs may be relatively strong. But it may be hard and even undesirable to provide regulation to express or protect the beliefs that unite the community. Values or beliefs are hard to translate directly into rules, or into any kind of unambiguous law. Ultimate values or beliefs need interpreting, but this easily produces controversy. And regulation is weak if it attracts serious controversy and interpretive impasses. Law expresses values, but legal reasoning usually avoids appealing to the broadest values and (as noted earlier) 'hides' in technicality. So the regulation of community of belief or values is always problematic, yet necessary. How are fundamental values to be expressed and guaranteed by law?

---

11   See e.g. E. Levy, 'The Reception of Highly Developed Legal Systems by Peoples of Different Cultures' (1950) 25 *Washington L Rev* 233.

Affective community poses the hardest regulatory problems of all. Perhaps ties of love or friendship can provide some of the strongest, most inclusive bonds of community, but how is love or friendship to be regulated? The very idea seems misguided. Yet law has to provide regulatory frameworks for social relations that are founded on affection, and to regulate the consequences of ending these relations. It also has to regulate relations created by pure hatred and bigotry, resistant to reason (as in racism). It frames altruism in the form of charity, welfare care and support, and fiduciary relations. In many ways law is concerned with the definition and analysis of relations based on emotion; relations that are powerful yet often quixotic, diffuse and hard to codify in terms of obligations and expectations; relations that – for Weber, at least – defied rational analysis.

Re-orienting Legal Theory

The tentative generalisations above are intended to suggest possible lines of inquiry for legal theory. They point to a need for sociological inquiries about social relations of community and their regulatory problems, and juristic inquiries about the forms that law can and should take in expressing these relations. They make no direct reference to the state, since networks of community exist both inside and across the boundaries of nation states. A law-and-community approach assumes that regulation of communities is not necessarily regulation by state law, though that will be of most interest to jurists. It sees regulatory problems as rooted in the very nature of community life – in all its variety. Hence legal studies not informed by sociological insight will be barren. Further, if the pure types of community interact in complex ways in actual social life, contradictory regulatory problems will often arise in these interactions. An emphasis on community does not imply an absence of conflict. Rather it highlights key foci of legal contradiction and controversy.

Two final claims to be made here address the main criticisms of legal philosophy and legal sociology presented earlier. Firstly, a law-and-community approach corrects the instrumentalist overemphasis of sociology of law, and directs attention to law's complex relations to culture, which legal philosophy often ignores or under-emphasises. Secondly, this approach restores the significance, in legal theory, of ethics and morality, seen in intimate but variable relation to law.

As has been seen, in a law-and-community approach, *instrumental* social relations are only one of four distinct social realms of regulation. The framework of analysis puts equal emphasis on tradition, beliefs and values, and emotion – matters underemphasised in most contemporary legal analysis but important to culture. Culture is often seen as embedded in beliefs and values, on the one hand, or traditions, on the other. It also has important affective aspects. People do not just consider instrumentally the culture they inhabit (as, for example when they talk of levels of material or technological culture). Culture is also a matter of cultural inheritances and cultural values, often overlaid with (nationalistic or other) emotional attachments. Law is called on to express and protect culture in these senses, no less than it is also required to frame economic life and serve instrumental or material aspects of culture.[12] A law-and-community approach recognises (i) that these different regulatory demands relating to culture may often violently conflict and (ii) that a legal focus on the promotion or protection of instrumental social relations alone would be a distortion of law's responsibilities as an expression of community life.

It may be that, partly because of the general legal problems (mentioned earlier) of regulating both community of values and affective community, there is a tendency for regulatory aspects of these two types of community to be reinterpreted as regulatory aspects of instrumental or traditional community. Thus, recent tendencies to reinterpret fiduciary relations of trust (which have affective aspects as relations of care and concern) as contractual relations can be noted.[13] Similarly, difficult questions of religious sensitivity (related to community of belief) may be turned into issues of public order (a kind of regulation of traditional community), in justifying laws on blasphemy[14] or incitement to religious hatred. If a law-and-community approach has an explicit moral-political message it is that law's relations with all types of community are important and that the vitality of the social requires law to engage sensitively with them all, recognising their distinct integrity.

One other aspect of a law-and-community approach is important here: its emphasis on law's close relation to ethics and morals, and its claim that these vary, taking different forms in relation to different types of community. In a community, morality specifies the shared understandings that allow mutual interpersonal trust to exist. Ethics concerns the individual's responsibilities. Some appropriate orientations of morals and ethics for each type of community can be tentatively suggested here (appropriate in the sense that they spring directly from the nature of the social bond involved). Thus, courtesy, civility and neighbourliness seem important to the morals of traditional community, together with an ethics of non-interference. Empathy, sympathy and an ideal of unbounded concern for the other seem morally important to affective community; the relevant ethics is one of altruism and care. Again, honesty and

---

12 R. Cotterrell, 'Law in Culture' (2004) 17 *Ratio Juris* 1.

13 J.H. Langbein, 'The Contractarian Basis of the Law of Trusts' (1995) 105 *Yale L J* 625.

14 C. Unsworth, 'Blasphemy, Cultural Divergence and Legal Relativism' (1995) 58 *Modern L Rev* 658.

fair dealing are morally important to instrumental community; and the relevant ethics is one of performance (meeting personal obligations undertaken). Finally, as regards community of values or belief, morality focuses on fellowship and respect for others' integrity; and ethics here demands personal integrity and discipleship.

Of course, it can be said that many of these moral and ethical principles have little to do with law, and it is not the responsibility of law to enforce them or reward their adoption. But law either mirrors aspects of them, or engages with them, turning them into practical rules or principles insofar as it can. Just as ultimate values resist precise legal expression, so law (in the form of rules, at least) merely approximates the general moral and ethical directions of community solidarity. Yet legal doctrine might be better understood as something socially vital, and less a matter of 'mere technicality', when its relation to the various moral dimensions of community is explored in depth.

As noted earlier, the regulatory problems of different types of community can conflict. So, complex networks of community may present a picture of moral confusion or contradiction, reflected in the law relating to these networks. Some overarching values, common interests or traditions, or shared emotional attachments are needed to hold networks of community together; to prevent unmanageable conflicts between them. It was claimed earlier that shared values or beliefs and mutual affection often provide the strongest communal bonds (as compared with instrumental or traditional bonds). But in considering large-scale networks of community, affect or emotion may be too unstable and volatile to consider as a primary basis of unity. So, if, by a process of elimination, the most promising source of bonding is common beliefs or values, where are these to be found?

In sociology of law, Philip Selznick has claimed that a universal humanism can guarantee an ultimate integrity of pluralistic community life;[15] but its source remains obscure. Durkheim suggests a sociological basis for a moral individualism (emphasising respect for others as individuals, and human dignity) appropriate to complex modern societies.[16] Others, such as Jürgen Habermas,[17] have speculated on historical conditions that have given rise, through painful experience, to unifying ultimate values in Western Europe. Here the problem of identifying such unifying values can only be indicated, not explored. But a law-and-community approach, tentative and undeveloped as it is at present, at least points clearly to the need to reconsider in depth law's

---

15 P. Selznick, *The Moral Commonwealth: Social Theory and the Promise of Community* (1992) ch. 4.

16 R. Cotterrell, *Emile Durkheim: Law in a Moral Domain* (1999) ch. 7.

17 See e.g. J. Habermas, 'Why Europe Needs a Constitution' (2001) 11 *New Left Review* 2nd ser. 5.

relations to morals, ethics and ultimate values. It raises many more questions than it answers, but this is because, as suggested at the beginning of this lecture, it is a methodology – a tool to open up legal theory to a sharp and sustained sensitivity to the variation of the social and the cultural meanings of law.

[3]
From 'Living Law' to the 'Death of the Social': Sociology in Legal Theory

Theoretically-minded lawyers—jurists—have actively reflected on sociology's potential throughout much of its modern history. They have often wondered whether sociology can be a resource to aid their inquiries about the nature and functions of law, or a competitor in these inquiries. The relations of juristic legal theory, in this sense, and sociology have been debated over many decades, at least by legal scholars.

A century ago sociology was in the process of becoming institutionalized as a modern discipline. Around that time, the vast diversity of possible attitudes of jurists to sociology was first clearly signalled. Eugen Ehrlich proclaimed in 1913 that legal theory *is* sociology of law. 'Since the law is a social phenomenon, every kind of legal science is a social science; but legal science in the proper sense of the term [as a theoretical study] is part of the theoretical science of society, of sociology. The sociology of law is the theoretical science of law.'[1] Hans Kelsen answered by bluntly declaring sociology irrelevant to a genuine science of law, which studies not social activity but norms governed by a specific coercive technique.[2] In sharp contrast, around the same time, Roscoe Pound attached the label 'sociological' to his entire legal philosophy to suggest its progressive outlook.[3]

In these and all later juristic engagements with sociology, the latter is usually taken as a given, its nature assumed to be well-understood. For Kelsen, Ehrlich's writings (and related work by Hermann Kantorowicz) were sufficient initially to represent sociology in its relation to law and allow an assessment of its prospects;[4] for Pound, early influences especially from the sociologists Edward Ross and Albion Small[5] gave

---

[1] E. Ehrlich, *Fundamental Principles of the Sociology of Law* (New Brunswick, 2002), 25.
[2] H. Kelsen, *General Theory of Law and State* (New York, 1945), 24–8.
[3] N.E.H. Hull, *Roscoe Pound and Karl Llewellyn: Searching for an American Jurisprudence* (Chicago, 1997), 84–5.
[4] See generally, R. Treves, 'Hans Kelsen et la sociologie du droit' (1985) 1 *Droit et Société* 15.
[5] Hull, n.3, above, 55; R. Pound, 'Sociology of Law' in G. Gurvitch and W.E. Moore (eds), *Twentieth Century Sociology* (New York, 1945), 297, 335.

sufficient indications to make the 'sociological' label initially meaningful for him; it was a term that was 'in the air' early in the twentieth century.[6] Matters have changed little since: the nature of sociology as a knowledge-field has remained largely unexamined in detail by jurists.

My chapter seeks to address this topic. It asks: what is sociology for legal theorists, especially for jurists pursuing theoretical inquiries about the nature of law as doctrine, ideas and reasoning? And, by contrast, what is sociology for sociologists? Can an inquiry into the awareness which sociology's practitioners have of its nature as a scholarly practice and field help to clarify relationships between legal theory and sociology? I think that it can, if only by raising issues about the nature of the kinds of social inquiry to which legal studies might relate.

Law as a scholarly field of juristic studies undoubtedly has important internal debates on methods and aims. But these usually seem very limited compared with the anguished self-examination which sociology regularly undergoes. From some standpoints, this is undoubtedly a weakness of sociology, raising doubts about its disciplinary status, its coherence and unity as a scholarly field, its usefulness (for what? to whom?), its scientific credentials and its identity and demarcation from other fields of knowledge. From another standpoint, however, sociology's incessant navel-gazing and its radical debates on methods, theory, aims and achievements are far from counter-productive. They are instructive—and not just for sociologists. In what follows I shall try to show that they can even help to clarify the very nature of theoretical legal studies.

Conceptualizing Sociology in Relation to Legal Theory

Sociology's intellectual discomforts suggest not its weakness but its inherently reflexive character. The aim of sociology is to study systematically and empirically the nature of the social (however much debate there is about how to do this). Consequently, it cannot help but reflect on its *own* research practices as social practices. So there is nothing paradoxical about the idea of a sociology of sociology.[7] The implication of it is that sociology seeks methods of critically examining its

---

[6] *Cf.* Benjamin Cardozo's use of the phrase 'the method of sociology' (the term 'sociology' remaining unexplained) in his *Nature of the Judicial Process* (New Haven, 1921) to suggest purposive, policy-oriented shaping of law.

[7] See, e.g. A.W. Gouldner, *The Coming Crisis of Western Sociology* (London, 1971), ch. 2. The idea of a law of law is not paradoxical either. Natural law can be seen as a (moral) law of (positive) law. Yet it is surely significant that law's reflexivity in the form of natural law theory is now pushed to the margins of legal scholarship, having little impact on much of it, while, as will be discussed below, sociology's self-critique seems never far from the centre of sociologists' concerns. The idea of sociology's reflexivity which is central to Pierre Bourdieu's influential work is treated by him as compatible with a strong sense of disciplinarity. See P. Bourdieu and L.J.D. Wacquant, *An Introduction to Reflexive Sociology* (Cambridge, 1992). I argue in this chapter that the full implications of reflexivity make that compatibility doubtful.

18

own methods; theory to explain its own theory; paradigms to upset the rigidities of its existing paradigms. This is not a recipe for comfortable existence. But it might be a necessary prescription for permanently reflexive practice in social research: practice that seeks to understand its own ambiguities, problems, and limits at any given time, but also is engaged in a continuous, never-ending effort to transcend them.[8]

These features of sociology will be illustrated later by considering aspects of sociologists' contemporary debates about the nature of their scholarly enterprise. But how could such matters be relevant to juristic concerns? I think jurists have often failed to consider sociology's complex nature sufficiently and so may have sometimes over-estimated and sometimes under-estimated possibilities for engaging with it, or failed to see problems. In particular, if sociology embraces (i) well-recognized common methods, theories and research traditions but also (ii) a permanent tendency to reject confinement within these, it can be conveniently seen for the purposes of legal theoretical inquiries in two contrasting yet related ways.

On the one hand, 'sociology' means the established products of sociology-as-discipline: the methods, theories, research, and writings of self-professed sociologists, accredited members of a distinct discipline. This is *professionalized sociology*—sociology as a self-consciously organized academic field and professional practice.

On the other hand, sociology's reflexive character, which often disturbs its self-perceptions as a discipline, suggests that its intellectual boundaries are often open and largely unpoliced. This situation makes it plausible to consider sociology as something beyond a specialized discipline or professional practice. It can be understood as any systematic, empirically-oriented study of the social (the human relations that make up social life), whether or not conducted by scholars who are identified or identify themselves in any way with sociology as a discipline, science, or profession.[9] Stjepan Meštrović described sociology as a 'wild discipline', that bursts free of attempts to contain it through agreed disciplinary protocols, resists organization, is the focus of work for scholars of any discipline or none, and draws on any knowledge-fields (including the humanities, and the natural and social sciences) that may be helpful.[10] Sociology in this second, wider sense, might be called *transdisciplinary sociology*—sociology as an aspiration and resource, unconstrained by and often oblivious to demarcations of academic fields and formal divisions of professional accreditation.

I suggest that both of these conceptions of sociology are relevant to legal theory. Because the nature and problems of sociology as an organized discipline have

---

[8] See generally R. Cotterrell, *Law's Community: Legal Theory in Sociological Perspective* (Oxford, 1995), ch. 3, and for further discussion and critique, D. Nelken, 'Can There Be a Sociology of Legal Meaning?', in Nelken (ed.) *Law as Communication* (Aldershot, 1996); D. Nelken, 'Blinding Insights? The Limits of a Reflexive Sociology of Law' (1998) 25 *Journal of Law and Society* 407.

[9] R. Cotterrell, 'Why Must Legal Ideas Be Understood Sociologically?' (1998) 25 *Journal of Law and Society* 171.

[10] S. Meštrović, Anthony Giddens: The Last Modernist (London, 1998), 209–11.

From 'Living Law' to the 'Death of the Social'—Sociology in Legal Theory 19

seldom been examined by legal scholars (and seldom been of much interest to them), legal scholarship has rarely sought a place in the concerns of professionalized sociology, or a means of integrating juristic viewpoints with them. But it has often allied itself with various kinds of transdisciplinary sociology, drawing on it, contributing to it, and even becoming integrated in some aspects with it.

Correspondingly, juristic issues (questions about the nature of legal doctrine and its interpretation, legal values, and concepts, relations of legal and moral ideas, etc) have rarely been a concern for social scientists. A few leading sociological theorists (notably Philip Selznick and Niklas Luhmann recently, and Emile Durkheim, Max Weber, and Georges Gurvitch among classical sociological theorists) have had a sufficient interest in juristic concerns to define a clear, prominent place for them in relation to sociology. But the primary link of professionalized sociology to law has been through empirical sociolegal studies using categories that social scientists, not jurists, have defined as research foci.

What seems clear is that when jurists first began to appeal in a sustained way to sociology or social psychology for enlightenment they saw primarily a transdisciplinary sociology of some kind, if only because professionalized sociology then hardly existed. Ehrlich's sociology of law is clearly a jurist's homespun (but insightful) sociology, largely unrelated to any sense of sociology as an organized discipline.[11] But his _Fundamental Principles of the Sociology of Law_ does not need re-labelling as a work of sociological jurisprudence.[12] Pound, for all the vagueness of his conceptual thinking, recognized that scholars such as Ehrlich aimed to contribute to a science of social life in a way that Pound's own sociological jurisprudence ultimately did not.[13] If Ehrlich's sociology of law is a jurist's sociology, it is sociology none the less. His concept of 'living law' was intended to identify normative structures of social life—that is, to pursue a sociological project of systematic empirical study of the social. But Ehrlich's sociology sought to wake lawyers up to their failure (as he saw it) in understanding social conditions that give law its substance.[14] Sociology could reveal and define social norms that lawyers should accept as part of the regulatory field their work addressed.

Half a century after Ehrlich wrote his great book on sociology of law, a strongly contrasting juristic invocation of sociology was made when H.L.A. Hart described his _Concept of Law_ as 'an essay in descriptive sociology'.[15] Sociolegal

---

[11] Ehrlich (n.1, above, 25), explicitly denies that sociology is a unitary field distinct from 'the social sciences as a whole'.

[12] _Cf._ R. Banakar, _Merging Law and Sociology: Beyond the Dichotomies in Socio-Legal Research_ (Glienicke, Berlin, 2003), ch. 7; R. Banakar, 'Sociological Jurisprudence' in R. Banakar and M. Travers (eds), _An Introduction to Law and Social Theory_ (Oxford, 2002).

[13] R. Pound, 'Preface' to G. Gurvitch, _Sociology of Law_ (London, 1947), ix, x, xv; Pound, 'Sociology of Law' (n.5, above), 297, 301–2. D. Nelken, 'Law in Action or Living Law? Back to the Beginning in Sociology of Law' (1984) 4 _Legal Studies_ 157 carefully highlights the differences between Pound's and Ehrlich's projects.

[14] K.A. Ziegert, 'The Sociology behind Eugen Ehrlich's Sociology of Law' (1979) 7 _International Journal of the Sociology of Law_ 225.

[15] H.L.A. Hart, _The Concept of Law_, 2nd edn. (Oxford, 1994), vi.

20

scholars have often treated Hart's claim as a simple category mistake, noting that his essay in legal philosophy lacks systematic sociology.[16] The elements most obviously missing are those associated with professionalized sociology, such as established social scientific methods, concepts, or theories. Yet the reason why Hart's claim to have written sociologically was mistaken is surely not that legal philosophy and sociology are *inherently* different enterprises or that legal philosophy cannot be sociological in some respects. It is that *The Concept of Law* is not seriously concerned with systematic empirical inquiry about the diversity—what Selznick calls 'variation'[17]—of the social (and, one might add, insufficiently reflexive about its own social practices of juristic speculation).

Shortly before Hart's book was published, Ernest Gellner labelled its main intellectual inspiration—Oxford linguistic philosophy—as 'pseudo-sociology' because its speculation on linguistic usage was claimed to be able to reveal features of social life. Gellner thought that 'some of its insights logically call for sociological inquiry, if indeed they do not imply that sociology should replace philosophy.'[18] Linguistic philosophy 'calls for sociology. If the meaning of terms is their use and context, then those contexts and the activities therein should be investigated seriously—and without making the mistaken assumption that we already know enough about the world and about society to identify the actual functioning of our use of words.'[19] Linguistic philosophy (including its juristic branch) might be empirically-oriented in its concern with 'ordinary usage'. But what particular part of the social world does this philosophy reflect? Whose ordinary usage is assumed? For Gellner, it was that of 'the [academic] folk of North Oxford, roughly.'[20]

There is no need here to pursue further Gellner's fascinating polemic. The point is to note how different senses of 'sociology' are invoked. Hart and some other philosophers claim to be doing a kind of social analysis—even sociology—by analysing certain social practices (of language use). Gellner, however, implies that a real sociology would show the emptiness of the philosophers' 'pseudo-sociology'. He appeals not necessarily to professionalized sociology but surely to methods and theories associated with it: these would be criteria of real rather than pseudo-sociology. But what if, today, sociologists themselves do not agree on what is real or pseudo-sociology? And if they adopt disciplinary definitions, why must these be accepted by jurists? If the idea of a transdisciplinary sociology is accepted, the criticism of Hart is not that his legal philosophy is pseudo-sociology, but that as sociology (systematic empirical study of the social) it is demonstrably weak, even if

---

[16] See, e.g. J.P. Gibbs, 'Definitions of Law and Empirical Questions' (1968) 2 *Law and Society Review* 429; S. Roberts, *Order and Dispute: An Introduction to Legal Anthropology* (Harmondsworth, 1979), 24–5; M. Krygier, '*The Concept of Law* and Social Theory' (1982) 2 *Oxford Journal of Legal Studies* 155; P. Fitzpatrick, *Modernism and the Grounds of Law* (Cambridge, 2001), 97–9.

[17] R. Cotterrell and P. Selznick, 'Selznick Interviewed' (2004) 31 *Journal of Law and Society* 291, 296.

[18] E. Gellner, *Words and Things* (Harmondsworth, 1968), 255–6.   [19] *Ibid*, 257.

[20] *Ibid*, 265.

From 'Living Law' to the 'Death of the Social'—Sociology in Legal Theory 21

its conceptual analysis may be useful in structuring certain kinds of sociological inquiry.[21]

Jurists and Sociologists

Some jurists have taken methods, theories, or traditions of professionalized sociology very seriously, adopting them directly in their work. Some of Lon Fuller's writings on the forms and functions of legal processes, the use by French jurists such as Léon Duguit, Paul Huvelin, and Emmanuel Lévy of Durkheim's sociology, and Gunther Teubner's developments of Niklas Luhmann's social theory, are varied illustrations of this.[22]

Indeed, relations between juristic study and sociology have occasionally been described—at least rhetorically—as relations of dependence, and not just of the former on the latter. Celestin Bouglé, a follower of Durkheim, proclaimed the study of laws and customs as essential to sociology, which 'must inscribe on the mansion it seeks to build: "No-one may enter here who is not a jurist."'[23] Such a claim now seems very strange, but it represents a particular sociological view that the theoretical study of law could be detached from its pragmatic ties to the concerns of lawyers and treated as an important, perhaps foundational social study in its own right, even where it was built on the work of jurists.[24] Conversely Ehrlich's and Pound's claims that legal theory relies on sociology presuppose a transdisciplinary sociology. Claims of dependence usually seem to presuppose a view that largely rejects the disciplinary distinctiveness of either sociology or legal studies.

Where, however, juristic study and sociology are seen in terms of strong disciplinary or scientific identities of some kind, the relation between them may often be simply one of indifference or, at most, mutual observation. Weber presented his sociology of law as essentially distinct from juristic studies,[25] and focused

[21] See, e.g. H. Ross, *Law as a Social Institution* (Oxford, 2001); E. Colvin, 'The Sociology of Secondary Rules' (1978) 28 *University of Toronto Law Journal* 195; Cotterrell and Selznick, n.17, above, 303–4, 305.

[22] See, e.g. W.J. Witteveen and W. van der Burg, *Rediscovering Fuller: Essays on Implicit Law and Institutional Design* (Amsterdam, 1999); E. Pisier-Kouchner, 'La sociologie durkheimienne dans l'oeuvre de Duguit' (1977) 28 *Année Sociologique*, new series 95; R. Cotterrell, 'Émmanuel Lévy and Legal Studies: A View from Abroad' (2004) 56/57 *Droit et Société* 131; R. Cotterrell, 'Durkheim's Loyal Jurist? The Sociolegal Theory of Paul Huvelin' (2005) 18 *Ratio Juris* 504; G. Teubner, *Law as an Autopoietic System* (Oxford, 1993).

[23] C. Bouglé, *Bilan de la socociologie française contemporaine* (Paris, 1935), 96. See also W. Schluchter, 'The Sociology of Law as an Empirical Theory of Validity' (2003) 19 *European Sociological Review* 537, 538, claiming that, for Durkheim, sociology 'is first of all a comparative sociology of law' focused on the comparative study of (primarily legal) rules.

[24] Kelsen (n.2, above, 175–7) claims that sociology of law depends on juristic legal science to specify its object 'law', but this seems incorrect unless sociology of law has to be restricted to the study of law as jurists define it. Kelsen gives no reason why it must be.

[25] M. Weber, *Economy and Society* (Berkeley, 1978), Part 2, ch. 1, and see Weber, *Critique of Stammler* (New York, 1977), 126–43 (distinguishing normative justification and empirical regularity). Kelsen (n.2, above, 175–7) essentially follows Weber in this respect.

22

mainly on the development and consequences of law's professional organization in different historical contexts. Luhmann stresses even more forcefully the separate discursive spheres of law and sociology and enshrines these in the terms of his systems theory.[26]

Sometimes more than indifference is involved. Nicholas Timasheff claimed (referring to Auguste Comte's writings) that the discipline of sociology 'was born in the state of hostility to law'.[27] The sense of disciplinary power may sometimes become imperialistic. 'Law is entering an age of sociology,' writes the sociologist Donald Black[28] and 'sociological justice' is now feasible: sociology will reveal the myths that pervade legal thought and how to reorganize legal practice realistically. Black even envisages sociology, as a way of thinking, replacing juristic ways.[29] Early in sociology's disciplinary career, Durkheim gave at least rhetorical support to some such imperialism: 'My aim has been precisely to introduce ... [the sociological idea] into those disciplines from which it was absent and thereby to make them branches of sociology.'[30] Durkheim's fierce advocacy of sociology as a distinct discipline (like Black's, many decades later) no doubt encouraged the widespread opposition to such imperialism among the jurists of his time. By contrast, Ehrlich's idea of 'sociologizing' law seemed to appeal to many progressive jurists, perhaps in part because he invoked a transdisciplinary, not a professionalized sociology—a cooperative, open effort in building knowledge of law.

The time of Ehrlich was one in which some progressive legal scholars could look to sociology with unlimited and, seen from today's perspectives, naive optimism; with a sense that anything might be possible in social research on law, even if the new territories opened up were vast. Reading Ehrlich one could be, as Karl Llewellyn noted, 'somewhat crushed in spirit, because he had seen so much'.[31] But optimism was encouraged by sociology's aura of a promise still to be realized.

Early sociology in the United States, where the subject first began to flourish as an organized discipline, had three particular elements that could appeal to legal scholars. Each of them contrasts with those primarily associated with American sociology as a discipline today. First was a strong social reform orientation which might relate to studies of law's social functions and of legal reform. Practical social reform foci (the concerns of 'damned do-gooders') tended to be much less prominent in sociology as it became a distinct, professionalized academic field, though they have never been

[26] See, e.g. N. Luhmann, 'Operational Closure and Structural Coupling: The Differentiation of the Legal System' (1992) 13 *Cardozo Law Review* 1419.
[27] N.S. Timasheff, *An Introduction to the Sociology of Law* (Cambridge, Mass., 1939), 45.
[28] D. Black, *Sociological Justice* (New York, 1989), 4.
[29] *Cf.* Cotterrell, n.8, above, 183–93.
[30] E. Durkheim, *The Rules of Sociological Method and Selected Texts on Sociology and Its Method* (London, 1982), 260.
[31] Quoted in Hull, n.3, above, 291; and *cf.* C.K. Allen's *Law in the Making*, 7th edn. (Oxford, 1964), 30–2, famously despairing of the unlimited range of Ehrlich's 'megalomaniac jurisprudence'.

excluded.[32] Second was an emphasis, notably in influential early Chicago-school sociology, on empirical social description which, while not atheoretical, avoided 'the inhibiting consequences of doctrines, schools of thought, and authoritative leaders'.[33] Correspondingly, 'fact research'—gathering data about social life—could appear as an aid to understanding law's effects; pursued or adopted by jurists it could readily inspire 'legal realism' or the study of 'living law' or 'law in action'.[34] Third was sociology's early professional catholicity including scholars from groups outside the academic establishment (e.g. women, black scholars, social and political campaigners and reformers).[35] Early sociology suggests an open club in which jurists might not feel complete outsiders if they sought some association with it.

A very different situation obtains in today's highly developed academic discipline of sociology, with its sophisticated research methods, elaborate theoretical traditions, distinctive professional training, qualifications and career paths, and numerous disciplinary specialisms. Nevertheless, certain factors limit the tendencies towards professionalization (and associated specialization and technicality) that have made it harder for sociology to appear as a general resource and locus of aspiration for legal scholars and others.

One is the enduring idea of a public sociology—the idea that sociologists should, to some extent, use their work to hold up a mirror to their society and explain it to itself, addressing its broadest, most widely-felt social concerns. Books such as David Riesman's million-selling *The Lonely Crowd* and, recently, Robert Putnam's *Bowling Alone*[36] exemplify writing that has achieved this in some way. Here sociology remains a resource for general reflection on the social. Yet some of this writing has been called 'expressive' rather than 'scientific' sociology[37] because of its popular, non-technical, non-specialist appeal as a kind of evocation, in arresting terms, of the widely-felt and the familiar.

The other phenomenon that has limited sociology's tendencies towards professionalism has been its already-mentioned insecurity about its character as a knowledge-field and research practice. A closer view of this matter is needed so as to be able to move towards some conclusions about relations of legal theory and sociology today.

---

[32] J.R. Feagin, 'Social Justice and Sociology: Agendas for the Twenty-First Century' (2001) 66 *American Sociological Review* 1, 6–10. The quoted words are Robert Park's: see *ibid* 8.

[33] J.F. Short Jr., 'Introduction', in Short (ed.) *The Social Fabric of the Metropolis: Contributions of the Chicago School of Urban Sociology* (Chicago, 1971), xi, xiv (quoting Albion Small).

[34] A. Nussbaum, 'Fact Research in Law' (1940) 40 *Columbia Law Review* 189; M. Rehbinder, 'The Development and Present State of Fact Research in the United States' (1972) 24 *Journal of Legal Education* 567; J.H. Schlegel, *American Legal Realism and Empirical Social Science* (Chapel Hill, N. Carolina, 1995).

[35] Feagin, n.32, above, 6–8; C. Lemert, 'Representations of the Sociologist: Getting over the Crisis' (1996) 11 *Sociological Forum* 379, 386 (emphasizing the institutional outsider status of many early sociologists).

[36] D. Riesman with N. Glazer and R. Denney, *The Lonely Crowd: A Study of the Changing American Character* (New Haven, 1950); R. Putnam, *Bowling Alone: The Collapse and Revival of American Community* (New York, 2000).

[37] R. Boudon, 'Sociology That Really Matters' (2002) 18 *European Sociological Review* 371, 372.

24

Sociology as Discipline

Professionalized sociology's self-examinations are, no doubt, partly fuelled by external perceptions. In Britain in 1989, A.H. Halsey noted 'the remorseless chill of received opinion about sociology'.[38] A mid-1990s commentator declared that 'sociologists have nothing worth saying about things that matter, in the here and now of contemporary politics, in the national conversation about identity and purpose.'[39] Paul Wiles has recently suggested that 'the reputation of sociology for practical utility is at an historical low and sociology is regarded as the least developed of the social sciences in terms of the rigour of its methods.'[40] In America in the 1980s sociology fell into a 'terrible reputational state'[41] and in 1994 Seymour Martin Lipset called it 'an endangered discipline'.[42] Yet it *continues to thrive*. There are more than 13,000 career sociologists in the United States.[43] The Paris-based sociologist Raymond Boudon claims that sociology has an 'identity crisis' but 'seems more solidly institutionalized than ever'.[44] In Britain, Ray Pahl notes, hostile political currents in the 1980s 'did no harm to sociology: staff, students and research all expanded rapidly.'[45] The image is of an insecure, embattled, yet flourishing research field; exactly what we should expect if sociology's reflexiveness, far from undermining it, helps to make it vibrant and rich, though always controversial.

One main theme of sociologists' current debates about their enterprise is about disciplinarity. A recent presidential address to the American Sociological Association called sociology 'a broad *interdisciplinary* field that draws on ideas from other social sciences, the humanities, and the physical sciences. Our intellectual and methodological pluralism, as well as our diversity of practitioners, are major virtues.'[46] Some writers stress sociology's 'disciplinary openness'.[47] But worries are expressed that social research training not anchored in any specific discipline may produce 'technologists ... equipped only with investigative skills',[48] and some sociologists are embarrassed to profess a discipline that is 'something of a rickety shed'.[49]

---

[38] Quoted in D. Walker, 'All Quiet on the Home Front' *Times Higher Education Supplement*, 17 March 1995, 21.   [39] *Ibid.*
[40] P. Wiles, 'Policy and Sociology' (2004) 55 *British Journal of Sociology* 31.
[41] Charles Lemert, quoted in R. Pahl, Book review, *Times Higher Education Supplement*, 23 August 1996. See also Lemert's (n.35, above) excellent critical discussion of sociologists' concerns about their field.
[42] Quoted in I. Deutscher, 'Sociological Practice: The Politics of Identities and Futures' (1998) 3 *Sociological Research Online*, No. 1, para 5.5 *http://www.socresonline.org.uk/socresonline/3/1/3.html*.
[43] J. Steele, 'Four Days in California' *Guardian*, 24 August 2004.
[44] Boudon, n.37, above, 371.   [45] Pahl, n.41, above.
[46] Feagin, n.32, above, 6 (my emphasis).
[47] H. Lauder, P. Brown and A.H. Halsey, 'Sociology and Political Arithmetic: Some Principles of a New Policy Science' (2004) 55 *British Journal of Sociology* 3, 6, 8.
[48] M. Williams, quoted in Lauder et al., n.47, above, 5.
[49] D. Voas, 'The So-So Construction of Sociology' (2003) 54 *British Journal of Sociology* 129.

From 'Living Law' to the 'Death of the Social'—Sociology in Legal Theory   25

There is also, however, a tendency to reject fixations with disciplinarity. For Paul Wiles, 'disciplines are simply the social organisation of the knowledge produced in response to yesterday's problems (usually for the purpose of teaching that knowledge to neophytes).'[50] It follows that cutting-edge work will often escape disciplinary bounds. Craig Calhoun argues that sociology's future will be stronger if 'we embrace rather than marginalize interdisciplinary projects'; disciplines, like nations, are committed to defending their turf and boundaries, 'promulgating myths about their essential internal unity and character and literally disciplining the individualistic and dissentient opinions and behaviours of their members.'[51] Disciplines 'exalt into matters of principle what are in fact matters of historical accident, gradual cultural change, networks of personal relationships, particular combinations of styles and . . . a never fully articulated system of socially constituted dispositions that guides agents in their perception and action. It is always and in every case impossible to identify a principle of belonging that unifies everyone in the discipline without also including others one intuitively thinks don't fit. Likewise, most of the disciplinary "principles" that matter most to us actually unify only some of the members of the discipline.'[52] Calhoun's observations suggest a sociology of sociology: a *transdisciplinary* sociology of *professionalized* sociology, but also of professional disciplinary organization in general.

But what follows from such disciplinary ambivalence? Certainly, one might hesitate to call sociology of law a sub-discipline of sociology when sociology debates its own disciplinarity in this way. But, of course, such debates in no way prevent a vast amount of research being pursued by sociologists in well-recognized fields, according to settled methods and by reference to familiar canons of established theory. This situation does, however, suggest that an important distinction is to be drawn between, on the one hand, recognizing the existence of relatively coherent sets of methods, theories, and research traditions (which is as easy to do for sociolegal studies or sociology of law as for sociology) and, on the other, making any strong claims about disciplinary identity, unity, or integrity.

Sociology as Science

Often debates about sociology focus on the idea of science. A leading British sociologist, John Goldthorpe, sees much sociology as 'pretend social science', more like 'social revelation' or 'social poetry' than science.[53] Another commentator

---

[50] Wiles, n.40, above, 33.

[51] C. Calhoun, 'The Future of Sociology: Interdisciplinarity and Internationalization', paper presented to the University of Minnesota Sociology Department at its Centennial celebration, 29–30 March 2002, pp. 1, 2 *http://www.src.org/programs/calhoun/publications/futureofsoc.pdf.*

[52] *Ibid,* 1, 2, 3–4.

[53] J. Goldthorpe, 'Book Review Symposium: The Scientific Study of Society' (2004) 55 *British Journal of Sociology* 123, 125.

26

sees 'the path of testable theory and empirical investigation' as the 'homeward route' for a discipline that has lost its way; scientific laws and value-free research in sociology are possible, he claims, but sociologists reject the 'scientific' label because of 'the dread' that they 'might then commit the sin of prediction'.[54] A natural science model is clearly being invoked here as the guarantor of scientific status and integrity. Other sociologists insist that scientific method or at least 'some special expertise' is needed to distinguish sociology from journalism or even novel-writing.[55]

Fears for sociology's scientific status were an important impetus for sociologists' efforts to separate it professionally from social reform activity so as to pursue 'the pure-science ideal' or 'a detached-science perspective'.[56] Both Weber and Durkheim devoted much attention to specifying scientific methods for social research. Later, functionalism was, for a time, advocated as sociology's distinctive scientific approach,[57] though it was always shared with other social studies. Today much argument centres on the merits of rational action theory (RAT) derived from rational choice theory in economics and advocated as a general sociological approach. The sense that sociology should learn from economics is no doubt encouraged by the relatively high status of the latter as a discipline of social explanation.

Goldthorpe defines RAT as any 'theoretical approach that seeks to explain social phenomena as the outcome of individual action that is construed as rational, given individuals' goals and conditions of action, and in this way made intelligible.'[58] Boudon identifies a range of postulates underlying various rational choice or rational action approaches. The most basic of these characterize methodological individualism, a sociological approach derived from Weber. They are: the centrality of the individual, an emphasis on understanding the meaning for individuals of their social actions, and a claim that that meaning explains why they act. Beyond this, other postulates can be added: consequentialism (actors' reasons always concern the effects of their actions), egoism (relevant effects for actors are those that impact on themselves), and cost-benefit balance (actors always choose alternatives with the optimum cost-benefit balance). Boudon suggests that these postulates are the basis of rational choice theory. But RAT adds yet other postulates because choice is sociologically too simple an idea unless social or psychological restrictions shaping choice are added. These postulated restrictions vary depending on the kind of RAT adopted.[59]

What may be of most interest here is the fact that, in both sociology and juristic studies, rational choice or rational action ideas have been advocated to address

---

[54] Voas, n.49, above, 130, 132.
[55] T. Tam, 'The Industrial Organization of Sociology' (1998) 3 *Sociological Research Online*, No. 1, para 3:6 *http://www.socresonline.org.uk/socresonline/3/1/4.html*; Wiles, n.40, above, 34.
[56] Feagin, n.32, above, 9, 10; Calhoun, n.51, above, 19.
[57] K. Davis, 'The Myth of Functional Analysis as a Special Method in Sociology and Anthropology' (1959) 24 *American Sociological Review* 757.
[58] J. Goldthorpe, 'The Quantitative Analysis of Large-Scale Data Sets and Rational Action Theory: For a Sociological Alliance' (1996) 12 *European Sociological Review* 109.
[59] R. Boudon, Book Review (2001) 17 *European Sociological Review* 451, 451–2.

From 'Living Law' to the 'Death of the Social'—Sociology in Legal Theory   27

perceived defects in the scientific, practical, or predictive power of traditional scholarship. But rational action scholarship in sociology is only 'a niche operation'[60] and, in legal studies, research models derived from economics have been very influential in some locations (especially in the United States) but so far much less so in Britain. Since much law is concerned to regulate instrumental relations and presupposes instrumental (means-ends) rationality it is unsurprising that rational action approaches in legal theory have an appeal.

Yet most jurists have tended to assume that there is more to the social world which law attempts to regulate than means-ends rationality. Debates in sociology make explicit the kind of problems that may induce juristic caution. Both Goldthorpe and Boudon stress the variety of forms of rationality but some sociological critics of rational choice theory note that it 'leaves little place for affect or emotional attachments'.[61] Weber's sociology, after all, not only postulated categories of what he considered non-rational action (action driven by blind habit or pure emotion) alongside (potentially conflicting) categories of rational action, but assumed that non-rational action was more socially pervasive than rational.[62] For one recent sociological commentator on RAT, economists 'assume away preferences and utility whereas sociologists ... want to know something about desires, preferences, beliefs, evaluations, expectations, and intentions when these are central in their explanations.'[63]

It is not hard to see a direct relevance for theoretical legal inquiries in controversies around RAT. Sociologists (like lawyers) usually accept the great significance of the kind of rational action on which RAT focuses. But many see the social as much wider and more diverse than rational choice approaches can grasp. And implicit in the resistance of many legal scholars to economic analysis of law may be a conviction that the social for law is better seen in the untidy, empirically complex way sociology usually presents it—in terms of combinations of many kinds of rational and non-rational action (judged as such from numerous perspectives)—than in terms of the rational structures through which economists tend to portray it.

Advocates of RAT tend to admit that it is only one method, which cannot address all sociological inquiries. Yet it often carries for them the hopes of 'scientific' sociology. Perhaps an appropriate conclusion is that no universal methods can cover the vast diversity of social inquiries. Science is an aim and aspiration to question all received assumptions and continually, systematically, to broaden perspectives on experience. But a search for absolute protocols for doing this is doomed to failure.

    [60] D.B. Grusky and M. Di Carlo, Book Review (2001) 17 *European Sociological Review* 457.
    [61] N. Smelser, 'The Rational and the Ambivalent in the Social Sciences' (1998) 63 *American Sociological Review* 1, 4.
    [62] R. Brubaker, *The Limits of Rationality: An Essay on the Social and Moral Thought of Max Weber* (London, 1984), ch. 2.
    [63] B. Laplante, Book Review (2002) 18 *European Sociological Review* 121, 122.

28

Sociology's Aims and Object

Other debates focus on sociology's aims. How far should it seek to be useful to policy-makers? Does a concentration on theory drive research away from practicality and towards useless abstraction? Boudon sees risks in policy-oriented or, as he calls it, cameral/descriptive sociology, which he contrasts with cognitive/ scientific sociology driven by a disinterested search for knowledge: 'Once the cameral orientation becomes dominant, the cumulative character of sociology is weakened. Sociology of the cognitive type is internally driven, but cameral sociology is externally driven.'[64] Goldthorpe, however, sees no necessary tension between these types of sociology. Both 'share ... a commitment to the same logic of inference or understanding of the relation of evidence and argument'.[65] Can theory in sociology progress? Goldthorpe has doubts because of 'the relatively high degree of mutability of social phenomena'.[66] He advocates studying the causes of specific social phenomena. But other sociologists suggest that sociology lost its way by devaluing its past agenda of social description in favour of attempts to explain the causes of what was described. Thus, endless debates were opened about the nature of social causality.[67]

Sociology's aims are thus varied and contested. Boudon distinguishes not only cognitive/scientific and cameral/descriptive sociology but also two other kinds.[68] Expressive sociology, as mentioned earlier, is writing that vividly expresses the widely-felt and the familiar in social life; for Boudon it is more art (literature) than science. Critical sociology, by contrast, aims at critiquing or changing society. Sociology is, on this view, not a single enterprise. It is many things and sociologists differ as to which of them is central. One can see the ghosts of early sociology as mentioned earlier (social reform, descriptive fact-gathering, professional diversity) refracted through contrasting categories of sociological work and views of sociology's aims.

One final theme from contemporary debates deserves mention. What object does sociology study? Traditionally the discipline has been called the science of 'society' but the concept of society is now widely seen as problematic. As Craig Calhoun notes, sociologists have imagined society primarily on the model of the nation-state; as, for example, British society or French society. The notion of society 'had largely to do with the idea that legitimate rule ought to reflect the interests of a more or less integrated population called a people' but we 'should ask when integration at any scale involves boundaries and some overall sort of order, and how that is achieved and ... not assume that the nation-state provides us with the image of the "whole" society.' The tendency to equate society and nation 'encouraged

---

[64] Boudon, n.37, above, 375.
[65] J. Goldthorpe, 'Sociology as Social Science and Cameral Sociology: Some Further Thoughts' (2004) 20 *European Sociological Review* 97, 100. [66] *Ibid*, 102.
[67] Grusky and Di Carlo, n.60, above, 458. [68] Boudon, n.37, above.

From 'Living Law' to the 'Death of the Social'—Sociology in Legal Theory   29

sociologists to think of whole and individual societies in a way at odds with manifest transnational relations and intranational divisions.'[69] An important question is thus: What is sociology's object? And the issue is no less acute for sociolegal studies and sociology of law, which have taken as their field the study of 'law and society' or 'law in society'. What exactly is it that law must be related to? What is the social? How should it be conceptualized? What are its boundaries and components?

Can sociology conceptualize Europe, for example, as a social entity and offer a means of studying this?[70] More prosaically, can it adjust to the decline of various expressions of a general society-wide social realm, such as social work, social welfare, social solidarity, and socialism?[71]

In a widely cited article, 'The Death of the Social?', Nikolas Rose notes the decline of a sense of the social where this refers to society-wide relations, activities, and policies such as those linked to the welfare state. He sees the social as losing importance as a specific primary field of government intervention, fragmenting into many localized sites where intervention and control take diverse forms.[72] For sociology the danger is of losing its focus if it can no longer identify a well-defined field of social relations distinct from (or more general than), for example, economic or political relations. Perhaps the answer is to associate the social not with society as a kind of unity, but with fundamental types of structured human relations (or community) that can exist on any scale (within or beyond nation-states) and in innumerable empirically observable combinations.

Legal Theory in the Mirror of Sociology

How do these debates about sociology bear on the nature and tasks of legal theory? This chapter began by noting Ehrlich's equation of legal theory with sociology of law. One might say he equates it with *sociology*, since his view of law, including 'living law' or social norms, is so broad. Certainly, he treats the theoretical science of law as the systematic empirical study of law as an aspect of social experience. Legal theory can still be seen in this way and, for the present writer, it is the most attractive way to see it. On such a view, sociology's disciplinary debates bear directly on the nature and tasks of legal theory. They suggest (i) that the theoretical study of law can be governed by established disciplinary protocols, conceptions of science and understandings of the nature of the social, but at the same time

---

[69] Calhoun, n.51, above, 2, 6, 10. See generally Z. Bauman, *Society Under Siege* (Cambridge, 2002).
[70] G. Delanty, 'Social Theory and European Transformation: Is There a European Society?' (1998) 3 *Sociological Research Online*, No. 1 *http://www.socresonline.org.uk/socresonline/3.1.1.html*.
[71] *Cf.* J. Simon, 'Law After Society' (1999) 24 *Law and Social Inquiry* 143, 144–7.
[72] N. Rose, 'The Death of the Social?' Re-Figuring the Territory of Government' (1996) 25 *Economy and Society* 327. Like many others, Rose links this development with a growing importance of the concept of community (rather than society): see also Z. Bauman, *Intimations of Postmodernity* (London, 1992), 36–7.

30

(ii) all of these can be challenged in the name of a transdisciplinary sociology to which legal inquiry must relate.

A vital lesson from sociology's disciplinary debates is, however, that sociological approaches to legal study are not unified by fundamental aims. This is the message of Boudon's fourfold categorization of the uses of sociology, as of earlier ones.[73] We should not expect to find unifying objectives of sociology of law or sociolegal theory. Sociology is irreducibly diverse in its very nature.

Is this diversity a feature of legal theory? It seems that it must be for any legal theory that, like Ehrlich's, ties itself to sociology. It will benefit from the characteristics of sociology that point towards open, transdisciplinary social inquiry. But what of other kinds of legal theory? Surely there are many kinds of juristic studies that need no relation with sociology? Their concern is not with 'living law' but with the positive law that lawyers identify as such. And debates on the 'death of the social' or other forms of sociology's self-questioning have little bearing on juristic researches that treat the social as merely whatever legal doctrine declares it to be.

Any juristic study is, however, a social practice, an intervention in the social world and a way of interpreting that world. So is sociology, but, as has been seen, sociology reflects in radical ways on its own social practice. As such it provides a model of reflexivity. When (juristic) legal theory asks interminably 'What is law?', it implies (but rarely answers adequately) a need to address fundamental questions about the nature of law as discipline, science and object: questions that parallel exactly those we considered earlier about sociology's character, aims, and object. And if legal theory is a highly diverse enterprise, Boudon's four categories of sociological practice suggest how legal theory might understand its own diversity. First, legal theory may be cameral, instrumental or policy-oriented in some way; it may aim at helping lawyers, administrators, or others to do their work better. Secondly, it may be expressive, perhaps presenting in a striking, reassuring or vivid way what is familiar about law to lawyers or citizens. Boudon's disparagement of 'expressive' literature which appeals to the emotions is paralleled memorably by, for example, Karl Llewellyn's scornful criticism of Pound for offering 'bed-time stories for the tired bar',[74] a kind of after-dinner-speech jurisprudence. Boudon's third 'critical' category is well represented in legal theory in, for example, much Marxist, feminist and postmodernist writing and critical race theory.

Finally, Boudon's cognitive/scientific category remains as vague for legal theory as for sociology because it raises all the issues discussed earlier about the methods, aims, and objects of science. It points simply to the inevitability of endless critical reflection on these matters. What David Nelken strikingly terms 'sociological blindness'[75] (the inherent limits of sociology's understanding) is, I think, simply

---

[73] See especially P. Abrams, 'The Uses of British Sociology, 1831–1981', in M. Bulmer (ed.), *Essays on the History of British Sociological Research* (Cambridge, 1985).
[74] K.N. Llewellyn, 'A Realistic Jurisprudence—The Next Step' (1930) 30 *Columbia Law Review* 431, 435.   [75] Nelken, 'Can There Be a Sociology of Legal Meaning?' (n.8, above) 118.

the impossibility of this process of reflection ever ending. Boudon's specification of good scientific theory (which might be adopted by some jurists also for legal theory) is that it 'explains a given phenomenon by making it the consequence of a set of statements compatible with one another and individually acceptable either because they are congruent with observation, or for all kinds of other reasons variable from one case to the other.'[76] The vagueness of this formulation merely illustrates that for all studies of the social (including the study of law) the worth of theory and research methods cannot be judged at an abstract level. They depend on the aims of research and the specific contexts of intellectual debate in which it takes place.

Legal theory is primarily the concern of jurists and sociolegal scholars who may occupy different positions in relation to the debates considered in this chapter. Legal studies, as social studies of a kind, may have all of the problems that are addressed in sociology's disciplinary debates. But whereas sociology pursues its self-analyses in a context in which official support is not guaranteed, law remains secure as a legitimated practice because of its connections with government, politics, and power. Legal studies are being increasingly freed from disciplinary demarcation disputes. Social theory, empirical sociolegal studies, and (to some extent) the indirect influence of sociology's disciplinary debates have greatly enriched the field of theoretical legal inquiries. Yet jurists inevitably remain tied, to some extent, to law's cocoon-like official existence, relatively secure from the kind of self-questioning that sociology reveals. Law achieves its discipline-effect and its status as juristic knowledge as much from its location in the power-knowledge complexes of the nation-state as from its own intellectual self-awareness. In my view, sociology, with its permanent self-doubts as well as its remarkable professional achievements, continues to offer important lessons for all legal theorists, whether or not they see their interests as allied to the agendas of sociolegal research.

---

[76] Boudon, n.37, above, 372–3.

[4]
Pandora's Box:
Jurisprudence in Legal Education

I

Perhaps jurisprudence has a moderately secure place in undergraduate law curricula in the UK at present—after much controversy and many local skirmishes in university law departments. If this is so, it is because it is thought to offer something important that other law school courses cannot or do not offer. But the nature of this 'something' and how important it is are far from clear. Sometimes the subject is one among many optional units in an undergraduate law curriculum; its position suggests that it offers something valuable, yet not essential to every law student's education. In many other single honours law programmes, jurisprudence is a compulsory subject; its curriculum status indicates that undergraduate legal education is officially considered incomplete without it. In yet other settings, it is one of a small number of 'protected' options from which undergraduates must choose in their law degree programme. In this last case, the curriculum placing suggests that jurisprudence exemplifies a *kind* of study necessary to a full legal education, but that the subject's specific material is not, itself, essential.

These conflicting messages about jurisprudence's significance, which the diverse (but now, it seems, relatively stable[1]) placings of the subject in the curriculum convey, indicate a lack of agreement among law teachers about its value. And teachers of jurisprudence themselves give a wide variety of views about the purpose of the subject. Yet the vast majority consider that it "makes students think about the nature of law" or "gives a broader perspective" on law as "an important social activity".[2] This suggests that jurisprudence presents material to inspire this radical thinking and provide this broadening of view.

How far does the subject really do these things? It should be noted, first, that in some respects taught jurisprudence (especially as reflected in the kinds of material presented in introductory textbooks) is a rather well settled body of theory. Whereas in many other scholarly fields the idea of a canon of classical or fundamental literature

180

is breaking down, or has already done so, in taught jurisprudence in the UK such a canon still clearly exists, as Hilaire Barnett's recent survey shows.[3] It includes: the classical utilitarian tradition (especially Bentham and Austin); Hart and Dworkin individually and locked in debate; classic writings on legal positivism and liberalism as a theoretical spine around which much else is arranged; key representatives of legal realism (now often supplemented by critical legal studies), Marxist legal theory and natural law as a combined 'official opposition' to the mainstream; modern US theories of social justice (Rawls and Nozick); and the Mill–Hart–Devlin debate on law's role as an agent of morality. The most important invader of the canon of established theoretical writings in recent years has clearly been feminist theory.

However radical jurisprudence is claimed to be, however much it is claimed to provide a window for law students on contemporary law in its changing social context, its body of ideas actually changes quite slowly. Austin is still taught in depth in 59% of jurisprudence courses in the UK. Hart's dominant position in the canon has not changed in 20 years. There is much diversity in what is covered in teaching, but a generally strong continuity with the perceived classics.

Some ways of viewing this pot-pourri of approaches, theories and foci may be more productive than others. Perhaps least productive is the approach that sees them as making up a unified intellectual field or even a discipline, perhaps labelled in the teaching context as 'legal philosophy' (which tends to imply a branch of philosophy). The problem for such an approach is that no unity of methods or aims unifies the material of taught jurisprudence. Nor are there constant epistemological or ontological bases of the theories typically brought together in this way. They have been created for different purposes at different times. In many cases the theories are the work of jurists who saw themselves mainly as addressing various practical lawyers' issues about law. Other theories, however, are the work of scholars with different primary intellectual allegiances—to moral or political philosophy, for example, or social theory of various kinds. It seems important to recognise clearly that jurisprudence is unified only by its place in legal education (which, as noted above, is a matter on which law teachers agree to disagree). A virtue of such a clear recognition is that it prevents anyone mistaking the canon of taught jurisprudence for an intellectually integrated whole, rather than the historically and geographically contingent collection of materials that it is.

One marker of this contingency is the overwhelming dominance of Anglo-American writings in the current mainstream or central theoretical spine of the UK jurisprudential canon, and the virtual absence in this role of important Continental European traditions of legal theory,[4] let alone theoretical materials from further afield. While many such traditions have been reflected in taught jurisprudence in the UK at various times, it seems that they tend gradually to be marginalised in it. Yet jurisprudence as a taught subject is not usually presented as being concerned exclusively with Anglo-American legal issues. It seems, however, that it does not have the role of explaining law's nature in some general and comparative way. Its scope appears to be determined pragmatically. It provides materials to illuminate a specific range of legal experience relevant primarily to the intending lawyer in a certain jurisdictional context.

If follows that a more modest, but also more realistic, way to view taught jurisprudence is as a rather disordered compendium of very disparate elements. So seen, it is a complex intellectual patchwork. It does not necessarily make any serious attempt to tie itself to any particular conception of philosophy as a discipline or tradition of inquiry, but makes space for the social and human sciences, linguistics, history and other knowledge fields, as well as for a range of more explicitly philosophical traditions. The appeal may for some teachers be to a specific discipline or approach, thought of as holding the key to theoretical 'truth' about law, but in taught jurisprudence this is often not the case. More often the course tends to be a sampling of a wide range of literatures.

In this situation, the jurisprudence teacher might be imagined as rummaging in a box of different knowledges, pulling out the shiniest items to catch the eye of students. The box is labelled 'law and other disciplines' or perhaps merely 'law and society'. It contains whatever has been put in it at various times by 'wandering jurists',[5] who have come across intellectual objects they thought legally interesting. Jurisprudence teachers often add their own personally treasured items. Some objects in the box were found on travels to scholarly fields considered remote from local legal professional experience (for example, psychoanalysis, geography, anthropology, semiotics and aesthetics). Some are commonplace domestic items (for example, common law traditions, the rule of law, legal positivism and concepts such as punishment or authority). The teacher's job is to take a cluster of objects (perhaps a very personal selection) from the box and tell a story that links them and holds students' attention. The approach relates to jurisprudence's role as what Julius Stone called the lawyer's 'extraversion',[6] a turning outwards to look at law's contexts, to locate law in the broadest and most diverse intellectual, moral and social settings, to stand (notionally) in those settings and see how law appears; perhaps to stand outside law in some way or, at least, outside the legal thoughtways becoming increasingly familiar to the law student through the study of legal doctrine in other law school subjects.

II

The image of the box of ideas is subversive. It implicitly denies the ideal of a fully integrated body of knowledge. What does jurisprudence add up to? For students this is often the hardest question. Perhaps as an undergraduate one can speak of mastering the law of contract: the mass of principles makes a kind of whole, or can be believed to do so (at least at examination time). But jurisprudence resists this result. The contents of the box of jurisprudential ideas could be arranged in an infinity of ways. And there is no necessary inventory of contents. The message of jurisprudence, viewed in this way, is of contingency and incompleteness, uncertainty rather than certainty, questions rather than answers, and the importance of personal discovery rather than the acceptance of authority. I think this is the key to the power which jurisprudence has to bring something important to legal education. Legal thought tends to seek closure; that is, rational consistency and authoritative solutions to legal and social issues. But the incompleteness—even arbitrariness—of the juris-

182

prudence canon ultimately conveys for the thoughtful student a disturbing message of law's own indeterminacy and unfinished nature as a form of social knowledge. Law as legal doctrine seeks the security of closure—a complete and reliable professional knowledge. But jurisprudence teaches (by its very nature as a law school subject and perhaps almost irrespective of the particular content of the course) that law is implicated at all times with diverse forms of knowledge which law itself cannot control or systematise. The message is that law orders the social world provisionally and contingently. Yet legal order is not insignificant; it is all the more remarkable in the face of the social complexity and contingency it must address.

Seeing jurisprudence in this intellectual context explains much, I think, about students' typical reactions to the subject. For the weakest students, the subject may be incomprehensible because its purpose is not understood. For more able ones, the subject is disturbing because it is seen to disrupt the certainties that much legal education otherwise fosters and relies on. It suggests, at least, that there is more to law than they had otherwise thought. But for the best students, jurisprudence's uncertainties directly inspire, eventually, a far richer understanding of law, built on new respect for the sheer complexity of law's ordering tasks in a world of contingency and complexity.

Because jurisprudence draws its material from many sources there is sometimes a tendency to see it as observation of law from 'the outside', or as a view of a moral or social context from 'inside' the lawyer's world (as with Stone's idea of the lawyer's 'extraversion'). But this inside–outside terminology is ultimately unhelpful; everything depends on where one stands when participating in or observing law. The inside–outside distinction reflects a particular professional viewpoint or theoretical preference in relation to legal analysis.[7] Nevertheless, taught jurisprudence certainly gets some of its strangeness (particularly for students) as a law school subject from the fact that it can easily be thought of as 'inside' law's domain, or 'outside' it, or (most commonly perhaps) somehow running in and out of this domain with bewildering indecision. Jurisprudence seems, on such a view, like a restless individual who cannot decide whether to stay inside the house and clean the rooms or go outside and repair the pointing.

It is easy to fall into using the metaphor of law as a structure with an inside and an outside, because so much of legal education reinforces the idea that law is such a structure. The law student is taught how to gain entry to what is presented as the lawyer's *professional* house of law; how to find the way around it, feel at home in it and look out of the windows at the world outside. After this induction, the outside world looks very different from the way it appeared before. It is easy to forget that there may be other, different houses of law which citizens inhabit.

I believe that jurisprudence as a taught subject has the task of preventing the student's existence inside this house of professionalised law from becoming too comfortable; that is, so comfortable that one forgets the need to step outside and breathe the air outdoors. It is necessary to see the social world not just through the windows of law's professional mansions. It is important to see more than the images of society that are reinforced in the dominant professional worlds of law. That means, in turn, challenging dominant professional images of law, because these images are themselves shaped in the wider context of lawyers' self-images as inhabitants of a social world conceptualised in terms of citizens or subjects, groups or individuals, communities or states. If one sees this social world only in terms of law's professional imagery it becomes hard to see the trajectories of law's development, the forces shaping it, its potential and limits and the varieties of legal experience.

Most law school subjects are taught now, or can be taught, in ways that actively seek to transcend familiar professional perspectives on those subjects. But jurisprudence surely has the special task of permanently challenging central and general assumptions of professional thought. It is always in the business of broadening legal perspectives, breaking down internal–external distinctions that legal thought creates, letting light into the professional house of law (that is, the currently dominant orientations of professional legal thinking) showing the house from many angles and perhaps emphasising that the professional house of law is not the only or the most important place in which law exists.

The image of a box of ideas from which the jurisprudence teacher selects is not intended to be a demeaning one—as though the teacher is to be seen as a trickster, magician or mere entertainer (though maybe there has to be something of each of those roles in portraying the complex reality of law). The ideas box is a useful image. It suggests that what is taught in jurisprudence is less important than how it is taught. One can teach classical jurisprudence (Austin or Hart, for example) 'in context'—the context of the political and professional needs to which in particular times and places it responded—and thereby tell a different story from the ones that have become professional orthodoxy. One can teach Durkheim or Habermas or Freud (or a host of other 'non-jurist' theorists) as jurists and thereby shine a different light on legal knowledge. The test of whether the story told is a good one in a jurisprudence course is whether it conveys powerfully something different about—a new perspective on—general assumptions about the nature of law that are often presupposed in other law school courses.

What should be conveyed? I think jurisprudence should be *constructively subversive*. It should question assumptions that underlie received professional wisdom about the nature of law in general, rather than about the nature of particular legal fields. It should do this in a way that enriches professional understanding by broadening it. It should require students to understand that the current view out of the window in the professional house of law is not the only available view of the social world that law inhabits. It should make clear that any house of scholarship and practice that law's professional guardians inhabit looks different when one steps outside it, and that the value and importance of this scholarship and practice become subject to criteria of assessment different from those that are often professionally encouraged or favoured.

Broadening perspectives on law certainly does not entail declaring dominant professional views of law to be wrong or misguided. The task is rather to reveal them as partial, as particular views of law that can co-exist with others; to show the student a plurality of perspectives, illustrated through different theories, or different readings of theories. A broadened perspective is one that makes it possible to

184

understand a range of viewpoints in themselves but also to locate them in relation to other viewpoints. This is why, ultimately, there is no 'inside' view of law to be contrasted with an 'outside' view, but only different kinds of experience of law (for example, of different categories of legal practitioners and different categories of non-lawyer citizens), which necessarily lead to different perspectives. Clearly, this poses problems for students seeking final answers. That there are no objectively right answers in jurisprudence may seem obvious to those who teach it but can be deeply disturbing for students: until, that is, they realise that it can be illuminating to see the favoured answers given in professional legal thought as limited. Then there is the prospect for them of realising that understanding the nature of law is a quest open to them using their own developing experience; not a matter of seemingly finished knowledge, like a House of Lords decision that cannot be appealed.

III

What jurisprudence has to offer, then, I think, is a permanent constructive challenge to existing professional legal thought. Not a destructive challenge but one declaring that there is a plurality of perspectives on law, and that any teaching suggesting only a single perspective to be available is false and dangerous. Jurisprudence, understood in this way, challenges received ideas. But received professional wisdom about the nature of law does not stay the same in all times and places. Even if we think only of jurisprudence teaching in the context of legal education in the UK (and, even more specifically, England), it is possible to see that the challenge that jurisprudence has offered has altered over time. It has been adjusted to reflect changing perceptions of law within the legal profession. This is a major topic for inquiry in its own right. But, for present purposes, three broad phases in the development of jurisprudence's constructive subversion—its challenge to legal professional accepted wisdom—might be identified.

In its earliest phase modern English jurisprudence challenged the idea that explicitly developed theory had no place in legal analysis. It challenged common law empiricism and pragmatism. Perhaps the most important contribution of Bentham and especially Austin in this context was simply to make a recognised space for legal theory—for explicitly developed general theory of the nature of law. Jurisprudence taught, for example, the importance of considering theoretically law's systematic and formal character, its bases of authority and its doctrinal unity or autonomy. In this way it facilitated comparison of legal styles and systems, and a more reflexive view of the nature of legal reasoning.

Once that battle was substantially won the task changed. I suggest that it became a task of challenging the idea of law as a self-contained discipline or mode of understanding or reasoning. Jurisprudence in this second phase was the flagship of interdisciplinarity and multidisciplinarity in legal education. Its practitioners took it upon themselves to look actively for insights in what their law school colleagues typically regarded as 'other disciplines' outside law. In this way, the reality of law as a disciplinarily weak field—but a rich focus for multidisciplinary debate—was registered explicitly in legal education. Jurisprudence teaching challenged law's apparent disciplinary autonomy, celebrated or assumed elsewhere in much of the teaching of other law school subjects.

It seems clear now that the battle for interdisciplinarity and multidisciplinarity in much of legal education has been substantially won, at least for the time being. It is hard to see how a counter-offensive could succeed in current conditions. Jurisprudence is no longer needed to proclaim a multitude of disciplinary faiths or deny allegiance to any. I think it was this development, above all, that made jurisprudence's position in the law curriculum in the UK uncertain after the establishment of 'law in context' teaching from the late 1960s. While the 'law and other disciplines' box had been a good resource for challenging the claimed insularity of legal thought, it had obviously become available not just to jurisprudence teachers but to all interested law teachers, whatever their legal field.

Where does this leave jurisprudence? I think that the box of resources on which it draws for its teaching resources has to be—if jurisprudence is to maintain its constructive challenge to orthodoxy—a Pandora's box; one that, once opened, lets loose troubles into the world of legal complacency. Merely appealing to an ever-widening range of knowledge fields as sources of insight about law is not enough any longer to provide that challenge. The important matter now, in what might be thought of as modern English jurisprudence's third phase, is to ask: Why do we seek to broaden theoretical perspectives on law? Why do we need to call on (for example) philosophy or social science in jurisprudence when this is already done in so many taught legal subjects? In what ways can the use of these resources still challenge complacency in legal thought, in the ways that jurisprudence has necessarily sought to do to earn its distinctive place in law teaching?

One important answer surely lies in contemporary jurisprudence's emerging concern with what may be called—to use a term well established in legal theory—legal pluralism, or—a less familiar term—perspectivism. Orthodox legal thought has still not yet come to terms with important changes taking place in the way legal authority is understood and experienced, and with radical changes in the range and variety of sources of law. Modern English jurisprudence as a taught subject, whose beginnings might be traced to John Austin's London lectures of 1829–33, arose as the nation-state consolidated its position as the author of virtually all law. Austin did not recognise the legal status of international law in his perspective of sovereign-subject legal relations within independent political societies. Equally, autonomous local legal systems and jurisdictions appeared to be subsumed relentlessly during the nineteenth century in the monolithic authority of state law.[8] Modern law marginalised all forms of legal experience except those related directly to the jurisdiction of the nation-state.

A century and a half later, matters appear somewhat differently. Transnational law, in many different forms, demands an adequate legal theory. The diversity of legal expectations and traditions within nation-states—reflected in multiculturalism, regionalism and more general demands for recognition of the distinctiveness and diversity of group life—similarly demands legal recognition as a central, not merely peripheral, aspect of legal regulation. Jurisprudence as the constructive subversion of professional orthodoxies needs now to reveal the inadequacies of centralist legal

186

thinking; that is, of theories that postulate monistic rather than pluralistic sources of legal authority and legal regulation. It needs to challenge the vacuum in legal thought that threatens to arise from the latter's excessively individualistic outlook. Jurisprudence surely needs to probe the inadequacy of legal understandings of the autonomy and variety of experience of group life and of autonomous sources of regulatory authority created within groups. It needs to examine how extremely diverse forms of legal authority are seeking mutual accommodation in an increasingly complex world; and how new sources of legal authority beyond or apart from those of the nation-state are gradually forming or changing their character. Perhaps jurisprudence must now express the idea that law is to be understood from various perspectives because it is experienced in a variety of ways, its authority is judged from a variety of communal standpoints and its diverse sources increasingly compete with and challenge each other in local, state and transnational jurisdictions.

If these ideas remain inchoate and open-ended it is because jurisprudence as a challenge to orthodox legal thought has no option but to raise problems and perspectives beyond those that professional legal thinking has accommodated. No doubt there are other forms of challenge to orthodoxy that jurisprudence as a component of the undergraduate law curriculum can and should make. The challenges of pluralism and perspectivism seem, to me, among the most urgent and important.

By making such challenges, jurisprudence ensures that its box of resources remains not just a store of interesting ideas but a Pandora's box. Opening it lets troubles into the world of professional law, via the examination of that world in legal education. But like Pandora's troubles these are challenges that, once accepted, can sometimes also promote wisdom. The subversion is constructive. In my view, jurisprudence's future role remains what it has always been: the constructive challenging of professional orthodoxy, in the service of broader legal understanding.

Further reading

On the importance of legal pluralism for contemporary legal theory, see Petersen, H. & Zahle, H. (Eds) (1995) *Legal Polycentricity* (Aldershot, Dartmouth), and Santos, B. de Sousa (1995) *Toward a New Common Sense* (London, Routledge). On the growth and significance of transnational law and some of its implications for legal theory see Teubner, G. (Ed.) (1997) *Global Law without a State* (Aldershot, Dartmouth). Some of the analytical challenges posed by local, national and other forms of legal diversity are discussed in Nelken, D. (Ed.) (1997) *Comparing Legal Cultures* (Aldershot, Dartmouth). Cultural and social diversity and difference as a challenge for contemporary law and politics are explored from a variety of standpoints in, for example, Kymlicka, W. (Ed.) (1995) *The Rights of Minority Cultures* (Oxford, Oxford University Press), Danielsen, D. & Engle, K. (Eds) (1995) *After Identity* (New York, Routledge) and Minow, M. (1990) *Making All the Difference* (Ithaca, Cornell University Press). For an interpretation of English jurisprudence in terms of its relationship to legal professional concerns, see Cotterrell, R. (1989) *The Politics of Jurisprudence* (London, Butterworths). On legal thought as a professional project of intellectual closure, see Cotterrell, R. (1995) *Law's Community* (Oxford, Clarendon Press), ch. 3 and 5; and for a sample of recent ideas on the theoretical problems of explaining how legal ideas structure social environments, see Nelken, D. (Ed.) (1996) *Law as Communication* (Aldershot, Dartmouth).

Notes

[1] See Barnett, H. (1995) The province of jurisprudence determined again!, *Legal Studies*, 15, 88–127.

[2] Barnett, loc. cit., 107.

[3] Barnett, loc. cit., 109–120.

[4] Even Kelsen's sophisticated work, which beyond the anglophone world is widely seen as fundamental in any serious consideration of positivist legal theory, remains less important in jurisprudence taught in the UK than Austin's much criticised theories, according to Barnett's survey.

[5] The term is William Twining's, implying for him both geographical and intellectual movement. See Twining, W. (1997) *Law in Context* (Oxford, Clarendon Press), ch. 1.

[6] Stone, J. (1968) *Legal System and Lawyers' Reasonings* (Sydney, Maitland), p. 16.

[7] See Cotterrell, R. (1998) Why must legal ideas be interpreted sociologically?, *Journal of Law and Society*, 25, 171–192.

[8] Arthurs, H.W. (1985) *'Without the Law': Administrative Justice and Legal Pluralism in Nineteenth-century England* (Toronto, University of Toronto Press).

Part Two

Sociolegal Theory and Theorists

[5]
Living Law Revisited: Communitarianism and Sociology of Law[1]

The concept of living law (*lebendes Recht*) was part of Eugen Ehrlich's ambitious "laying of foundations" (*Grundlegung*) for legal sociology (Ehrlich 2002). It is the seminal idea which most obviously takes us "back to the beginning in sociology of law" (Nelken 1984). At what seems the very start of the modern history of empirical socio-legal inquiry (Rottleuthner 1998, 227), Ehrlich used this concept to affirm a view of law that would be adopted in different ways by many other scholars: the view that law, even in the context of modern nation states, should be thought of as something more than, and in certain respects very different from, the regulatory products or techniques of the state and its judicial, legislative, or administrative agencies.

The idea of living law locates law's doctrinal sources, regulatory authority, and normative essence in communal life, understood in some way as a realm of shared moral understandings or social interaction, and not primarily (if at all) in the purely political authority and coercive power of the state. Law "lives" insofar as it grows from, and is shaped, tested, and sanctioned by the collective experience of individuals interacting in particular social fields or contexts. The forms of social regulation that arise in the many different kinds of association in which people interrelate are forms of living law. The important implication is that, by contrast, state law is *not* alive except in so far as it directly expresses these forms of regulation. It is the hierarchically organized, centrally coordinated, and systematized official law of the state, promulgated and enforced only by its legislative, judicial, and administrative agencies. It may even be *morally dead*; existing not in citizens' moral consciousness and guiding their practices but found only in texts that document

34

the norms guiding decisions (*Entscheidungsnormen*) by state agencies, including courts.

The concept of living law haunts sociology of law. Like a ghost it is neither actually present in contemporary debates nor spiritually absent from them. It expresses insights that have been considered important, perhaps central, to sociological inquiry about law and it is still referred to frequently in the literature. Yet it has been substantially banished from serious theoretical analysis in sociologically oriented writings about modern Western legal systems.

Why might there be profit now in reconsidering this "ghost" in the machine of socio-legal studies? One reason is that it helps to direct us toward alternatives to the dominant paradigm of law underpinning much socio-legal inquiry in contemporary Western (and many other) societies. Many writers, in different contexts and different ways, imply that this paradigm is gradually becoming exhausted. The paradigm of modern Western law has been the law of the nation state considered as a politically produced, rationally unified, normatively distinctive, and primarily instrumental system of regulation, and as a form of knowledge and understanding that is inevitably and appropriately monopolized by lawyers. But this focus now seems less satisfactory than in the past.

The reasons are many. Among them are uncertainties about the capabilities and technical suitability of state law as a directive instrument (see, e.g., Teubner 1987), about its identity, integrity, and relation to other kinds of regulation (Foucault 1991; Ewald 1990; Rose and Valverde 1998), and about the social foundations of its legitimacy (Habermas 1996, 427–46, 449–50). Hence, a consideration of forms of regulation beyond the paradigm case of state law seems increasingly important. Also notable are calls—reflecting felt moral and political needs—to reexplore relationships between law and culture so as to focus more clearly on issues about popular experience and consciousness of law (see, e.g., Merry 1995). It has seemed important, for example, to consider how in the face of the sometimes oppressive power of the state and its law, opportunities for resistance and assertion of freedom can arise from confrontations between professional and popular legal consciousness (see, e.g., Ewick and Silbey 1998; Yngvesson 1993; Merry 1990). Given such priorities, the legal arena may be viewed as extending far beyond the institutions or even the doctrine of state law itself. Finally, it is now generally recognized that old theoretical oppositions between "law" (as state law) and "society" are too simple to address many specific issues in socio-legal research (see, e.g., Nelken 1986). It is important to understand law *in* society (as an aspect of society, rather than an "external" force acting on it). But this may involve reconsidering the nature of law in broad terms. To treat law as an agency of the state seems inadequate, because that is merely to beg the question of the nature of the field of experience which law represents.

In this changing perspective on law, insights about legal pluralism, which the concept of living law helped to focus within sociology of law, and which legal anthropologists have long used in studying non-Western law, now seem increasingly important in studying the law of Western-style nation states. But pluralistic views of the law of contemporary political societies represented by nation states raise a difficult theoretical problem. What concept of *law*, what general view of law's nature, is appropriate to contemporary legal sociology?

The ambiguous position of the idea of living law in the literature of sociology of law is a symptom of this unresolved difficulty. I shall argue that the ambitions which underlay the development of the concept of living law are still important and that these are essentially *moral* ambitions which place questions of values close to the heart of the task of determining an appropriate sociological concept of law. For this reason some philosophical debates about the nature of community and the moral structure of contemporary Western societies are relevant to sociology of law's projects. I shall suggest finally that, despite its notorious vagueness and difficulty, the concept of community (implicit in the idea of living law) has to be returned in some form to the heart of the concept of law itself.

THE "GHOST" OF LIVING LAW

Around 1913, when Ehrlich fully elaborated the concept of living law (Ehrlich 2002), related ideas resonated in the work of many European critics of orthodox legal thought (Rottleuthner 1988; Nussbaum 1940; and see, e.g., Petrazycki 1955; Gierke 1955). But these ideas appeared in the literature at what might seem in retrospect to have been a very inappropriate historical moment. Thus, the advocacy of them often seems, in retrospect, tinged with nostalgia. Max Weber's major writings on sociology of law (Weber 1978) were published only a few years after Ehrlich's work. Weber's sociology was informed by an acute sensitivity to the nature of modern Western state power, and it adopted a sharply contrasting and seemingly far more realistic view of modern law. Weber made the relationship of law and state central to an understanding of modern law. He linked the basis of authority of the modern nation state with the development of modern, formally rational law and treated the relationship between modern law and modern state as essentially symbiotic. Weber associated law, in a "disenchanted" modern world, not with community and the interplay of social interaction and association but with the sort of formal rules that structure modern bureaucracy (in business enterprises no less than state agencies). Law's main link with social (especially economic) relationships was not as their expression but as a

36

state-guaranteed framework of norms available to give them calculability and predictability.

Unlike Weber, Ehrlich offered no systematic sociology, despite his erudition. He presented social insights touristically, with the enthusiasms of the sightseer (Ehrlich 2002, 10–11; and see Ziegert 1979, 228). He may have had only limited appreciation of political and social circumstances beyond his local sphere (Ziegert 1979, 232). Above all, his view of social life was that of a lawyer (ibid., 228, 230, 231). And it has often been remarked that Ehrlich's sociology of law was guided by very practical lawyers' concerns. Immediate experience, for Ehrlich, was the experience of a law professor observing the complex coordination of vastly different social and ethnic groups in an isolated region of the dying Austro–Hungarian Empire at the beginning of the twentieth century. This experience suggested that overloaded expectations were attached to state law and should be reduced (Ehrlich 2002, 71–72; Nelken 1984, 167). The study of living law would assist state officials, including judges, in decision making (Rottleuthner 1988, 232). It would inform state law—the law that lawyers know and use—and help to make it more realistic and more meaningful when applied in everyday social settings.

Ehrlich (2002, 43) writes that sociology of law is not bound by practical considerations. It is a pure science quite different from lawyers' unsystematic methods of analysis. Yet, implicitly, it is a *lawyer's* social science of law. It passionately rejects the social and theoretical preeminence of state law (ibid., 71); yet is produced by a jurist in the service of that law. The German school of "free law finding" of which Ehrlich was a founder, attempted to find a more secure authority for creative development of law by courts, drawing on the social forces surrounding legal institutions, so as to escape mere reliance on the state bureaucratic tradition. It sought to reinforce the status of lawyers and especially judges (Rottleuthner 1988, 239) in circumstances in which the continental European judge's work seemed to have become "a nearly bureaucratic execution of statute orders and prefabricated, codified decisions" (Ziegert 1979, 227). And when Ehrlich's ideas were first promoted in the English-speaking world, it was for their apparent usefulness in showing how to reinvigorate the common-law judge's creativity, then perceived as somewhat moribund (Page 1914, 75). Indeed, Roscoe Pound, Ehrlich's American champion, saw sociology as just such an aid to common-law methods.

This situation—inside the world of state law, yet also outside it—explains many of the incoherences and inadequacies of the concept of living law. There is no way to delimit the concept's scope, except to recognize it as embracing all forms of social regulation, actually operative in any given social field, that are generally regarded as of great social importance and clearly obligatory (Ehrlich 2002, 164–65). Living law can develop in any kind of social association as its internal means of regulation. Such associations can include families, business firms, clubs, partnerships, contracting parties, social classes, corporations, cities, localities, churches, professions, political parties, nations, and international groupings of nations (ibid., 26–27, 54–55). No effort is made to distinguish theoretically these vastly different social and legal contexts (cf. Gurvitch 1973, 117, 121).

Thus, the concept of living law gains coherence only from its polemical purpose: that of setting alongside state law (especially private law) an infinity of types of informal regulation that parallel specific fields of state or lawyers' law. Living law is the ever-present *conscience* of state law; it is the normative evidence of moral life available to monitor lawyers' law and where necessary shake it from moral sterility or social irrelevance. The unity of living law is given only as the *alter ego* of lawyers' law. It has no theoretical unity or precision outside this context.

Before we dismiss the hopelessly incoherent idea of living law, however, we should recognize parallel problems in its contemporary offspring, the concept of legal pluralism—especially as applied to contemporary Western societies in what has been generally termed the "new" legal pluralism (Merry 1988). Legal pluralism emphasizes the diversity of normative systems or regimes interacting with state law and demands that, for purposes of analysis, at least some of these should themselves be recognized as kinds of law. In this context we still have to ask: "What is law and where is it?" (Santos 1987, 281) and "Where do we stop speaking of law and find ourselves simply describing social life?" (Merry 1988, 878). One writer suggests we might need a new Hohfeld or Kelsen to organize the insights of legal pluralism into a general legal theory (Chiba 1989, 3). The problem of living law—what a critic of Ehrlich once called the problem of "megalomaniac jurisprudence" encompassing everything without adequate theoretical discrimination (Allen 1964, 32)—may thus survive in contemporary form. Indeed, Ehrlich notes, with seemingly total unconcern, that the difficulty is like trying to catch a stream and hold it in a pond (Ehrlich 1922, 133; 2002, 488). And it *could* remain a matter of unconcern for a practical-minded jurist. An incoherent notion of living law could serve well enough to marshal critical resources around the lawyer's *coherent* understanding of legal doctrine applied in state courts. For Ehrlich, the only concept of law that needed to be genuinely rigorous was the lawyer's concept of state law.

Contemporary concepts of legal pluralism are, of course, not usually constrained by the lawyers' concerns that explain Ehrlich's situation. The traditions of legal pluralist analysis have been developed primarily by anthropologists, who have been, presumably, relatively free of professional allegiances to lawyers' views of law. The problem for contemporary legal pluralism has been different. Western anthropologists' (and sociologists') paradigm experience of law—suggesting its fully developed form—has usually been that of state law (Snyder 1981, 163–64); whether in settings where customary law has been officially subordinated, incorporated, adapted, or

38

exceptionalized by state law (see Mastura 1994, esp. 474–75; and Chiba 1989); or in the pluralistic legal life of advanced Western societies to which anthropologists (and sociologists) have increasingly directed attention (see, e.g., Greenhouse 1982). To escape the "brooding omnipresence" of the state-law paradigm it has, indeed, often seemed appropriate to cease to talk in terms of law at all when analyzing nonstate forms of regulation (Roberts 1979, chap. 2; and see Snyder 1981, 66–67, 69). The issue, ultimately, is not one about defining law, but rather about the variety of moral settings and sources of regulation and about the kinds of authority that this regulation is able to command.

I want to conclude this brief discussion of the concept of living law on a positive note that will, I hope, suggest why, despite all its problems, the concept captures certain matters of enduring importance. Why was living law so important to Ehrlich that he declared its preeminence over state law even while directing all his work in the service of the latter? I think it was because the accident of the time and place in which he worked gave him an insight into moral and technical problems of state law, which may have seemed much less pressing to most lawyers in stable Western societies in his era than they did to him, but which have gradually come to seem increasingly important. At the time and place in which he wrote, on the edge of an empire whose state was about to disintegrate with the splitting apart of the extremely diverse national, cultural, and ethnic elements of that empire, Ehrlich was acutely aware of the fragility of state law as an effective regulator and of the *moral precariousness* of its authority. His parochial context gave him a very different view of the state and its law from, for example, Weber in Imperial Germany. But it was a view that might have received some sympathy from the other great contemporaneous founder of sociology of law, Émile Durkheim. Writing in a France wrecked by economic and cultural conflicts, Durkheim well understood the fragility of social solidarity and the moral authority of the state (Durkheim 1984, 291–328; Cotterrell 1999, chap. 2; Magraw 1983, chap. 3).

Ehrlich's situation allowed him to see, in a way that seemed archaic through most of the twentieth century but now appears prescient, the particular legal importance of the nation and the community as social associations and hence as moral entities. Ehrlich describes in detail the nation's social complexity as an association in which numerous smaller social associations (for example, economic, cultural, political, religious, and local) exist. Each association or community is portrayed as having its own legitimacy as a system of normatively ordered social relationships. Each has its own problems of maintaining internal integrity and external relations; of regulating its members' conduct in relation to each other and to the association as a whole; of maintaining their allegiance and ordering their participation within it. Ehrlich saw that social associations or communities, giving rise to their own structures of regulation, can exist beyond the scope of the nation, and hence the nation state. He recognized transnational regulation as part of the infinite variety of living law.

Most important is the idea that the state is to be conceptually distinguished from the nation and all other social associations. While allegiance to the state is a matter of the reach of its political authority, allegiance to the nation and other social associations depends on what we might call their broadly moral authority. This authority may be grounded in mutual recognition of congruent personal interests, in emotional attachments, in common traditions or environments, or in shared values or beliefs. But ultimately it is guaranteed by the member's need or wish to remain a part of the association, to stay within its jurisdiction. The ultimate sanction available to enforce the living law of social associations is the threat that the miscreant will be excluded from them. For Ehrlich, it seems, the nature of authority is inseparable from the nature of the types of social relations out of which authority arises. Implicit also are further difficult questions. If law is most truly the living law of social associations, and finds the moral basis of its authority in them, what authority does the lawyer ultimately serve? And where does the citizen's ultimate allegiance lie?

What remains disastrously missing from Ehrlich's picture of law is a specification of the theoretical relationship between the state and social associations. To theorize successfully this relationship would have been to alter lawyers' understanding of the nature of law (as state law) in the light of the sociological insights of living law. Through such an alteration Ehrlich would have cemented the importance of the study of living law for lawyers, as part of their essential intellectual world and professional outlook. But this did not happen. Living law did not disrupt juristic conceptions of law. Lawyers could dismiss Ehrlich's work by saying that living law, however sociologically interesting or relevant in legal policy debates, was simply not a matter of law as far as they were concerned, because it had no defined, specific, and invariant relation to the tasks of the state's legal agencies.

We can thus understand the ghostly presence and absence of the idea of living law in contemporary sociology of law. It is absent because lawyers can bypass it and sociologists are likely to find scant value in its conflation of many different social phenomena in a concept that almost wholly lacks sociological rigor. Nevertheless, the ambition remains for a radical reconceptualization of law in terms of its social conditions of existence and for the purpose of making it more morally responsive to those it purports to regulate. The concept of living law symbolizes that enduring ambition in sociology of law. It captures a part of the critical spirit of the research field. As such it remains powerfully present. The ghost is not likely to be exorcized; nor would it be good to banish it.

40

THE STATE, THE INDIVIDUAL, AND SOCIAL ASSOCIATIONS

Pluralist perspectives have begun to encourage a reconceptualization of state law in complex Western societies. To take one example from a wide literature, Peter Fitzpatrick (1984) has argued that the coherence of state law is, in certain respects, dependent on the parallel existence of certain other normative fields structured according to normative principles radically different from those of state law. The rule of law doctrine in state law may, for example, depend for its viability as a principle of social ordering on the very differently structured regimes of discipline existing in the workplace or in the prison, which influence the conditions of "docile citizenship" on which the operation of the rule of law depends. Thus state law and other techniques of normative ordering are mutually sustaining. They interpenetrate and shape each other in complex ways (see also Henry 1983; Cooper 1998).

But what principles should guide efforts to rethink state law by reference to other normative systems? We noted that the concept of living law emerged out of worries about the destiny of state law and the techniques, skills, and crafts (especially judicial) that went with it. The effort to import sociology into legal inquiry was an effort to change the direction of state regulation, to reinvigorate its methods of regulation, and make them more responsive to social context. The impulse was to confront state law with its necessary moral conditions of existence and, in the process, to show that, in the context of the modern nation state, these conditions could not sustain a state law with the regulatory ambitions that it had come to assume. Ehrlich associated the over-extended reach of state law in Western European societies with its individualist ethos: the "culmination of individualism is the principle that every man is an end unto himself. . . . The ideal of justice of individualism is the individual and his property, the individual . . . who recognizes no superior but the state, and is not bound by anything but the contracts he has freely entered into" (Ehrlich 2002, 235).

These impulses toward the rethinking of the nature of state law are, above all, moral impulses; to breathe moral life into law, to put it in touch with the sources of its normative authority in everyday moral experience. Similar impulses are found in Durkheim's work, as well as similar serious doubts about the capacity of the state, and of centralized or hierarchically structured state law, to provide morally meaningful regulation.[2] Such worries, linked to observation of state law's frequent remoteness and ineffectiveness, are reflected in some contemporary demands for responsive law (Selznick 1992, 463–76), the product of the state somehow acting in moral partnership with the regulated citizenry.

It is this kind of impulse to rethink the nature and scope of state law that the rest of this chapter seeks to pursue. But because the rethinking is largely motivated by the demand that law embody certain *values* (responsiveness, appropriateness to local contexts, respect for the integrity of community life in some sense, sensitivity to the diversity of moral experience of the regulated population), it easily moves outside the accepted scope of an empirically oriented sociology (and anthropology) of law. After all, value choices are involved in deciding how far to treat living law phenomena as "law"; how much attention to pay to these types of regulation in legal debates; how to think about the state in relation to law; how to conceptualize social associations. Legal sociologists and anthropologists have been prepared increasingly to structure and justify their empirical researches in terms of value-guided critique of law. But there has remained an understandable reluctance to engage in philosophical discussion of ideal social institutions.

Nevertheless, much social inquiry about law, developed within the shadow of the dominant paradigm of state law, *already presupposes* certain foundational values embedded in that paradigm. The paradigm reflects long centuries of lawyers' interpretations of legal ideas and theorization of the nature of law, as well as broader currents of political thought, moral understanding, assumptions about the fundamental character of social life, and reflections on specific historical experiences. It is a paradigm embedded in the modern history and intellectual traditions of Western societies, the societies in which the dominant orientations of sociological inquiry about law have been developed. Ehrlich tried to present living law as morally meaningful law that should force a reconsideration of the dominant paradigm of state law. We need to confront the intellectual resources that inform that paradigm if we are to pursue comparable aspirations.

One way of doing so is through elements of communitarian theory developed in contemporary political philosophy. I do not wish to suggest that communitarian theory as such should be adopted to guide the aspirations of sociology of law. Certainly, much of it inhabits realms of speculation distant from the careful empirical observation of particular conditions of social interaction that has typified the best sociology. But it provides certain valuable themes.

The starting point is a reconsideration of the political and moral situation of the individual citizen. Communitarianism examines analytically the structure of Western liberalism and its individualist legal orientations that Ehrlich noted. For communitarians, the individual is not, as Western liberalism asserts, a socially "unencumbered self" but a social being formed in association with others within communities (Sandel 1984; Taylor 1992, 45). On this view, autonomous individuals gain their very autonomy from the possibility of conceiving of alternative choices and courses of action. And these choices and possibilities are given by the social civilization in which the individual develops (Taylor 1992). Such a claim may entail the suggestion that the support of individual autonomy and freedom is found at least as much in community structures of some kind, as in the state's coercive powers. If the sustaining

42

structures of community wither, the regulatory task entrusted to the state becomes unmanageable. Thus Michael Sandel (1984, 92), a prominent communitarian theorist, observes "what appear simultaneously as the power and
powerlessness of the nation state," experienced as "an overly intrusive presence" yet "disempowered," incapable of discharging the regulatory burdens
heaped on it. Solutions to problems of state regulation might, therefore,
sometimes lie in strengthening structures of community on which the realization of individual autonomy depends.

At the level of individual life, communitarianism observes a sense of loss
and longing (ibid., 94–95), so that people are more entangled yet less attached to each other than ever before. In this condition democracy itself becomes enfeebled and lifeless. Democracy becomes less meaningful as the
centralization of the regulatory power of the state proceeds (ibid., 93–94).
This is because democracy depends on a vital sense of community that
makes participation in the processes of shaping regulation worthwhile and
important (Selznick 1992, 363–64, 522–24). Hence the meaning of citizenship is a central focus for some communitarian writers (Miller 1992; cf.
Bubeck 1999). Particularly important in this context are questions of allegiance and authority. We noted earlier how Ehrlich separated the concept of
state from that of nation, seeing the latter as a social association that could
thus be the creator of a living law contrasted with state law. Contemporary
communitarians sometimes similarly distinguish allegiance to the nation as a
community from allegiance to the state (MacIntyre 1985, 254; Miller 1992,
88). Philip Selznick, applying his long experience with issues of sociology of
law to develop in detail a communitarian perspective, also stresses a certain
moral primacy of community over state (Selznick 1992, 505–10).

From the wealth of communitarian ideas, one other theme is of major importance here. The view of the basis of individual autonomy that communitarianism encourages often entails a different view of rights from the view
that predominates in liberal thought and informs much thinking in sociology
of law and legal theory. Since the individual is, for communitarianism, not a
presocial being but a being whose very essence is socially given through the
character of the community in which the individual grows to personhood, it
follows that social relations are not to be seen as structured solely or even
mainly by the interplay of rights existing independently of some sense of
communal good (Taylor 1992; but cf. Miller 1992, 94). Other connections between individuals are stressed by communitarians as reflecting more appropriately the communal structures within which individuality is formed.
Hence friendship or care have been emphasized especially by feminist writers as more appropriate models of community relationships (Friedman 1989;
Bubeck 1999). From another standpoint the idea of trust, and especially mutual interpersonal trust, might seem a basic element of community (Cotterrell
1995, 325–32).

What should socio-legal scholars make of these ideas? Is communitarianism essentially an idealistic but unrealistic response to the sense of "loss and longing" that its exponents notice and perhaps themselves feel? Empirically oriented legal sociologists are likely to point out the difficulty in treating community as a focus of regulation in the conditions of advanced societies. Contemporary societies are increasingly atomistic; at least, the complexities of legally regulating them seem frequently to involve assuming that they are. The concept of community is applied most easily to premodern social forms—the *Gemeinschaft* and the self-regulating guild, the isolated neighborhood and the clan. Perhaps, then, "'community' stands for the kind of world which is not, regrettably, available to us" (Bauman 2001, 3).

In much communitarian literature a fundamental vagueness about the scale and scope of the communities under discussion persists (Bauman 1993, 44). Sometimes analysis is in terms of the whole range of social associations that Ehrlich had in mind. Often, however, discussion focuses on the polity— the political society of the nation state—as the community. Sometimes it is asserted that no other focus of significant regulatory authority is really viable (Miller 1992). What is important, in this view, is to understand the moral nature of the nation as a focus of allegiance, and the means by which the nation is presented as a focus of moral allegiance.

Very important matters, clearly understood by Ehrlich, seem neglected in much communitarian literature. Is it really possible to think of the whole national political society as a community? Perhaps contemporary experience in many parts of the world confirms that it is; the deep emotions that can attach to the sense of nation are too often underestimated. In most Western nation-state political societies, however, it is difficult to think of the strong consensus on values that has often been associated with the idea of community in the past. Often what exists is a political rhetoric of community values (Cotterrell 1995, 242–43), community constructed or imagined for specific political projects. Alasdair MacIntyre links ideas of community with traditional virtues that he sees modernity as having undermined. MacIntyre (1985, 252) asserts: "our [Western nation-state] society cannot hope to achieve moral consensus"; there are simply too many competing moral concepts—views of justice—that cannot be rationally resolved. Thus, for MacIntyre, community—understood as the locus of morality—has to be thought of in terms of a different (if variable) scale from that of the nation state.

Communitarianism, nevertheless, usefully encourages a radical rethinking of the relationship between state and individual. It challenges the view of this relationship that underpins much Western philosophy and legal thought and has been carried into the paradigm informing much socio-legal scholarship. Communitarianism does not provide adequate resources for this rethinking partly because—as a philosophical movement—it lacks sufficient sociological commitment to the empirical examination of social differences,

44

the sheer diversity of Ehrlich's social associations. But in its alternative view of rights, individual autonomy, and the location of regulatory authority, it challenges foundational assumptions about the character, functions, and limits of state law and the forms of justice it offers.

It is worth mentioning here the very important discussion in Michael Walzer's book *Spheres of Justice* of the complexity and variety of principles of justice and of their application that arise in different social spheres in complex modern societies (Walzer 1985). Walzer's concern is not with differences between localities or specific social or cultural groups, which have been the traditional focus of much pluralist writing about legal regulation. He looks rather at many different types of social goods (for example, commodities, offices of responsibility, work, leisure, education, respect and recognition, and political power) in connection with which a modern state must establish regulatory principles of justice for their distribution. Walzer addresses the important point that social relationships requiring regulation and the appropriate principles of their regulation may vary greatly as between these different spheres of distribution.

Where then do communitarian ideas take us if we introduce them into sociolegal studies? They carry into modern debate a sense of dissatisfaction with the unmediated relationship of state and individual: the same sense that made Ehrlich use the concept of living law to try to prise apart that relationship. In some forms they import a conservatism—a reverence for traditional ways and social forms—which is also present in some of Ehrlich's thinking. But, although critical thought in legal scholarship may be an effort to break away from some of the agendas of modernity, it cannot properly lead to efforts to return to the past. It may, indeed, be important to see law as an institution supporting communication across cultural diversity, as much as an instrument for politically steering society (Habermas 1986, 1996). But law today cannot be the law of some reinvigorated *Gemeinschaft*. In any case, few people would welcome such a possibility.

One way of avoiding a drift to conservatism is to affirm that, in general, community structures meriting legal protection or expression or even, in some cases, possessing a degree of regulatory authority of their own in partnership with that of the state, should be open and voluntary. Thus, they will allow, as far as possible, free movement into them and, certainly, out of them. Where unfettered freedom of entry is impracticable, qualifications for entry should be based on achieved merit, not ascribed status. Such general propositions are, however, not always applicable. At the very least, they require much elaboration not possible here. Indeed, it is a further virtue of some writing on communitarian ideas that it explores contrasting principles of group membership arising in such diverse social associations as clubs, families, neighborhoods, and nations.[3]

Another way to limit the conservative aspects of communitarian perspectives is to reduce the traditional emphasis on shared values as a central defining aspect of any community. Ehrlich's view of social associations has some continuing merit here, too. He focuses on mutual interaction as the essence of these associations, though, of course, that may involve—or be premised on—adherence to commonly held values or beliefs. Some modern communitarians stress that in seeking community bonds in national culture, "the common culture we are looking for must be of a relatively thin kind" (Miller 1992, 93). Unifying values may be limited.

If, for example, the idea of mutual trust is taken as central to community, then the shared values essential to community will only be those needed to enable this trust to exist and flourish. They will vary depending on the nature of the trusting relationships that characterize different types of community. From such a standpoint it is appropriate to think of communities not as social groups or populations but rather as *types of social relations* intertwined in often intricate ways to create social networks (Cotterrell 1997). Social life can be more or less communally organized depending on the extent of the development of mutual trusting relationships within it. And regulation—informed by the insights of socio-legal research—might be consciously shaped to foster and support such relationships.

A third way to counter the conservatism of some invocations of community is to stress that relations of community are always to be understood, from a certain standpoint, as relations of power. A focus on community cannot properly displace a concern with the analysis of power and its links to law, but makes this central. Communities are sites of conflict, as much as of harmony. The idea that they could be regulated to make them never the former and always the latter has often led, in practice, to unlimited repression (Bauman 2001, 4–5, 96–97). As relations of dependence, mutual trusting relationships are rarely evenly balanced. Nevertheless, solidarity and stability in relations of community, and the possibility that those relations can provide a source of moral authority for regulation, rely on a *limiting* of extremes of power and on the existence of *mutual* reliance and the recognition of *cross*-dependencies (Cotterrell 1995, 330). So power, productively pervading social relations but also giving rise to "major dominations" (Foucault 1979, 93–96), must be studied as an aspect of community.

Legal sociologists are accustomed to working with specific, concrete hypotheses. Abstract ideas in sociology of law are usually and properly developed not from general philosophical speculations but in relation to particular projects of empirical inquiry. The material introduced in this chapter may seem remote from such necessary foci of research. Nevertheless, it seems clear, from a variety of general discussions of socio-legal studies—especially perhaps from many recent assessments of American law-and-society research—that there is a sense of a need to reconsider directions of effort.

I certainly do not wish to suggest that socio-legal studies should incorporate the philosophical outlook of communitarianism; nor that they should shift their focus from the numerous pressing problems arising in the analysis

46

of contemporary forms of state law in advanced nation states. As a field that has been shaped by the broad aspirations of social science, however, socio-legal scholarship has established its credentials in relation to particular paradigms of both science and law. These paradigms now seem to be changing fundamentally. The idea of science that has typified the modern age has been the idea of science overcoming nature, and so dispelling the dangers that unregulated nature presents for humankind. The comparable modern idea of law has been that of law overcoming culture, and so dispelling the ignorance and irrationality which modern thought has often associated with the traditional in culture.

Nowadays there is a tendency to emphasize a need to protect nature against science, and perhaps to protect culture against law. This tendency should not be allowed to weaken the commitment to a social science of law. But it should make us recognize that socio-legal studies must treat with great seriousness the need to nurture diverse moral conditions of human interaction and, indeed, of human interaction with nature. I have argued that a certain ambition was implied in the founding conceptions of modern sociology of law with which this chapter has been concerned. It was to require state law to cooperate pluralistically with other forms of regulation precisely in order to respect and regulate moral diversity and so preserve and enhance law's own regulatory authority. Such an ambition remains no less relevant today, nearly a century after the concept of living law began its complex intellectual history.

NOTES

1, This chapter is a substantially revised version of a paper originally presented at the meeting of the International Sociological Association Research Committee on Sociology of Law, Kobe, Japan, in August 1995.

2. See Cotterrell 1999 for detailed analysis of Durkheim's sociology of law and morality.

3. See especially Walzer 1985, chap. 2; and cf. the contrast drawn between genetic and voluntary associations in Ehrlich 2002, 28.

REFERENCES

Allen, Carleton K. 1964. *Law in the Making*. 7th ed. Oxford: Oxford University Press.
Avineri, Shlomo, and Avner de-Shalit, eds. 1992. *Communitarianism and Individualism*. Oxford: Oxford University Press.
Bauman, Zygmunt. 1993. *Postmodern Ethics*. Oxford: Blackwell.
———. 2001. *Community: Seeking Safety in an Insecure World*. Cambridge: Polity Press.

Living Law Revisited: Communitarianism and Sociology of Law   47

Bubeck, Diemut. 1999. A Feminist Approach to Citizenship. In *Gender and the Use of Time*, ed. Owlen Hufton and Yota Kravaritou, 401–28. The Hague: Kluwer Law International.

Chiba, Masaji. 1989. *Legal Pluralism: Toward a General Theory through Japanese Legal Culture*. Tokyo: Tokai University Press.

Cooper, Davina. 1998. *Governing Out of Order: Space, Law and the Politics of Belonging*. London: Rivers Oram Press.

Cotterrell, Roger. 1995. *Law's Community: Legal Theory in Sociological Perspective*. Oxford: Oxford University Press.

———. 1997. A Legal Concept of Community. *Canadian Journal of Law and Society* 12:75–91.

———. 1999. *Émile Durkheim: Law in a Moral Domain*. Stanford: Stanford University Press.

Durkheim, Émile. 1984. *The Division of Labour in Society*. Trans. W. D. Halls. London: Macmillan.

Ehrlich, Eugen. 1922. The Sociology of Law. *Harvard Law Review* 36:130–45.

———. 2002. *Fundamental Principles of the Sociology of Law*. Trans. Walter L. Moll [1936]. Repr. New Brunswick, NJ: Transaction Publishers.

Ewald, François. 1990. Norms, Discipline, and the Law. *Representations* 30:138–61.

Ewick, Patricia, and Susan S. Silbey. 1998. *The Common Place of Law: Stories from Everyday Life*. Chicago: University of Chicago Press.

Fitzpatrick, Peter. 1984. Law and Societies. *Osgoode Hall Law Journal* 22:115–38.

Foucault, Michel. 1979. *The History of Sexuality*, vol. 1, *An Introduction*. Trans. R. Hurley. London: Allen Lane.

———. 1991. Governmentality. In *The Foucault Effect: Studies in Governmentality*, ed. Graham Burchell, Colin Gordon, and Peter Miller, 87–104. Hemel Hempstead: Harvester Wheatsheaf.

Friedman, Marilyn. 1989. Feminism and Modern Friendship: Dislocating the Community. *Ethics* 99:275–90.

Gierke, Otto von. 1958. *Natural Law and the Theory of Society*. Trans. E. Barker [1934]. Repr. Cambridge: Cambridge University Press.

Greenhouse, Carol J. 1982. Nature Is to Culture as Praying Is to Suing: Legal Pluralism in an American Suburb. *Journal of Legal Pluralism* 20:17–35.

Gurvitch, Georges. 1973. *Sociology of Law*. Repr. [1947]. London: Routledge and Kegan Paul.

Habermas, Jürgen. 1986. Law as Medium and Law as Institution. In *Dilemmas of Law in the Welfare State*, ed. Gunther Teubner, 203–20. Berlin: Walter de Gruyter.

———. 1996. *Between Facts and Norms: Contributions to a Discourse Theory of Law and Democracy*. Trans. W. Rehg. Cambridge: Polity Press.

Henry, Stuart. 1983. *Private Justice: Towards Integrated Theorising in the Sociology of Law*. London: Routledge and Kegan Paul.

MacIntyre, Alasdair. 1985. *After Virtue: A Study in Moral Theory*. 2nd ed. London: Duckworth.

Magraw, Roger. 1983. *France 1815–1914: The Bourgeois Century*. London: Fontana.

Mastura, Michael O. 1994. Legal Pluralism in the Philippines. *Law and Society Review* 28:461–75.

48

Merry, Sally E. 1988. Legal Pluralism. *Law and Society Review* 22:869–96.

——. 1990. *Getting Justice and Getting Even: Legal Consciousness among Working-Class Americans*. Chicago: University of Chicago Press.

——. 1995. Resistance and the Cultural Power of Law. *Law and Society Review* 29:11–26.

Miller, David. 1992. Community and Citizenship [1990]. Repr. Avineri and de-Shalit, 85–100.

Nelken, David. 1984. Law in Action or Living Law? Back to the Beginning in Sociology of Law. *Legal Studies* 4:157–74.

——. 1986. Beyond the Study of "Law and Society": Henry's *Private Justice* and O'Hagan's *The End of Law*. *American Bar Foundation Research Journal*: 323–38.

Nussbaum, Arthur. 1940. Fact Research in Law. *Columbia Law Review* 40:189–219.

Page, William H. 1914. Professor Ehrlich's Czernowitz Seminar of Living Law. In Proceedings of the 14th Annual Meeting of the Association of American Law Schools, December 28, 29, and 30, 1914, 46–75. Chicago: Association of American Law Schools.

Petrazycki, Leon. 1955. *Law and Morality*. Trans. Hugh W. Babb. Cambridge, MA: Harvard University Press.

Roberts, Simon A. 1979. *Order and Dispute: An Introduction to Legal Anthropology*. Harmondsworth: Penguin.

Rose, Nikolas, and Mariana Valverde. 1998. Governed by Law? *Social and Legal Studies* 7:541–51.

Rottleuthner, Hubert. 1988. Three Legal Sociologies: Eugen Ehrlich, Hugo Sinzheimer, Max Weber. In *European Yearbook in the Sociology of Law 1988*, ed. Alberto Febbrajo, 227–59. Milan: Giuffrè.

Sandel, Michael. 1984. The Procedural Republic and the Unencumbered Self. *Political Theory* 12:81–96.

Santos, Boaventura de Sousa. 1987. Law: A Map of Misreading: Toward a Postmodern Conception of Law. *Journal of Law and Society* 14:279–302.

Selznick, Philip. 1992. *The Moral Commonwealth: Social Theory and the Promise of Community*. Berkeley: University of California Press.

Snyder, Francis G. 1981. Anthropology, Dispute Processes and Law: A Critical Introduction. *British Journal of Law and Society* 8:141–80.

Taylor, Charles. 1992. Atomism [1979]. Repr. Avineri and de-Shalit, 29–50.

Teubner, Gunther. 1987. Juridification: Concepts, Aspects, Limits, Solutions. In *Juridification of Social Spheres: A Comparative Analysis in the Areas of Labor, Corporate, Antitrust and Social Welfare Law*, ed. Gunther Teubner, 3–48. Berlin: Walter de Gruyter.

Walzer, Michael. 1985. *Spheres of Justice: A Defence of Pluralism and Equality*. Repr. [1983]. Oxford: Blackwell.

Weber, Max. 1978. *Economy and Society: An Outline of Interpretive Sociology*. Trans. Ephraim Fischoff et al. [1968]. Repr. Berkeley: University of California Press.

Yngvesson, Barbara. 1993. *Virtuous Citizens, Disruptive Subjects: Order and Complaint in a New England Court*. New York: Routledge.

Ziegert, Klaus A. 1979. The Sociology behind Eugen Ehrlich's Sociology of Law. *International Journal of the Sociology of Law* 7:225–73.

[6]
Emmanuel Lévy and Legal Studies: A View from Abroad*

Summary

Emmanuel Lévy is almost entirely unknown in the Anglophone world, yet his originality deserves international recognition. His work can be compared with radical legal theory in other societies but is more subtle than that of some better known jurists. His ideas about the political practice of law and about the social significance of legal thought predated, by many decades, similar views of the American critical legal studies movement. His understanding of law as grounded in potentially unstable beliefs resonates with themes of postmodernist legal studies. Where Lévy is ambiguous or unclear, the cause often lies in the profoundly contradictory influences that shaped his thought.

. . . .

[132] To be invited to contribute, as a writer from the common law tradition, to this symposium on a remarkable French legal scholar is an honour. Yet the task is daunting because vast intellectual distances must be bridged. Emmanuel Lévy's ideas, developed early in the twentieth century, are far removed from current tendencies in both Francophone and Anglophone legal scholarship and his work (none of it translated into English) is almost entirely unknown in English-language literature on law.

Until very recently, the only introduction in English to Lévy was in a translated adaptation of Georges Gurvitch's *Élements de sociologie juridique* published in London as *Sociology of Law* in 1947. For theoretically-oriented researchers in England who, like the present writer, committed themselves to legal sociology in the 1970s, Gurvitch's book was essential reading to gain perspective on pioneer socio-legal theorists. But it criticised Lévy without explaining his ideas fully. Misleading translation of some key words (e.g. *valeurs, créances*) also made the discussion opaque.

---

* Originally published in (2004) *Droit et Société*, no 56–57, pp. 131–41. Numbers in bold print inside square brackets indicate the original pagination. The original text is unaltered except for the addition, in square brackets in footnotes, of English translations of some French quotations.

At that time, Jean Carbonnier's *Sociologie juridique* (1978) surveyed the pioneers of sociology of law and briefly but intriguingly noted Lévy's originality and his socialist notoriety. Then André-Jean Arnaud's valuable *Critique de la raison juridique I: Ou va la Sociologie du droit?* (1981) and some of Lévy's articles and pamphlets introduced me to his ideas. Later I found copies of Lévy's *Les fondements du droit* and *La vision socialiste du droit*, dusty, fragile and yellowing in the basement of a London library. The books had clearly lain undisturbed for many years.

Learning about Lévy over two decades, I realised that his situation and achievement had no parallels in the common law world, but his moral integrity and intellectual honesty seemed to shine like a beacon. The mixture of activism and scholarship in his career, and his apparently unquenchable idealism and personal tenacity, suggested that it would be good to know more about the details of his biography. Then, a decade-long project of research on Émile Durkheim's legal sociology convinced me of Lévy's importance in radicalising aspects of Durkheimian legal thought, transforming it into a philosophy of political action by fusing and challenging it with other intellectual influences.[1] I felt that although Lévy's work had no direct relations with Anglophone legal scholarship, comparisons with 'realist' and 'critical' common law traditions were potentially worth exploring. This paper offers a few suggestions about possible directions for this exploration.

I. Between Marx and Durkheim

The main influences on Lévy's legal thought might be divided broadly into two clusters. One is the range of socialist thinking – related to but [133] often in tension with Marxism – that contributed to *socialisme juridique* in France and elsewhere in Europe at the beginning of the twentieth century.[2] The other is the sociological influence of Durkheim and the Durkheim school, of which Lévy was an active, committed and longstanding member. Neither of these intellectual movements has left a living legacy for contemporary legal scholarship, so that the terrain in which Lévy worked might be thought to have become barren. But it would be far too negative and too unfair to Lévy's achievement to leave the matter at that.

---

1 Roger Cotterrell, *Émile Durkheim: Law in a Moral Domain*, Edinburgh: Edinburgh University Press/ Stanford: Stanford University Press, 1999, pp, 188–194 and *passim*.

2 Nicole and André-Jean Arnaud, 'Le socialisme juridique à la "Belle Époque": visages d'une aberration' in André-Jean Arnaud (with Nicole Arnaud-Duc), *Le droit trahi par la philosophie*, Rouen: CESPJ, 1977, pp. 115–144.

He wrote: '*Au point de vue école, j'ai trouvé chez Durkheim confirmation de ceci: nous vivons de croyances.*'[3] In stressing the link between law and collective belief, Lévy focused on a matter that has become central to critical legal theory long after he wrote. The idea that we live by beliefs, and that law must be understood in its relation to collectively held convictions or understandings is an idea that is widespread in recent legal theories, though they explain that relation in many different ways.

Lévy's fusing of Durkheimian and socialist thought allows him to adopt a complex theoretical position. The path he traces runs between theories of ideology, on the one hand, and Durkheimian understandings of the nature of collective representations (*répresentations collectives*), on the other. But these very different approaches to understanding the nature of shared beliefs or understandings suggest contrasting kinds of legal theory: on the one hand, theories of law as an instrument or reflection of ideology; on the other, theories of law as a repository of social values, an expression of shared morality or bonds of solidarity.

Theories of 'law and ideology' tend to emphasise law's mystificatory functions or its contribution to the maintenance of dominant ideological currents. Legal doctrine and legal practice are seen as helping to promulgate broad systems of ideas and beliefs. The theoretical image of law is as a site of struggle for hearts and minds, a struggle between world-views, or between interpretations of the nature of social life. In Marxist terms, the conflict of ideas and beliefs is clearly part of class struggle. Law is both a prize and a weapon in this struggle.[4] The state is, in part, a mechanism through which ideological control is exercised.[5]

Theories of 'law and collective representations', derived from Durkheimian traditions, are likely to have a very different orientation. Law is not seen primarily as a site of struggle or a weapon but as an expression of [134] moral conditions. Law embodies the moral realities of social life. It represents collective convictions. Law's task is to define, rationalise and make explicit the currents of moral understanding and belief existing in society. Law expresses, in a public and codified form, social ideas that are otherwise inchoate and diffuse. The state is a mechanism for discovering, refining and expressing

---

3   Emmanuel Lévy, *Les fondements du droit*, Paris: Alcan, 1933, p. 168. ['From the viewpoint of scholarship, I found in Durkheim confirmation of this: we live through beliefs.']

4   Bernard Edelman, *Le Droit saisi par la photographie: Éléments pour une théorie marxiste du droit*, 1973, translated as *Ownership of the Image: Elements for a Marxist Theory of Law*, London: Routledge & Kegan Paul, 1979.

5   Louis Althusser, 'Idéologie et appareils idéologiques de l'État', translated as 'Ideology and Ideological State Apparatuses' in Althusser, *Essays on Ideology*, London: Verso, 1984, pp. 1–60.

collective representations in a normative and institutional form, strengthening them and enabling them to foster social integration and solidarity.[6] The most serious ambiguities of Lévy's work arise from the fact that it uneasily combines the influences of these contrasting basic approaches to the relations of law and belief. But both approaches remain strongly present in current theoretical analyses of law. Certainly, in the Anglophone legal world, ideas about legal ideology, hegemony and the struggle of ideas conducted through law are now discussed in terms of critical legal studies (of many different kinds)[7] and rarely in terms of explicitly socialist legal thought or even less in terms of Marxism. Correspondingly, ideas about law's relation to morality, and about the importance of shared values expressed through law and serving as a foundation for solidarity, are rarely discussed at present in terms of Durkheimian sociology. But they are much debated in the language of communitarianism or republicanism.[8]

The ambivalence in Lévy's approach can easily be noticed in his views on the state. On the one hand, he sees it as having the Durkheimian task of expressing and clarifying collective beliefs – especially those affecting credit, security, property and contracts. Where these beliefs are unstable, the state *'participe à l'instabilité des valeurs; le droit devient perpétuellement en rupture.'*[9] Law and state reflect the shifting currents of collective belief. Law attempts to measure and reconcile conflicting representations. But Lévy sees the state itself becoming diffuse (even internationalised)[10] as it seeks to support a society that has become increasingly a regime of securities (*régime des valeurs*) depending entirely on unstable collective convictions (*croyances*) that cannot be contained within the borders of state jurisdiction.

Implicit in this view is the idea that changes in collective beliefs entirely determine the nature and function of the state and the role and content of law. Just as for Durkheim, *'les idées morales sont l'âme du droit'*,[11] so for **[135]** Lévy *'la croyance crée le droit.'*[12] Law is rooted in belief: it is *'un substitut*

---

6   Cotterrell, *Émile Durkheim, op. cit.*, chs. 4 and 10.

7   See e. g. David Kairys, ed., *The Politics of Law: A Progressive Critique*, New York: Basic Books, 3rd edn., 1998; Dan Danielsen and Karen Engle, eds., *After Identity: A Reader in Law and Culture*, New York: Routledge, 1995.

8   See e. g. Philip Selznick, *The Communitarian Persuasion*, Washington D.C.: Woodrow Wilson Center Press, 2002; Selznick, *The Moral Commonwealth*, Berkeley: University of California Press, 1992.

9   Lévy, *Fondements, op. cit.*, p. 81. [The state 'is implicated in the instability of values; law becomes perpetually disrupted.']

10   *Ibid.*, p. 152.

11   Émile Durkheim, *La science sociale et l'action*, Paris: PUF, 2nd edn., 1987, p. 150. ['Moral ideas are the soul of law.']

12   Lévy, *Fondements, op. cit.*, pp. 96, 165. ['Belief creates law.']

pratique de la religion' and judges are its priests.[13] One senses that '*croyances*' might break law apart and force it into new forms. The state would have no option but to acquiesce in what might be called the social or cultural creation of law.

On the other hand, Lévy (citing Lassalle in support) suggests that law and rights *depend utterly* on the state. They are politically created and have no existence except through the state's directive force. '*Seul l'État assure ou enlève aux individus leurs droits...C'est la loi qui donne, c'est la loi qui ôte, la loi, c'est à dire la volonté de l'État (législateurs, administrateurs, juges).*'[14]

Thus, while one strand in Lévy's thought treats the state, as Durkheim did, as a deliberating 'brain' distilling collective representations into legal form[15] and dependent on these representations, another strand treats the state as sovereign 'will' without which collective representations cannot acquire legal force. The question is: is law ultimately dependent on the state which gives it force and authority, or is the state merely the servant of culturally or socially produced law? Putting it more bluntly: are law's sources essentially political or moral?

Lévy's ambivalence on the relations of law, state and society (the legacy of the conflicting theoretical influences on him) is unresolved because he leaves key ideas vague. His central concept of '*croyances*' is unclear, as Georges Gurvitch emphasised[16] and Lévy does not explain how collective beliefs arise, change and have effects. So their sociological character remains obscure: are they rooted in class interests (as ideology) or in conditions of social integration (as collective representations)? How does law 'measure' collective convictions? By what processes are conflicts between them reconciled – by public deliberation (Durkheim) or by coercion or ideological mystification (Marx)? How does law express '*croyances*'? Does law alter them in the process because legal thought and doctrine have their own special qualities? As a lawyer, Lévy could hardly be unaware of this issue, yet he has little to say about it. And these matters are not just of historical interest. Today the question of how far law reflects

13 *Ibid*, pp. 35–6; Lévy, *La vision socialiste du droit*, Paris: Giard, 1926, pp. 117–118. ['a practical substitute for religion'].

14 Lévy, *Fondements, op. cit.*, p. 53. ['Only the state guarantees to individuals or removes from them their rights... It is (enacted) law that gives and that takes away; in other words, the will of the state (legislators, administrators, judges).']

15 Émile Durkheim, *Leçons de sociologie*, Paris: PUF, 2nd edn., 1995, ch. 4; Cotterrell, *Émile Durkheim, op. cit.*, ch. 10.

16 Georges Gurvitch, 'Les fondements et l'évolution du droit d'après Emmanuel Lévy' in Gurvitch, *L'expérience juridique et la philosophie pluraliste du droit*, Paris: Pedone, 1935, pp. 190–191.

or mirrors collective understandings and how far it 'constitutes' (defines and shapes) them remains a matter of debate.[17]

[136] Can law and morality be distinguished clearly? For Lévy the distinction is that law provides a 'measure' to limit, define and reconcile moral or other beliefs. But does morality not also 'measure' (i.e. fix degrees of merit or responsibility) and address conflicts of beliefs or understandings? Durkheim treats the difference between law and morality as only one of degree, legal rules being moral rules that have been institutionalised in certain vaguely defined ways.[18] Marx, by contrast, sees legal ideas and morality mainly as parallel expressions of ideology. Neither the Durkheimian nor the socialist traditions, on which Lévy draws, justifies any sharp separation of law and morality such as he seems to assume.

Despite its problems, Lévy's work has enduring value for current legal studies. First, it stresses in a most striking way the *fragile* grounding of law's structures of meaning, and its *dependence* on social currents of belief and understanding that may combine (from the lawyer's standpoint) rational and irrational judgments. Secondly, Lévy's work is valuable for its provocative analysis of the conditions of stability and change in these social currents. It stresses that law is grounded in certain *faiths* that are not timeless, and that its legitimacy is never to be taken for granted.

Lévy's view of law is profoundly populist, asserting that law's strength lies ultimately not in the expertise of lawyers and judges who serve the state legal system but in the ideas of citizens at large. Eugen Ehrlich famously declared that the centre of gravity of law lies not in courts or legislation but in society itself.[19] Lévy goes much further: law's centre of gravity lies not just in 'the social', understood as the patterns of social relations that make up society. It lies in the shifting social understandings and convictions of society's members: in collective psychology rather than observable patterns of social action.

Hence, in a striking radicalisation of legal thought, Lévy privileges, in every important respect, the understandings of non-lawyers over those of lawyers. Because he asserts that legal ideas depend for their legitimacy and ultimate meaning on the pre-legal convictions (*croyances*) of citizens, he cleverly turns on their head all traditional assumptions about ultimate control of law. It is hardly surprising, then, that he should have provoked such antagonism to his theories among jurists; and that he should have wanted primarily to address

---

17 See e. g. Roger Cotterrell, 'Law as Constitutive' in Neil J. Smelser and Paul B. Baltes, eds., *International Encyclopedia of the Social and Behavioral Sciences*, New York: Elsevier, 2001, pp. 8497–8500.

18 Cotterrell, *Émile Durkheim, op. cit.*, pp. 60–61.

19 Eugen Ehrlich, *Fundamental Principles of the Sociology of Law*, Cambridge, Mass.: Harvard University Press, 1936, Preface.

non-lawyers (socialist activists, industrial workers and, not least, the citizens of Lyon whom he served as deputy mayor) through his work. **[137]**

II. Lévy and Critical Legal Studies

What connections exist between Lévy's ideas and modern legal thought? Can there be points of contact with an international world of legal scholarship that has dismissed or, more often, simply been unaware of his work?

Lévy can be regarded as a remarkable precursor of modern critical legal studies in some of its aspects. More than seven decades before the critical legal studies (CLS) movement came into being, initially in the United States, Lévy (with other adherents of *socialisme juridique*) emphasised the central CLS idea that legal concepts reflect broader social currents of thought and that as part of the process of challenging these broader currents, legal ideas themselves can be turned to new purposes and reinterpreted in new, more liberating and just ways. Long before CLS, Lévy saw legal argument as a form of political practice.[20]

From the time of his thesis on *Preuve par titre du droit de propriété immobiliaire* (1896), he held the view that property rights existed only through the well-founded conviction of property owners in the soundness of their title. This conviction is made well-founded only by the general collective conviction as to what acts and circumstances are appropriate to give good proprietary title. Lassalle had argued that legal entitlements depend on and vary with collective belief in them: Lévy added to this the idea that these entitlements (or their value) could be destroyed by the *withdrawal of belief*.

Nearly a century after Lévy, CLS saw the political potential of forms of legal practice that aim to secure this withdrawal of belief in legal certitudes. CLS describes the establishment of these legal certitudes as the 'reification' of legal ideas – their tendency to appear as solid, unshakeable and 'thing-like'. To challenge reification involves a radical legal practice aiming to secure the withdrawal of belief in dominant interpretations of legal ideas. CLS describes this practice as one of attacking legal 'hegemony'.

For CLS, legal ideas can potentially be turned upside-down by able, politically-aware, critical legal argument. Assumptions that underpin previous interpretations of them can be undermined and the possibility arises that judges might be forced to see these ideas in a radically new way. Concepts of 'property', 'ownership', 'contract', 'responsibility', etc., might have to be reinterpreted in

---

20   One of the clearest and fullest general accounts of CLS as a form of political practice focused on law is Robert Gordon, 'Some Critical Theories of Law and Their Critics' in Kairys, *Politics of Law, op. cit*, pp. 641–661.

ways not foreseen by the court but brought forcibly to its attention. In the specific circumstances of a case, they might have to be broadened or narrowed to take account of changes in the social realities that the concepts presuppose.

As early as the beginning of the twentieth century, Lévy's prescription for radical legal practice in the service of the working classes was, in all [138] essentials, the same as these CLS positions. To have thought through such ideas so long before American CLS scholars discovered and widely popularised them makes Lévy more than just a precursor. Even to call him a prophet seems inadequate. Although his analyses in simple class terms now seem archaic, his view of the social sources of the stability of legal ideas and his advocacy of a legal practice based in understanding those social sources has striking contemporary resonance. His work in this respect is truly prescient.

Interestingly, Lévy's work also shows some similar faults to that of CLS. For all his proletarian sympathies, his political activism and his disdain for orthodox legal scholarship, Lévy's legal thought (like much CLS scholarship) is rooted in a law school environment. His analysis of the transformations of property and credit rights is in terms of juristic technicalities. Lévy devotes little attention to detailed social inquiry, despite his sympathy for sociology. The content of *'croyances collectives'* is largely assumed. He takes, from the socialist tradition and from Durkheimian sociology, broad assumptions about social change, using them as a generally unstated background for his juristic analysis. In a very similar way, American CLS writers cite the work of social theorists (e.g. Gramsci, Foucault, the Frankfurt School) often without engaging very much, themselves, in rigorous social analyses. In general, neither Lévy nor CLS recognises that a politics of law needs to be based on detailed empirical social inquiries about law's sources and effects and about the specific practices by which it is created, interpreted and enforced.

Lévy differs fundamentally, however, from CLS in the deterministic nature of his thought. This reflects both its Durkheimian and socialist origins. This determinism is perhaps the clearest marker of the decades that divide his thought from contemporary legal studies. CLS generally rejects any kind of social determination, any idea of history's inevitable movement in certain directions.[21] For Lévy, however, the movement from the traditional social regime of property rights to the modern social regime of credit rights and rights to securities is a structural movement, which he takes for granted as an historical process. Understood and interpreted correctly, this process guarantees, in Lévy's view, that the rights of labour will eventually absorb the rights of capital: the future is preordained.[22] Lévy's optimism about the role of

---

21 See e. g. Mark Tushnet, 'Critical Legal Studies: An Introduction to Its Origins and Underpinnings' (1986) 36 *Journal of Legal Education* 505.
22 Lévy, *Fondements, op. cit.*, pp. 38–42.

law in ensuring the triumph of socialism is founded in his view that a historical transition in forms of wealth is occurring. In his analysis, this will inevitably benefit organised employees at the expense of capitalist employers. Whereas CLS insists that nothing is preordained and no laws of history make the future predictable, Lévy's theory is left in the dilemma that always haunted Marxist theory: how far is social change structurally [139] determined and how far can it be produced by political initiative (for example, through law)?

Lévy's work has disturbing implications for orthodox jurists not only because he turns the practice of law into a radical political practice. Perhaps more fundamentally, his idea that law rests only on subjective belief appears to *remove all objectivity* from juristic analysis. Legal edifices, on this view, are not just built on sand. A better metaphor would be that they float like hot-air balloons – and can collapse quickly if the thin fabric of belief is suddenly punctured. Otherwise, they can sink slowly if the air of conviction supporting them gradually cools. Similarly disturbing ideas about the radical 'ungroundedness' of legal ideas were expounded during Lévy's lifetime (though after his main ideas were formed) by 'legal realists' in the United States and other countries. More recently, in a different way, the idea has been associated with postmodern legal theory.

The American Felix Cohen wrote that any legal concept 'that cannot pay up in the currency of fact, upon demand, is to be declared bankrupt, and we are to have no further dealings with it.'[23] It is nothing more than 'transcendental nonsense'. The response of Cohen (and other legal realists) to the apparently ungrounded character of many legal ideas was, however, different from Lévy's.

For Lévy the convictions that underpin law are not entirely free-floating. In some way, they reflect structural conditions of society. As we have seen, Lévy's view of the nature and determinants of these conditions remains unclear (because of the ambivalence of his appeal to both Durkheimian and socialist traditions). A task of legal practice and legal analysis, however, is to help to bring law and the '*croyances*' it reflects more closely in touch with these structural conditions.

For American legal realists such as Cohen, legal practice and legal analysis must bring law into touch with 'fact', meaning actual social behaviour. On the one hand, this involves discarding broad concepts and categories in favour of narrower ones that reflect distinctions in social practice (such as different kinds

---

23 Felix S. Cohen, 'Transcendental Nonsense and the Functional Approach' [1935] in Lucy Kramer Cohen, ed., *The Legal Conscience: Selected Papers of Felix S. Cohen*, New Haven: Yale University Press, 1960, p. 48.

of contracting).[24] On the other, bringing law into touch with facts involves focusing on judicial behaviour (what judges do, rather than what they say) and analysing distinctions and categories employed by judges in deciding cases, even where these distinctions and categories are not recognised in orthodox legal concepts.[25]

[140] From a certain viewpoint, Lévy's theoretical approach to making law 'realistic' is much more sophisticated than that of some American realism in his era. Instead of requiring that legal ideas 'pay up in the currency of fact', Lévy asks that these ideas be attuned to theoretically explicable tendencies of social change. Though he offers no sociology himself, Lévy's legal theory presupposes a need for sociological interpretation of the environment in which law exists. In general, American legal realism made no such connections to social theory. Instead, its strength lay in its focus on the judicial function understood in behavioural and institutional terms.

III. Faith in Law

Lévy makes the dramatic claim that law is grounded in faith and that it has no substance beyond this. His legal theory, indeed, was sometimes called *fidéisme*.[26] This position may give him a limited affinity with aspects of postmodernist writing on law. Contemporary postmodernist scholars devote much attention to showing law's lack of ultimate foundations, and that its authority resides in myth or circular reasoning.[27] Some scholars are much concerned with the theoretical dependence of law on faith.[28]

Here, Lévy may even offer useful correctives to recent tendencies in postmodernist thought about law. He sees law as grounded in (sometimes irrational) faith but he sees this grounding in the same constructive way that Durkheim does. Faith in law, if it is to be a living faith, must reflect the

---

24 See e. g. the Introduction to Karl N. Llewellyn, *Cases and Materials on the Law of Sales*, Chicago: Callaghan, 1930.

25 See e. g. Karl N. Llewellyn, *The Common Law Tradition: Deciding Appeals*, Boston: Little, Brown, 1960; and Llewellyn, *The Case Law Method in America*, Chicago: University of Chicago Press, 1989.

26 Paul Roubier, 'Emmanuel Lévy (1871–1944)' in *Annales de l'Université de Lyon en 1943-1944. Fascicule Spécial*, Lyon: Imprimerie Bosc, 1945, p. 62.

27 Jacques Derrida, 'Force of Law: The "Mystical Foundation of Authority"' in Drucilla Cornell, Michel Rosenfeld and David G. Carlson, eds., *Deconstruction and the Possibility of Justice*, New York: Routledge, 1992; Peter Fitzpatrick, *Modernism and the Grounds of Law*, Cambridge: Cambridge University Press, 2001.

28 See Peter Oliver, Sionaidh Douglas Scott and Victor Tadros, eds., *Faith in Law: Essays in Legal Theory*, Oxford: Hart, 2000.

requirements of solidarity in society and must demand that these requirements be met through law.

In one sense, as some postmodernists claim, law is empty, supported only by fragile beliefs. Legal statuses may be masks to disguise the lack of more solid or meaningful bases of social relations.[29] It is as though a puff of wind could blow away the whole edifice. On the other hand, postmodernist legal writing often suggests that despite (or even because of) its lack of foundations, law is *strong*. When all social knowledge has been revealed as lacking foundations and the age of 'grand narratives' has passed, law's transience, disposability and infinite adaptability seem congenial. Its moral emptiness makes it a form of knowledge entirely appropriate to a morally empty world.

[141] For Lévy too, law can be morally empty, a mere shell, supported only by a lingering faith in its rationality or its elusive authority. This is how he sees the credit rights (*droits de créance*) of capital, when finally confronted by the credit rights of labour.[30] As law continues to ignore the social conditions of solidarity it must become ever more empty. One might even imagine that Lévy would not have been surprised at postmodernism's picture of the barrenness of contemporary law, a law that so often flies in the face of moral demands for just social relations.

Against the implications of much postmodernist writing, however, Lévy insists that law does not have to be like this. Something has to stand behind the mere faith that supports legal ideas as legitimate. Law need not be morally empty. Indeed, for Lévy, following Durkheim, law's vitality depends on it being morally rich. And this means that law should express the normative requirements of social solidarity, in the various social relations of community that law is called on to regulate. Lévy's tragic failure was that he thought this process was predetermined: that the movement of history would eventually ensure that law would reflect the conditions of solidarity. One can only imagine his anguish as experience (perhaps especially the experience of two world wars) surely eventually made him realise his mistake.

The legacy of Lévy's work for current legal studies is in its fertile suggestiveness more than in its specific positions. He reminds us of law's dependence on faith and belief. He stresses that the conditions of its legitimacy are ultimately moral. He emphasises that law's vitality depends on its contribution to social solidarity, and he insists that legal practice as a form of political practice should promote that contribution. Lévy suggests (through his own theoretical ambivalence, noted above) the problematic relation of law and the state. Very importantly, he stresses that the social forces shaping law now

---

29 See Peter Goodrich, *Languages of Law: From Logics of Memory to Nomadic Masks*, London: Wiedenfeld and Nicolson, 1990, pp. 295–296, 299–301.

30 Lévy, *Fondements, op. cit.*, pp. 29–30, 38–39.

increasingly escape limitation by national boundaries. All these orientations in his work are highly relevant to current legal theory.

As is so often noted by those who read Lévy's writings, they are frustratingly allusive, unclear and ambiguous: full of rich but undeveloped observations. We can regret, as Durkheim did,[31] that Lévy, *'plein de dispositions'*, did not write more and complete his projects more satisfactorily. Yet, given the still profoundly stimulating qualities of many of his ideas, this fascinating French jurist surely deserves to find some of the international recognition that has eluded him for a century.

---

31 Émile Durkheim, *Lettres à Marcel Mauss*, Paris: PUF, 1998, p. 253.

[7]
Durkheim's Loyal Jurist?
The Sociolegal Theory
of Paul Huvelin

I. Introduction

As is well known, law was an important interest for Émile Durkheim in his
project of developing what has come to be recognised as one of the great
classic systems of sociology. But the nature and purposes of his engagement
with law remain somewhat unclear and have often been misunderstood.
Among jurists and legal sociologists, understandings of this engagement
have usually been shaped by almost exclusive attention to the treatment of
law in his first book *The Division of Labour in Society*. Here, Durkheim seems
to approach legal materials mainly for their capacity to provide, in the
documentary form of ancient and modern codes, "visible symbols" of social
solidarity; an "index" or measure of this elusive phenomenon. *The Division
of Labour* contains his most sustained discussion of legal doctrine from many
societies and eras, but the comparative and historical study of law is promi-
nently presented in it as a methodological device for examining something
that is, apparently, of greater sociological significance than law itself. So the
sociological study of law appears as central and peripheral at the same time;
a vital means to an end rather than an end in itself.

Durkheim's later writings (including his many reviews of books on legal
subjects), as well as the approach and contents of the journal, the *Année sociologique*, under his direction, make clear that, from a Durkheimian standpoint, law is far from being a secondary or derivative phenomenon. For
Durkheim himself and several of his co-workers, it was a major topic for
sociological study; an aspect of social life related (but not reducible) to
morality, religion or the changing conditions of social solidarity. Matters are,

however, complicated by the changing position of religion in Durkheim's sociology as it developed. In his early work, law appears sometimes to be "a practical substitute for religion"[1] in modern society, as religion loses its regulatory power. But, in his later work, where the need even in modern society for something like religion is asserted (Durkheim 1915), law's significance again becomes ambiguous or, at least, its function is harder to define. An idea of law as co-ordinating social functions in complex, diverse, modern societies coexists in his work with an idea of law as expressing a value system or set of beliefs to underpin such complexity.[2]

This paper is concerned with law in the Durkheimian tradition: with Durkheim's approach to law and some ambiguities and limitations of this approach. What follows is part of an ongoing consideration of this subject, centred on the way that Durkheim's ideas were adapted to serve the purposes of professional jurists who collaborated with him in producing the *Année sociologique*. Several members of Durkheim's *Année* team had legal qualifications (Vogt 1983, 177–8), but only two, Paul Huvelin and Emmanuel Lévy, were actually professors of law. Colleagues in the law faculty of the University of Lyon for almost the whole of their academic careers, both were active contributors to the journal. Lévy was in contact with Durkheim from 1896 and, as an editor and book reviewer, contributed to all volumes of the *Année*'s first series from its commencement in 1898. Huvelin, whom Lévy first put in touch with the Durkheimians, began his association in 1899 and contributed from the sixth volume, published in 1903, until the end of the first series (1913).

It is clear that Durkheim valued very highly the contribution of the two jurists from Lyon, admitting to his closest collaborator Marcel Mauss that he would not know how to replace Lévy in the *Année* team (Durkheim 1998, 49). Huvelin, however, was a more prolific contributor than Lévy. He wrote a major article (Huvelin 1905–1906) and more than 40 book reviews (Besnard 1983, 32). After Huvelin's premature death in June 1924, Mauss wrote, "the loss of Huvelin is irreparable for us" (Mauss 1969a, 497). Although these jurists have received relatively little discussion in Durkheimian literature, they were clearly much respected members of the team[3] and, recently, they have begun to attract attention among French intellectual historians.[4]

Both Lévy and Huvelin were sympathetic to Durkheim's sociology and saw its powerful relevance for legal studies. Yet both felt a need to depart

---

[1] The phrase is by one of his followers, the jurist Emmanuel Lévy (1933, 14, 35).
[2] For detailed discussion of these and related matters see Cotterrell 1999.
[3] See the effusive praise of Lévy in Mauss 1997. As regards Huvelin, Durkheim thought his ideas made him "very close to us" and lost no time in enlisting his help for the *Année*: See Durkheim 1998, 319. See also Durkheim's letter in support to Huvelin's Paris chair candidature in 1907 (Durkheim 1979).
[4] On Lévy, see the symposium in *Droit et Société* nos 56–57, 2004, the documentation in *Jean Jaurés cahiers trimestriels* no 156, 2000, and Frobert 1997. On Huvelin, see the documentation in *Revue d'histoire des sciences humaines* no 4, 2001, and Audren 2001.

506

from Durkheim in important ways to make their scholarly work realistic and practically useful. I have discussed Lévy's contribution elsewhere (Cotterrell 2004). This present paper therefore concentrates on Huvelin's work as a response to, and adaptation of, Durkheim's sociology. I use a study of Huvelin to illustrate certain problems which Durkheim's ideas posed for sympathetic jurists. The paper considers how one particular legal scholar tried to overcome these, using elements of Durkheim's thinking to develop general sociological insights about law and its history.

II. Durkheim on Law

When he first began to teach sociology, Durkheim made clear his wish to reach out to lawyers and welcomed law students to his lectures (Durkheim 1987a, 108–9). Building bridges was a necessary strategy given the hostility his ideas soon provoked from some law faculties. Many jurists were sceptical of Durkheimian sociology. They often caricatured it as focusing on the social rather than the individual, on social forces rather than individual responsibility, and on an unrelenting questioning of traditions and established institutions (Cotterrell 1999, chap. 3). Durkheim, for his part, advocated the reform of legal education to make law "something other than conceptual games" and to show its cultural roots (Durkheim 1975d, 244). But he also assumed that sociology could learn much from jurists and legal historians. In 1904, reviewing a book by the comparative lawyer Édouard Lambert, Durkheim even equated the study of comparative legal history with sociology of law at least in some of its aspects (Durkheim 1975b, 266). Comparative legal history could thus be a site of intimate cooperation between sociology and legal studies.

Durkheim's own thinking on law has to be understood as undergoing major changes during his career and leaving unresolved problems for those who have at various times attempted to construct a rigorous theory of law from his work. "Moral ideas are the soul (*l'âme*) of law," he writes (1987c, 150), but law is distinguished from morality by a degree of organisation, especially as regards the process of sanctioning breaches of social rules. Legal rules are "instituted by definite organs and under a definite form and [. . .] the whole system which the law uses to realise its precepts is regulated and organised" (Durkheim 1975c, 320–1). But the only organisation always found in relation to law is a court (*un tribunal*), which might be an assembly of the people as a whole, or an elite of judges (Durkheim 1984, 52). So law's essence is adjudication and judgment, not legislation.

Compared with repressive law, restitutive law has much more extensive organisational needs. Modern law, mainly restitutive, is characterised by boards, administrative agencies, specialised officials, enforcement systems and detailed demarcations of jurisdictions. All of which seems to point towards the idea of law as an instrument of government and to a linking of law and politics. Indeed, Durkheim's early thinking in *The Division of Labour* suggests this (Durkheim 1984). Ultimately, law is not just a reflection or index of moral bonds (of solidarity) but helps form them or even create them. The underlying morality of restitutive law might be considered a kind of official "governmental morality," aimed at ensuring a good, integrated functioning of social life, rather than a popular morality or a reflection of a collective consciousness (Cotterrell 1999, 109–12). Law, in this image, is separated more and more from popular moral convictions insofar as these are society-wide. Modern law lives, for the most part, increasingly in regions remote from the heart of the collective consciousness (Durkheim 1984, 69–70).

So it might appear that modern law is to be viewed as an active, powerful agent of governmental steering of society. But this seems not to be Durkheim's view. For him, law as a moral framework is hardly seen politically in any sense. Thus, a sociology of law and morals (these being intimately related) takes the place of a political sociology in the Durkheimian scholarly schema (cf. Favre 1983). Durkheim sees organic solidarity as the normal state of affairs for complex modern societies; anomie and the forced division of labour are abnormal forms. So law's task is not to arbitrate between dominant political interests but to fine-tune society, checking aberrations and freeing normal social processes of development when they become obstructed. Lawmakers, we might say, are like gardeners tending a plant. They do not make it grow and have limited knowledge as to why or how it does. They can only protect and nurture spontaneous processes of development over which they have relatively little control. Sociological laws, not juridical ones, produce solidarity. Social structure and the emergence of appropriate functional relations are the key to this process, not legal intervention as such.

In his work after the publication of *The Division of Labour*, Durkheim pulls back even more from the idea of law as a political force or a directive instrument of government. Two elements in his work, which contrast strongly with the approaches of his earlier writings, are central here. First is his reaffirmation of the value system of individualism as the unifying moral foundation of complex modern societies (Durkheim 1987b). Second is his implicit recognition that all modern law (not just surviving repressive or penal law) is an expression of the specifically modern individualistic content of the collective consciousness (Cotterrell 1999, chap. 7). So law is seen eventually by Durkheim in modern (no less than simple or ancient) societies as deeply rooted in culture, in the sense of general beliefs, values, outlooks, attitudes and traditions of thought. The moral value system of individualism is implicit in modern social interaction and necessary to it as the differentiation of societies proceeds. But it is a contingent product of history in certain societies at certain periods. Law, it seems, has the general function of supporting and elaborating this value system; at least, this much is implicit in

508

Durkheim's writings on contract, property, criminal and inheritance law (Cotterrell 1999, chaps. 5, 8, and 9). Hence law's task is, it seems, primarily an expressive one. Law is to be seen (in modernity as in earlier societies) as a distillation of moral values rather than a political instrument of governmental intervention in social relations. Where the latter use of law is appropriate it is as a derivation from the former.

III. Huvelin and Durkheimian Sociology

For jurists wishing to import Durkheimian ideas into their legal scholarship a main problem has been how to find a significant, well-defined place for law in the general picture of modern society which Durkheim's sociology offered. The modern lawyer is typically concerned with using law to make things happen: to right wrongs, achieve justice, promote interests, or secure rights. Many jurists in Durkheim's time, no less than now, would be dissatisfied with an image of law as a reflection of the established character of moral life or an index of social solidarity, or as explicable in its operations in terms of a long historical development of social structure (the shifting combinations of forms of social solidarity).[5] If they felt the need for a social theory of law at all, it would most likely be for a theory that could recognise an active role of law in shaping society, engaging with power and intervening in or mediating political struggles. Durkheim's view of law might not seem to offer this possibility.

On the other hand, as has been noted, his work emphasises law's rootedness in values, its secure place in culture and its links with deep-rooted beliefs. These ideas, in some respects, elevate law to a place of great moral and cultural significance. Especially if their conservative aspects were stressed, they could be attractive to traditionally-minded lawyers. But since Durkheimian sociology advocated examining the social foundations of values that might be associated with law, it could appear threatening to conservative lawyers. It was to progressive, reformist jurists that it offered more attractions, insofar as it suggested that law, to be strong, must be rooted firmly in popular experience and understandings and could be understood as a social force only through empirical study of social change. The status of (conservative) jurists' doctrines might be usefully challenged by a sociological theory that saw the centre of gravity of law not in juristic disputes but in everyday social conditions and popular belief systems.

Paul Huvelin's contact with, and eventual membership of, the Durkheim School may have been promoted initially as much by his restless intellectual curiosity and desire to challenge traditional ideas in his legal field

[5] It is significant that both Lévy and Huvelin were far more active in practical politics than Durkheim, though in Huvelin's case this activity was a late phase in his life and a brief one because of his early death.

(Appleton 1924, 698), as by any wider sociological ambitions. Having obtained his doctorate in law for a thesis on an aspect of the history of commercial law (the law of markets and fairs), he joined the University of Lyon law faculty in 1899, aged 26, and stayed there for the rest of his career, becoming a full professor (of Roman law) in 1903.

Continental jurists were necessarily interested in Roman law as a primary historical foundation of European legal thought. Legal history, which Huvelin taught, was presented to French students largely as the reception, transmission and adaptation of Roman law into French civil law. But tracing the roots of current legal conceptions or traditions to distant sources such as the Twelve Tables of early Roman law (451–450 BC) could seem arbitrary unless one continued to ask where the concepts of this ancient law had come from. The whole approach of using history to expound legal tradition involved a reading back from the ideas of the present to those of the past. So it could appear as a search for origins that might, for a curious and radical scholar, lie beyond the earliest documentary sources of Roman law themselves. Many Roman law specialists might dismiss such ultimate inquiries as merely speculative. Huvelin, however, pursued them in a scholarly and imaginative way, using not just specifically legal materials but also information gleaned from other ancient literature. His work combined prodigious erudition with "a pronounced taste for researches that give free flight to the imagination, where the ingenuity of conjectures can be given unfettered scope" (Appleton 1924, 701).

Huvelin asks about the sources of Roman law itself in "pre-legal" ideas, focusing on the field then designated as "very ancient Roman law"; that is, the earliest conceptions of Roman law of which any evidence exists. These ancient legal conceptions are intermingled with religion, myth and magic (cf. Faralli 1993). Early Roman legal procedures seemed to invoke magical elements (ritual being considered to produce specific effects on individuals' circumstances). To understand this ancient law required a process of imaginative reconstruction. Sketchy evidence of certain procedures and legal concepts was available, but often knowledge was lacking about the full meaning of the concepts or the significance of the procedures.

Huvelin was much impressed with the essay by Marcel Mauss and Henri Hubert on the nature of sacrifice, published in the *Année sociologique* in 1899. With the encouragement of Lévy, Huvelin wrote to Mauss in June of that year, explaining that he now saw the sociology of religion as a key to pursuing his studies. Sociological explanation of the nature of ritual seemed to him very relevant for an understanding of early legal procedures and he asked Mauss for guidance on relevant literature (Huvelin 2001b). More generally, Huvelin thought that the work of the Durkheimian scholars might help in understanding how private law—especially the law of property, contract and civil wrongs (tort/delict)—emerged from the general religious matrix of early law which Durkheim had explained in *The Division of Labour*.

510

For Huvelin, the interesting question was how, in societal development, private law (essentially the law of individual claims protecting private interests) became distinct from the general regulatory structures of the collective consciousness. What processes in history made this separate legal development possible?

IV. Law and Magic

It was the later essay by Mauss and Hubert "Outline of A General Theory of Magic" that gave Huvelin the clue he thought he needed. Mauss and Hubert saw religion and magic as having common sources in social belief but acting as opposing forces; magic rites do not unite society but are sometimes illicit and often secret, private activities. Magic is close to religion but turns away from the social cohesive function of religion and is a distortion and private appropriation. Magic becomes more individualistic and "tends towards the concrete" and practical, while religion remains abstract and oriented to the collectivity. Magic is "an art of doing things," a childish skill, the forerunner of techniques that would later discard all mystical elements. Belief in it is utilitarian, its value being only in its effects. Its kinship is with religion, on the one hand, and technology, on the other (Mauss and Hubert 1972, 174–5). As a primitive technology, it shows how a collective phenomenon can assume individual forms.

Soon after Mauss' and Hubert's essay was published in 1904, Durkheim invited Huvelin (a contributor to the *Année sociologique* since 1902) to write a full paper for the journal. Huvelin took the opportunity to produce an extremely learned piece on the origins of ideas of individual rights in magic (Huvelin 1905–1906). He did not rely solely on Mauss and Hubert because he had already been exploring the idea that the procedures of early Roman law had magical elements and had published a long paper on the subject some years before (Huvelin 1929). Nevertheless, Mauss' and Hubert's idea of magic's technical power applicable to private ends, but closely related to religion, was of great importance. In "Magie et droit individuel," Huvelin sees magic as distinguishable from religion by its purposes (Huvelin 1905–1906, 3).[6] A social phenomenon becomes potentially illicit if it is turned to anti-social ends. Thus magic may or may not be illicit or anti-social, depending on how it is used. Huvelin's paper aims to show that one of its uses has been to provide technical resources necessary for the earliest development of private law.

First, magic gives individuals access to the power of spiritual forces that can be turned to their chosen private purposes. Second, magic can be a weapon of the wronged against the wrongdoer (for example, where the

---

[6] Cf. Durkheim's essential distinction: religion centres on a church, magic does not (Durkheim 1915, 42–7); cf. Mauss and Hubert 1972, 30.

The Sociolegal Theory of Paul Huvelin   511

wrongdoer cannot be identified, magic rites allow some action to be taken against the unknown person). Third, magic can be harnessed as a guarantee of restitution. With the agreement of both parties to a transaction, a magic incantation or procedure provides for a sanction against one party which is to take effect only if that party defaults on undertakings given. Fourth, contracts can be enforced through the power of magical sanctions; future compliance with promises is guaranteed by the invocation of magical bonds between the parties. Fifth, through magic, writing assumes special importance in solemn procedures, the magical power of writing being well understood in many ancient civilisations. Huvelin's essay illustrates these and related processes, with a wealth of detailed comparative examples from ancient history and the early legal (or law-like) practices of many civilisations.

In this way, "in lending its own force to individual activity, magic prepared the way for legal sanctions" (Huvelin 1905–1906, 42). In early stages of legal development, magic allows individual activity to find a place in the purview of a law otherwise inspired by the collective sense of religion. Thereafter, Huvelin suggests, two possibilities present themselves. Sometimes, eventually, magical practices are prohibited once law becomes strong enough to do this. It becomes able to rely on its own resources of enforcement, which shed spiritual or magical elements. Otherwise, law co-opts magic rites and rituals, as in the use of oaths, ordeals, formalities of writing and seals, and symbolic transfers of property relying on precise rituals.

Huvelin's analysis is speculative, yet thoughtful and carefully documented. But is it Durkheimian? For Durkheim, law is social and moral in nature, not private and utilitarian. Yet these latter seem to be magic's characteristics in Durkheim's understanding (1915, 42, 44–5). So how can society's law be built (in part) on magic? The thesis of "Magie et droit individuel" is, in essence, Huvelin's effort to link restitutive law (indirectly) to religion and the collective consciousness in a way that Durkheim seemed unable to do in The Division of Labour in Society; Huvelin's argument is that the link is historical or developmental. He seeks to overcome what, in The Division of Labour, appears as the mystery of modern law's moral foundations (Cotterrell 1999, chap. 7). For Durkheim (1984, 69–71, 82), restitutive law is not connected to the collective consciousness in any significant way. But Huvelin claims that individual right (the foundation of all restitutive law) derives indirectly from religion or, more broadly, from the matrix of beliefs and understandings that make up the collective consciousness. Over the ages this religious aspect is partly transformed into pure regulatory technique; magic is the medium that enables this to happen. Law distances itself from the religious matrix as technique, but the religious matrix itself makes possible a social evolution that allows this freeing of law in the form of individual rights.

512

Huvelin preserves what lawyers typically want to see in law—its power and freedom as a technique for providing security and facilitating projects, transactions and relationships. At the same time, he affirms Durkheim's view of law's origin in the religious matrix of early society. The approach was no doubt useful to Huvelin to ground his researches on very ancient Roman law, helping to answer the questions: Where did this law come from and how was it shaped? It might also have seemed appropriate for a modern jurist anxious to see law as somehow independent of social structure or social experience so as to be able to act on these.

Nevertheless, Huvelin's thesis is ultimately unstable. Is law a moral phenomenon or not? Durkheim (1975a, 276, 277) is clear that it is: Law is entirely implicated with morality and inseparable from the conditions and needs of social solidarity; law is not a private resource. Huvelin's answer, however, seems to be both yes and no. On the one hand, law's moral nature is explicable ultimately in terms of its links to religion; on the other hand, private law's origins are, it seems, in utilitarian technique. Magic provides the template for private law's mechanisms of control. It provides a model for law as a resource for private ends and as a privately appropriated technique. Law, it seems, takes on something of the utilitarian character of magic. This is surely something that Durkheim could not have accepted. For him, the utilitarian view of (a part of) law, implicit in Huvelin's explanation of its origins, would be incompatible with his essentially non-utilitarian conception of morality and with the assumption that law (inseparable from morality) must share morality's character in this respect.

V. Human Bonds

A decade and a half later, just a few months before he died, Huvelin published his most striking effort to adapt Durkheim's thinking to a juristic outlook. He had planned to write an *Introduction to the Study of Law* drawing on his sociological interests. In April 1923, he gave six lectures at the University of Brussels on "The Spirit of French Law." The sociological introduction to the course would have been incorporated into the planned book but ultimately it was the only part published, under the title "Les cohésions humaines" (Huvelin 2001a).

In this lecture, Huvelin addresses in general sociological terms the question underlying his "Magie et droit individuel" essay. What predates law? What, in sociological terms, provides the conditions for and shapes the social tasks of law? What gives rise to and makes possible human bonds (*cohésions humaines*)? And what is the place of law in securing and supporting these bonds? This is, of course, another way of posing Durkheim's question about the place of law in supporting or expressing social solidarity. But ultimately

Huvelin answers this question in a very different way from Durkheim, whom he calls in the lecture "my teacher." Without Durkheim, declares Huvelin, there would be no sociology of law and, as regards method, "we still rely on him, even when, as in my case, it is necessary to abandon some of his conclusions" (Huvelin 2001a, 137).

Huvelin tries to visualise the beginnings of civilization in his inquiry, just as he had in studying ancient Roman law. Law is not the source of social cohesion; something precedes it. The givens of sociological inquiry are (i) individuals in contact with each other, interacting and belonging to groups of many kinds, and (ii) societies. A society is the totality of individuals in a certain field of interaction, or encompassed by the same network of reciprocal influences (ibid., 134). The basis of all human bonds, Huvelin claims, is sympathy, a resonance that draws individuals together and produces positive feelings for another; not feelings of love (which seeks to possess or conquer the other) but of understanding, concern or liking. Sympathy expresses itself in sensitivity to the other and, to some extent (as a derivative characteristic) in imitation of others' ways or situations. It derives from two conditions, often interrelated: proximity and similarity. Thus, a moral unity often naturally arises among neighbours in frequent contact who become accustomed to each other, or among people who perceive themselves as having similar characteristics.

Solidarity, for Huvelin, is "the totality of conscious and unconscious attractions deriving from sympathy" (ibid., 137). This is the basis of all social groupings in which people voluntarily link their individuality with that of others. Drawing such conclusions, he sees no problems with Durkheim's concept of mechanical solidarity which he associates with the human bonds of attraction he describes. Yet it is clear that he understands the basis of this solidarity somewhat differently from the "teacher," since sympathy provides for him an intermediate psychological element added to Durkheim's own association of similarity and proximity with mechanical solidarity.

As regards organic solidarity, however, Huvelin appears to break dramatically with Durkheim. He simply denies the existence of this kind of solidarity. The progress of the division of labour (differentiation of occupational roles and social functions) gives rise to individuality which, for Huvelin, undermines solidarity based on sympathy. Remoteness and dissimilarity are sources of antipathy, not sympathy. The appearance of originality is frequently seen as a source of trouble or scandal; society acts against the innovator who is often seen as a heretic of some kind. But differentiation cannot be prevented; this tendency is an incontestable fact. Organisation becomes more elaborate with societal development and takes the form of the creation and interrelating of specialised techniques or instruments (*outils*) to secure interdependence. Crucially, Huvelin insists, the division of labour does not

514

produce sympathy and so cannot give rise to solidarity. The exchange of services leads to the effort to exploit others and dominate them.

Here then is the fundamental divergence from Durkheim. Durkheim notes that the division of labour can produce solidarity only if it is not forced (as in a master-slave relationship). But where, asks Huvelin, can we find authentic, voluntary specialisation or fully free vocations? "One sees the birth and growth of originality, heresies, the spirit of invention, sectarianism. Sympathy born of similarity sees its scope curtailed by increasing differentiation. Antagonisms multiply" (ibid., 139). In such conditions, interdependence exists but specialisation creates an unstable environment, where reactions of antipathy may be dangerously unpredictable. So it is appropriate, in the context of a highly developed division of labour, to speak of *organic interdependence* but not organic solidarity.

In these conditions, according to Huvelin, law has precisely the powerful, directive role that Durkheim's sociology seems reluctant to accord it. Order is maintained in conditions of organic interdependence by two essential forces. The first is "organised social constraint" (law), which requires a sovereign power to impose peace by means of a specialised force (ibid., 141). Thus Huvelin denies that contractual relations create or express solidarity between the parties, who are likely to be concerned only with their own individual benefits; it is law that provides enforcement and "a good number" of parties fulfil their contracts not through sympathy but fear (ibid., 142).

The other force maintaining the always precarious order of organic interdependence is that of common sensibilities or outlooks (*des états d'âme communs*) (ibid., 142). Interdependence can produce feelings of sympathy among individuals who exchange services in similar conditions. Similarity of situation and proximity can create spontaneous solidarity (perhaps Huvelin is thinking particularly of solidarity of classes, occupations or professions). In particular, common ideas and convictions can develop, even in conditions of elaborate division of labour. Some of these take on a "religious veneer" as notions of justice, probity and honour (ibid., 142) and enter into law in various ways.

Indeed, law alone is not powerful enough to control the potential anarchy of the increasing division of labour. The "religious imperatives" of justice, probity and honour, produced and strengthened in the enclaves of spontaneous solidarity in modern life, are necessary to support legal imperatives. Without them law would fail. It is vital to understand that law without moral support is "almost nothing" (ibid., 143). Both moral and legal elements of order in modern society are indispensable. But the balance of attraction and constraint varies with the nature, history and conditions of social groups, and the direct roles of law and morals are inversely proportional: One compensates for the lack of the other. Huvelin calls this the rule of legal-moral compensations (*loi des compensations juridico-morales*) (ibid., 143).

The Sociolegal Theory of Paul Huvelin   515

VI. Conclusion: Durkheim and Huvelin

Finally, therefore, Huvelin strongly affirms what is perhaps the central point of Durkheim's legal theory as a whole: that law is inseparable from morality and that its function is to express and support this morality, which is the normative framework of solidarity (in modern societies no less than earlier or simpler ones). But he departs from Durkheim in interesting ways. He wants to use a Durkheimian framework but (i) to avoid what he plainly sees as Durkheim's complacency about the nature and possibility of social solidarity in complex societies and (ii) to portray law as having a much more active role in fostering social cohesion than Durkheim explicitly recognises.

Mauss (1969c, 27), reviewing "Les cohésions humaines" in the *Année sociologique*, noted clear differences from Durkheim's positions but was sure that Huvelin's text would have interested Durkheim. Praising it warmly, he saw its framework as allowing interesting comparisons of societies in terms of their aptitude for organisation and spontaneous sociability. Mauss (1969b, 12) thought that, had it been completed, Huvelin's book would have been an important discussion of the question of the state.

Yet a comparison with Durkheim's positions shows the problems of Huvelin's ideas. In *The Division of Labour*, Durkheim treats the content and authority of law as given by society's structural development. Law is tied to morality and expresses the conditions of solidarity. Thus, law is the moral structure of society expressed in particular organisational forms. In Durkheim's later work law is no longer discussed in terms of direct links between types of law and types of solidarity. Instead, the content of law (in modern and pre-modern societies alike) is considered in terms of the value system of the collective consciousness. In modern complex societies this value system is that of moral individualism. Law is thus a public expression of society's basic values and its central (officially promulgated) belief system.

By contrast, for Huvelin, law is influenced by morals but not derived from either the logic of the division of labour (creating the structural conditions of organic solidarity) or from popular morality. Law's function is not expressive but *corrective* of the sociologically "normal" social order (which in complex modern societies is potentially one of chaos and disorder). Huvelin thus portrays law as a political force, somehow external to social life. Law is available to control the natural tendencies of societal development, which are *away* from solidarity.

Huvelin, therefore, needs an "independent" explanation—that is, an explanation outside the terms of the logic of Durkheim's sociology—of where law originates and gains its directive, controlling character. In "Les cohésions humaines" he offers no such explanation. The earlier essay on magic and individual rights suggests, consistently with Durkheimian sociology, that law's origins are in the collective consciousness of early societal

516

development, dominated by religion. Magic is the social phenomenon that eventually "frees" law for future pragmatic development as a regulatory technique. Religion and magic thus provide the resources to support the development of legal ideas and institutions. Yet Huvelin's thesis does not actually explain the sociological origins of law, but only the social phenomena that created conditions conducive to its emergence and development. Again, "Les cohésions humaines" only suggests sociological reasons that make law necessary and give it its tasks. A sociological explanation of how law arises and develops is still missing.

Huvelin's effort to explain law's independent effectiveness and power is therefore unconvincing. Within the framework of Durkheimian explanation, law remains a cultural reflection and expression, rather than a sociologically intelligible instrument of societal guidance or control. This is not, however, to suggest that a Durkheimian view of law is unfruitful. Far from it, because Durkheim's emphasis may be very important in highlighting law's interrelation with culture in many forms. It also properly insists on the significance of moral components in legal thought, practices and institutions, and in guaranteeing law's ultimate authority and defining its social functions.

But it is precisely what Paul Huvelin found missing in Durkheim's legal theory—an explanation of law's connections to power and politics in their historical settings—that later critics have almost always seen as its central problem. Mauss (1969a, 497) admired Huvelin's "taste for the practical and for ideas while being a master of legal dialectics" and he always saw the jurist as fully part of the Durkheim group. But the main interest of Huvelin's work today lies in the fact that he tried, sympathetically and thoughtfully, to solve the fundamental problem of the place of power and politics in Durkheim's legal thinking and so to save the "teacher" from himself.

Department of Law
Queen Mary and Westfield College
University of London
Mile End Road
London E1 4NS, UK
E-mail: R.B.M.Cotterrell@qmul.ac.uk

References

Appleton, C. 1924. Huvelin romaniste. *Revue historique de droit français et étranger* 3: 696–704.
Audren, F. 2001. Paul Huvelin (1873–1924): juriste et durkheimien. *Revue d'histoire des sciences humaines* 4: 117–24.
Besnard, P. 1983. The "Année sociologique" Team. In *The Sociological Domain: The Durkheimians and the Founding of French Sociology*. Ed. P. Besnard, 11–39. Cambridge: Cambridge University Press.

Cotterrell, R. 1999. *Émile Durkheim: Law in a Moral Domain*. Stanford, CA: Stanford University Press.

Cotterrell, R. 2004. Emmanuel Lévy and Legal Studies: A View from Abroad. *Droit et Société* 56/57: 131–41.

Durkheim, É. 1915. *The Elementary Forms of the Religious Life*. Trans. J. W. Swain. London: Allen & Unwin.

Durkheim, É. 1975a. Définition du fait moral. In É. Durkheim, *Textes*, vol. 2: 257–88. Paris: Minuit. (1st ed. 1893.)

Durkheim, É. 1975b. Review of Lambert, "La Fonction du droit civil comparé." In É. Durkheim, *Textes*, vol. 3: 266–71. Paris: Minuit. (1st ed. 1904.)

Durkheim, É. 1975c. Review of Neukamp "Das Zwangsmoment im Recht . . ." In É. Durkheim, *Textes*, vol. 3: 319–21. Paris: Minuit. (1st ed. 1900.)

Durkheim, É. 1975d. Sur la réforme des institutions judiciaires: l'enseignement du droit. In É. Durkheim, *Textes*, vol. 1: 243–5. Paris: Minuit. (1st ed. 1907.)

Durkheim, É. 1979. Letter. *Revue française de sociologie* 20: 115.

Durkheim, É. 1984. *The Division of Labour in Society*. Trans. W. D. Halls. London: Macmillan.

Durkheim, É. 1987a. Cours de science sociale: leçon d'ouverture. In É. Durkheim, *La science sociale et l'action*, 77–110. 2nd ed. Paris: Presses Universitaires de France. (1st ed. 1888.)

Durkheim, É. 1987b. L'individualisme et les intellectuels. In É. Durkheim, *La science sociale et l'action*, 261–78. 2nd ed. Paris: Presses Universitaires de France. (1st ed. 1898.)

Durkheim, É. 1987c. Sociologie et sciences sociales. In É. Durkheim, *La science sociale et l'action*, 137–59. 2nd ed. Paris: Presses Universitaires de France. (1st ed. 1909.)

Durkheim, É. 1998. *Lettres à Marcel Mauss*. Paris: Presses Universitaires de France.

Faralli, C. 1993. Magie. In *Dictionnaire encyclopédique de théorie et de sociologie du droit*. Ed. A.-J. Arnaud et al., 355–7. Paris: Librairie Générale de Droit et de Jurisprudence.

Favre, P. 1983. The Absence of Political Sociology in the Durkheimian Classification of the Social Sciences. In *The Sociological Domain: The Durkheimians and the Founding of French Sociology*. Ed. P. Besnard, 199–216. Cambridge: Cambridge University Press.

Frobert, L. 1997. Sociologie juridique et socialisme réformiste: note sur le projet d'Emmanuel Lévy. *Durkheimian Studies* (n.s.) 3: 27–41.

Huvelin, P. 1905–1906. Magie et droit individuel. *Année sociologique* 10: 1–47. (Published in 1907.)

Huvelin, P. 1929. Les tablettes magiques et le droit romain. In P. Huvelin, *Études d'histoire du droit commercial romain*, 219–71. Paris: Sirey. (1st ed. 1901.)

Huvelin, P. 2001a. Les cohésions humaines: La place qu'y tiennent la contrainte juridique et l'attraction morale. *Revue d'histoire des sciences humaines* 4: 131–44. (1st ed. 1923.)

Huvelin, P. 2001b. Letter to Marcel Mauss. *Revue d'histoire des sciences humaines* 4: 125–6.

Lévy. E. 1933. *Les fondements du droit*. Paris: Alcan.

Mauss, M. 1969a. In memoriam: l'oeuvre inédite de Durkheim et ses collaborateurs. In M. Mauss, *Œuvres*, vol. 3: 473–99. Paris: Minuit. (1st ed. 1925.)

Mauss, M. 1969b. La cohésion sociale dans les sociétés polysegmentaires. In M. Mauss, *Œuvres*, vol. 3: 11–25. Paris: Minuit. (1st ed. 1931.)

Mauss, M. 1969c. Review of Huvelin's "Les cohésions humaines." In M. Mauss, *Œuvres*, vol. 3: 26–7. Paris: Minuit. (1st ed. 1925.)

Mauss, M. 1997. Emmanuel Lévy, juriste, socialiste et sociologue. In M. Mauss, *Écrits politiques*, 729–32. Paris: Fayard. (1st ed. 1926.)

518

Mauss, M. and Hubert, H. 1968. Essai sur la nature et la fonction du sacrifice. In M. Mauss, *Œuvres*, vol. 1: 193–307. Paris: Minuit. (1st ed. 1899.)

Mauss, M. and Hubert, H. 1972. *A General Theory of Magic*. Transl. R. Brain. London: Routledge. (Reprint 2001.)

Vogt, W. P. 1983. Obligation and Right: The Durkheimians and the Sociology of Law. In *The Sociological Domain: The Durkheimians and the Founding of French Sociology*. Ed. P. Besnard, 177–98. Cambridge: Cambridge University Press.

[8]
The Rule of Law in Transition: Revisiting Franz Neumann's Sociology of Legality

THE RULE OF LAW is a concept with which so many writers have wrestled that it might be thought that little remains to be said. This article adopts a special focus to try to develop some manageable and relatively neglected themes in a vast, much discussed subject. It takes, as a basis, central ideas from the German jurist Franz Neumann's important but still insufficiently discussed work[1] on the Rule of Law and tries to pursue a tentative but specific inquiry in the spirit of Neumann.[2]

Neumann's historical study of the Rule of Law (1986; and see 1957), written in the 1930s, was strongly coloured by the experience of the constitutional turmoil of the Weimar Republic through which he had lived and worked as a practising lawyer and law teacher (see also Kirchheimer and Neumann, 1987). His work was concerned, in part, with exploring the changing social and political contexts in which the Rule of Law ideal, variously interpreted in different nations but with a certain common core of meaning, was invoked. For Neumann, it was important to emphasize in legal theory the emergence of a distinctively modern form of society – such as that of Germany of the 1920s but exemplified in important aspects by advanced western industrial nations in general – in which corporate organization of life had acquired important new forms. In this kind of society, which we might

452

call 'corporate society', social and economic change, and especially the
growth of monopolistic corporate economic power, had, in Neumann's view,
undermined radically some of the most crucial social assumptions on which
the ideal of the Rule of Law had been founded.

This article attempts three things: first, it tries to suggest in the idea of the
Rule of Law a core of meaning reflecting the universal social as well as legal
importance attached to this idea – whatever name is given to it in the various
languages of western Europe. Second, it speculates as to how Neumann's
thesis about the changing social conditions of existence of the Rule of Law
in the modern (corporate) society of his time might be assessed and reinterpreted in the light of recent characterizations of contemporary (or, according
to familiar current terminology, postmodern) western societies. Finally, it
suggests how traditional thinking about the Rule of Law might be modified
to take account of certain changed social and economic conditions of legal
regulation in contemporary advanced western societies; conditions which can
be directly related to those Neumann analysed. What follows is admittedly
tentative: limited by space and time and the fact that any theoretical discussion, however confined, of the Rule of Law must cover much ground and
refer to a very wide range of legal and social experience.

DIMENSIONS OF THE RULE OF LAW

The English idea of the Rule of Law seems to combine central elements of
the German *Rechtssicherheit* (legal certainty or security) and *Rechtsstaat*[3]
(legally regulated state) and related concepts in other legal systems (see
Aubert, 1989: 66ff). For Neumann, the essence of the Rule of Law was the
fusion or reconciliation of two vital elements of law which he termed *voluntas* and *ratio* (Neumann, 1986: 45–6; 1944: 440ff, 451–2; 1957: 26ff). *Voluntas*
refers to the political authority which gives law its power of command, its
non-optional, politically enforceable status. *Ratio* refers to the broad rationality of legal doctrine, the quality that makes it possible to reason with and
analyse legal ideas in a principled and general way. Thus, the Rule of Law
refers, for Neumann, to law that is not only reliably enforced but also general
in application, applied uniformly to all cases within its terms. It is, therefore,
predictable and calculable in its general consequences, permitting a sphere of
freedom to the citizen. The Rule of Law is thus the enemy of particularistic
regulation and administrative discretion.

Dicey's much earlier English statement of the Rule of Law (Dicey, 1959)
has been strikingly called an 'unfortunate outburst of Anglo-Saxon
parochialism' (Shklar, 1987: 5). Rather than prefiguring Neumann's abstract
formulation of elements of a Rule of Law that might unite various meanings
of the term in different western legal systems, Dicey had focused on specific
features of the English common law as the essence of the Rule of Law. He
gives the idea of generality of law a particular twist. Not only must law apply
generally to citizens but they must be able to enforce all of their legal rights

through a uniform system of ordinary common law courts (Dicey, 1959: 193–5). The stress on generality here becomes a prohibition on specialized expertise, for in Dicey's view continental administrative courts, with their special jurisdictions, are the enemy of the Rule of Law. General courts of common law can deal with the threat to liberties posed by administration.

In Dicey's vision, judges and the general common law principles they serve are ranged against executive discretion (see 1959: 188). Common-law judges as 'experts in non-expertise' (Kirchheimer, 1967: 435) are qualified as protectors of civil society – the common law community – from state infringement of the negative liberties of citizens. Courts express, as a by-product of their decisions on individual rights, the fundamental principles of the constitution. Common-law thought, developed in everyday judicial practice, sustains an environment of legal culture in which the problem of executive lawlessness has been largely dispelled. The 'rule, predominance, or supremacy of law' is 'the distinguishing characteristic of English institutions' (Dicey, 1959: 187). The implication seems to be that somehow *only* common-law courts can achieve such a happy state. And behind this implication seems to lie the familiar common-law mythology that puts the judge (merely by virtue of *being* a judge) in the centre of a notional moral and national community, as both its protector and spokesperson (see Postema, 1986: 32; Cotterrell, 1989: 33–5).

One great value of Franz Neumann's work for a British lawyer ought to lie in making it possible to hold Dicey at a distance and think of the Rule of Law in broader, less parochial terms. Neumann's writing portrays the long historical evolution of the *Rechtsstaat* and of the idea of government subject to law. In a similar context Judith Shklar (1987) has emphasized two contrasting themes running through the history of Rule of Law ideas.[4] One of these themes, which she traces to Montesquieu, is that of institutional restraints on government. The other, associated with Aristotle, is that of the Rule of Law as the 'rule of reason'.

The Aristotelian Rule of Law has vast ethical and intellectual scope ('an entire way of life') (Shklar, 1987: 1), but applies only to a limited range of persons who are (as office-holding citizens) full participants in the collective organization of the polity (see Barker, 1946: 93–5). It is concerned with the need to organize life collectively in a principled manner and seems indirectly reflected, for example, in Ronald Dworkin's contemporary conception of the Rule of Law as primarily embodied in the principled decision-making of courts (1978; 1986: 93–4). By contrast, Montesquieu's Rule of Law refers to 'a limited number of protective arrangements which are, however, meant to benefit every member of the society, though only in a few of their mutual relations' (Shklar, 1987: 2). These protective arrangements provide security against arbitrary exercises of discretionary power by government. But they are intended to protect also, indirectly, against other citizens and collectivities, insofar as the law that defines individual rights and duties is made secure from invasion by arbitrary discretions.

Montesquieu's version tends to dominate in lawyers' thought about the Rule of Law, since it emphasizes controlling rules and regulated institutions

454

– the kind of matters of planned social arrangements with which lawyers are typically most comfortable. But I argue that part of the problem of adjusting expectations of the Rule of Law to contemporary conditions lies in the need to recover the interrelation between the two directions of Rule of Law thought that Shklar usefully distinguishes.

The Rule of Law is the 'will-o'-the-wisp of political history' (Hutchinson and Monahan, 1987: ix). It is claimed as an 'unqualified human good' (Thompson, 1975: 266), yet is said to be almost impossible to explain without raising a doubt that it still exists as a practical virtue (Nonet, 1987: 127). No interest group is organized specifically to support it (Lowi, 1987: 56). If this is its situation, the reason may be that the Aristotelian version of the Rule of Law seems to entail such difficult challenges to deliver principle in an unprincipled world that only a few of the most ambitious philosophers now accept these challenges, and never with uncontroversial results. At the same time, Montesquieu's version of the Rule of Law demands protective arrangements that seem inadequate on at least two fronts.

On the one hand, they seem inadequate because their failure to safeguard citizens generally against arbitrary power appears increasingly transparent. The Rule of Law does not provide, at least for substantial sections of the population and in significant circumstances, the protection against governmental discretion, in the broadest sense, that is its apparent *raison d'être*. On the other hand, the emphasis on protection from public power through checks and balances in government and the limitation of governmental regulatory authority seems to ignore – or at least fail to address directly – problems of *private* power which are of no less significance for individual security, in particular the power of corporate capital to shape the lives of individuals, as consumers and employees as well as citizens.

In such circumstances a sense of insecurity may arise not from any disregard of the virtues of protective arrangements such as those associated with Montesquieu's version of the Rule of Law. It arises more typically from the apparent impossibility of applying the idea of the Rule of Law to important contexts in which relations of power require stabilization through regulation.

In contexts of social life where traditional regulation in the form of stable, relatively general rules operates, the Rule of Law often seems to represent an experienced reality. This will often be the case in the protection of traditional property entitlements and private transactions in a stable civil society not subject to restructuring on the basis of radical redistributive policies. So too, the reality of the Rule of Law is recognizable in the sense of general security felt at least in neighbourhoods where policing is considered to be 'by consent' and police discretions are exercised in 'reasonable' ways in the spirit of legal rules seen as maintaining a consensually supported status quo. The Rule of Law as limited but universal protective arrangements seems in general to remain a meaningful idea at least where the pace of regulatory change is slow, where populations are homogeneous and cases of conflict or dispute and claims of entitlement are relatively standardized, and where the values underlying regulation are generally understood and approved by the regulated population as a whole.

Over time, however, the images of law and society which could sustain a faith in the Rule of Law have been changing. Regulation now takes a wide variety of forms and is expected to do so. At one extreme it tends towards detailed technical prescriptions applicable to very specific cases; at the other it embraces the broadest, most open discretions. The lines between law and administration, and between legal and technical standards, seem to become increasingly hazy, and this development is no longer seen as a matter of aberrations which lawyers have long criticized but as a defining component of a changed general perception of legality (Cotterrell, 1995: ch. 13). Thus, in many fields of welfare or public-order regulation, it is assumed that governmental strategy can be expressed in almost any regulatory form, however technical and narrowly focused or however open and permissory it may be in controlling official actions. The Rule of Law remains theoretically intact as the presence of legal controls, 'protective arrangements' against unlawful applications of power. Yet much regulation slips through the guarantees of the Rule of Law, like sand through the fingers, because it seems impossible to say conclusively how general or how specific a lawfully established legal precept must be to be consistent with the Rule of Law's protective arrangements. The diversity and flexibility of contemporary regulatory forms make the practical meaning of the Rule of Law increasingly indeterminate.

Accompanying this general perception of change in the character of regulation is the sense of a significant pattern in the social contexts in which different kinds of regulation are used – a sense that the kinds of setting in which particular forms of regulation are often applied are not random but betray a sociological consistency. Typically, the more particularistic and discretionary forms of regulation are applied extensively, though certainly not exclusively, to areas beyond the assumed stable core of civil society. They are applied to what may be seen by government and lawmakers as 'problem populations', defined as appropriate objects of regulation. These regulatory forms tend to operate especially in areas where implementation of policy seems too urgent a matter to be trammelled routinely by clear rules, general in application; where direct and precise control of action may be more important than guiding citizens' autonomous decision-making; and where traditional ideas of legal protection may even seem a hindrance to effective resolution of pressing governmental tasks.

REINTERPRETING CORPORATE SOCIETY

One way to approach these issues is through Neumann's thesis on the Rule of Law. Neumann tried to relate the legal ideal of the Rule of Law to a specific historical context. Influenced by Max Weber, he linked the rise of the legal rational state, the *Rechtsstaat*, with the development of entrepreneurial capitalism. The competitive society of commodity traders and freely

456

interacting property owners was favoured by the Rule of Law, which provided security of property holding and calculability and predictability in the
legal consequences of transactions.[5] Neumann saw, controversially, the doctrine of precedent in the common law as providing the kind of legal security
established in continental Europe by rational legal codes (1986: 241ff). It may
be doubted whether he was any more successful than Weber in identifying a
consistent link between the development of capitalistic economic activity and
the establishment of a particular form of law. His interest, however, was not
so much with the character of legal doctrine as with the more general values
associated with it, which emphasized legal security and predictability, and
non-intervention in private activity except insofar as necessary to secure a
framework of known rules.

Accordingly, the Rule of Law supported the extension of markets, free
access to them by entrepreneurs, the guarantee of general peace and security
in which to trade and accumulate capital, and the security of capital acquisi-
tions. Alongside its economic significance, the Rule of Law, in Neumann's
view, enshrined virtues transcending the needs of the competitive society of
entrepreneurial capitalism. It embodied an ideal of liberty that is of enduring
value. Cherishing the legal conditions of individual freedom, the Rule of Law
became, in the words of later writers, 'the central jewel in liberalism's crown'
(Hutchinson and Monahan, 1987: ix).

The transition from the competitive society of entrepreneurial capitalism
to a corporate society[6] of monopoly capitalism, dominated by cartels, giant
business enterprises and other mass organizations, marked, in Neumann's
analysis, conditions of crisis for the liberty-creating role of the Rule of Law.
In a society no longer to be thought of as composed mainly of freely interrelating individuals, but rather as increasingly shaped by corporate interests
and commitments powerfully influencing the conditions of life of citizens,
the ideal of the generality of law favoured the corporate interest at the
expense of the individual.

The Rule of Law emphasizes formal, not substantive, equality. Thus, in
Neumann's view, it served the ends of equal liberty where the economic and
social power of legal actors was not so unbalanced that formal legal equality
and reliance on equal rights would merely entrench substantive inequality. In
entrepreneurial capitalism the Rule of Law embraced the entire bourgeois
class even if it failed to reach subordinate classes. But in modern society, the
enfranchisement as citizens of those who had earlier been excluded from legal
protection within the polity brought their demands for legal security and
liberty into the political arena. At the same time, the concentration of capital
in corporate structures removed the social conditions that had enabled the
formal legal equality enshrined in the Rule of Law to parallel and promote a
reasonable substantive equality in the life chances of citizens.

Corporations and cartels could benefit from the Rule of Law to protect
their property and hence their economic power. They could use this power
freely in bargaining and contracting with citizens and could counter government efforts to control it through special regulation, insofar as this regulation

would fall foul of the corporation's right, as a legal person, to be treated legally in the same way as individual citizens. Thus, corporations could resist expropriation or other interference with their property using the same arguments that individual citizens might use – arguments grounded in the sanctity of individual liberty protected by the Rule of Law (see Kirchheimer, 1983).

The term *corporate society*, while useful to encompass what Neumann saw as defining conditions of modern society, seems inadequate today. 'Corporate' implies only certain aspects of the complexity of contemporary life and not necessarily the most significant. Indeed, the tendency today is to view corporate power more neutrally, not condemning or praising but treating it as socially inevitable. Power in general tends to be thought of in more positive terms than it was by Neumann during and immediately after the Weimar years. Again, aspects of corporate organization that were familiar to Neumann have become less so today. Trade unions, for example, play a less prominent role in social life in many contemporary western societies. And we tend to think in terms of disorganized capitalism (see Offe, 1985), recognizing a much less homogeneous economic organization than seemed apparent to radical social critics of Neumann's time. We speak less of corporate society than of consumer society, with its implications of individuals united only in their purchasing situation (Baumann, 1992: 49–53) and having a realm of individual choice that invalidates the idea of homogeneity produced by corporate constraints.

Nevertheless, the idea of corporate society remains important if supplemented appropriately. The consumer society is, after all, a society where what is chosen for consumption is, to a considerable extent, what is offered and promoted by corporate interests. Kinds of corporate economic structures that were familiar in Weimar times still exist, although their forms may have changed. But they must now be reconsidered in a much more international perspective. Their power is no longer shielded so much by Rule of Law principles of the nation state as by transnational economic imperatives that constrain state lawmakers.[7] Powerful nation states themselves can be regarded as pursuing their own corporate interests as political societies, sometimes through extraterritorial law enforcement, for example, in the imposition of terms in contracts of supply to contractors in other countries, whose freedom to resell products is thereby restricted as a condition of contracting. Again the political, and even military, power of nations is sometimes used to protect the nation's economic interests abroad, for example, as represented through multinational corporations, and to restrict the ability of less powerful states to control these corporations. In such ways the dominance of individual life by corporate interests may be made even harder to counter than the Rule of Law ideology seemed to Neumann to make it in Weimar times.

Correspondingly, however, corporate characteristics of other aspects of social organization have lost prominence since Neumann wrote. The privatization of life is reflected in the reduced influence of organized mutual welfare associations as foci of collective action. Postmodern society is held to

458

be characterized in part by the decline of stable collective loyalties and the fragmentation of moral and political organization into loose, continually shifting interest group activity (Baumann, 1992: 181–3). The ideology of individual choice is seen to replace that of moral allegiance. The political party composed of committed activists dissolves into a myriad of single issue groups; national involvement transmutes into more local (or even merely individual) concern. The individual life is portrayed as increasingly atomistic. More may be known about the intimate personal circumstances of media stars and politicians (and, in Britain, at least, royalty) than about the lives of immediate neighbours. The moral bonds linking individuals into collectivities seem to weaken in the most rapidly developing patterns of contemporary social life, as sociological research has shown (Baumgartner, 1988).

Yet most of these developments can be seen as an extension rather than a reversal of the tendencies which Neumann and others associated with modern society. The political ideology of consumer choice offers a strictly limited perspective on social relations in a society dominated by corporate interests, which can express themselves far more effectively today than in Neumann's era. Corporate interests that dominate a market often seek to narrow the range of choice available to the consumer and standardize consumer demand so as to minimize corporate risk. The alliance between the public corporate interests of the state and the private corporate interests of capital, which Neumann emphasizes, is no less relevant than in his time. It is now cemented through the promotion of the ideology of the free market as both a political project (symbolizing political freedom) and an economic one (symbolizing future wealth). Half a century ago, Theodor Adorno and Max Horkheimer wrote of the 'world of the administered life' – a society structured by an alliance of bureaucracy and technology extending its normalizing controls into all aspects of social and cultural life (Adorno and Horkheimer, 1986). Today the notion of the administered life seems largely fused with a more general idea of 'mass society' – a society of homogeneous tastes and shared outlooks, promoted by global mass media controlled by a limited number of corporate organizations. The seemingly atomistic society of individual consumers thus exists alongside – indeed, as the other side of the coin from – the vast extension of Neumann's society of corporate interests.

LEGALITY IN CONTEMPORARY SOCIETY

Writers on postmodernity frequently portray contemporary western societies as marked by a profound loss of faith in the underpinnings of modernity. Five such underpinnings, in particular, might be identified: first, science as the intellectual basis of modernity; second, economic expansion as its material basis; third, the nation state as its affective, cultural basis; fourth, historical progress as its inspirational basis; and fifth, humanist and individualist morality as its moral basis. Modern law could be seen to a large extent as the instrument of all of these aspects of modernity; the expression, in part, of all of these foundations of modern life. In the perspective of *post*modernity, however, law tends to be seen as set free from the projects of modernity, which no longer appear as convincing underpinnings or justifications of legal regulation.

In this perspective, the situation of law seems profoundly ambiguous. Legal regulation is ubiquitous yet morally and culturally empty. For example, Jack Balkin, writing about United States constitutional law, remarks on the almost total divorce between, on the one hand, the prosaic, pragmatic practices of constitutional adjudication in the current United States Supreme Court and, on the other, the attempts of academic constitutional commentators to elaborate profound cultural meanings of the American constitution (Balkin, 1992: 1985–6). While philosophical efforts are made to infuse law with moral meaning, the reality of law as practised, produced and elaborated in the business of contemporary government is extremely mundane. In the most pessimistic postmodern views, law may be all there is to believe in. But that is not much, if something of greater cultural significance is sought than the endlessly pragmatic adjustment of regulation to increasing social complexity.

In particular, law is not much to believe in if what is held out as the object of belief is Montesquieu's version of the Rule of Law, as characterized by Shklar. We noted, earlier, the apparent inadequacy of this idea both in the light of perceived changes in the character of regulation – in the very image of legality that prevails (see Cotterrell, 1995: ch. 13) – and in the light of perceived social discrimination; that is, in the seemingly patterned application of different kinds of regulation to different kinds of social population.

If, however, we build on some of Neumann's themes, the vistas of so-called postmodern law and society can be approached with less hopelessness than many postmodernist analyses convey. The first matter of importance is to notice, as Neumann did, the Rule of Law's 'decisive ethical function' (1986: 256–7; 1957: 42). The Rule of Law implies not just specific political contexts or institutional structures but an appeal to transcendent *ideals*, which do not derive their validity from specific social conditions but are worth pursuing whatever the social context.

The moral essence of the Rule of Law in this sense lies in three values: equality, individual autonomy and security (Bobbio, 1987: 143–4). Equality refers mainly to procedural equality, or fair and equal governmental treatment of citizens; not to equal treatment of citizens in terms of substantive benefits. Individual autonomy refers to the treatment of the citizen as an independent, freely reasoning being, responsible personally for, but only for, his or her own rationally chosen actions and inactions. This value is typically expressed through the insistence that ignorance of the law is no excuse, through the requirement of intention (*mens rea*) generally in criminal law, and through the assumption that the discretion in action denied to government by the Rule of Law is available to citizens as the range of free decision left to them by clear general rules. Security, the third transcendent value of

460

the Rule of Law, may be expressed in many other terms: as certainty, predictability, order or safety (see Aubert, 1989: 76). The guarantee to citizens
of security, for example, of transactions, of property or of liberty, is one to
which the state commits itself[8] by limiting its regulation to general, abstract
rules.

The enduring project of the Rule of Law should be to promote these values
even in the changed conditions of contemporary social life. Each of them,
however, is challenged by contemporary conditions in a way that goes significantly beyond the challenges Neumann identified in corporate society.

Take first the value of *equality*. Formal equality before the law as an ideal
has developed through several broad phases historically. Premodern notions
of legal rights as dependent on personal status – itself determined by, for
example, class, caste, religion, gender or age – were replaced by the modern
idea of formal legal equality of all citizens. But lack of access to courts for
subordinate sections of the population meant that the promise of the Rule of
Law was mainly realizable only by the middle and upper classes. The class
differentials in law application and enforcement in English history described
by Weber (1968: 814) illustrate what can be termed the phenomenon of the
'dual state'. This involves the practical restriction of Rule of Law safeguards
to certain population categories, and the regulation of other categories by
means that do not incorporate such safeguards. But this familiar phenomenon
has remained largely underemphasized in most celebrations of the Rule of
Law, except when the duality has been instituted formally, even *de jure*, as in
apartheid or other politically segregated societies (Shklar, 1987: 2).[9]

In contemporary western societies, particularly those where the institutions of the welfare state are weak or seriously challenged, the establishment of a *de facto* dual state is an ever-present threat. Judith Shklar (1987: 14)
sees the reappearance of the dual state in the conditions of formal representative democracy as 'a constant possibility in our century'. It may exist
insofar as sections of the population, often identified as a permanent 'underclass', become almost wholly separated, in terms of life-chances, economic
resources, practical access to the legal system and political allegiances, from
other citizens in civil society.[10] In such conditions their opportunities to
benefit from the protections offered by the Rule of Law may be significantly
less than those of other population groups.

Lack of resources (not merely economic but also resources of knowledge
and of networks of support and aid) may make it very difficult to invoke the
protections that the Rule of Law offers. Indeed, the Rule of Law is sometimes
seen, from a governmental perspective, as threatened by the very existence of
such an 'underclass'.[11] In fact, the term *underclass* seems to define a collective object of regulation rather than individual citizens as autonomous subjects of regulation. Control of the 'underclass' is often thought of from this
perspective as an administrative matter no less than one of balancing rights
and duties in terms of general legal rules. Consequently, control is achieved,
to a significant extent, through a mixture of police and welfare discretions
and highly particularized regulation. As noted earlier, these regulatory

phenomena are not easily brought within the focus of Rule of Law protections.

Typically lacking any philosophy of action, any real possibility of engaging with the power and resources of law and the state except through isolated confrontations, many of those categorized as the 'underclass' may consider that they have little choice but to make a life substantially outside the scope of legal protections; a life either largely indifferent to the demands of law (living anarchistically) or sometimes calculatedly flouting those demands for purposes of survival (living through crime). What seems relatively new in this state of affairs in advanced western societies in recent times is that the underclass is both defined explicitly out of civil society in a host of ways and includes a great diversity of people who, deliberately, define themselves out. Hence, for this part of the population, the special characteristics of corporate society as well as its postmodern accretions may be largely irrelevant. The contemporary dual state adds to the inequalities of power existing in corporate society the inequalities that arise from the substantial exclusion of whole sections of the population from corporate society itself.

Consider next the Rule of Law's value of *individual autonomy*. The great achievement of liberal thought in what Neumann termed the competitive society of entrepreneurial capitalism was to remove special group statuses and elevate the individual human being as the explicit focus of almost all legal concern. But a recognition of the business corporation as a legal person, whose legal status was to be assimilated to the universal legal status of the individual citizen, made possible legally the inequalities of contractual and property-owning power that Neumann associates with modern (corporate) society (see Cotterrell, 1992: 123–30). Thus, the extension of legal individualism to accommodate the economic importance of the business corporation set in train a legal development, under the cloak of the Rule of Law, that has gradually undermined the legal significance of the autonomy of the individual citizen.[12] The internationalization of corporate power, previously noted, has subsequently further increased this power in ways that mainly escape Neumann's perspective, which is largely restricted to the context of the nation state.

At the same time, the idea that the individual person (whether citizen or business corporation) remains the necessary locus of rights and duties prevents constructive thought along lines that might strengthen the situation of citizens collectively, faced with overbearing concentrations of corporate power and the reinforcement through this power of the homogenizing features of 'mass society'. The value of individuality, as it has typically been interpreted in law, distracts attention from a full recognition of the importance of communities, however defined; groupings that might provide legally sanctioned forms of mutual support and collective action to protect and enhance the conditions of life of their individual members.

The development of corporate society has, as noted earlier, seen the individual's status enhanced as a consumer. But the value of individual autonomy has somehow been turned against itself, in the mass society of consumers,

462

towards a celebration of privatized lifestyles. In contemporary society, economic developments have merely highlighted in new ways the elusiveness of individual autonomy as a legally promoted value.

Finally, consider the value of *security*. Security is provided legally through the consistent use of known rules, procedures and formalities.[13] In the competitive society of small entrepreneurs, legal security, according to Neumann, arises from the maintenance of a stable framework of general rules through which individuals can pursue their own lawful projects. With the emergence of large corporate economic interests, Neumann saw the need for government to act to control and organize these interests, not merely holding the ring but intervening with particularistic regulation to control specific concentrations of corporate power in the general interest of maintaining the security of the individual citizen. Indeed, government *has* increasingly intervened in economic planning and regulation, not necessarily to promote the security of the individual but to stabilize and control national economies, employment patterns, trade and commerce and industry in conditions determined increasingly by the internationalization of the corporate organization of economic life.[14]

This is merely a recent phase in the development of governmental management of society: 'the right disposition of things, arranged so as to lead to a convenient end'.[15] Michel Foucault (1991: 95) suggests that for such management purposes 'the instruments of government, instead of being laws, now come to be a range of multiform tactics'. Whether we call these instruments law or not, they are certainly in no way restricted to general legal rules. A traditional 'core' legal structure of civil society is provided by relatively general rules – clustered in fields of legal doctrine that often continue to be seen as the heart of law for the purposes of the academic education of lawyers. But around this traditional core – the heartland of the Rule of Law – a periphery of different forms of regulation extends. And the periphery seems in practice, if not in academic legal consciousness, to be turning into the core of regulation, while the traditional legal core is displaced to the periphery of regulatory experience for many citizens.

A general threat to the value of security in this state of affairs is the entrenchment of a wholly instrumental view of law and regulation (see Weinrib, 1987: 61). In such a view security is guaranteed not so much by maintenance of a stable framework of general rules as by appropriate ad-hoc regulatory responses to problems. When legality is viewed as an instrumental matter, there is a risk that the values of the Rule of Law themselves will be seen in purely instrumental terms. For example, court decisions identifying illegal acts of government officials and agencies may be treated as creating merely technical problems for government, rather than issues of principle.[16]

What has been previously stated is coloured by a certain interpretation of British experience, but the range of circumstances discussed can be put together to suggest an emerging general contemporary context of the Rule of Law which is not Neumann's corporate society, but recognizably derived from it. This context might be sketched, in necessarily highly schematic terms, as a kind of sociolegal hierarchy, to suggest how it provokes important further questions about the Rule of Law.

At the level of *the state*, contemporary conditions seem to encourage an instrumental view of legal regulation in general so that lines between law and policy, and between legal forms of regulation and other forms, are not only blurred but even increasingly regarded as unimportant. The consequence, when viewed in terms of the requirements of the Rule of Law, is that legality means something very different from what it meant to Neumann or, for that matter, Dicey. Legality as a virtue tends to lose its connection with moral demands rooted in cultural conditions. It becomes almost solely a matter of efficient government regulatory action.

At the level of *civil society*, dominated, on the one hand, by corporate entities and interests and, on the other, by a substantially privatized and atomistic life of individual citizens, law tends to be experienced increasingly as complex technicality. As such, it may be resented when it appears as the instrument of state agencies pursuing government policies that appear transient, remote from the moral conditions of everyday life, and at times ignorant, irrelevant or oppressive. The ordering in civil society is provided partly through instrumental lawmaking to ensure coordination and planning of complex social and economic conditions. However, insofar as government recognizes the limits of policy-driven law but appears largely unable to envisage any other form of legal innovation, it tends to rely also on promoting self-regulation, especially among the corporate entities that are seen as holding the keys to economic well-being in contemporary society.

Hence the Rule of Law is typically promoted as the rule of *minimum* law among those key sections of society that are considered able and motivated to regulate themselves largely without the state's intervention. But the combination of deregulation and the moral privatization of social life creates the possibility that individuals will be both morally isolated and legally unprotected; unable and unwilling to call either on legal agencies of the state or their fellow citizens for aid. Furthermore, while discriminatory law enforcement as between different sections of the populations participating in civil society is not a new phenomenon, the privatized character of social life may reduce sources of communal support and solidarity that otherwise provide some protection against or a means of compensating for the consequences of discriminatory legal ordering.

Finally, 'below' and outside civil society stand the various population sectors viewed from a certain governmental or law enforcement perspective as the *underclass*. As applied to this part of the population the Rule of Law may be taken to mean primarily the rule of strong discretionary controls or intricate particularized regulation. In contrast to the self-regulating subjects of civil society, the members of the 'underclass' are widely seen as appropriate *objects* of regulation. The Rule of Law appears in one aspect as a weapon to ensure adequate control of them. While in theory in contemporary democracies they can appeal to its protection no less than can other citizens, in practice their appeal will often be weakened not only by the inadequacy of Rule of Law protections in relation to the particular kinds of regulation often used against them but by the assumption that these populations threaten the conditions of general security, one of the central values associated with the Rule of Law.

THE RULE OF LAW AS A CONTEMPORARY PROJECT

The preceding discussion may seem wholly negative, since it sketches in general and schematic terms some largely unfavourable conditions in which the idea of the Rule of Law seems to exist today. Nevertheless, if emphasis is put on some long-standing traditions of Rule of Law thought and an effort made to relate them specifically to the kinds of social conditions that have been discussed a more productive view of possibilities is indicated.

Earlier a contrast was noted between traditions of Rule of Law thought linked, in Shklar's discussion, respectively with Aristotle and Montesquieu. The Aristotelian rule of reason indicates principled, fair and just government, though its benefits might not be extended to all within the regulated territory. The conception associated with Montesquieu emphasizes limited institutional protections for all citizens. What may need to be recaptured is the explicit combination of the universality of protection of the latter conception and the broad moral principle of the former. The jurist Lon Fuller, attempting to infuse a discussion of legality with explicit reference to moral principle, suggested that the lawmaker who governs through principles of the Rule of Law, as Fuller elaborated them (1969: ch. 2), thereby adheres to a relationship of reciprocity between rulers and ruled. The relationship is one of mutual trust, in which the authority of the lawmaker is founded on, or underpinned by, the confidence of citizens in the legislator's good faith. The idea that those who make law are no less subject to the laws, as made, than are other citizens is a powerful component of this confidence and trust.

The equal protection of the laws should not, therefore, be considered only as an affair of procedural technicalities but is, indeed, a matter of moral principle influencing not only the design of institutions to secure checks and balances but also the kinds of legal regulation created, the purposes for which it is created, and the manner in which its content is determined. The Montesquieu-derived conception of the Rule of Law properly insists on the protection of *all* by law, a situation rendered impossible by the existence of a formal or informal 'dual state' and of a population labelled as 'underclass' and substantially excluded from participation and protection as citizens.[17] At the same time, the value of individual autonomy as an object of the Rule of Law can, in contemporary conditions, be effectively promoted only by using law to aid citizens in confronting the corporate and bureaucratic power that shapes their lives by building *collective* strength through mutual support.

Hence the fulfilment of the promise of the Rule of Law requires not only the *universal* protection of the rights of all citizens to participate as members of the polity as a whole but also the *specific* protection of degrees of autonomy of groupings of citizens in partially self-regulating *communities* of many different kinds. The possibility for citizens to take more control of their lives can be enhanced through conditions of self-regulation, but only insofar as law ensures possibilities for all members to participate as full members of the communities to which they belong. Equally, government and law need to guarantee the minimum conditions of material life for individuals that make this participation worthwhile and that give them a serious stake in the various communities with which they may associate.

What of the problems for the Rule of Law posed by particularized and discretionary regulation? It might be suggested that a general problem here (leaving aside many specific justifications of these regulatory forms) is the frequent overextension of regulatory jurisdiction. Regulation by centralized government of frequently changing 'local' (for example, functionally or geographically specific) conditions may be possible only by creating extensive local official discretions. Conversely, attempts to legislate centrally to control 'local' complexity may sometimes lead to the temptation to cover every case or variation by a mass of particularistic regulation. The *general* issue in seeking to limit discretionary and particularistic regulation may be that of ensuring that the creation of regulation takes place in *reasonable proximity to the contexts to be regulated*. What is required is more extensive devolution of the creation of regulation from seemingly remote agencies of the centralized state to more local agencies representative of functional or geographical communities. Created, within certain limits of general principle, in these more localized settings, regulation might 'naturally' be particularized to local conditions. At the same time, necessary regulatory discretion might be better monitored democratically through greater proximity between regulator and regulated.

It seems ironic that ultimately the pursuit of these conditions requires, in pursuance of the Rule of Law, a further step that appears directly contrary to its doctrine. It has been argued earlier that the Rule of Law requires the equal treatment of individuals before the law of the state, but also the greater possibility of self-regulation within communities. In addition, however, and as a condition necessary to make these other requirements feasible and significant, the Rule of Law requires specific regulatory controls on corporate economic power. In recognizing the diversity of corporate structures and their effects, this regulation may need to dispense with the generality of legal rules addressed to individual citizens.[18] The equality, security and individual autonomy that exist as values served by the Rule of Law, may sometimes be promoted by the *unequal* or at least relatively particularistic treatment of large corporate entities. This is so where they dominate substantial sectors of economic life and their control in the general public interest needs to be specifically adapted to the perhaps unique patterns of their activities and social or economic effects.[19] Such an approach may undermine to some extent the security and autonomy of these entities. It does so, however, in the interests of the equality, autonomy and security of individual citizens at large, and of promoting the vitality of numerous forms of collective organization and

466

cooperation not characterized by extensive capital accumulation and economic power. It recognizes, indeed, that large concentrations of capital and powerful corporate business enterprises should be treated – because of their special economic power – merely as instruments to serve the welfare of individual citizens generally.[20]

Thus, the Rule of Law is not only something to be preserved by negative controls imposed by legal doctrine on governmental processes. These aspects remain of great importance. Beyond them, however, are other matters that in contemporary conditions are even more fundamental. The Rule of Law needs to be *created* and *shaped* by positive acts of government and lawmaking. To speak of a society governed by the Rule of Law is hollow talk unless law's protection in practice reaches all sections of a population, giving enforceable rights and powers as well as imposing duties and constraints. The Rule of Law as a moral principle of government necessarily rejects any 'dual state'. At the same time, the Rule of Law as an embodiment of mutual trust between those who make laws and regulations and those who are subject to them requires for its fulfilment positive action to create and extend the conditions of this mutual trust – to enhance the conditions of reciprocity between rulers and ruled. The effort to promote democratic participation within communities that are able, as far as possible, to shape their own regulation and, thus, to take moral responsibility for it seems important here.

The Rule of Law is not an idea too vacuous to be taken seriously. Its seemingly unsatisfactory character derives partly from being considered merely as a set of institutional or procedural requirements divorced from a broader moral context. When the values of equality, individual autonomy and security implicit in it are given appropriate prominence, it ceases to appear as a limited requirement of procedural propriety and appears instead as an ambitious programme for responsible and responsive government.

Dissatisfaction with traditional modes of thought is deepened by attempts to work with familiar ideas of the Rule of Law in radically changed social and political circumstances. The society of freely interacting individuals, presupposed in much traditional thinking about the Rule of Law, has been replaced by the complex fusion of large-scale corporate organization and moral privatization that characterizes contemporary advanced western societies. Given these conditions, the Rule of Law should be seen as a dynamic project and not a static doctrine. Treated in this way much of its promise remains to be fulfilled. The corporate society of Neumann's time did not herald the end of the Rule of Law. It marked an historical moment in a process of sociolegal change which has made the reconstruction of the Rule of Law a contemporary necessity.

NOTES

This article is an adapted and extended version of the text of a lecture delivered at the Netherlands Instituut voor Sociaal en Economisch Recht (NISER), University of

THE RULE OF LAW IN TRANSITION 467

Utrecht, on 27 October 1994. I am grateful to Roel de Lange, Anne-Marie Bos, Brian Tamanaha, Linda Cotterrell and Alan Norrie, in particular, for helpful comments and criticisms.

1. On Neumann's life and career see Jay, 1986; Wiggershaus, 1994: 223–9; Neumann, 1953a.
2. The following discussion builds on ideas in Cotterrell, 1995: ch. 8.
3. In the sense of the liberal (formal), rather than social, *Rechtsstaat*. See Böckenförde, 1991: ch. 3.
4. It is not necessary here to assess whether Shklar correctly identifies the sources of these contrasting themes in the history of ideas. The claim being made is only that the enduring tension between them is fundamentally important.
5. Neumann, 1986: 255–6; 1957: 40. See also Aubert, 1989: 81–3.
6. Neumann usually wrote in terms of 'monopoly capitalism' or, simply, 'modern society'; see 1986: ch. 15; 1957.
7. For a classic case study, see Carson, 1981.
8. 'Every legal rule also constitutes a guarantee to the legal subjects that the state is itself under an obligation for as long as the rule remains in force. . . . Before its subjects the state commits itself through the creative legal act – irrespective of how the law originates – to apply and enforce the law' (G. Jellinek, quoted in Aubert, 1989: 66).
9. Fraenkel, 1941, analysing the nature of the Nazi state, uses the term 'dual state' in a different sense to indicate parallel regimes of legality and political or administrative expediency, the last being cloaked by the former.
10. Among the now substantial literature focused – from a variety of political perspectives – on the concept of an 'underclass' in relation to US and UK society, see e.g. Auletta, 1982; Dahrendorf, 1985: ch. 3; MacNicol, 1987; Field, 1989; Mann, 1992; Morris, 1994, especially ch. 4.
11. In the remainder of this article, I use this controversial term (*underclass*) to indicate not a sociologically distinct group or social class but diverse categories of people often treated by governments and agencies of social control and public order as constituting a 'problem population' because of their perceived lack of a significant stake in the dominant economic order of society.
12. For important discussions of the empirical conditions in which corporate power may significantly limit the practical possibilities for individuals to enforce rights, secure redress or assert demands effectively through legal processes, see e.g. Galanter, 1974; Wanner, 1975; Hagan, 1982; Atkins, 1987; Wheeler et al., 1987.
13. On the contribution of legal formality to security see Fuller, 1941.
14. See e.g. Thompson, 1984a; 1984b; and, for a longer comparative perspective, Hall, 1986.
15. Guillaume de la Perriere, *Miroir Politique*, quoted in Foucault, 1991: 93.
16. See Zellick, 1985: 288–93, discussing examples of governmental practices in dealing with 'technical' illegalities.
17. At its broadest this problem is central to debates about the extension of social rights and benefits that have long surrounded the concept of the social *Rechtsstaat*. At its narrowest it refers to specific issues of access to justice, i.e. access to the machinery of justice through courts and other tribunals and to reliable legal advice and assistance.
18. For a discussion of related themes, see Lustgarten, 1988.
19. See Neumann, 1957: 52: 'The postulate that the state should rule only by general laws becomes absurd in the economic sphere if the legislator is dealing not with equally strong competitors but with monopolies which reverse the principle of

468

the free market.'
20. See Neumann, 1953b: 183, discussing limits on the 'civil right' of 'corporate property'.

REFERENCES

Adorno, T. and M. Horkheimer (1986) *Dialectic of Enlightenment*, 2nd edition. (tr. J. Cumming). London: Verso.
Atkins, B. (1987) 'A Cross-National Perspective on the Structuring of Trial Court Outputs: The Case of the English High Court', pp. 143–61 in J. R. Schmidhauser (ed.), *Comparative Judicial Systems: Challenging Frontiers in Conceptual and Empirical Analysis*. London: Butterworths.
Aubert, V. (1989) *Continuity and Development in Law and Society*. Oslo: Norwegian University Press.
Auletta, K. (1982) *The Underclass*. New York: Random House.
Balkin, J. M. (1992) 'What Is a Postmodern Constitutionalism?', *Michigan Law Review* 90: 1966–90.
Barker, E. (ed.) (1946) *The Politics of Aristotle*. Oxford: Clarendon.
Baumann, Z. (1992) *Intimations of Postmodernity*. London: Routledge.
Baumgartner, M. P. (1988) *The Moral Order of a Suburb*. New York: Oxford University Press.
Bobbio, N. (1987) *The Future of Democracy: A Defence of the Rules of the Game* (tr. R. Griffin). Cambridge: Polity.
Böckenförde, E.-W. (1991) *State, Society and Liberty: Studies in Political Theory and Constitutional Law* (tr. J. A. Underwood). Oxford: Berg.
Carson, W. G. (1981) *The Other Price of Britain's Oil: Safety and Control in the North Sea*. Oxford: Martin Robertson.
Cotterrell, R. B. M. (1989) *The Politics of Jurisprudence: A Critical Introduction to Legal Philosophy*. London: Butterworths.
Cotterrell, R. B. M. (1992) *The Sociology of Law: An Introduction*, 2nd edition. London: Butterworths.
Cotterrell, R. B. M. (1995) *Law's Community: Legal Theory in Sociological Perspective*. Oxford: Clarendon.
Dahrendorf, R. (1985) *Law and Order*. London: Sweet & Maxwell.
Dicey, A. V. (1959) *An Introduction to the Study of the Law of the Constitution*, 10th edition, by E. C. S. Wade. London: Macmillan.
Dworkin, R. (1978) 'Political Judges and the Rule of Law', pp. 9–32 reprinted in R. Dworkin (1985) *A Matter of Principle*. Cambridge, MA: Harvard University Press.
Dworkin, R. (1986) *Law's Empire*. London: Fontana.
Field, F. (1989) *Losing Out: The Emergence of Britain's Underclass*. Oxford: Blackwell.
Foucault, M. (1991) 'Governmentality' (tr. R. Braidotti), pp. 87–104 in G. Burchell, C. Gordon and P. Miller (eds), *The Foucault Effect: Studies in Governmentality*. London: Harvester Wheatsheaf.
Fraenkel, E. (1941) *The Dual State: A Contribution to the Theory of Dictatorship* (tr. E. A. Shils, E. Lowenstein and K. Knorr). New York: Oxford University Press.
Fuller, L. L. (1941) 'Consideration and Form', *Columbia Law Review*, 41: 799–824.
Fuller, L. L. (1969) *The Morality of Law*, revised edition. New Haven, CT: Yale University Press.

Galanter, M. (1974) 'Why the "Haves" Come Out Ahead: Speculations on the Limits of Legal Change', *Law and Society Review* 9: 95–160.

Hagan, J. (1982) 'The Corporate Advantage: A Study of the Involvement of Corporate and Individual Victims in a Criminal Justice System', *Social Forces* 60: 993–1022.

Hall, J. A. (1986) 'States and Economic Development: Reflections on Adam Smith', pp. 154–76 in J. A. Hall (ed.), *States in History*. Oxford: Blackwell.

Hutchinson, A. C. and P. Monahan (eds) (1987) *The Rule of Law: Ideal or Ideology.* Toronto: Carswell.

Jay, M. (1986) 'Foreword: Neumann and the Frankfurt School', pp. ix–xiv in F. L. Neumann, *The Rule of Law.* Leamington Spa: Berg.

Kirchheimer, O. (1967) 'The *Rechtsstaat* as Magic Wall', pp. 428–52 reprinted in F. S. Burin and K. L. Shell (eds) (1969) *Politics, Law and Social Change: Selected Essays of Otto Kirchheimer.* New York: Columbia University Press.

Kirchheimer, O. (1983) 'The Limits of Expropriation', pp. 85–129 reprinted in O. Kirchheimer and F. L. Neumann (1987), *Social Democracy and the Rule of Law* (tr. L. Tanner and K. Tribe). London: Allen & Unwin.

Kirchheimer, O. and Neumann, F. L. (1987) *Social Democracy and the Rule of Law* (tr. L. Tanner and K. Tribe). London: Allen & Unwin.

Lowi, T. J. (1987) 'The Welfare State, the New Regulation, and the Rule of Law', pp. 17–58 in A. C. Hutchinson and P. Monahan (eds), *The Rule of Law.* Toronto: Carswell.

Lustgarten, L. (1988) 'Socialism and the Rule of Law', *Journal of Law and Society* 15: 25–41.

McLennan, G., D. Held and S. Hall (eds) (1984) *State and Society in Contemporary Britain: A Critical Introduction.* Cambridge: Polity.

MacNicol, J. (1987) 'In Pursuit of the Underclass', *Journal of Social Policy* 16: 293–318.

Mann, K. (1992) *The Making of an English 'Underclass'?: The Social Divisions of Welfare and Labour.* Milton Keynes: Open University Press.

Marcuse, H. (ed.) (1957) *The Democratic and the Authoritarian State: Essays in Political and Legal Theory by Franz L. Neumann.* Glencoe, IL: Free Press.

Morris, L. (1994) *Dangerous Classes: The Underclass and Social Citizenship.* London: Routledge.

Neumann, F. L. (1944) *Behemoth: The Structure and Practice of National Socialism 1933–1944.* New York: Octagon reprint, 1983.

Neumann, F. L. (1953a) 'The Social Sciences', pp. 4–26 in F. L. Neumann et al., *The Cultural Migration: The European Scholar in America.* Philadelphia: University of Pennsylvania Press.

Neumann, F. L. (1953b) 'The Concept of Political Freedom', pp. 160–200 reprinted in H. Marcuse (ed.) (1957), *The Democratic and the Authoritarian State.* Glencoe, IL: Free Press.

Neumann, F. L. (1957) 'The Change in the Function of Law in Modern Society', pp. 22–68 in H. Marcuse (ed.), *The Democratic and the Authoritarian State.* Glencoe, IL: Free Press.

Neumann, F. L. (1986) *The Rule of Law: Political Theory and the Legal System in Modern Society.* Leamington Spa: Berg.

Nonet, P. (1987) 'The Rule of Law: Is That the Rule That Was?' pp. 125–40 in A. C. Hutchinson and P. Monahan (eds), *The Rule of Law.* Toronto: Carswell.

Offe, C. (1985) *Disorganised Capitalism: Contemporary Transformations of Work and Politics.* Cambridge: Polity.

Postema, G. J. (1986) *Bentham and the Common Law Tradition.* Oxford: Clarendon.

470

Shklar, J. N. (1987) 'Political Theory and the Rule of Law', pp. 1–16 in A. C. Hutchinson and P. Monahan (eds), *The Rule of Law*. Toronto: Carswell.
Thompson, E. P. (1975) *Whigs and Hunters: The Origin of the Black Act*. London: Allen Lane.
Thompson, G. (1984a) 'Economic Intervention in the Post-War Economy', pp. 77–118 in G. McLennan, D. Held and S. Hall (eds), *State and Society in Contemporary Britain*. Cambridge: Polity.
Thompson, G. (1984b) ' "Rolling Back" The State?: Economic Intervention 1975–82', pp. 274–98 in G. McLennan, D. Held and S. Hall (eds), *State and Society in Contemporary Britain*. Cambridge: Polity.
Wanner, C. (1975) 'The Public Ordering of Private Relations: Part 2 – Winning Civil Court Cases', *Law and Society Review* 9: 293–306.
Weber, M. (1968) *Economy and Society: An Outline of Interpretive Sociology* (tr. E. Fischoff et al.) Berkeley: University of California Press edn, 1978.
Weinrib, E. J. (1987) 'The Intelligibility of the Rule of Law', pp. 59–85 in A. C. Hutchinson and P. Monahan (eds), *The Rule of Law*. Toronto: Carswell.
Wheeler, S., B. Cartwright, R. A. Kagan and L. M. Friedman (1987) 'Do the "Haves" Come Out Ahead? Winning and Losing in State Supreme Courts, 1870–1970', *Law and Society Review* 21: 403–45.
Wiggershaus, R. (1994) *The Frankfurt School: Its History, Theories and Political Significance* (tr. M. Robertson). Cambridge: Polity.
Zellick, G. (1985) 'Government beyond Law', *Public Law*?: 283–308.

[9]
The Representation of Law's Autonomy in Autopoiesis Theory

What is at stake in current debates in socio-legal literature about the nature of law's 'autonomy'? The first part of this paper tries to sketch an answer to this question. Then the remainder of the paper will, as its main focus, suggest some strengths and weaknesses of autopoiesis theory's particular effort to portray the autonomy of law as discourse. This theory has stimulated attention to a very important matter - the nature of the discursive structuring of legal doctrine - which modern legal sociology has neglected for too long. Nevertheless, autopoiesis theory has been much criticised. This paper restates some criticisms and tries to extend them. The argument to be developed is that, despite the ambition and power of autopoiesis theory, some of its most important claims about the nature of law as discourse or communicative practice are misleading and even harmful as guides for the progress of socio-legal studies unless qualified to such an extent as to remove much of the theory's distinctiveness.

Debating legal autonomy

The question of how far and in what way law might be 'autonomous' as a normative or discursive field was neglected for a long time in sociology of law. Indeed, legal sociology found space for its own academic existence mainly by denying any interest in identifying this autonomy, implying the insignificance of the matter and leaving it to jurists. Even when Marxist legal theory, imported into social studies of law, postulated law's 'relative autonomy' (Jessop, 1992), the key word was probably 'relative', rather than 'autonomy'. The object was to preserve an idea of law's ultimate explicability in social analysis in terms of something (for example, class or productive relations) other than the distinctive practice lawyers typically understand it to be, and to do this in the face of doubts as to whether such a strategy was really possible in explaining specific legal decisions, doctrines, procedures or institutions.

At the other end of the theoretical spectrum, Durkheimian views treated as self-evident the postulate that law - though having certain (contingent) organisational characteristics - is a branch of morality as social regulation (Cotterrell, 1999), and impossible to consider in isolation from more general and fundamental social phenomena of which it forms part. On this view, characteristics that make law 'autonomous' are merely provisional identifiers of a sociological field. Even Max Weber - focusing strongly on modern law's formal rationality as doctrine - closely linked this, for purposes of sociological analysis, with the broader empirical phenomena of bureaucratic organisation (Gerth and Mills, 1948: 216; Weber, 1978: 975). Certainly, when law was treated in functional terms its functional distinctiveness might be strongly emphasised (Bredemeier, 1962; Parsons, 1977; 174-6). But functional distinctiveness seems a different matter from the normative or discursive autonomy that lawyers often attribute to law.

Thus, despite a focus of classic literature on legal doctrine and lawyers' practices, most legal sociology treated as self-evident that law was to be analysed in terms of something (politics, morality, economics, administrative structure, professionalisation, disputing behaviour, etc.) other than the distinctive discursive features lawyers typically attribute to it. Modern empirical sociology of law, from the mid-twentieth century, established its claim to offer useful knowledge largely by ignoring lawyers' professional learning. It set in place a sharp division of labour to legitimise a field of research entirely its own. Largely avoiding doctrinal concerns, legal sociology mainly focused on law as behaviour. At the extreme, sociology has sometimes been considered as merely seeing its own established disciplinary concerns reflected in law (Ewald, 1995; Cotterrell, 2001).

In fact, the refusal to address most questions about law's discursive autonomy allowed socio-legal studies to achieve much. It enabled socio-legal scholars temporarily to avoid the thickets of jurisprudence, and to use research methods that allowed fresh understandings of legal practices and institutions, radically different from those typical of lawyers. Legal doctrinal debates might collapse in casuistry, circularity or deadlocked rhetoric, or be terminated only by the fiat of judicial or legislative authority. Behavioural researches gave (and continue to give) insights into law, as a mechanism of government and social control, that may be more important, practically and theoretically, than decades of lawyers' doctrinal interpretation.

Yet the very success (and, therefore, increasing ambition) of socio-legal research has now made the old, convenient division of labour between jurists and legal sociologists impossible to sustain. That division depended ultimately on acceptance of some kind of 'internal/external' distinction in legal studies. Typically, the jurist would be the unchallenged 'insider' in the interpretive community of law; the social scientist's role would be as 'outside' observer of behaviour and institutional structures. But as socio-legal research has extended its scope it has begun to insist on the inadequacy of lawyers' typical general understandings of law. The so-called external perspective has refused to stay external; the barbarians have entered the citadel! Social inquiries about law have shown the inadequacy of legal philosophy's perspectives in interpreting contemporary changes in the conditions and character of legal practices and regulation; they have begun to challenge juristic perceptions of law's bases of authority and jurisdiction and of the nature and conditions of its interpretive practices.

To take only a few themes: studies of transnational legal developments raise issues about the location of law's interpretive communities, and of the centres of gravity of legal authority (Dezalay and Garth, 1996; Petersen and Zahle, 1995; La Torre, 1999; Teubner 1997). They portray legal authority, in certain increasingly important contexts, as permanently contested, no longer to be analysed adequately in the terms of traditional jurisprudence. Again, serious questions arise as to what (if anything) legal autonomy should be taken to mean in a world in which state sovereignty is an increasingly problematic concept (MacCormick, 1993; Jackson, 1999) and regulation takes many forms, many of them barely supervised by the state. Regionalism, multiculturalism, separatist movements, devolution, international human rights regimes, proliferating cross-border regulation and transnational financial and economic systems all provoke queries as to how the social context of law is now best to be understood, what law's typical jurisdictional scope is coming to be, and what are the ultimate bases of its authority in the contemporary world (Santos, 1995; Cotterrell, 1998). As will appear, this links with broader issues about the nature of participation and interpretation in law.

Ideas of legal autonomy are closely related to the concept of an internal/external dichotomy. Indeed, insistence on law's autonomy (whatever this might mean), always implies the acceptance of some version of this dichotomy. Legal sociologists content to see themselves as 'outside' observers of law, accepted, at least implicitly, that there was an 'inside' beyond their reach, even if it might be regarded as (relatively or absolutely) insignificant sociologically (Black, 1989).

Many legal philosophers also accept the importance of an internal/external dichotomy. But their use of the dichotomy is usually diametrically opposed to that of the legal sociologist. For legal philosophy, in general, an 'internal' view of law, however that view is defined, is far from insignificant. Indeed, it is often seen as giving access to the centre of legal reality, that which makes law meaningful as a normative or interpretive realm. Thus, an 'external' description cannot capture the reality of law as a social phenomenon unless it somehow incorporates - or combines with - the 'internal' understanding typical of participants in legal reasoning. Some legal philosophers go further: this insiders' world is the entirety of law; law cannot be grasped at all except in terms of its protocols (Dworkin, 1986). Law is thus the possession of a community of interpreters. One must be a part of this world of interpretation, a participant in it, to have any understanding of law's reality. One need not be emotionally or morally committed as an insider, although one might be.

For much contemporary legal philosophy, an internal perspective of some kind is the marker of law's autonomy. It indicates the gateway that must be passed through in order to enter the world of law in some real or full sense. Thus, the Dworkinian interpretive community of law is the community of insiders (judges, legal philosophers, lawyers and - to a somewhat indeterminate extent (Dworkin, 1978: ch. 8; Dworkin, 1985: ch. 4) - ordinary lay citizens) who reason with law and subscribe to the legal system as their universe of practical reason and social evaluation in matters of shared public concerns. For Hartian positivism, the internal view of rules is the view of someone who understands the rules with a critical reflective attitude as guides to conduct. It is the view of players of a game, of people committed to playing by the rules or who, at least, can think about rules as if they have such a commitment to them (Hart, 1994).

The distinction between Hart's and Dworkin's very different views of what it means to be 'inside' law is very significant in considering different ways in which an internal/external dichotomy might be used. Hart's legal theory, concerned with understanding law as a social phenomenon of rules, treats external as well as internal views as necessary to this understanding. The 'external' sociological observer gains and uses important knowledge of law from a behavioural perspective. No doubt this can be combined in complex, variable ways with 'internal' insight into rule-governed practices. For Dworkin, by contrast, understanding law can only be understanding within legal discourse. One must join the discourse in order to comprehend law. For Hart, internal and external perspectives complement each other to constitute complete legal understanding; for Dworkin they are separate, different understandings, hence not necessary to each other. The sociologists (behavioural observers of law) 'have so far been barred from competing' (cf. Honoré, 1987: 32) in the game of legal interpretation (as though they need some permission to do so). On this view, insiders and outsiders simply cannot engage in communication about law. Law's autonomy has become a postulated autonomy of discourse. If law is a closed discourse of some kind, it follows that the internal/external divide is absolute. Either one communicates within this discourse, or not.

Questionable and very important assumptions are, however, being made here. To accept legal autonomy and the related internal/external dichotomy in these terms one must first accept the idea that law is or can be a distinctive discourse. To make this idea rigorous one must specify what is meant by a discourse, what the characteristics of a discourse are, what would define its distinctiveness. One must ask in what sense and under what conditions law is identifiable as a discourse, what must be taken to follow from this and why. One must ask what requires us to accept that it is a single discourse, or that all who participate in law do, indeed, participate in it as a single discourse. Many other questions present themselves.

The point is that they are ultimately empirical questions; questions about how people communicate with each other in relation to the enterprises of government and social control that we term law. Ultimately they are questions about what it means to participate in law (understood as these enterprises), what different ways of participating there can be, and also what social distinctions can be usefully drawn in general and abstract terms between participating and observing. Sociological analysis might lead us to ask, indeed, whether any firm separation is to be drawn between participation and observation. The lawyer participating in courtroom argument, and in a trial process more generally, relies on observation of the behaviour of others (judge, jury, witnesses) in the courtroom as well as a more diffuse general knowledge of typical workings of the legal system (typical behavioural patterns, institutional structures, processes and procedures). No lawyer, or other social actor, can participate without observation, or knowledge founded on other people's observations. Equally, the observer is necessarily in some sense a participant. It is hard to imagine anyone functioning consistently and permanently as a Hartian 'external observer' of legal rules, without any (probably considerable) normative understanding (Shiner, 1992: 149-50; Waluchow, 1994: 27-9). Observation and participation continually intertwine in actual experience. What Michel Van der Kerchove and François Ost (1994: 9) call a 'moderate' external point of view (which necessarily also appreciates the internal view) is surely complemented by a 'moderate' internal point of view which necessarily observes in order to participate.

What is it to participate? Do scholars of Roman law today participate in any sense in a legal system that no longer exists? They may participate mentally no less than do jurists interpreting the rules of their own contemporary legal order. But they are also observers of a legal regime that no longer regulates social action. Do they constitute part of an interpretive community with the long dead jurists of Roman times? Or are they merely observers of history? What, indeed, constitutes membership in an interpretive community? What are the qualifications for membership? Can there be many different qualifications - for example, being a practising judge or lawyer, a citizen living 'under law', a jurist studying a (perhaps defunct) system, a sociologist or historian seeking understanding of legal consciousness?

What, as a practical matter, defines an interpretive community, and defines positions within it? In law, political authority may determine relative status in such a community (for example, giving appellate courts more weight in legal interpretation than lower courts). But so may economic or other power (for example, affecting status between nation states or other corporate actors operating within transnational regimes of commercial law); or intellectual reputation (between judges of the same court, or scholars of the same legal field). How do these and other determinants interrelate in practice? And what determines precedence or relative status between legal interpretive communities where several such communities exist in the same society or social group?

The questions are unending and, in many cases provoked by changes in social experience in a world in which questions about the nature of interpretation, jurisdiction and authority in law are becoming increasingly complex. I list some of them here solely to suggest how deeply problematic is the internal/external dichotomy in relation to legal thought and scholarship (Cotterrell, 1998). Participation and observation of law may require a wide range of variable, shifting perspectives and practices. To speak of these as 'internal' or 'external' is meaningless without specifying: internal or external to what? And there is surely no single 'what'! The same issues make the idea of law's autonomy puzzling. What does it mean to say law is autonomous when law is taken to exist in so many different interpretive settings and sites and when participation in law can take so many forms? Today socio-legal studies can no longer leave lawyers and jurists to theorise about law's autonomy, doing so in a way that may be conservative and at least partially outdated in terms of contemporary legal experience. If law is characterised as a discourse or interpretive practice it is not automatically to be assumed that it is best understood as a unitary discourse or practice: the shared, unchallenged possession of a single interpretive community. Nor does characterising law in this way necessarily tell us anything at all about its purported autonomy.

Nevertheless, despite all complexities, the great power of law as discourse (or rather, as a variety of discourses) has to be clearly recognised. Various theories of legal ideology have strongly emphasised this aspect of law's power. And critical legal studies have built on the advances of some such theories by stressing that law constitutes, through its discursive power, social relations. But theories of legal ideology are not necessarily also theories of legal doctrine or legal interpretation. Something more is needed, which hermeneutic approaches have tried to provide. But these often fail to focus on the sheer diversity of settings, sites and contexts of legal interpretation and discourse, referred to above. More empirically oriented studies of institutional practices are required to identify this diversity. And these studies have to overcome, in one way or another, the old analytical distinctions between participation and observation which, for reasons given earlier, are often unhelpful if the diversity of legal experience is to be recognised.

Autopoietic law?

On one view, all of this leads to autopoiesis theory, which has rightly been regarded as among the most important recent theoretical developments relevant to legal sociology. But it is interesting that autopoiesis theory seems to have entered legal scholarship much more as a response to a perceived weakness of legal sociology than as an expression of the increasing power and ambition of the socio-legal enterprise, stressed above. In part this theory responds to claims about misguided, ignorant or inefficient social uses of law (excessive juridification and the 'regulatory trilemma') (Teubner, 1987: 21-7). In part, it claims also to remedy a purported inability of legal sociology to predict and explain regulatory failure or the unanticipated consequences of regulatory activities (the long-recognised 'social limits of law') (see, for instance, Allott, 1980; Pennock and Chapman, 1974).

In addressing these matters, autopoiesis theory presupposes a very different agenda for socio-legal studies from that suggested above. I have presented socio-legal scholarship as needing to engage with legal discourse to take further legal sociology's insights which have already added much to those of juristic legal scholarship but now highlight the need for new theories of law in a changing world of jurisdiction, legal interpretation and legal authority. By contrast, autopoiesis theory presumes a legal sociology on the defensive, that must atone for its predictive and analytical failures by finally paying obeisance to law's discursive power.

Certainly autopoiesis theory applied in socio-legal studies is very important because of what it attempts. It takes extremely seriously the problem of characterising what lawyers may think of as law's autonomy. It reinterprets the internal/external dichotomy in law as a matter of social practice and theorises this in a manner more sophisticated than anything to be found in the modern literature of legal philosophy.

Yet I think that autopoiesis theory suffers from opposite faults from those of the older legal sociology. The latter often paid insufficient attention to the character of legal doctrine and so disabled itself from confronting directly jurists' understandings of law. Not only that, but it failed to understand much of the central social reality of law which resides in its discursive presentation and cognitive ordering of the social world. By contrast, autopoiesis theory tends to *reify* lawyers' (and other orthodox) understandings of law, including, above all, the idea of law's discursive autonomy, the internal/external dichotomy and the metaphor of system as applied to law. Each of these it interprets in a certain way, but treats them largely as givens for social scientific understanding of law, as well as givens of legal experience.

In what way does the theory tend to reify these matters? Autopoiesis theory always stresses contingency. Matters could be different from the way they are. Nothing is pre-ordained in some way theoretically. The theory does not dictate empirical outcomes but claims to offer a way of understanding them. Nevertheless it focusses attention firmly on certain matters and requires that we approach social research with certain presumptions. Law is not inevitably an autopoietic social system of communication, or a self-observing, self-producing and self-reproducing discourse, but in modern conditions, according to the theory, it tends to become such and *functional necessity drives this tendency*. The possibility of thinking of law's relations with other aspects or fields of social life in terms of influence, interpenetration, interdependence and interaction is not ruled out. But it is firmly marginalised in a theory which is oriented to explaining why such linkages are, in contemporary conditions, increasingly implausible and, ultimately, impossible. Hence the idea of law possessing uniform and powerful characteristics given *by its system-character* becomes a theoretical presumption. And because this presumption (and its theoretical elaboration) is the central contribution that the theory appears to offer for legal analysis, it is hard to displace. Perhaps, indeed, the theory must firmly resist its displacement, because to do otherwise would be to cast fundamental doubt on the theory's practical utility. Hence presumed ideas tend to be reified, becoming for the theory a kind of 'reality' about law, which is then presented as the basis for predictions, policies or strategies, and sometimes as an adequate explanation in itself of certain social consequences of legal interventions.

Autopoiesis theory thus tends to treat as the very basis of its analysis what might otherwise be seen as merely contingent objects of analysis. I mean here (as such objects) especially certain ideological constructions - taken for granted ways of understanding legal phenomena that present themselves as 'reality', irrespective of the diversity, complexity and contradictions of empirical experience. Indeed, these constructions purport to provide self-evidently 'correct' characterisations of this experience. They include ideological constructions about law's functions, the 'blind' unguided character of its evolution, the uniform coding of its decisions as autonomous of politics, economics, etc., or its nature as a normatively closed system. Certainly, these constructions may be of great value for purposes of professional (and other) legitimation. But autopoiesis theory seems to present them as sociological necessities, although it recognises that they are the outcome of historical processes. It sees radical system-differentiation as required functionally to deal with the complexity of modern society. Even more fundamentally, this differentiation is ultimately dictated by the theory's claims about the way in which the communication of meaning in modern society is possible at all.

Yet law's apparent system-differentiation might be treated in other ways. It might be seen, in part - *but only in part*, as an aspect of a contingent, often contested and far from consistent (Posner, 1987; Cotterrell, 1995: ch. 3) professional project of lawyers in particular times and places. In other respects, what appears as the system-differentiation of law might be analysed as an aspect of a more general political development of particular societies, perhaps especially linked with the development of liberalism and individualism. Autopoiesis theory might appear to marginalise the difficult task of explaining such matters empirically because it treats law's autonomy (in a specific sense) as the functionally necessary result of evolutionary processes considered analytically apart from questions of human agency (Luhmann, 1986: 112).

What, from a different sociological point of view, needs explanation thus risks becoming, for autopoiesis theory, what is taken for granted. In so far as a project for sociology of law arises from the theory, it is surely that of finding means of adjustment to the situation of law's autopoietic system-differentiation and self-reproduction. But the theory assumes this situation because its conception of the nature and conditions of existence of meaning in systems of communication necessarily predicts such a state of affairs. It assumes law's autonomy as a social fact, rather than as, for example, a political and professional aspiration. But all of this is a matter of controversial theoretical deduction rather than empirically-grounded observation.

Autopoiesis theory is valuable to legal sociology because it presents in the starkest way social presuppositions that underlie a certain kind of extreme view of legal autonomy. It characterises legal autonomy not in terms of normative structure or reasoning as in much legal philosophy but in the dynamic terms of systems of communication. Hence it has promised a means of analysing sociologically - in terms of social processes - characteristics of legal doctrine and its elaboration that are familiar to all Western lawyers. Autopoiesis theory presents law's 'rational strength' (Lawson, 1951) as an effect of the intensity of its communications in a seemingly self-reproducing realm of discourse. Law's cognitive openness allows continual responsiveness to stimuli (economic, cultural, scientific, administrative, etc.) that provoke (but do not determine) the creation of new legal decisions and hence legal ideas. At the same time, using its own binary code of legal/illegal (legally right or wrong), it appears to produce decisions from decisions, normative judgments from normative judgments. On this view, law regulates the processes of its own creation (Kelsen, 1989: 71, 221). But law also may appear to provide the materials for its own creation. Law is produced from law, because existing legal discourse provides normative resources that can be recycled - and, in the process, elaborated in ever more complex and detailed forms - into new normative resources.

For those who inhabit the world of academic law, as well as the world of social science, this imagery of professionalised, sophisticated legal discourse is, at least at a certain level of generality, familiar and realistic. It seems initially accurate in its portrayal of some of the intellectually and morally closed-off worlds of professional legal discourse. For law teachers who have devoted much of their careers to trying to break down law's splendid isolation as an intellectual product and encouraging law students to see ways in which legal knowledge depends upon and can be enriched by knowledge fields often considered 'external' to law, autopoiesis theory seems to confirm the reality of barriers to achieving this. It offers an image of law which suggests that legal strategies will be frequently ineffective in regulating 'other systems' such as the economy, or that law will 'resist' or merely ignore the various kinds of scientific or technical knowledge and practice that may confront it. Where these are brought into the courtroom, in juvenile justice or social welfare contexts, or where law is required to confront the understandings of psychology, biology, economics or other sciences as evidence, autopoiesis theory predicts that law will interpret these understandings in its own ways for its own distinctive purposes, treating them merely as 'irritants' (see, for example, King and Piper, 1995). It may be spurred to decisions of some kind, but not necessarily those that seem reasonable or predictable from the standpoint of practitioners of the sciences in question. Autopoiesis theory dramatises our deep disappointment that more cannot be done with law to effect social regulation, that law is too unresponsive to a world of problems urgently requiring regulatory solutions and that when law does act, the results seem frequently tangential or arbitrary in relation to the problems it purports to address.

90   *Law's New Boundaries*

Most importantly, perhaps, autopoiesis theory dramatises law's 'system character' in a way that is likely to ring true for many lawyers. Law students who come to law initially expecting it to be full of dramas of human interest, its decisions richly coloured with passion and engagement, soon learn that it is an important part of law's regulatory technique to drain away these elements into dry abstraction. Passionate law is controversial law, thus of doubtful acceptability. Law depends, especially in highly pluralistic, complex and rapidly changing societies, on abstraction; a calculated distancing from its specific human settings. In this way it nurtures its 'objectivity' and so its special authority. Yet it must be stressed that this is a strategic distancing. It is required because legal doctrine must give generalised normative meaning to social institutions and relationships while recognising their particularised significance in the subjective experience of those who participate in them. Legal practice relies on its own abstractions, yet cannot carry them beyond a certain point because law's social meaning, and so its ultimate authority, depends on a great diversity of forms of understanding and evaluation over which it has no final control.

Autopoiesis theory's picture of contemporary positive law's apparent autonomy is, in important respects, plausible. But one must ask: what does the theory offer that goes beyond lawyers' practical observation of typical experiences of reasoning with rules where a degree of communicative precision and predictability in regulatory and adjudicative practice is sought? These experiences certainly promote practical efforts to secure some kind of autonomy of legal reasoning and doctrine. Regrettably, I think that much of what the theory offers beyond this is harmful in so far as it is used to guide socio-legal inquiry. I say regrettably, because I much admire, for example, Gunther Teubner's effort to bring new rigour to sociologically-oriented legal theory and to use this theory, built especially on Niklas Luhmann's work, in legal analysis. This is important not least in relation to the theorisation of transnational law, and some central concerns of current comparative law (Teubner, 1997; Teubner 1998; Ladeur, 1999). In the rest of this paper I shall try to explain where, from the standpoint of a legal sociologist, I think that the harm in autopoiesis theory applied to law most clearly lies.

Autopoiesis as explanation?

As suggested earlier, the theory observes key features of law in an initially persuasive manner. In my view it does not, however, offer substantial sociological explanations of these features. Rather, it provides analytical models of them but then *takes the models as a kind of reality in themselves.*

The Representation of Law's Autonomy in Autopoiesis Theory   91

Thus, law's postulated autonomy is modelled in a complex and sophisticated manner in terms of the capacity of law to observe, constitute and ultimately reproduce itself as a system of communications. But Teubner's important general statement of autopoietic legal theory offers no substantial sociological account of the interplay of forces that give rise to this autonomy in particular times and places (Teubner, 1993: ch. 4).[1] Of course, it is precisely his point that no general sociological explanation of the development of legal autopoiesis is possible. Strictly speaking, legal development is a matter *only* of legal development (significantly he finds support in Alan Watson's profoundly anti-sociological analyses of legal evolution) (Teubner, 1993: 40, 50, 58). Here one must either accept the theory or not. But it is hard to see how, in this context at least, it can offer much help to a sociology of law, viewing law in terms of general social processes.

All that the theory seems prepared to say of these processes in specific terms is that they are processes of communication, and, in the case of law, communication is about legality or illegality, conceived as a binary opposition. In itself, this may not be much help to lawyers' juristic science which has its own sophisticated understandings of what it takes to be institutional processes of legal doctrinal development, and of the complex formulations, gradations and contextualisations of juristic categories of legality or illegality. Indeed, adjudicative and interpretive practice in law might well be seen by many lawyers as focused on a very diverse range of matters often far removed from what autopoiesis theory identifies as law's distinctive binary coding. Lawyers are well aware that the meaning and use of any such coding are themselves matters for permanent interpretation and reinterpretation. If law's binary coding is taken, in some simple sense, as distinctive of legal discourse it might be best understood as a signal (like alternation between a red and green light) provided to influence the actions of enforcement agencies, citizens, etc. If so this can be seen as a functional output, but hardly as adequately characterising or defining the complex discourses of legal practice.[2]

---

[1]What is important for the theory is that evolution is 'blind' and regulated only by 'filter mechanisms' of variation, selection and retention. 'Structural coupling' between systems may (but may not) inspire developments but it seems that the way this comes about will be, in terms of the theory, inexplicable. And contingency is preserved in the idea that functional equivalents are always possible. The possibility of explaining historical development in terms of the play of social forces is recognised but treated as refering to an entirely different level of analysis to be distinguished from the theory's own focus on functional analysis (Teubner, 1993: 50, 51).

[2]Following autopoiesis theory's own claims, the theory could, indeed, have no influence on

The audience for autopoiesis theory is surely intended, therefore, to be legal sociologists or socio-legal scholars. But the theory's explanatory potential, as regards social processes, seems to me to reduce to very little; perhaps even to tautology. Legal communications are about law: the theory seems to revel in its acceptance of law's circularity and self-reference. Law endlessly creates law out of law (even if in response to social stimuli). This is claimed as almost the entire key to its functioning as a social system. Legal sociology (as an enterprise dedicated to explaining this functioning) is surely therefore rendered redundant, having - through autopoiesis theory - achieved its theoretical goal of declaring why this redundancy arises (or at least modelling it analytically). Are we to accept this with enthusiasm or resignation? The answer is not clear.

I think that Teubner, at least, has been determined to resist this outcome. That is surely why he wrestles in such a strange way in Chapter 6 of his major book on autopoiesis theory (Teubner, 1993) with what he presents as the problem of conflict between law and other subsystems of society. Everything written earlier in the book should suggest, as far as I can see, that in this context 'conflict' in any *strict* sense is impossible. There are simply no points of *direct* contact between subsystems. Therefore there cannot be conflict. Law reads an event in its (legal) terms; the economy reads the same event in its own (different) terms. There cannot be conflict because each system sees normatively only in its own way. Each *sees nothing to oppose.* Law reads the economic environment in legal terms; the economy reads the significance of legal regulation in terms of its own coding. Conflict implies the possibility of (unwelcome) influence. But autopoiesis theory denies the possibility of any influence, as such. Interference (as contrasted with influence) is not a matter of conflict because interference is not perceived by the system as something oppositional but merely as an occurrence that may or may not provoke the system to react to the interference. The system decides on its response and this will always be on its own normative terms.

It seems that Teubner very much wants to reintroduce the idea of system-conflict despite the fact that autopoiesis portrays a world of systems that do not conflict because they do not interact. He wants to do so because this is to reintroduce central concerns of legal sociology into the analysis - above all the issue of the 'limits of effective legal action' on which so much of legal sociology has been founded. As an issue (of the uncertain outcome of conflicts) it might be addressed through empirical study, whereas if taken as a given (an aspect of law's systemic nature) it surely needs no further

---

juristic thought or practice. Autopoiesis theory could register here only as a 'perturbation', a perception of external 'noise', when the discourse of law observes what it takes to be that of social science.

empirical examination. I believe that Teubner is deeply committed to the empirical enterprise of legal sociology and sees autopoiesis theory as uniquely suited to present the discursive construction of social reality as the underpinning of law as an empirically-examinable practice.

However, to reintroduce system-conflict, arguments that seem inconsistent with autopoiesis theory are required. Conflict can arise, he suggests, between external descriptions of a system (for example, law's description of the economy), on the one hand, and 'the way in which a system [for example, the economy] actually operates', on the other (Teubner, 1993: 103). But, in a constructivist theory such as autopoiesis theory, what is meant by the way a system *actually operates*? Surely there is no *accessible* objective standpoint from which this can be recognised or determined? The legal system cannot experience any such 'actual operation', nor even the economy's own self-understanding, but only law's own 'legal reading' of its environment. Thus, reference to 'actual economic processes', 'ways in which the surrounding systems actually operate', or 'real operations of the surrounding systems' (Teubner, 1993: 103), seems a kind of sleight of hand in which objective (actual, real) criteria are postulated to serve as common reference points between systems. Yet surely this is fundamentally at odds with the constructivist nature of the theory. There is no objective meaning (surely no 'actuality', or 'reality' in any trans-system sense) but only meaning within and for specific systems of communication.[3]

Teubner uses his analysis of conflict to paint a picture of law potentially in crisis, at risk even of disintegration because of conflict with other systems. There is, as a result of such crises, a 'dramatic increase in the indeterminacy of law' (Teubner, 1993: 105). But, on the one hand, this seems a manufactured crisis in terms of autopoiesis theory, since, as suggested above, the theory does not appear to allow a place for such crises to exist. On the other hand, if we discard the models that autopoiesis theory has set up, it may seem an overblown, sensational portrayal of crisis (Rottleuthner, 1989). From

---

[3]Luhmann and Teubner have both insisted that a 'materiality continuum' is 'presupposed as a basis of system operations' and has 'real contact' with them. Indeed, system operations are 'founded on' it (Teubner, 1993: 85). Its nature seems mysterious, however. Not only do Teubner and Luhmann disagree fundamentally as to what it includes (Teubner, 1993: 85) but there seems to be no precise explanation of how it operates on systems. Perhaps some theories of ideology might be helpful here. One of their more important insights has been that the nature of 'material reality' is always interpreted in any particular structure of ideological thought (what autopoiesis theory might identify as a discursive system) in ways consistent with that thought. Thus, ideological understandings collapse only when the emotional and intellectual resources that support them fail (Cotterrell, 1995: 7-14). This is a matter, at least in part, of psychological conditions, including especially those relating to personal and group morale.

any standpoint other than that of autopoiesis theory, law's negotiation, absorption, rejection, modification, colonisation of, or adaptation to moral, scientific, economic, historical, political and other evaluations is normal; the stuff of everyday legal experience, which legal sociology has confronted with varying degrees of success since its modern beginnings. This situation is an inevitable recipe for crisis only if we treat law's discourse as 'pure' in some narrow sense - focused on its legal/illegal coding but not on a host of other valuations that are necessary to wise regulation and are, in fact, taken on in much legal decision-making in routine ways. These valuations, in fact, often involve the use of what autopoiesis theory sees as distinctive codes of other systems (efficiency criteria, for example).[4]

Could it be suggested that autopoiesis theory reflects a peculiarly continental conception of law's 'rational strength' as a form of conceptual or doctrinal purity - an all-or-nothing view of law, very different from common law legal thinking? Much Anglophone discussion of the theory has confronted it with the empiricist traditions of the common law world (Nelken, 1987; Lempert, 1987). But a different aspect of common law thought might be invoked here. The tradition of common law 'law-finding' (now admittedly heavily overlaid with a completely different, modern, 'scientific' legal positivism) is to see law deeply rooted in culture, that is, moral experience in some broad all-encompassing sense. Autopoiesis theory flatters much positivist legal philosophy by 'super-autonomising' this positivist philosophy's 'autonomising' portrayals of law. The problem is that such portrayals of law's autonomy make it hard to see how vital as a practical matter law's direct moral links to the various communities of social interaction are. Positivism in this guise does not make these links central to analysis - quite the opposite; hence it risks promoting the false and, indeed, dangerous idea of positive law's adequate self-referentiality and self-reproduction. This idea leaves law a dead-letter morally, rather than (to paraphrase Durkheim) 'an effective [moral] discipline of wills' (Durkheim, 1975: 277). It denies or ignores the rooting of law in the general and diverse moral experience of citizens, which should be the basis of legal sociology's concern with law.

---

[4]This is certainly not to suggest that, typically, all is well in law's relations with its social environment. But the crisis tendencies of law, as I see them, have causes almost diametrically opposed to those that adherents of autopoiesis theory identify. Crises (of law's authority, and respect or support for law), when they arise, are likely to be rooted in the effort to sustain the mirage of positive law as self-validating or self-legitimating, or requiring merely political authority, rather than acknowledging its dependence on moral groundings arising from the specific social (communal) contexts of its historical existence.

The Representation of Law's Autonomy in Autopoiesis Theory   95

Autopoiesis and agency

I have claimed that analysis of law must focus on law's roots in the diverse moral experience of citizens. It follows that, on this view, the motivations of individuals in relation to law and the contexts it regulates are centrally important for legal sociology. It is important to relate law to the subjective meaning which, as Weber (1978: 22-6) emphasised, individuals attach to their actions in social contexts. People relate to each other in terms of very varied motivations - expressing combinations of emotional attachment, common or convergent interests, shared values or beliefs, or common experience of some kind. But it hardly needs to be said that systems have no motivations; nor can they accept responsibility, set projects, or form attachments. Instead, they have (in the view of autopoiesis theory) functions and are repositories of meaning, understood entirely in their own system-terms.

Zenon Bankowski has raised the very important question of how individuals relate to systems (Bankowski, 1996). Strictly speaking, and despite all protestations to the contrary, it seems that, for autopoiesis theory, they do not. The importance of the individual in a system-oriented world is said, by Teubner, to be reinstated by autopoiesis theory (Teubner, 1993: 45) because individuality can itself be thought of in terms of 'psychic systems' that have an existence entirely independent of social systems. Bankowski's critique, however, is that because individuals have no direct access to social systems (psychic systems lending themselves to autopoiesis no less than social systems) it is impossible to see how individuals engage with social systems, including law. 'How, and by what principle, do we attribute bits of communication to human beings' (Bankowski, 1996: 70). In what way then can individuals be responsible for the consequences of social systems? For example, in a contemporary world conscious of the power of impersonal systems, no one can, it seems, be held responsible for 'globalisation' and its burgeoning transnational legal regimes; yet people and organisations strongly promote this system (however characterised), benefit from it, suffer as a result of it, or struggle against it in various ways. It must be stressed that autopoiesis theory in no way denies the significance of responsibility in relation to the consequences of systems. It is rather that there seems no place for serious consideration of this issue in terms of the theory.[5]

---

[5]Autopoiesis theory can, it seems, postulate the responsibility of social systems, which might be understood as a form of collective responsibility. The implication would be that all who are agents of the system share its responsibility. This idea was suggested to me in discussion. But I find it hard to understand how responsibility, in any usual sense of the word, can be attributed to or accepted by a system of discourse or communication. Responsibility would

96 *Law's New Boundaries*

John Paterson has replied to Bankowski that autopoiesis theory actually strengthens the individual's situation (Paterson, 1996). From the standpoint of the individual as psychic system, social systems exist as an array of constructs in relation to which specific choices of action may or may not be thematised. Thus, in the fictional illustration provided by Gabriel García Márquez' celebrated story *Chronicle of a Death Foretold* (1996), it is not that the 'honour system' impels the killing of the transgressor of this system. Nor is it that the killers lack individual responsibility or the possibility of personal choice ('the system did it'; 'there was no option'). Rather the choice is one of how the matter should be thematised - as a matter within the honour system (which requires the killing), or within the entirely different terms of the legal system (which prohibits it). Responsibility remains. In terms of autopoiesis the psychic system negotiates its internal adjustments (for example, individuals make sense of their situation and make their decisions) while responding to the 'interference' or 'noise' produced by the various operative social systems, including law.

Surely, however, we learn little from this particular analysis as to how and why individuals thematise situations in particular ways. While it would be possible to analyse 'agency' in terms of the autopoietic requirements of psychic systems this would still not link the agency of individuals - and so issues of motivation or responsibility - to law. Yet law's attributions of responsibility and its claims about the mental states involved in action must involve, to some extent, an effort to 'see inside' what autopoiesis theory calls psychic systems (although the effort is, admittedly, limited by practicalities of evidence and the need for presumptions that can form a basis for general rules). Equally, law is not merely a system waiting to have situations thematised in relation to it. It is continually being constructed and reconstructed as practice and doctrine through the (particularly judicial) effort to understand actions, responsibilities and intentions of individual litigants and to use this understanding to give meaning to public regulation.

It is not difficult to identify the exact point in the logic of autopoietic legal theory where, in my view, it takes its fundamental wrong turning in reifying 'system' in law and effectively excluding agency from its horizon of social explanation. This point arises in answering a basic question: how can the concept of autopoiesis be extended beyond its original biological application (in analysing processes of life - the cell, the central nervous system, etc.) to the analysis of social systems? If systems of organic life may be self-

---

require the system to 'respond' (give an answer or account) to something or someone outside itself, but this would involve a communication process of which, according to the theory, it is not capable.

The Representation of Law's Autonomy in Autopoiesis Theory 97

producing and self-reproducing it is harder to see this as a parallel feature of social systems. Consequently many adherents of autopoiesis theory among natural and social scientists refuse to apply it to social phenomena. Again, while the autopoiesis of living systems might be understood as an all-or-nothing affair, there is no agreement as to how this aspect of autopoiesis applies to social systems (Luhmann apparently sees legal autopoiesis as all-or-nothing; for Teubner it can be a matter of degree) (Teubner, 1993: 27).

The more serious problem, however, is that for social systems, such as law, to be autopoietic their components *must* be distinct from living beings that are themselves analysed as autopoietic systems; otherwise a social system could not be self-producing and self-reproducing, but would be dependent on processes external to itself. For this reason, Teubner must insist that higher-order autopoietic social systems such as law 'can be formed in such a way that emergent unities are constituted which provide their elements' (Teubner, 1993: 29). Crucially, these emergent unities are entirely distinct from living beings. Thus 'communications (not human beings or cognitive systems)' are the elements of social systems (Teubner, 1993: 29). The banishment of living beings, it must be stressed, is an absolutely necessary step in order to apply the theory of autopoiesis to law. The basis of social systems is thus 'not life' (Teubner, 1993: 30). Legal (communicative) acts are the elements of a legal system (Teubner, 1993: 41-2) but the system itself defines the concept of action (Teubner, 1993: 43). In this way the system drags itself into autopoiesis, with human beings as the bearers of communicative acts whose essential nature is (increasingly, as the system moves towards autopoiesis) given by the system itself.

It is of great interest in this context that John Paterson and Gunther Teubner have recently sought to clarify how these ideas can guide empirical socio-legal research (Paterson and Teubner, 1998). Using the example of regulation of the British North Sea Oil industry they show very convincingly the sharp contrasts between discourses of legislators, regulators, operators and engineers. It is, indeed, highly plausible to suggest that different 'codings' or criteria of value or appropriateness apply in each of the identified discourses. Autopoiesis theory offers an interesting framework for conceptualising these discursive contrasts, a set of predictions about the way discourses will relate, and guidance about relatively successful and unsuccessful legal strategies for regulation of the industry.

It seems to me, however, that, in order to provide this impressive illustration of autopoiesis theory's empirical power and to show how it relates to questions of agency some subtle modifications to the idea of 'system' in the theory are being made. Thus, it now appears that the existence of any system (including presumably the system-character of law as a practice of regulation) is not to be assumed but depends on observation of 'concrete interactions in legislative chambers and lobby halls and the technological processes in our implementation field in order to discover the systemicity of our research object' (Paterson and Teubner, 1998: 459). A regulated area might be defined by many systems, 'the exact number being a matter for empirical observation' (Paterson and Teubner, 1998: 471).

On the one hand, therefore, systems are real - one might say they are Durkheimian social facts - and present themselves to empirical observation. One has only to look to see them and then count them up! The concept of system has been reified into an object to be observed. On the other hand, 'system' as the model that provided the entire structure of claims about discursive autonomy, predictions of regulatory effects, prescriptions for regulation and warnings about failure is downgraded to *a mere pattern* that might appear to some indeterminate degree mixed with many others and *with no strong system integrity* of its own. Therefore, the researcher will construct systems by observing and interpreting human actions. But is it unfair to say that what is now offered as guidance and method is little more than legal sociology has worked with - institutional structures, patterns of action, currents of ideology - in empirical research without need of help from autopoiesis theory? What then becomes of 'system'? It exists, like beauty, in the eye of the beholder - no longer a social fact but a way of talking about perceived patterns of action. The powerful claims and predictions disappear when the theory refuses to assume the existence of autopoietic systems in operation, but recognises instead the empirical impossibility of closure, the intermingling of discourses and the empirical specificity of sites and settings of interpretive practice.

Nevertheless, the theory cannot for long, it seems, give up its powerful and dramatic claims - and as soon as they re-enter they defeat any attempt to supply open analytical frameworks that facilitate empirical research rather than close off the need for it. Thus, in the same paper, Paterson and Teubner refer to Boaventura De Sousa Santos' subtle attempt to explain how and why laws 'misread' reality (Santos, 1987), reinterpreting his thesis in terms of autopoiesis theory. This theory shows, they assert, that such a misreading is 'inevitable', indeed that it is 'impossible' to avoid (Paterson and Teubner, 1998: 461). In the face of such unqualified and universal claims, empirical researchers might as well give up, it seems. Nothing much remains to be discovered when conclusions are so definite and sweeping in advance of research.

Conclusion

It is appropriate finally to return to the point from which this paper started. Legal sociology progressed by denying the social significance of certain features of law treated as important by most lawyers - especially law's 'internal' discursive or doctrinal nature. When legal sociology observed law as a system it saw lawyers and administrators dealing with cases in their offices, regulatory agencies making decisions on law enforcement, police on patrol, judges, advocates or legislators at work, citizens making (or failing to make) complaints, and disputes being processed. It identified system, provisionally and for theoretical convenience, in such matters as collective understandings, organisational needs and aims, informal patterns of regular social interaction, and professionalisation strategies - all of these observed in specific empirical settings. Today it is important to stress the key part of law that old-style legal sociology too often left out of account: the social significance of legal doctrine, including the general structures of social understanding which it supports. For myself, I think that the concept of ideology (reformulated in certain ways) still remains useful (though not necessarily sufficient) in doing this. Some other researchers prefer to think in terms of legal culture and use this concept in productive ways.

But it is by no means apparent that we need to think about these matters in the strong systems-terms of autopoiesis theory. The danger is of reifying systems (especially of reifying law's autonomy as a discursive system); treating as a social phenomenon what is best thought of as a model of convergent and interlocking practices and contingently interrelated understandings and perceptions. Whatever may be the case for biological systems (Zolo, 1992: 79), the concept of *social* systems is useful only as a *metaphor*. Social systems (including legal systems) cannot be observed or even experienced as such. What are experienced (and may be metaphorically described in system-terms) are stable patterns of action and understandings, associated with particular groups or social environments, or embodied in organisations, agreements for co-operation or peace, or policies and strategies; co-operating individuals with distinct but interconnected objectives; social hierarchies of power, influence or authority; and relationships between people linked to each other on the basis of shared beliefs or values, mutual affection, or the familiarity of common experience. In other words, we should think always, in my view, in terms of people[6] and use the concept of social system only as a convenient way of

---

[6]This is not a reification of subjectivity. It presupposes only an empirical recognition that human beings are discrete entities in a way that (without elaborate conceptualisation) social systems are not.

conceptualising sustained convergences of action of individuals, and the varied patterns of organisation of groups. Used in this way 'system' is obviously a concept of great value, probably indispensible in legal and social theory. If the notion of system implies assemblages, relations and unities in phenomena (Van de Kerchove and Ost, 1994: 5-6), its use allows a focus on these matters in interpreting the aims or consequences of social action. The notion of system, in this sense, is, undoubtedly, a device by which lawyers organise practices of legal interpretion, especially when questions of legal validity are being addressed (Raz, 1980: ch. 8).

Instead of reifying the idea of system in law, we should focus on practices and motivations that promote, and make plausible, ideas of law's autonomy, including the radical claims to autonomy that autopoiesis theory highlights. We should also look at, and behind, the various intellectual, moral and professional interests that have been served by advocacy of different versions of the internal/external dichotomy in relation to legal studies or legal practice. Then, perhaps it will become possible to dust off and re-present in fruitful new ways some old insights of sociology of law - dating back as far as Eugen Ehrlich (1975). I include here the insight that being 'inside' or 'outside' regulatory experience is a matter of being inside or outside particular groups;[7] as well as the further insight that there is, realistically speaking, no single group of legal insiders, but that everything depends on perspective. Hence, it is necessary to look at the many different kinds of social groups that, today, are engaged in the interpretation of law or the promotion or invocation of regulation. Some groups (judiciaries, jurists) may claim a monopoly of interpretation; yet they themselves might be seen to be divided into sub-groups in competition. Within the state as an organisation of governmental power there may be a range of groups (for example, sections within judiciaries; specialised administrative or enforcement staffs) seeking in different ways to interpret law, not necessarily in harmony with each other and sometimes in sharp if often unadmitted opposition.

In society at large, where autopoiesis theory sees incommensurable social systems, it might be better to see a host of different interpretive communities relating in various ways to law, perhaps understanding law in different ways. Sociology of law can examine action in such communities; its conditions, motivations and constraints. Perhaps, indeed, the idea of a single, discursively distinctive or normatively unified legal system, which the reification of the idea of system encourages us to treat with great seriousness, ought to be viewed with suspicion in formulating the

---

[7]But understood as a process in continual flux, not a rigid status; relations are typically with different groups at different times and invariably with several groups simultaneously.

The Representation of Law's Autonomy in Autopoiesis Theory   101

contemporary agendas of legal sociology. Its replacement would be a recognition of a wide and very diverse array of practices, expectations, doctrines, sites and settings of legal interpretation. Such a focus emphasises - as I think the best work in legal sociology has always done - the complexity and contingency of law as a field of experience marked by endless conflict and competition around vested interests, ideals and aspirations. Viewed sociologically, legal authority, jurisdiction and interpretation are always potentially contested - ultimately not the technical preserve of jurists but the site and stake of social conflict or competition.[8]

References

Allott, A. (1980), *The Limits of Law*, Butterworths, London.
Bankowski, Z. (1996), 'How Does It Feel To Be On Your Own? The Person in the Sight of Autopoiesis' in D. Nelken (ed.), *Law as Communication*, Dartmouth, Aldershot, pp. 63-80.
Black, D. (1989), *Sociological Justice*, Oxford University Press, New York.
Bredemeier, H. (1962), 'Law as an Integrative Mechanism' in W. M. Evan (ed.), *Law and Sociology: Exploratory Essays*, Free Press, Glencoe, Ill., pp. 73-88.
Cotterrell, R. (1995), *Law's Community: Legal Theory in Sociological Perspective*, Clarendon Press, Oxford.
Cotterrell, R. (1998), 'Law and Community: A New Relationship?', 51 *Current Legal Problems*, pp. 367-91.
Cotterrell, R. (1999), *Emile Durkheim: Law in a Moral Domain*, Edinburgh University Press, Edinburgh.
Cotterrell, R. (forthcoming in 2001), 'Is There a Logic of Legal Transplants? in D. Nelken (ed.), *Adapting Legal Cultures*, Hart Publishing, Oxford.
Dezalay, Y. and B. G. Garth. (1996), *Dealing in Virtue: International Commercial Arbitration and the Construction of a Transnational Legal Order*, University of Chicago Press, Chicago.
Durkheim, E. (1975), 'Définition du fait morale' in *Textes*, vol 2, Les Éditions de Minuit, Paris, pp. 257-88.
Dworkin, R.M. (1978), *Taking Rights Seriously*, Duckworth, London.
Dworkin, R.M. (1985), *A Matter of Principle*, Harvard University Press, Cambridge, Mass.
Dworkin, R. M. (1986), *Law's Empire*, Fontana, London.
Ehrlich, E. (1975), *Fundamental Principles of the Sociology of Law*, Arno, New York.
Ewald, W. (1995), 'Comparative Jurisprudence II: The Logic of Legal Transplants', 43 *American Journal of Comparative Law*, pp. 489-510.
Gerth, H.H. and Mills, C. W. (eds), (1948), *From Max Weber: Essays in Sociology*, Routledge and Kegan, London.
Hart, H.L.A. (1994), *The Concept of Law*, 2nd edn., Clarendon Press, Oxford.
Honoré, T. (1987), *Making Law Bind*, Clarendon Press, Oxford.
Jackson, R. (ed.), (1999), 'Sovereignty at the Millenium: Special issue', 47 *Political Studies* No 3.

---

[8]I am grateful to the participants in the Cardiff workshop on autopoiesis theory, and especially to Gunther Teubner, Michael King and Zenon Bankowski, for much valuable comment on and criticism of this paper as originally presented.

102   Law's New Boundaries

Jessop, B. 'The Economy, the State and the Law: Theories of Relative Autonomy and Autopoietic Closure', in G. Teubner and A. Febbrajo (eds), (1992), *State, Law and Economy as Autopoietic Systems*, Giuffre, Milano, pp. 187- 263.

Kelsen, H. (1989), *The Pure Theory of Law*, Peter Smith, Gloucester, Mass.

King, M. and Piper, C. (1995), *How the Law Thinks About Children*, 2nd edn., Gower, Aldershot.

La Torre, M. (1999), 'Legal Pluralism as Evolutionary Achievement of Community Law', 12 *Ratio Juris*, pp. 182-95.

Ladeur, K. H. (1999), *The Theory of Autopoiesis as an Approach to a Better Understanding of Postmodern Law: From the Hierarchy of Norms to the Heterarchy of Changing Patterns of Legal Inter-relationships*. EUI Working Paper LAW 99/3, European University Institute, Florence.

Lawson, F. H. (1951), *The Rational Strength of English Law*, Stevens, London.

Lempert, R. (1987), 'The Autonomy of Law: Two Visions Compared', in G. Teubner (ed.), *Autopoietic Law: A New Approach to Law and Society*, de Gruyter, Berlin, pp. 152-190.

Luhmann, N. (1986), 'The Self-Reproduction of Law and Its Limits' in G. Teubner (ed.), *Dilemmas of Law in the Welfare State*, de Gruyter, Berlin, pp. 111-27.

MacCormick, D. N. (1993), 'Beyond the Sovereign State?', 56 *Modern Law Review*, pp. 1-18.

Marquez, G. G. (1996), *Chronicle of a Death Foretold*, Penguin, London.

Nelken, D. (1987), 'Changing Paradigms in the Sociology of Law', in G. Teubner (ed.), *Autopoietic Law: A New Approach to Law and Society*, de Gruyter, Berlin, pp. 191-216.

Parsons, T. (1977), *The Evolution of Societies*, Prentice-Hall, Englewood Cliffs, NJ.

Paterson, J. (1996), 'Who Is Zenon Bankowski Talking To? The Person in the Sight of Autopoiesis' in D. Nelken (ed.), *Law as Communication*, Dartmouth, Aldershot, pp. 81-104.

Paterson, J. and Teubner, G. (1998), 'Changing Maps: Empirical Legal Autopoiesis', 7 *Social and Legal Studies*, pp. 451- 86.

Pennock, J. R. and Chapman, J. W. (eds), (1974), *The Limits of Law*, Lieber-Atherton, New York.

Petersen, H. and Zahle, H. (eds), (1995), *Legal Polycentricity: Consequences of Pluralism in Law*, Dartmouth, Aldershot.

Posner, R. A. (1987), 'The Decline of Law as an Autonomous Discipline: 1962-1987', 100 *Harvard Law Review*, pp. 761-80.

Raz, J. (1980), *The Concept of a Legal System: An Introduction to the Theory of Legal System*, 2nd edn., Clarendon Press, Oxford.

Rottleuthner, H. (1989), 'The Limits of Law: The Myth of a Regulatory Crisis', 17 *International Journal of the Sociology of Law*, pp. 273-85.

Santos, B. de S. (1987), 'Law - A Map of Misreading: Toward a Postmodern Conception of Law', 14 *Journal of Law and Society*, pp. 279-302.

Santos, B. de S. (1995), *Toward a New Common Sense: Law, Science and Politics in the Paradigmatic Transition*, Routledge, London.

Shiner, R. A. (1992), *Norm and Nature: The Movements of Legal Thought*, Clarendon Press, Oxford.

Teubner, G. (1987), 'Juridification - Concepts, Aspects, Limits, Solutions', in G. Teubner (ed.), *Juridification of Social Spheres: A Comparative Analysis in the Areas of Labour, Corporate, Antitrust and Social Welfare Law*, de Gruyter, Berlin, pp. 3-48.

Teubner, G. (1993), *Law as an Autopoietic System*, Blackwell, Oxford.

Teubner, G. (ed.), (1997), *Global Law Without a State*, Dartmouth, Aldershot.

Teubner, G. (1998), 'Legal Irritants: Good Faith in British Law or How Unifying Law Ends Up in New Divergences', 61 *Modern Law Review*, pp. 11-32.

The Representation of Law's Autonomy in Autopoiesis Theory   103

Van der Kerchove, M. and Ost, F. (1994), *Legal System Between Order and Disorder*, Oxford University Press, Oxford.

Waluchow, W.J. (1994), *Inclusive Legal Positivism*, Clarendon Press, Oxford.

Weber, M. (1978), *Economy and Society*, University of California Press, Berkeley.

Zolo, D. 'The Epistemological Status of the Theory of Autopoiesis and Its Applications to the Social Sciences' in G. Teubner and A. Febbrajo (eds), (1992), *State, Law and Economy*, Giuffre, Milano, pp. 67-124.

[10]
Images of Europe
in Sociolegal Traditions*

The referenda rejections in 2005 of the proposed European Union constitution, and their immediate consequences, have been described as the biggest crisis that the Union has faced. Contrary to what some have claimed, however, these referenda results have not derailed the European project, if this is taken to be an increasing political, economic and social integration of Europe. The momentum towards this integration may be unstoppable and there are no ultimately attractive alternatives to it. Nevertheless, recent events indicate that fresh thinking and new directions are needed. As much as at any previous time, Europe as an idea or as an image of the future demands examination. Many issues essential to this examination are about regulation – its scope and legitimacy, its democratic and cultural foundations and its social and economic effects. So it is clear that sociolegal scholars have an essential part to play in re-imagining Europe. Many are currently actively engaged in it.

In pursuing that engagement it should be remembered that concern with the nature of Europe goes back to the beginnings of modern social theory. Within the broader theme of European 'ways of law' this paper revisits general ideas of Europe that can be found in the work of some of the greatest sociolegal theorists. I hope to show that classic writings are still relevant to current issues about the European project; they help to link these issues to sociolegal traditions. What follows examines the images of Europe that are present in the work of three founders of these traditions – Eugen Ehrlich, Max Weber and Emile Durkheim – writing at the beginning of the twentieth century when Europe as a legal entity was only a dream. Then the paper contrasts these images with Jürgen Habermas' recent ideas on the European Union as a vehicle for a kind of cosmopolitanism. My argument is that – by imagining Europe as a sociolegal entity – these past and present sociolegal theorists together provide a valuable map of issues about regulatory aspects of the European project that remain centrally important today.

* A revised version of the text of a plenary lecture delivered at the First European Sociolegal Conference, Oñati (Gipuzkoa), Spain, July 6th 2005. I am grateful to Kenneth Armstrong for valuable references on European Union law.

Ehrlich and the End of Empire

Eugen Ehrlich's significance here is in pioneering the study, in modern European law, of legal pluralism – 'the presence in a social field of more than one legal order' (Griffiths 1986: 1). The 'living law' that Ehrlich studied empirically grows out of everyday life rather than being imposed or codified by the state. Intimately embedded in custom and experience and varying between different population groups, it is learned not in law schools but in 'the university of life' and needs no state legitimation to give it authority (Ehrlich 1936). It points to social diversity confronting juristic universals.

Ehrlich's distinction between living law and state law is formulated in a specifically European context, that of the old Austro-Hungarian Empire, made up of many nationalities, languages and cultures. Ehrlich's academic base, the Franz-Josef University of Czernowitz in the Bukowina, now part of Ukraine, was often seen, in a late-nineteenth century Western European imagination, as a symbolic bastion of German culture at the eastern edge of Europe (Likhovski 2003: 640) Some Austrian settlers in the Bukowina thought they were there to protect 'Europe against the wild hordes who kept breaking in from the East.'[1] As for Ehrlich, the loyal servant of a fragile state, all his cultural and intellectual allegiances seem to have been turned westwards. His reference point was the European community of German-speaking jurists and, beyond that, modern Western law and culture as a whole. But his geographical placement made him aware that modern European law must address multiculturalism, and the varied regulatory expectations of different populations held together in a single legal frame. As David Nelken (1984) has insisted, Ehrlich is not a theorist of 'law in action', like Roscoe Pound. He wished not so much to impose state law effectively as to negotiate legal unity through appreciation of difference. In a sense, he is a prophet of subsidiarity, or perhaps of a Europe of the regions. But these political-administrative notions seem pale and thin, set alongside Ehrlich's passionate cultural concern with the diversity of social associations.

Although he is a great pioneer, we should not ask more of his work than it can offer. It quickly attracted criticism for its conceptual imprecision and failure to connect with wider sociological scholarship (Vinogradoff 1928: 224). Living law is an opaque idea, mixing values, traditions, affective and instrumental elements indiscriminately. It treats the social as an analytically undifferentiated phenomenon, the categories of living law being given meaning only by their correspondence with lawyers' legal categories (Cotterrell 2006b). If Ehrlich points to a need to consider Europe pluralistically, the question of what constitutes this plurality for regulatory purposes remains unanswered.

---

1   Gregor von Rezzori, quoted in Likhovski 2003: 640.

In more recent times, legal pluralism has often been invoked in sociolegal studies of Europe. Europe clearly contains many kinds of 'official' regulation or 'lawyers'' law. Recent literature discusses the interrelation of different types of regulation, sometimes contrasting European 'hard' law with 'soft' law, 'co-regulation' and self-regulation (see e.g. Senden 2005). Official law in the European context is sometimes seen in a hierarchy, with national law viewed as most developed, European Union law as intermediate and international law as least developed (Zürn and Wolf 1999). Writers such as André-Jean Arnaud (1995) and Massimo La Torre (1999) have characterised the interpenetration of regimes of European regulation in explicitly legal pluralist terms (see also Delmas-Marty 2002: 147–9). Joanne Scott and David Trubek have explored tensions between what they call the 'classic Community method' of legal regulation and various kinds of 'new governance' in the European context (Scott and Trubek 2002). Christopher Harding has surveyed Europe's 'rich and interrelated patchwork of legal "regimes", "orders" or "spaces"' (Harding 2000: 129), these being best seen as distinct normative fields rather than legal systems. For Francis Snyder (1999), Europe is a meeting place of regulatory regimes that have sources or centres not necessarily inside its boundaries. For Volkmar Gessner (1994), acute legal cultural differences within Europe pose major problems for European legal integration.

Few of these studies have direct links to Ehrlich but underlying issues that they imply have long been discussed in relation to his work. What is a legal pluralist approach for? For Ehrlich it is to remind the state about the existence of the social, and to remind jurists and philosophers that talking about 'society' without empirically studying its diversity is inadequate. He was well placed to issue these warnings. A scholar of legal pluralism should be, like Ehrlich, central and peripheral at the same time: an *insider-outsider*, engaged with and expert in the various types of official law but also mentally distanced from them and sensitive to many kinds of social regulation that are entirely outside lawyers' normal experience. To be such an insider-outsider consistently is not easy. This is surely one reason why social scientific legal pluralism remains less intellectually central in sociolegal studies than it deserves to be. European lawyers usually know much more about the law of the Union than about its diverse populations and their expectations. Yet this must surely change if the remoteness of European institutions from Europe's populations is to be reduced.

Ehrlich was one of the first modern writers to study empirically the *moral distance* between regulators and regulated. Law morally distanced from the regulated appears inflexible, impressionistic (ignorant of social facts), too generalised, too absolutist in its values or democratically weak (Cotterrell 1995: 305). Often it is all of these. In Europe these problems are clear enough.

But, in addressing them, Ehrlich's living law concept needs replacing with more precise characterisations of basic types of communal relations (built on shared values, common heritage, convergent projects or emotional ties) (see generally Cotterrell 2006a). The different regulatory problems which these abstract types of relationships pose need to be separated, and sociolegal inquiry should analyse the ways in which the types combine in complex ways in social experience.

Ehrlich's social scientifically-oriented legal pluralism requires empirical study of social life combined with sensitivity to juristic concepts. By contrast, what has been called juristic legal pluralism requires the study of different *juristically-recognised* legal regimes co-existing in the same social space (Griffiths 1986). Juristic legal pluralism is easily seen in Europe with its many overlapping, intersecting forms of state and European law. But a clear distinction between juristic and social scientific legal pluralism is hard to make today. As new forms of regulation and governance develop, sharp lines between juristic law and social regulation become controversial. It may be that Europe is now a particularly important laboratory in which the reshaping of the very idea of law is taking place.

Juristic legal pluralism has been associated with the treatment of indigenous law in colonial territories, or with situations where 'the sovereign commands different bodies of law for different groups of the population varying by ethnicity, religion, nationality, or geography' or where 'parallel legal regimes are all dependent on the state legal system' (Merry 1988: 871). None of these cases is that of contemporary Europe. But conflicts, disagreements or inconsistencies arise as different European and state agencies create and interpret official law and regulation. Unresolved differences in the effective meaning of legal rules or procedures may arise through contrasting practices of different governmental agencies (e.g. Graver 1990; and see Dalberg-Larson 2000: 103–14), for example between courts and administrative or enforcement agencies, or between different court systems. And contrasts in legal interpretive cultures may exist between different member states in the European context (Gessner 1994: 134–6). The potential is for a legal plurality that is official in some senses, unofficial in others, and demands both juristic and sociological recognition.

The pluralist message in sociolegal inquiry still remains the same as it was in Ehrlich's time: law's meaning and authority are never to be taken for granted and are often a matter of competition and struggle. In this context, the diverse perceptions of the regulated are important because law must have moral meaning for those it addresses. Ehrlich's still salient challenge is to minimise moral distance and ensure law's meaningfulness in this sense. The crucial political issues are: What should be seen as the 'units' of plurality? And how much plurality must European law recognise or deny, if it is to be both authoritative and responsive?

Weber and European Government

Sociolegal scholars know Max Weber best as the classic theorist of modern legal rationality and for his historical studies of rationalisation processes – in, for example, economy, government, law, religion and art – which he associated with the West's uniqueness. European history is Weber's primary focus. 'The tremendous after-effect of Roman law... stands out in nothing more clearly than the fact that everywhere the [European] revolution of political management in the direction of the evolving rational state has been borne by trained jurists. This also occurred in England, although there the great national guilds of jurists hindered the reception of Roman law.' Weber insists: 'There is no analogy to this process to be found in any [other] area of the world.' Thus, Europe's governmental traditions are unique and pervaded by the 'spirit of the jurists' (Weber 1948: 93, 94).[2]

This idea of a Europe of juristically-managed official rules merges easily with familiar Weberian images of bureaucratic and technical administration and the 'iron cage' (Weber 1930: 181) – the regulation and routine that he sees as becoming the welcome prison of modern individuals who 'need "order" and nothing but order' and are 'nervous and cowardly' whenever this order is threatened (Weber quoted in Mayer 1956: 127-8). Formal legal rationality underpins the legitimacy and efficiency of the modern European bureaucratic state, even if substantive demands on law can disrupt it and even if rational administration is actually only an island in a sea of non-rational (for Weber, non-rule governed) social action in citizens' everyday lives (Brubaker 1984).

Though formal legal rationality and the bureaucratic state are the topics of Weber's work that are most familiar in sociolegal scholarship, they are only part of the picture of modern government that he provides, and arguably, for Weber himself, the politically less important part. To appreciate this, we should look more closely at his idea of legal domination (authority based on a system of formally integrated rational rules) and then at what must supplement it.

Legal domination provides, for Weber, the basic legitimacy of modern administrative structures such as those of European states. This legitimacy requires no sovereign power and so it can surely apply to a rule system and bureaucracy extending beyond states, such as that of the European Union. But this is not simply legitimacy produced by legality. Apart from customary or

---

2   For an interesting discussion of the ambiguities of Weber's views on Europe's uniqueness see Harrington 2003: 12–16.

purely emotional bases of allegiance, which Weber distinguishes from legal domination, allegiance to an order (or regulatory structure) as legitimate can, for him, be purpose-rational (that is, instrumental) or value-rational (that is, the order represents ultimate values which are themselves accepted as legitimate). Weber saw natural law theory as the last viable value-basis of political legitimacy in Europe. Thus, after the decline of natural law, legal domination could only be instrumentally based (Cotterrell 1995: ch 7).

In other words, the web of rules, the iron cage, is accepted because its overall *usefulness* is accepted. It provides a framework of order in which individuals' projects can be pursued and their security guaranteed. If positive law's authority in the modern state seems unassailable this is because the sheer complexity and scale of this law normally prevent anyone seeing enough of it to be able realistically to question its utility as a whole, that is, to deny the worth of the established rule of law.

Could, however, the seemingly self-sustaining character of legal domination break down when a *choice* becomes possible between rule-systems, for example between the laws of European member states and the regulatory structures of the European Union? Perhaps some issues in the 2005 referenda on the European constitution can be seen in this light. Individuals may sometimes have the chance to choose which prison of order and security to inhabit, which iron cage to submit to. My argument is that Weber's logic does not necessarily point to the idea of law as a self-founding system – an idea that leads towards contemporary autopoiesis theory or some postmodernist positions. His ultimate sociological focus on the individual social actor prevents a move to systems-thinking as such.

We might go on to ask why the iron cage is, in Weber's portrayal, such a dismal place. Surely it is not because of its rule-governed nature, which should provide a framework for individual freedom and security. It is because of its changelessness, its inertia and cocoon-like stillness. This must be why Weber's political sociology devotes so much attention to the question of *leadership* – the capacity for dynamic political action. If this question is rarely addressed by sociolegal scholars it may be because Weber's ideal of political leadership seems to stand in stark opposition to the governance of rules.

In a famous conversation with the military commander General Ludendorff, at the end of World War I, when the question of a new form of government for Germany needed to be settled, Weber unequivocally advocated plebiscitarian democracy, under which the people directly elect a leader. They give him a free hand in government ('…the chosen man says, "Now shut your mouths and obey me."'). Then, at the end of his term of office, the people judge, again by plebiscite, throwing him from power if they think he has failed.[3] Such a leader

---

3   The Weber-Ludendorff conversation is quoted in Marianne Weber 1975: 653.

stands above parliamentary processes or bureaucratic structures, exemplifying a kind of charismatic rather than legal domination (Weber 1968: 266–9). On a different occasion, speaking as a sociologist rather than a political advocate, Weber noted that a plebiscitary process of leader election (which he observed in the United States and some European countries) may in practice be a caucus system, involving exchanges of favours and party machines (Weber 1948: 103–11). The process may be one of public acclamation or private bargaining. Either way, leaders, good or bad, emerge. Weber's value-free sociology merely observes this process as a necessary complement to legal domination.

What significance do these ideas have in today's European context? Weber's advocacy of the plebiscite – or referendum – is linked with his ambivalence about parliamentary government. His plebiscite preserves democracy of a kind against the impasse of irreconcilable conflicts of interest in a diverse population and is a means of directly, if only momentarily, linking leaders and led, leap-frogging over the layers of rule-bound bureaucracy that often characterise modern European governmental structures. Weber's emphasis on a populist rather than parliamentary basis of democracy brings to mind Carl Schmitt here. Schmitt's solution to what he saw as the impasses of liberal parliamentarianism was to call for a homogeneity of the populace (and so of leaders and led) at least as regards acceptance of the unifying mythical bases of sovereignty (e.g. Schmitt 1988). By contrast, Weber seems to accept social, political and cultural diversity and conflict as normal and to seek a strong legitimation of leadership despite these. The message is surely that, while the iron cage is here to stay and more or less legitimates itself in normal conditions, modern political societies need direction from leaders created and given legitimacy by means that escape everyday bureaucratic routine or ad hoc compromises.

Weber has remarkably little to say about constitutions. Can there be a plebiscitarian *constitutionalism*? This seems to be what was recently attempted in the European Union – legitimation of a constitutional document by referendum. But how is a constitution's legitimacy to be judged in Weberian terms? Alongside its instrumental aspects as part of a structure of legal domination, the constitution's symbolic aspects are surely relevant (see e.g. Cotterrell 1996; Witteveen 1993). An aura surrounds a successful constitution. This is projected on to it, as assumed qualities are projected on to a charismatic leader. Assumptions are made about its provenance and what it stands for. This aura is a basis of emotional allegiance as in Weberian charismatic domination – ideas and associated feelings are created that go beyond the words of the document, just as legends of the charismatic leader's prowess or wisdom may outstrip the evidence that supports them. But how is it possible to imbue a document with charisma? For Weber, charisma is irrational, a crystallisation of emotional power that social science cannot predict. How to ensure an adequate supplement to legal domination in contemporary politics thus remains, for Weber, unfathomable.

Yet he provides lessons worth remembering in a European context. Utility is surely a very important basis of legitimacy: a legal order that is assumed to be compatible with the best chance of personal security and prosperity derives powerful legitimacy from that assumed compatibility. But European law is not inevitably self-legitimating and its legitimacy based on utility can sometimes be questioned. In any case, this kind of legitimacy is enough only for those who are content to be sleepy, docile inhabitants of the iron cage.

Durkheim and European Legal Values

Emile Durkheim declared in 1907 that 'beyond this country [France], there is another in the process of forming, enveloping our nation; it is the country of Europe [*patrie européenne*] or of humanity' (Durkheim 1987: 294). Weber, at much the same time, viewed Europe as a continent of competing states, his own, Germany, standing between Anglo-American power and, as he thought, the threat of Russia (Jaspers 1989: 53–54). Durkheim doubted that separate European states would disappear, yet his vision of Europe's future is entirely different from Weber's. It is not arrived at through analysis of structures of state power but by elaborating a view of European *values*: Europe, in Durkheim's view, could become unified in so far as its nation states gradually turned to cultivate these values which were objectively necessary for each of them as complex modern societies. The appropriate values of each nation would tend to become the uniform values of all. Thus, the distinction between cosmopolitanism and nationalism would break down. Durkheim sees European nations as, in certain respects, 'all part of the same society, still incohesive, it is true, but one becoming increasingly conscious of itself' (Durkheim 1984: 76–77, 337). Twenty-one years after he published these words in *The Division of Labour in Society*, World War I broke out and the 'short' twentieth century (Hobsbawm 1994) began. In it, European nation states tried, by every available means, to dominate, defeat or destroy each other.

What is to be made of Durkheim's ideas today? He is not a federalist: a confederation of European states could be only 'like an individual state, having its own identity and its own interests and features. It would not be humanity' (Durkheim 1957: 74). He might be called a cosmopolitan nationalist. If each state aimed not to expand its borders at the expense of others, he suggests, 'but to set its own house in order and to make the widest appeal to its members for a moral life on an ever higher level, then all discrepancy between national and human morals would be excluded... civic duties would be only a particular form of the general obligations of humanity' (1957: 74). Societies could 'have their pride, not in being the greatest or the wealthiest, but in being the most just, the best organised and in possessing the best moral constitution' (1957: 75). But this, he recognises, is only an ideal: Europeans' allegiance, for now, is to their own state and its well-being, if necessary at the expense of others.

Ultimately Durkheim's sociology of law grounds these ideals, suggesting reasons for their appropriateness. But sociolegal readings of Durkheim have generally been misleading, being centred mainly on the treatment of law in his first book, *The Division of Labour* (Durkheim 1984). Little attempt has been made until very recently to explore the wholly different and much more satisfactory approach taken in the fragmentary but extensive discussions of law in his later writings. Durkheim 'Mark I', the Durkheim familiar in sociolegal studies, is the Durkheim of the index thesis, which rigidly links a distinction between mechanical and organic solidarity with one between repressive and restitutive law. Durkheim 'Mark II', who starts to emerge around 1897–8, some four years after *The Division of Labour* was first published, no longer writes about repressive and restitutive law as indices or visible representations of solidarity and avoids use of the mechanical/organic solidarity opposition altogether. Instead, he writes about law, in all its forms, as an expression of values. He associates modern (European) society with a particular, distinctive value system, which he calls the 'cult of the individual' or – with overtones of Comte and Rousseau – the religion of humanity (Cotterrell 1999: ch 7).

The cult of the individual, or *individualism* (Durkheim 1969) is entirely opposed to contemporary neo-liberal celebration of the individual, which speaks incessantly of individual freedom and choice and rarely of individual duties to others. Durkheimian individualism demands respect for the autonomy and dignity of all individuals, whoever and whatever they are. If it celebrates individual rights, these are, at base, human rights, for which each person qualifies equally. And it demands that one should promote *other* individuals' rights at least as much as one's own. The cult of the individual is the opposite of a cult of egoism. Durkheim plots the halting progress of this altruistic individualism in contract, criminal, property, succession and family law and in penology (Cotterrell 1999: chs 5, 7, 8 and 9). Whereas, in *The Division of Labour*, forms of law are seen as directly reflecting forms of social solidarity, Durkheim's later work suggests no such automatic link. One can say only that complex, diverse, modern societies are most likely to achieve solidarity under a value system that recognises and welcomes difference (for example, in beliefs, ambitions, experiences and allegiances) between individuals but treats every individual as deserving equal respect and dignity. If such a value system is in fact developing in Europe it is for complex and unique historical reasons, with religious (primarily Christian), economic, political and other influences. But in advanced European societies, where occupational specialisation and functional differentiation have developed very extensively, such a value system is more conducive to social solidarity than any other. So it might be expected to be favoured officially and elaborated in law.

When or if a 'European nation' materialises, for Durkheim it is less likely to be unified politically than by common adherence to the cult of the individual, the only value system that can be universally meaningful in a modern European society. Is his view of the possibility of value consensus naive? I do not think so. He narrows shared values down to the minimum; the most basic, irreducible formula. And his writings are cautious (or at least ambiguous) as to whether the cult of the individual will ultimately be internalised by Europe's populations, or remain only an official value system which the state will try (no doubt with numerous lapses) to apply in policy and law. In fact, many aspects of individualism as Durkheim understands it are invoked in literature on the idea of Europe, and treated as 'European values' in some sense.

For example, taking an individual's life is a gross affront to the cult of the individual, which condemns all assaults on an individual's body. So Europe's firm current rejection of capital punishment is clearly mandated by it. So also is the general discarding of corporal punishment. Consumer protection and controls on unfettered market freedom are aspects of Durkheim's idea of 'just contracts'. Welfare rights contribute to a universalisation of individual dignity and autonomy, and so express individualism. Clearly this is also true of such basic protections as the principle of no punishment without trial, and no punishment without a proven crime. Most obviously, the cult of the individual is expressed in human rights. Thus, the sociologist Göran Therborn claims, Europe has become 'an area of human rights, more binding than in any other area of the world' (quoted in Habermas 2001b: 20). He also refers to trade unionism, collective bargaining, universal welfare provision and the rights of women and children as 'all held more legitimate in Europe than in the rest of the contemporary world' (quoted in Habermas 2001b: 10). If there has been a recent decline in support for the first three of these it goes along with suspicions that in practice they have tended to favour sectional interests. Scepticism here is often consistent with Durkheimian individualism and not a rejection of it.

Is the cult of the individual simply liberalism? I think not. Durkheimian individualism is rooted in a specific historical context and related only to a particular kind of society. It is sociologically, not philosophically justified, by its relevance to the distinct characteristics of that society – vastly diversified, complex, heterogeneous, technologically and economically advanced. By contrast, liberalism tends to treat its outlook as universally valid, not tied to specific historical conditions. Liberals often demand democracy, elections or human rights everywhere in the world, and see no need to reinterpret values in relation to specific social contexts. But, for Durkheim, values are never philosophical absolutes. They are justified by the nature of the kind of society in which they exist. His writing about the cult of the individual is always in a modern western European context. Liberal human rights are universal and absolute, but for Durkheim all rights are socially produced, as is the very idea of the individual in the fullest sense (Durkheim 1960).

I think that the complacency at the heart of Durkheim's thinking lies not in his analysis of the cult of the individual but in his assumption that social solidarity *must* be significant in complex contemporary societies. Is solidarity needed? Is extensive mutual trust necessary to social life? Or does impersonal confidence in systems replace personal trust in each other (cf Luhmann 1979: Part 1)? Could the pursuit of Weberian purpose-rationality by citizens following rational law be enough to secure order in society without solidarity? Durkheim does not provide an adequate sociological explanation of what he treats as nascent European values, and so of European law and society. Neither can he give much guidance in understanding and confronting the gross affronts to moral individualism that historical emergencies often provoke. But he reminds us that a certain idea of solidarity does *matter* in modern European culture. By relating it systematically to law and legal values he highlights its practical relevance to the building of European institutions.

Habermas and European Cosmopolitanism

Why does solidarity matter? Recently, Jürgen Habermas (2001b: 20, 21) has suggested that a 'painful learning process' has led Europeans to value solidarity and build institutions to foster and protect it: 'In the course of painful, if not fatal struggles, [Europe]... has learnt how to cope with deep cleavages, schisms and rivalries between secular and ecclesiastical powers, city and countryside, faith and knowledge, and how to get along with endemic conflicts between militant religious confessions and belligerent states.' Perhaps it has learnt by direct *experience* that modern nations cannot bomb or terrorise each other into permanent submission, and that the best way to live is to respect *difference*, to co-ordinate it in structures of *interdependence* and to frame it with legal protections of individual *dignity* and *autonomy*. Habermas sees, as part of contemporary European political culture, a tendency to self-criticism and an avoidance of absolutes that history has often shown to be disastrous. The excesses of nationalism have given way to a willingness to pool sovereignty in European Union institutions; the futility of class conflict has given way to a pride in welfare states (Habermas and Derrida 2003: 294, 297). This characterisation of European values is consistent with Durkheim's, but historical rather than sociological. Maybe the difference is not great: both writers see distinctively European conditions as making these values meaningful.[4] Habermas maps what he sees as a European outlook. Secularisation is relatively far advanced and there is a relative trust in the state's organisational and steering capacities, as well as a recognition of the limits of what markets can achieve, a preference for welfare state guarantees of social security, and a desire for a multilateral and legally regulated international order. The benefits of technological progress are not seen with naive optimism and there is a relatively low threshold of tolerance of the use of force against individuals (Habermas and Derrida 2003: 295–6). Each listed item seems to invite a comparison with Europe's great moral competitor across the Atlantic and words are not minced. Europe must confront 'the blunt hegemonic politics of its ally', which are 'the unilateral, world-ordering politics of a self-appointed hegemon'. In international relations, 'the normative authority of the United States of America lies in ruins' and its recent actions have set disastrous precedents for the world's future superpowers to follow (Habermas 2003: 703, 706; Habermas and Derrida 2003: 295).

Given the centrality of law in Habermas' work it is unsurprising that he discusses European legal structures in the light of his general sociolegal theory. He sees legal and moral rules as complementary but distinct kinds of action norms, valid action norms being those 'to which all possibly affected persons could agree as participants in rational discourses' (Habermas 1996: 107). Morality, on this view, is a diffuse cultural knowledge justifiable discursively, but law has a more focused institutional dimension. It requires a procedure of democratic lawmaking: 'only those statutes may claim legitimacy that can meet with the assent of all citizens in a discursive process of legislation that in turn has been legally constituted' (1996: 110). Citizens must be able to see themselves as authors of the rules they live by. In this process of law creation, not just a universalistic morality is relevant, but also pragmatics (reasoning aimed at securing particular chosen goals) and ethics (values specific to the particular individual or community). Thus, while morality relates to humanity as a whole, legal rules always relate to 'a concrete society... a geographically delimited legal territory' (1996: 124).

---

4   James Whitman (2000) argues that, while contemporary European law strongly emphasises 'human dignity', this concept is largely absent from American legal culture. A Durkheimian approach would, however, suggest that some notion of individual human dignity and autonomy should be a key value for all highly developed, complex, differentiated societies. A Habermasian approach, by contrast, might emphasise the significance of Europe's distinctive history in shaping its particular contemporary understanding of human dignity as a legal idea.

Pablo De Greiff (2002) has pointed out the ambiguity in Habermas' formulations here. Norms are valid only if all potentially affected persons could agree on them; the legitimacy of legal norms, however, is determined in a delimited territory. But many laws apply extraterritorially or affect people beyond their jurisdiction. Does this mean that, to secure full legitimacy, law should eventually become *cosmopolitan*, both its applicability and its validity judged in processes that transcend the borders of all nation-state legal systems? Does it mean that state law should at least be supplemented by cosmopolitan law – a world law of humanity, not limited by jurisdictional boundaries – given that in contemporary conditions the effects of laws can be felt anywhere? Or does it mean only that a universal morality is available as a reference point for critique of state law? In any case, Habermas suggests, the nation state is too weak in the face of transnational economic, political and other influences adequately to protect democracy, human rights and its own mechanisms of solidarity, such as the welfare state.

Habermas defends a strong politico-legal structure for Europe as a way of defending European values and bases of solidarity in the face of globalisation and the declining power of nation states (Habermas 1999; Grewal 2001). A fully cosmopolitan law may be impossible because any 'political community that wants to understand itself as a democracy must at least distinguish between members and non-members.... This ethical-political self-understanding of citizens of a particular democratic life is missing in the inclusive community of world citizens' (Habermas 2001a: 107). In other words, cosmopolitanism abolishes boundaries but any legitimate (democratically founded) legal system requires them. The European Union, however, has such boundaries and Habermas (2001b: 23) insists that any constitution for it must clearly delimit these. In part, therefore, the EU seems to be envisaged, perhaps in the absence of anything better, as a legal bearer of cosmopolitan values (Fine and Smith 2003: 482-3),[5] alongside a reformed United Nations (Zolo 1999).

For Habermas, any process of constitution-making is a public discourse in which free and equal participants seek to agree about the rights they must mutually recognise to regulate their common life legitimately by law (Habermas 2000: 523). And, for him, a constitution should be, in itself, a focus of patriotism. Its universal moral aspect is its affirmation of human rights and democratic participation. Its 'local' element is its elaboration of these principles in a specific political culture (Fine and Smith 2003: 471). Habermas seems to envisage that 'constitutional patriotism' could be wholly or partly detached

---

5 Habermas' linking of Europe and cosmopolitanism can be compared with Durkheim's no less bizarre occasional use of 'Europe' and 'humanity' as near synonyms. Ultimately, however, Durkheim's sociological interpretation of individualism ties it not to humanity but to modern, complex, highly differentiated societies.

from nationalism, and this is what the European Union must eventually aim to achieve. If it can do so, it bypasses all 'no-*demos*' arguments; that is, it would show that a European *demos* (a homogeneous people) is not needed for European politico-legal identity. A different focus of unity – appropriate to Europe's multicultural, mobile and diverse society – could be secured via a constitution.

The key to this argument is in Habermas' civic conception of the nation 'which exists neither independently nor prior to the democratic process from which it springs' (2001b: 15). Civic (as opposed to ethnic) solidarity is produced in a circular process by which democracy and the nation state stabilize each other. Thus, democratic citizenship establishes an abstract, legally mediated solidarity between strangers and a constitution can play a vital role in the process by which a stable polity is created. A European constitution, for example, could have a 'catalytic' effect, changing the foci of European politics and social movements. Quite apart from the fact that it is needed to govern a newly enlarged European Union, the process of making it would provide 'a unique opportunity for transnational communication... a Europe-wide debate' (2001b: 16, 17). Thus, such a constitution has an innovative role. Its catalytic effect might be the equivalent of the inspirational role of Weber's charismatic leader.

Conclusion

Clearly, for the moment, things are not turning out as Habermas envisages. Recent debates on the proposed European constitution were often not Europe-wide as far as the general public was concerned. They were, for the most part, firmly based in national and local contexts, despite the efforts of Habermas and others to speak across frontiers to rally a 'European' opinion (e.g. Habermas and Derrida 2003). Law needs meaningful substance as well as form, and the substance of European law must come from the European society that it is to regulate. Habermas' view seems to be that a constitution can help to form a *demos* (see also Grewal 2001: 121). But empirical sociolegal scholars are likely to seek much more concrete evidence of processes of European will-formation and opinion-formation than Habermas' mainly abstract references to communication and discourse provide. There seems a deep complacency in Habermas' claims about the potential of a constitution produced by 'officials', and presented ready-formed for the acclamation of a vast, disparate European populace.

The shadow of Carl Schmitt has not entirely disappeared. The issue of sovereignty remains. When European states pool part of their sovereignty, it is necessary to ask where the pooled part resides, and how it is to be conceptualised.

Weber's ideas on charisma and leadership remain significant here. The idea that charisma might attach to a constitution is close to Habermas' idea of the constitution's catalytic effect. But charisma is, for Weber, inexplicable and constitutional catalysis might be wishful thinking. Certainly Habermas does not explain its source or even its nature. Much more analysis is needed to identify what a particular constitution represents – as an expression of ultimate values or beliefs, a framework for the pursuit of citizens' interests and an embodiment of traditions. Most problematic here are emotional aspects of allegiance. It is the *emotional* character of charisma that makes it, for Weber, so resistant to sociological analysis. But the European Union, like any state, needs symbols, memories and myths that can be the foci or catalysts of emotional attachment.

None of the theorists discussed in this paper implies clear solutions to Europe's notorious democratic deficit. For Ehrlich, living under a benevolently pragmatic autocracy governing through compromises, the problem was not purely one of lack of democracy, but more generally of moral distance: how are regulators to rule with a sophisticated understanding of and sympathy for the regulated? Both Durkheim and Habermas toy with the idea that democracy is as much about effective, conscientious and well-informed deliberation to serve a common good as it is about formal popular representation (Habermas 2001a: 110–11; Fine and Smith 2003: 476–7; Cotterrell 1999: ch 10). Again the central problem is perceived as one of moral distance and the key to legitimacy is in varied mechanisms for overcoming it in different contexts.

As we have seen, Durkheim and Habermas also have much to say about European *values*. The building of Europe may well depend on clarifying, defending and strengthening these values by setting them in both a functional sociological context and a critical interpretation of Europe's history. But nothing justifies claims that these values are unalterable, uncontroversial, secure, consistently applied or free from ambiguity or hypocrisy. The trajectory of history that, for the moment, makes a commitment to a certain kind of moral individualism a reasonable outcome of 'painful learning' may not continue to do so. As Durkheim recognised, the cult of the individual needs continuous reinforcement through law, education and collective reflection on experience. Again, while certain core European values can be identified, they are strictly limited in scope, as a basis for regulation. They cannot justify coercion to life-style uniformity – as, for example, in the prohibition of all religiously-mandated forms of dress (see e.g. Shadid and Van Koningsveld 2005) or behaviour.[6] Rather, they are a blueprint for unity within difference, the moral integration of

---

6   An important test would surely be whether these forms substantially prevent or seriously impede processes of social communication and interaction that are fundamental in fostering mutual respect, and individual dignity and autonomy, for all citizens within a diverse society.

social and cultural diversity, and for promoting mutual respect. Durkheimian individualism is necessarily a *thin* value system but its protection and extension throughout Europe should nevertheless be central to the European project. The appeal to a common European history and experience that underpins some of Habermas' discussions also emphasizes the continuing significance of shared *tradition*, in a broad sense, in European identity. But Europe is divided as well as united by its collective memory. For example, contemporary views of Europe as an environment of co-existence are inevitably influenced by different understandings of the history of changes in its internal and external political, national, linguistic and other boundaries. Up to a point, law can mediate between or influence these understandings or their effects (Misztal 2003).

By contrast, Weber's emphasis on the legitimating power of rules that seem to guarantee order and security within which people can pursue their projects, reminds us of the importance of purely *instrumental* foundations of European cohesion. European Union regulation must be designed so that in general it seems to its citizens to be an appropriate overall framework in which to pursue their economic and other projects, and more obviously appropriate than any alternative general structure of legal regulation that could realistically be envisaged.

Perhaps it can be said at least, on the basis of this paper's account of classic and contemporary theory, that sociolegal traditions allow us to identify many different regulatory aspects of European organisation. These resources help in clarifying problems and in pointing out directions for their possible solution. Most importantly, they illustrate, through their contrasting emphases, that the European project in its regulatory aspects demands attention to tradition, to ultimate values or beliefs, to the everyday demands of utility and to elusive emotional components of association and allegiance. In this irreducible complexity lie both the difficulty and the promise of the idea of Europe today.

References

Arnaud, A.-J. (1995) 'Legal Pluralism and the Building of Europe' in H. Petersen and H. Zahle eds., *Legal Polycentricity: Consequences of Pluralism in Law*, pp. 149–69 (Aldershot: Dartmouth).

Brubaker, R. (1984) *The Limits of Rationality: An Essay on the Social and Moral Thought of Max Weber* (London: George Allen & Unwin).

Cotterrell, R. (1995) *Law's Community: Legal Theory in Sociological Perspective* (Oxford: Clarendon Press).

— (1996) 'Some Aspects of the Communication of Constitutional Authority' in D. Nelken ed., *Law as Communication*, pp. 129–51 (Aldershot: Dartmouth).

Roger Cotterrell 161

— (1999) *Emile Durkheim: Law in a Moral Domain* (Stanford: Stanford University Press / Edinburgh: Edinburgh University Press).

— (2006a) *Law, Culture and Society: Legal Ideas in the Mirror of Social Theory* (Aldershot: Ashgate).

— (2006b) 'Living Law Revisited: Communitarianism and Sociology of Law' in P. Van Seters ed., *Communitarianism in Law and Society*, pp. 17–32 (Lanham: Rowman and Littlefield).

Dalberg-Larson, J. (2000) *The Unity of Law: An Illusion? On Legal Pluralism in Theory and Practice* (Glienicke, Berlin: Galda & Wilch Verlag).

De Greiff, P. (2002) 'Habermas on Nationalism and Cosmopolitanism' 15 *Ratio Juris* 418–38.

Delmas-Marty, M. (2002) *Towards a Truly Common Law: Europe as a Laboratory for Legal Pluralism*, transl. N. Norberg (Cambridge: Cambridge University Press).

Durkheim, E. (1957) *Professional Ethics and Civic Morals*, transl. C. Brookfield (London: Routledge & Kegan Paul).

— (1960) 'The Dualism of Human Nature and Its Social Conditions' in K.H. Wolff ed., *Essays on Sociology and Philosophy by Emile Durkheim et al.*, pp. 325–40 (New York: Harper & Row reprint, 1964).

— (1969) 'Individualism and the Intellectuals' reprinted in W.S.F. Pickering ed., *Durkheim on Religion: A Selection of Readings with Bibliographies*, pp. 59–73 London: Routledge & Kegan Paul, 1975).

— (1984) *The Division of Labour in Society*, transl. W.D. Halls (London: Macmillan).

— (1987) *La science sociale et l'action*, 2nd edn. (Paris: Presses Universitaires de France).

Ehrlich, E. (1936) *Fundamental Principles of the Sociology of Law*, transl. W.L. Moll (New Brunswick: Transaction Publishers reprint, 2002).

Fine, R. and Smith, W. (2003) 'Jürgen Habermas's Theory of Cosmopolitanism' 10 *Constellations* 469-87.

Gessner, V. (1994) 'Global Legal Interaction and Legal Cultures' 7 *Ratio Juris* 132–45.

Graver, H.P. (1990) 'Administrative Decision-Making and the Concept of Law' in A. Görlitz and R. Voigt eds., *Postinterventionistisches Recht*, pp. 177–94 (Pfaffenweiler: Centaurus Verlagsgesellschaft).

Grewal, S.S. (2001) 'The Paradox of Integration: Habermas and the Unfinished Project of European Union' 21 *Politics* 114–23.

Griffiths, J. (1986) 'What Is Legal Pluralism?' 24 *Journal of Legal Pluralism* 1–55.

Habermas, J. (1996) *Between Facts and Norms: Contributions to a Discourse Theory of Law and Democracy*, transl. W. Rehg (Cambridge: Polity).

— (1999) 'The European Nation-State and the Pressures of Globalization' 235 *New Left Review*, 1st ser. 46–59.

— (2000) 'Remarks on Erhard Denninger's Triad of Diversity, Security and Solidarity' 7 *Constellations* 522–8.

— (2001a) *The Postnational Constellation: Political Essays* (Cambridge: Polity).

— (2001b) 'Why Europe Needs a Constitution' 11 *New Left Review* 2nd ser. 5–26.

— (2003) 'Interpreting the Fall of a Monument' 4 *German Law Journal* 701–8.

Habermas, J. and Derrida, J. (2003) 'February 15, or What Binds Europeans Together: A Plea for a Common Policy, Beginning in the Core of Europe' 10 *Constellations* 291–7.

Harding, C. (2000) 'The Identity of European Law: Mapping Out the European Legal Space' 6 *European Law Journal* 128–47.

Harrington, A. (2003) *Concepts of Europe in Classical Social Theory: Themes in the Work of Ernst Troeltsch and his Contemporaries and their Status for Recent Conceptions of Modernity in Europe* EUI Working Paper SPS 2003/15 (Florence: European University Institute).

Hobsbawm, E. (1994) *Age of Extremes: The Short Twentieth Century 1914–1991* (London: Michael Joseph).

Jaspers, K. (1989) *On Max Weber*, transl. R.J. Whelan (New York: Paragon House).

La Torre, M. (1999) 'Legal Pluralism as an Evolutionary Achievement of Community Law' 12 *Ratio Juris* 182–95.

Likhovski, A. (2003) 'Czernowitz, Lincoln, Jerusalem and the Comparative History of American Jurisprudence' 4 *Theoretical Inquiries in Law* 621–57.

Luhmann, N. (1979) *Trust and Power*, transl. H. Davis, J. Raffan and K. Rooney (Chichester: John Wiley).

Mayer, J.P. (1956) *Max Weber and German Politics: A Study in Political Sociology*, 2nd edn. (New York: Arno reprint, 1979).

Merry, S.E. (1988) 'Legal Pluralism' 22 *Law and Society Review* 869–96.

Misztal, B.A. (2003) 'Durkheim on Collective Memory' 3 *Journal of Classical Sociology* 123–43.

Nelken, D. (1984) 'Law in Action or Living Law? Back to the Beginning in Sociology of Law' 4 *Legal Studies* 157–74.

Schmitt, C. (1988) *The Crisis of Parliamentary Democracy*, transl. E. Kennedy (Cambridge, Mass: MIT Press).

Scott, J. and Trubek, D. (2002) 'Mind the Gap: Law and New Approaches to Governance in the European Union' 8 *European Law Journal* 1–18.

Senden, L. (2005) 'Soft Law, Self-Regulation and Co-Regulation in European Law: Where Do They Meet?' 9 *Electronic Journal of Comparative Law*, no 1 (January) <http://www.ejcl.org/>.

Shadid, W. and Van Koningsveld, P.S. (2005) 'Muslim Dress in Europe: Debates on the Headscarf' 16 *Journal of Islamic Studies* 35–61.

Snyder, F. (1999) 'Governing Economic Globalisation: Global Legal Pluralism and European Law' 5 *European Law Journal* 334–74.

Vinogradoff, P. (1928) 'The Crisis of Modern Jurisprudence' in H.A.L. Fisher ed., *The Collected Papers of Paul Vinogradoff*, pp. 215–25 (Oxford: Clarendon Press).

Weber, Marianne (1975) *Max Weber: A Biography*, transl. H. Zohn (New Brunswick: Transaction reprint, 1988).

Weber, Max (1930) *The Protestant Ethic and the Spirit of Capitalism*, transl. T. Parsons (London: Unwin reprint, 1985).

— (1948) 'Politics as a Vocation' in H.H. Gerth and C.W. Mills eds. and transl., *From Max Weber: Essays in Sociology*, pp. 77–128 (London: Routledge & Kegan Paul).

— (1968) *Economy and Society: An Outline of Interpretive Sociology*, transl. E. Fischoff et al. (Berkeley: University of California Press reprint, 1978).

Whitman, J. Q. (2000) 'Enforcing Civility and Respect: Three Societies' 109 *Yale Law Journal* 1279–1398.

Witteveen, W.J. (1993) 'The Symbolic Constitution' in B. van Roermund ed., *Constitutional Review: Theoretical and Comparative Perspectives*, pp. 79–104 (Deventer: Kluwer).

Zolo, D. (1999) 'A Cosmopolitan Philosophy of International Law? A Realist Approach' 12 *Ratio Juris* 429–44.

Zürn, M. and Wolf, D. (1999) 'European Law and International Regimes: The Features of Law Beyond the State' 5 *European Law Journal* 272–92.

PART THREE

INTERPRETING LEGAL IDEAS SOCIOLOGICALLY

[11]
The Development of Capitalism and the Formalisation of Contract Law

Introduction: Sociological Interpretation of Legal Doctrine

The object of this paper is to consider, in the particular context of the development of legal doctrines of contract, some aspects of the relationship between historical patterns of doctrinal legal development and changes in socio-economic structure. In this paper law is taken to mean, centrally and primarily, legal doctrine, that is, the concepts, rules, principles and patterns of reasoning which define legal discourse and are present in, and shape, lawyers' arguments, the style and reasoning of judicial decision making, and the terminology and conceptual structure of certain forms of legislation and of the legal theories and commentaries of jurists. The existence of legal forms does not, however, depend on the existence of all of these specific practices and institutions within which legal discourse finds its expression in various societies and historical periods since the conditions under which power is exercised through the medium of rules are historically extremely varied. The reason for focusing here on legal doctrine is to enable us to take seriously, and indicate ways of examining, the claim made by writers as different as Weber and Pashukanis that law is not merely synonymous with state coercion and that legal forms have a certain specific effectivity which justifies attempts to analyse law as a distinct social phenomenon. Treating such a claim seriously involves no denial of the fact that legal institutions and doctrines occupy an important part of the territory of political struggle and serve as instruments of political domination under definite historical conditions. Nevertheless the distinctive character of law is not to be found in these matters alone since the territory of political struggle is not *exclusively* occupied by law, and neither is law the only medium through which political power can be exercised.

The kinds of reductionist accounts of law which have been widely influential include those which reduce law to a more or less direct expression of class interests (as, for example, in Stuchka's early Soviet legal theory (Babb, 1951) heavily criticised by Pashukanis) or view it as a 'neutral', resource-allocating, interest-balancing mechanism of social integration passively reflecting the imperatives of the social system it serves (as in crude functionalism). Other approaches treat law merely as the state's technical apparatus of control or as a part of it identifi-

Capitalism and the Formalisation of Contract Law   55

able as a set of functionally defined specific institutions. But, unless
legal form or legal reasoning is seen as having distinctive characteristics
which emerge with the historical development of legal institutions and
doctrine and which can be treated as raising sociological questions
about its possible independent effects on social and economic changes,
theoretical questions about law become merged into attempts to
construct general theories of the state and law as such ceases to be an
object of sociological interest. Accounts of historical changes in the
relationships of classes in the transition from feudalism to capitalism
in Western Europe often tend to see law in various territories and
historical periods as, on the one hand, a set of more or less formalised
customary practices and, on the other, a machinery of coercion the
controllers of which are of interest for historical and sociological
analysis but the internal mechanisms of which are regarded as raising
problems only for lawyers concerned with technical maintenance of a
machine which, in theory, is available to serve any master. By contrast,
following Marx's analysis of fetishised forms in *Capital*, Pashukanis and
some other Marxist writers have provided an analysis of law which
affirms the specificity of legal form as the distinctive form of the
relations of commodity exchange (Pashukanis, 1978). But the 'relative
autonomy' of the law is bought at a high price, the price of acceptance
of an 'ideological theory of ideology' (Hirst, 1972) which analyses
ideological forms as being in some way 'created by' the real. The
'autonomy' of the legal is thus an autonomy which frees it from reduc-
tion to an expression of 'the demands of powerful social actors' only
to reduce it to a necessary expression of 'the systematic requirements of
capitalism'. (Balbus, 1977). Law is thus an alien form in non-capitalist
systems, present to the extent that commodity exchange is present. To
the extent that law exists in, for example, feudalism, it can be analysed
only in relation to what it may become: an imperfect realisation of a
specific form which reaches full development — the realisation of its
essence — with capitalism. Law in pre-capitalist or non-capitalist
societies can thus be analysed only in relation to the legal essence
revealed in its fullness in capitalism alone, and the possibility of comprehensively analysing the patterns of legal ideas present in systems other
than those of capitalism, in all their variety and in the complexity of
their development, and of identifying important continuities in the
development of legal ideas which are not necessarily dependent on the
continuity of particular economic systems or patterns of social
relations, is effectively excluded. Further, in a theory of the autonomy
of legal form such as Pashukanis', the effectivity of law is limited to
expressing, fulfilling and guaranteeing the relationships of commodity
exchange, the 'social relationships between things' which are the
fetishised 'real' forms of social relationships under capitalism. Law can

56   *Capitalism and the Formalisation of Contract Law*

have no other function or effects since the form and function of the
law are reflections of each other. Legal form is determined by the logic
of capital and, at the same time, expresses and guarantees the relationships of capital.

Such a view must be rejected. Legal forms and the characteristics
of legal doctrine and discourse cannot be wholly explained by reference
to matters external to legal process themselves.[1] Thus a recent radical
critique of classical Marxist concepts accurately states:

Capitalist relations of production presuppose a legal system which
allows the formation of particular kinds of contractual relations and
exchanges. The concept of the legal conditions of existence of capitalist relations of production therefore imposes definite constraints
on the type of legal system compatible with the conditions of
capitalist production. But it cannot tell us precisely how the
necessary forms of contract will be provided for nor what other
properties the legal system might possess. (Cutler, Hindess, Hirst and
Hussain, 1977, p. 219)

Elsewhere, Hindess and Hirst have written that the transition from
feudalism to capitalism involves a 'double transformation: in conditions
of representation of the bourgeoisie and the landowning class at the
political level; in the articulation of commodity relations in the
structure of the economy as a whole' (1975, p. 307). They add that
'certain necessary transformations at the ideological level' are also
required. The patterns of specific relations of production which are held
to characterise capitalism have determinate conditions of existence
which involve not only economic transformations but also political and
ideological transformations which cannot be reduced to or wholly
explained in terms of economic change or the internal logic of
structures of economic relations. The coercive aspect of law obviously
makes it a potent weapon in political struggle and in establishing and
maintaining forms of political control. But strictly, if we are to treat
seriously the hypothesis that law has an independent effectivity, the
coercive power of the law must be treated primarily as the power of a
political authority *guaranteeing* the law and, at the same time, directing
and channelling its power *through* legal doctrine.

Law is thus, as Pashukanis correctly observed, not to be explained
merely as coercion, although the effectiveness of law depends to a
significant extent on coercion applied by political authorities. If law has
any autonomy it is to be understood not merely as a device for the
exercise of power but as a system of ideas at once legitimating and
channelling the exercise of power. Analysis of the historical patterns
of the development of legal doctrine is thus part of the field of study

Capitalism and the Formalisation of Contract Law   57

of the formation, modification and disintegration of ideologies. But it is a particularly important part because in legal doctrine major ideological supports of social order find expression and in legal practice and lawyers' rationalisations components of this ideological structure are elaborated in detail and often in remarkably explicit form. The impetus towards such elaboration derives largely from the more or less dramatic confrontation between these elements of ideology and everyday social experience which occurs in the specially constructed environment of the law court; a supposedly 'neutral' territory in which legal ideology battles against opposed ideologies, in which it struggles to impose its own meanings on, and therefore its exclusive control over, social and economic relationships of all kinds. Institutional legal history is primarily the record of the development of the conditions under which these ideological confrontations can take place and doctrinal legal history is, in its most important form, the record of the struggles themselves and their outcome.

At a humbler but still significant level doctrinal legal history is a record of the development of *techniques* by which power can be directed and applied through the medium of rules. Weber writes that

> the absence of an economic need is by no means the only explanation of the lack of certain legal institutions in the past. Like the technological methods of industry, the rational patterns of legal technique to which the law is to give its guarantee must first be 'invented' before they can serve an existing economic interest. Hence the peculiar kinds of technique used in a legal system or, in other words, its modes of thought, are of far greater significance for the likelihood that a certain legal institution will be invented in its context than is ordinarily believed. Economic situations do not automatically give birth to new legal forms; they merely provide the opportunity for the actual spread of a legal technique if it is invented (1954, p. 131)

This is important but not to be exaggerated. Legal history shows the discovery, loss and rediscovery of specific ideas and techniques over time, the best-known example being the development, decline and medieval renaissance of the doctrines of Roman private law. It is extremely difficult to pick out clear lineal patterns of development of legal techniques so as to be able to relate them confidently and exactly to the existence or non-existence of particular forms of economic or social relationships and particular procedures and kinds of transactions at specific moments in history. As the history of commerce shows, legal techniques may be created in the course of development of particular spheres of economic activity while legal systems claiming

58   *Capitalism and the Formalisation of Contract Law*

general territorial jurisdiction over areas in which such activities occur
have no place for such techniques within their body of legal doctrine.
The history of the development of doctrinal techniques in different
systems may thus tell us much about the nature of conflicts of jurisdiction between the several different kinds of legal orders which may
compete for dominance at particular moments in history and in relation
to particular territories or particular categories of legal claims and
relationships. These conflicts may, in turn, have a significance for
political developments, where various systems of courts controlling
different jurisdictions are themselves the legal instruments of different
political authorities.

    If, therefore, law does have a degree of 'autonomy' and 'independ-
ence', it seems most likely that the key to an understanding of its
autonomous character will be found in the characteristics of its 'internal'
processes of doctrinal development, notwithstanding that in many,
probably most, cases of major developments in doctrine it is possible
to identify political or economic circumstances or developments which
provide the impetus towards doctrinal change.

Weber and the Development of the Legal Concept of Contract

Among the patterns of doctrinal development in legal history the evolution of contract is of major significance not only for an understanding
of the ideological transformations associated with the development of
capitalism but also as a unifying theme in the sociological interpretation
of legal history as a whole. At the most basic level contract is the legal
concept which most directly links law and economy because of the
significance of the numerous forms of exchange transactions for economic development. Further, contract in its developed form embodies
central ideas of modern Western law – the idea of legal obligations and
legal rights, the creation and modification of legal relationships through
agreement, the concept of the will and responsiblity of the legal
subject.

    For these reasons contract provides a convenient doctrinal focus for
an attempt to assess the 'relative autonomy' of the law and the specific
effectivity of legal doctrine. But, at the same time, it cannot be
assumed that characteristics of one strand of legal doctrine, a roughly
severed segment from the complex of doctrinal legal history, can be
mechanically generalised as characteristics of a unified legal ideology or
of legal doctrine in its entirety.

    Among social theorists of comparable stature, only Weber analyses
contract in relation to general concepts of a sociology of law in a
manner which genuinely seeks to take full account of the complexities

and ambiguities of doctrinal legal history and, for this reason, his work provides a useful basis for further analysis. The themes which run through Weber's convoluted treatment of the development of contract law are, of course, chosen in the context of a sociology of law concerned to relate developing patterns of legal rationality to an ideal type of capitalism formulated in terms of rational economic conduct orientated to the market. If we reject this typification of capitalism and replace it with a concept of capitalism distinguished by a dominance of specific social relations of economic production having definite legal and political conditions of existence, Weber's themes still remain relevant for an analysis of the emergence of certain technical prerequisites of economic development and of the cultural conditions of existence of capitalism. But his central concern with a single problem – that of 'rationality' – and his linking of law and capitalist development primarily in terms of the concepts of 'calculability' and 'predictability' limit and distort some of the important inferences he draws from doctrinal legal history.[2]

In his methodological essays Weber suggests that legal concepts can serve in appropriate cases as ideal types of social action (1949, p. 43 and *passim*). In his writings on contract, as elsewhere in his sociology of law, Weber frequently and implicitly does use legal ideas in this way, and here, as elsewhere in the descriptive passages of his sociological writings, there is a tendency for ideal type and 'concrete reality' to be confused. Doctrinal legal developments are, therefore often treated as though it can be assumed that they reflect or are reflected in actual changes in patterns of behaviour, actual economic changes, etc. Thus, for Weber, the relationship between the legal development of contract and expanding capitalism is relatively straightforward.

> There exists, of course, an intimate connection between the expansion of the market and the expanding measure of contractual freedom or, in other words, the scope of arrangements which are guaranteed as·valid by the legal order or, in again different terms, the relative ·significance within the total legal order of those rules which authorize such transactional dispositions. (1954, p. 100)

But because of the limitations of the key linking concepts between law and economy on which his sociology of law is based he cannot systematically explore this 'obvious' relationship further. For this reason Weber's intricate account of the historical development of the concept of legal obligation arising from agreement is primarily an exercise in the writing of highly compressed 'pure' doctrinal history without any systematic explanation of the reasons for or sociological significance of particular doctrinal developments.

60   Capitalism and the Formalisation of Contract Law

A few historical landmarks stand out. The development of money
provides the impetus for legal interpretation of bilateral transactions
dependent on rigid ceremonies and verbal formulae as in the Roman
law *stipulatio* dating from before the fifth century BC. Such legal
forms mark points of transition between major eras of legal history.
Economic demands give rise to new legal possibilities yet the new
forms preserve and are dependent on the irrational 'magic' sanctions of
what Weber calls the 'pre-contractual stage' of legal development
(1954, p. 115). It is the magic ceremonies which create legal bonds,
not the agreement of the parties nor their mutual reliance. Many
centuries later the spread of international Roman commerce gave rise
to legal recognition of informal consensual contracts. But the formal
contracts and those arising merely as a result of delivery of possession
continued to form part of the law so that Roman law never developed
a unified universally applicable contract form (Buckland, 1963,
pp. 412ff.).

    Throughout his treatment of contract, Weber's object is to demon-
strate long-term continuities of legal development which are not
reducible to mere reflections of patterns of economic development.
Contract in some form, Weber claims, existed in the earliest periods of
legal history. The development of market relations produced not a
wholly new form but a radical development and change of character
in an existing one. Yet the distinctions Weber makes between the
status contracts of early law and the purposive contracts peculiar to
market economies, are far more important legally and sociologically
than the continuities. Only with purposive contracts, 'neither affecting
the status of the parties nor giving rise to new qualities of comradeship
but aiming solely . . . at some specific (especially economic) performance or result' (1954, pp. 105-7), can the idea of limited, narrowly
defined reciprocal legal obligations, fundamental to the legal elaboration of the consequences of market transactions, arise. 'Fraternization'
contracts, the dominant form of status contracts, require that the
'person "become" something different in quality (or status) from
the quality he possesses before . . . Each party must thus make a new
"soul" enter his body' (1954, p. 106). The 'total legal situation' and
social status of the contracting parties are altered by their agreement.
The purposive contract with its potential for reducing all contracting
parties to identical legal units provides a prototypical framework for the
development of formal legal rationality. Implicit in Weber's rigid distinguishing of status contracts and purposive contracts is the attempt to
specify doctrinal landmarks in the historical emergence of the kind of
legal thought which Weber associates with the ideal type of formal legal
rationality.

    The distinction between generalised, unspecific, 'fraternal' status relationships and limited, legally defined instrumental contractual relationships underlies Weber's discussion of the legal effects on 'third parties' of contractual ties and of the legal consequences of group membership – particularly in relation to the legal development of forms of incorporation. Since many of these group forms are created or developed to serve economic purposes, the elaboration of their consequences and characteristics is presumably significant in relation to economic development and it is in this area that Weber's linking of legal forms and capitalist development through the concepts of 'calculability' and 'predictability' and the emergence of formal legal rationality should receive its most direct test.

Yet he makes no serious and systematic attempt to specify the economic effects of various kinds of legal structure of groups or organisations in different historical periods. He stresses that the relations of the market are 'fundamentally alien to any type of fraternal relationship' such as that which characterises the internal membership relations within various kinds of group (1954, p. 193) and he discusses in very general terms the problems of representation of the group and fixing of liabilities which may be solved through the concept of corporate juristic personality. But this concept can be traced in various forms to ancient and, in Weber's terms, presumably 'irrational' sources (see Lobingier) and it is not easy to see how Weber's arguments about the legal forms of groups are directly related to his thesis concerning the significance of formal legal rationality. In fact, he notes that '[m]any of our specifically capitalistic legal institutions are of mediaeval rather than Roman origin, although Roman law was much more rationalized in a logical sense than mediaeval law' (1954, p. 131) and he recognises powerful *irrational* forces at work in their development. For example, the development of negotiable instruments (pp. 124-5), solidary group responsibility towards outsiders and the recognition of many different kinds of special funds (p. 131) were all favoured by irrational modes of thought. The 'backwardness' and illogicality of legal thought prevented the establishment of rigid conceptual systems in mediaeval law and hence promoted 'a far greater wealth of practically useful devices than had been available under the more logical and highly rationalized Roman law' (p. 131).

What Weber's analysis of contract shows is that elements which he understands as rational *and* irrational enter into the construction and elaboration of legal ideas in highly complex combinations when legal development is viewed in a broad historical perspective. He shows, in relation to contract, that there are striking continuities in the development of legal doctrine over long periods and that the processes and consequences of doctrinal change cannot be *wholly* explained by economic developments. All this is of value. But, as Albrow remarks, by

62 *Capitalism and the Formalisation of Contract Law*

Weber's 'own historical analysis it is difficult to show any clear relation-ship between formal law and the modern economy'. (Albrow, 1975, p. 29). The development of formal legal rationality does not underpin key phases in the development of capitalist enterprise, as Weber under-stands this development, in the direct manner which the use of his concepts of calculability and predictablity in relation to both law and economic action suggests. Furthermore, the distinction between pur-posive and status contracts, so important to him because of its implica-tions for his classification of modes of legal thought, is much less clear-cut than his ideal types of contract encourage us to believe.

This is only a symptom of the more fundamental problem that Weber's analytic distinctions of rational/irrational and formal/substantive legal thought are not adequate for the tasks to which they are applied. The development of contract shows a blending of rational and irrational elements and formal and substantive concerns sufficiently complex to cast doubt on the utility of his classification even as an admittedly ideal typical formulation. Formal rationality is defined in such a way as to exclude consideration of the values of the law and the way they are developed and generalised throughout legal doctrine (cf. Albrow, 1975, p. 21). So Weber does not see the processes of development of legal doctrine as processes by which political ideology can be developed and elaborated in forms which make it applicable for the official definition and control of all socially significant relation-ships. And the typification of formal and substantive legal rationality allows him to present these types as excluding each other; as different *kinds* of legal thought rather than as different *facets* of legal thought. The complex character of legal reasoning and its ideological significance are thus obscured.

The Legal Ideology of Contract

The primary ideological significance of legal contract form is twofold. Firstly, it lies in the idea of legal *equivalence*, the exact legal balancing of reciprocal rights and obligations of formally equal contracting parties assumed to be acting freely. In this way the law systematically interprets actual relations and conditions of inequality and substantial unfreedom as relations of equality and free choice, and attaches legal consequences accordingly.[3] Secondly, the ideological significance of legal contract form lies in the idea of its *universality*. It is, in its devel-oped form in capitalism, capable not only of being applied to the inter-pretation of economic relations of distribution and production but to other relations not directly concerned with economic production and it lends itself to generalisation and further abstraction as a major

Capitalism and the Formalisation of Contract Law   63

political ideology, supported and elaborated in the detail of legal
rules.[4] In the hands of a practically minded legal profession, legal
doctrine may be developed through creative modification deriving its
impetus from many sources including the need to compete with rival
legal jurisdictions (e.g. in England the powerful competition of
ecclesiastical, commercial and other court systems, at various times,
encouraged doctrinal innovations in the common law applied by the
royal courts). Such developments may involve and rely on *irrational* as
well as rational tendencies in legal thought. But, at the same time,
unified professional 'guardianship' of a legal system seeking, and, by
virtue of the political authority supporting it, capable of eventually
acquiring jurisdiction over all legally significant social relations, fosters
tendencies towards the application of broadly consistent modes of
thought throughout *all* areas of developing legal doctrine within such a
legal order. The importance of legal contract to capitalism is thus not
primarily in the provision of technical devices to support the developing
complexity of economic relations. Although such devices must be
developed they often emerge in the internal norms of economic groups
or institutions and are only later reflected in formal law recognised by
courts of general jurisdiction not controlled by commercial authorities
themselves. And while the developing rationality of the law is an element
contributing in various ways to the achievement of the ideological
functions of legal doctrine it is not necessarily of pre-eminent importance in all phases of social and economic development. The pervasive
legal ideology of contract, slowly created over a long period of history,
promotes the breakdown of all major status differentials unconnected
with the needs of an economy based on market exchanges and confirms
and defines the particular form of individualism in terms of which
capitalist social relations are conceptualised.[5]

    What then are the historical conditions which contribute towards
the creation of this ideology and its progressive legal elaboration? The
most basic legally relevant needs of commerce are, firstly, the guarantee
of peace and order within its area of operations. This involves the
internal guarantee of security of transactions through enforcement
procedures and the *external* guarantee protecting commercial arrangements and relationships from 'outside' attack, for example from those
outside the commercial community or hostile to its activities. Secondly,
commerce requires conceptual devices for the construction of forms of
transaction and structures of business organisation suitable to its operations. But the satisfaction of these needs as they exist at various stages
of the development of commerce does not necessarily demand reliance
on legal resources external to the commercial community itself. Private
courts of commercial communities play an important role in the
development of enforceable norms of commercial conduct and the

64   *Capitalism and the Formalisation of Contract Law*

political authority of the autonomous community may be adequate
to secure enforcement. Hence the stability of the autonomous structures of the German medieval sodalities. As regards the development of
transactional techniques and concepts, for example in relation to
credit, agency and negotiable instruments, much more flexibility may
be possible in the elaboration of techniques within the commercial
community than could be possible within an evolving system of legal
doctrine of courts of general territorial jurisdiction not merely
concerned with commercial affairs. A major restraining influence in
the development of legal doctrine, and one important cause of resort to
legal fictions (Fuller, 1967, pp. 60-2; Pound, 1921, pp. 166ff.), is the
problem of unforeseen and perhaps undesired consequences, in various
and possibly disparate areas of law, arising as a result of doctrinal
development in a seemingly narrow area.

Development beyond the stage of legal development of contract-
based transactions centred on commercial enclaves towards a 'contract-
ualisation' of societies seems to depend on such situations as the
following:

1. A situation in which further economic development requires a
system of norms and enforcement procedures beyond those which
commercial communities can create for themselves. For example, the
development of multiple group membership breaks down the system of
personality of laws, the system under which legal jurisdiction over
individuals is determined by their group membership which determines
status. Because of the complexities of determining which law is to be
applied to a person who is a member of several groups the need for
certain common legal principles, a *ius gentium* co-existing with the
norms of particular groups, is required (Weber, 1954, pp. 142-3).

2. The establishment of the dominance of a single system of law within
a territory which can support an integrated market economy as the
basis of its economic structure. This development depends, in turn, on
political factors, particularly on the establishment of centralised political
authority and the emergence of a legal profession centred on the courts
controlled by that authority. England provides the obvious example
with the development of such authority from the time of the Norman
Conquest and, much later, the victory of the common law enforced by
the King's courts over other competing systems (see e.g. Milsom, 1969,
pp. 1-25).

3. The existence of conditions under which those who control the
creation of legal doctrine of such a dominant legal system are prepared
to provide a system of rules and doctrines to support and guarantee the

Capitalism and the Formalisation of Contract Law 65

expansion of market activity. Thus, well-known accounts of the alliance of royal power and bourgeois interests in particular historical periods, particularly in England, and the alliance of bourgeoisie and common lawyers in the English Revolution, are of obvious relevance (see e.g. Tigar and Levy, 1977; Hill, 1965; cf. Malament, 1977).

4. The availability of doctrinal legal techniques to transform the existing doctrine of the dominant legal system so as to secure economic needs in a manner sufficiently compatible with existing political and cultural conditions (cf. Pound, 1921, p. 11). In this context the *fief-rente*, a legal device of the twilight of Western European feudalism, seems to provide a good example of a long-lasting and significant transitional legal form reflecting the ties of personal loyalty of the disappearing feudal bond of tenure as well as emerging contractual relations to be developed with the returning money economy. Involving the grant of an annuity to secure military service, it arose at a time when legal relations of service were inconceivable except in relation to feudal ties of homage and fealty and, surviving from the twelfth to the early fifteenth century, the legal relationship of *fief-rente* is said to have 'paradoxically enabled feudalism to survive . . . far beyond the time when based solely on land it would have ceased to exist' (Lyon, 1957, p. 273). Just as the Roman law *stipulatio* and other formal contracts established legal relations relevant to a money economy but in commercially inconvenient forms (Watson, 1977, pp. 12ff.) reflecting the impossibility of breaking with inherited modes of legal thought circumscribed by magic, so transitional legal devices involved in the movement from feudal relations to the contract relations of a money economy show the complex processes of modification of legal thought; processes which have, themselves, social and economic effects.

Indeed, legally, there are significant continuities between the legal conceptualisation of relations of lord and tenant in the feudalism of Western Europe and some important characteristics of contract as it features in the legal ideology of capitalism. The feudal bond is patently a relationship of unequals which eventually forms the focus of a class struggle more important for the break-up of feudalism than the struggle between bourgeoisie and feudal lords focused on the growth of commerce (see e.g. Dobb, 1963). Yet it is interpreted legally as a structure of reciprocal obligations (Milson, 1976, pp. 38ff.) and the oath of fealty becomes 'a detailed contract, carefully drawn up' (Bloch, 1962, p. 219). The feudal 'contract' is not even *legally* a relationship of equals, yet in this bond, affecting virtually all levels of society throughout Western Europe (cf. Poggi, 1978, pp. 23, 27-8), is a germ of

66   Capitalism and the Formalisation of Contract Law

the socially pervasive legal ideology of contract with its systematic obscuring of factual inequalities which makes the notion of free agreement creating reciprocal obligations a legal construction of major ideological significance.

The development of a pervasive legal ideology of contract as a centrally significant component of the cultural conditions within which capitalist social relations develop is thus, it may be suggested, partly the consequence of certain important legal doctrinal continuities traceable through pre-capitalist phases of social development – and particularly within Western European feudalism – which furnish ideological 'residues' influencing, and being modified in, further legal development. It is also partly the result of the gradual universalisation of legal ideas originally developed in specific commercial contexts (and themselves traceable at least to some extent to historical origins in modes of thought developed in spheres unconnected with specifically economic transactions). The creation of the historical conditions for this universalisation in particular societies depends on a variety of determinate political, economic and cultural developments which cannot be explained theoretically as the necessary consequence of any single unifying historical process.

This is not, it must be stressed, a claim that developed ideas of contract are wholly the result of legal development and legal processes. But their modern systematisation into an elaborate complex of generalised reciprocal obligations capable of abstract and exact interpretation irrespective of the realities of economic relationships or power relationships is primarily the result of legal doctrinal development. Partly on these foundations, ideological edifices are built (Nenner, 1977; Hill, 1965, pp. 268-9) to extend their consequences far beyond the confines of the law court while remaining grounded in the developing detail of legal interpretation of specific social and economic relationships. It has been argued that

> during the sixteenth and seventeenth centuries . . . many European nations obtained knowledge of their history by reflecting . . . upon the character of their law; that the historical outlook which arose in each nation was in part the product of its law, and therefore, in turn, of its history . . . (Pocock, 1957, pp. vii-viii)

In so far as patterns of legal doctrine have been interpreted in particular societies in particular historical periods to shape images of history, the forms in which social relations are conceived and the terrain of political controversy, their ideological significance is clear and where long historical continuities in the development of legal doctrine can be demonstrated law's ideological significance can be substantially enhanced.

Capitalism and the Formalisation of Contract Law   67

The 'relative autonomy' of the law thus appears as the significant effects of the processes of reasoning promoting continuities in the development of legal doctrine. 'Legal ideas have their own strength' (Milsom, 1969, p. xi) and the patterns of their development are not always predictable. One can understand fears such as those of Frederick William II of Prussia which impelled him, in the decree introducing his 1794 General Land Law for the Prussian States, to forbid the judges 'to indulge in any arbitrary deviation, however slight, from the clear and express terms of the laws, whether on the ground of some allegedly logical reasoning or under the pretext of an interpretation based on the supposed aim and purpose of the statute' and to threaten severe sanctions on any judicial miscreant (cf. Zweigert and Kötz, 1977, p. 81). In 1790 in France, in an attempt to protect the supposed consequences of the Revolution, a statute required that judges must seek the advice of the *corps législatif* 'whenever they believe it necessary either to interpret a law or make a new one' (ibid.). But such attempts at control invariably fail unless political authorities have the power, the will and the skill to exercise total and permanent control over all aspects of the creation and application of legal doctrine. These conditions have frequently not been satisfied through the historical development of legal ideas. For this and other reasons law has been able to develop 'autonomous' characteristics through its 'internal' processes of development in various ways, to varying extents, in various societies and historical periods. The gradual construction of the legal ideology of contract, as a particular product of legal development in certain societies,demonstrates one particularly important form in which the specific effectivity of law as regards social and economic change can manifest itself in the development of ideology to channel and legitimise the exercise of state power in a manner supportive of the patterns of social relations constitutive of capitalism.

Notes

1. I.e. the processes of the institutions concerned with the application and interpretation of rules through which political power is channelled.
2. Hunt (1978, pp. 128ff.) considers the treatment of contract in Weber's sociology of law to be set apart from and perhaps merely incidental to the major themes of his sociological analysis of law. Yet, in a sense, it is one of the central testing grounds of his theories because modern contract, as Weber interprets it, embodies directly in legal form, and thereby guarantees, the central characteristics of economic rationality upon which his conception of capitalism is constructed.
3. Modern contract law is the classic legal embodiment and support of the notion that 'in the modern state "vertical", power-focused, and power-activated relations could obtain only between the state itself and private individuals; among

68   Capitalism and the Formalisation of Contract Law

the latter, all relations were supposed to be "horizontal", contractual, and
power-free' (Poggi, 1978, p. 94). Furthermore, legal notions of contract have a
potential for development into an ideological interpretation of the relationship of
state and individual (or state and 'people' or, specifically, the state and a
particular class or classes) in 'horizontal' terms (Nenner, 1977; cf. Hill, 1965,
pp. 268-9).
    4. On the importance of private law concepts in the formulation of major
political controversies in seventeenth-century England see Nenner '[R] elationships
between King and Parliament and King and people were consistently reduced to
analyses based upon the lawyer's understanding of property, contracts, and
trusts' (1977, p. 198). Nenner makes clear that it was the developing legal
doctrine of contract which was the ideological herald of the new age while nevertheless retaining certain continuities with an earlier medieval order (see pp. 39ff.).
    5. To say this is to speak only of a particular area of legal doctrine – a
particular component of legal ideology – and it is not to be assumed that the
characteristics of the legal ideology of contract are the only characteristics of legal
ideology as a whole, nor that characteristics of other aspects of legal ideology are
necessarily compatible with those of legal contract ideology.

References

Albrow, M. (1975) 'Legal Positivism and Bourgeois Materialism: Max Weber's
    View of the Sociology of Law'. *British Journal of Law and Society*, 2, p. 14.
Babb, H.W. (1951) *Soviet Legal Philosophy* (translated). Harvard University Press
Balbus, I.D. (1977) 'Commodity Form and Legal Form: An Essay on the "Relative
    Autonomy" of the Law'. *Law and Society Review*, 11, p. 571
Bloch, M. (1962) *Feudal Society* (translated by L.A. Manyon, vol. 1). Second
    edn, Routledge and Kegan Paul
Buckland, W.W. (1963) *Textbook of Roman Law*. Third edn, Cambridge
    University Press
Cutler, A., Hindess, B. Hirst P. and Hussain, A. (1977) *Marx's 'Capital' and
    Capitalism Today*, vol. 1. Routledge and Kegan Paul
Dobb, M. (1963) *Studies in the Development of Capitalism*. Revised edn,
    Routledge and Kegan Paul
Fuller, L.L. (1967) *Legal Fictions*. Stanford University Press
Hill, C. (1965) *Intellectual Origins of the English Revolution*. Oxford University
    Press
Hindess, B. and Hirst, P.Q. (1975) *Pre-Capitalist Modes of Production*. Routledge
    and Kegan Paul
Hirst, P.Q. (1972) 'A Critique of Rancière's and Althusser's Theories of Ideology'.
    Unpublished mimeo
Hunt, A. (1978) *The Sociological Movement in Law*. Macmillan
Jolowicz, H.F. (1978) *Historical Introduction to Roman Law*. Third edn,
    Cambridge University Press
Lobingier, C.S. (1938-39) 'The Natural History of the Private Artificial Person:
    A Comparative Study in Corporate Origins'. *Tulane Law Review*, 13, p. 41
Lyon, B.D. (1957) *From Fief to Indenture*. Harvard University Press
Malament, B. (1977) 'The "Economic Liberalism" of Sir Edward Coke'. *Yale Law
    Journal*, 76, p. 1321
Milsom, S.F.C. (1969) *Historical Foundations of the Common Law*. Butterworth
—— (1976) *The Legal Framework of English Feudalism*. Cambridge University
    Press

Capitalism and the Formalisation of Contract Law   69

Nenner, H. (1977) *By Colour of Law.* University of Chicago Press
Pashukanis, E.B. (1978) *Law and Marxism: A General Theory* (translated by
    B. Einhorn). Ink Links
Pocock, J.G.A. (1957) *The Ancient Constitution and the Feudal Law.* Cambridge
    University Press
Poggi, G. (1978) *The Development of the Modern State.* Hutchinson
Pound, R. (1921) *The Spirit of the Common Law.* Marshall Jones
Tigar, M.E. and Levy, M.R. (1977) *Law and the Rise of Capitalism.* Monthly
    Review Press
Watson, A. (1977) *Society and Legal Change.* Scottish Academic Press
Weber, M. (1949) *The Methodology of the Social Sciences* (translated by E. Shils).
    Free Press
—— (1954) *On Law in Economy and Society* (translated by E. Shils and
    M. Rheinstein). Harvard University Press
Zweigert, K. and Kötz, H. (1977) *An Introduction to Comparative Law* (translated
    by T. Weir), vol. 1. North Holland

[12]
The Law of Property and Legal Theory

What can legal theory offer to the understanding of contemporary property law? This paper seeks to suggest some answers to this question. But the analysis of property and property law is used here primarily to illustrate a view of the nature of legal theory and of some of its applications. So this paper is more concerned with outlining and illustrating a conception of legal theory than with unravelling contemporary problems of the property law field. Nevertheless it attempts to show how theory may help to clarify some of these problems.

Property law provides a particularly interesting field within which to explore the relationship between legal theory and legal doctrine. In the traditional view at least,

> the law of property, and more especially the law of real property, presents in almost every respect a marked contrast to the rest of the law. . . . It is logical and orderly, its concepts are perfectly defined, and they stand in well recognised relations to one another. . . . Above all, this part of the law is intensely abstract. . . . The various concepts had, and still have, when properly understood, a very necessary relation to the economic facts of life, but once created and defined they seem to move among themselves according to the rules of a game which exists for its own purposes. . . . More than anywhere else we seem to be moving in a world of pure ideas from which everything physical or material is entirely excluded.[1]

Property law offers richly stocked and highly developed fields of doctrine in which to test legal theory's claim to aid the understanding and interpretation of legal ideas.

However, when we move from the traditional core of property law – real property – to its expanding periphery where rights to many new, or newly recognized and debated, forms of wealth are in issue the image of property law as a game played according to known and well-tried rules seems less appropriate. Even the nature and purposes of the game itself may be seriously in issue. The meaning of the term 'property' or the utility of invoking it as a basis of legal intervention and as an organizing concept for legal doctrine may seem increasingly questionable. Furthermore, even in the traditional core doctrinal areas of rights in land, fundamental questions about the appropriate objects of legal protection

82

have re-emerged in Anglo-American law in recent years to remind us that property law is the basic legal expression of the nature of economic life in all its aspects. Here, as in all other areas of law, doctrine has to be understood in relation to the social context in which it gains its significance as a mode of regulating behaviour.

Legal doctrine in the property field thus has a formidable 'rational strength'. At the same time its central social and economic importance in changing Western societies creates tensions within it which appear increasingly serious. If we are to understand both the power of doctrinal abstractions in this area and their limits – when social, economic or other pressures break through them and force us to revise or discard them – we need aid from outside legal doctrine itself. We need methods of interpreting it and showing the wider context in which its characteristics and problems are formed. Legal theory may provide the means. But what kind of legal theory?

In the following sections an attempt will be made, first, to outline a conception of legal theory which may be of service in this context; secondly, to identify some general contemporary problems in the property law field as they present themselves in ordinary legal analysis; and thirdly, to consider how legal theory may provide aid in understanding the nature and causes of these problems.

THEORY AND DOCTRINE

What kind of legal theory can provide a means of interpreting legal doctrine in the ways suggested above? It would seem to need to be theory which is both 'inside' legal doctrine as lawyers[2] comprehend and use it, understanding the manner and techniques of lawyers' interpretation of doctrine in legal reasoning and discourse, and also 'outside' it, understanding its significance in the wider society beyond the limited professional world in which it is typically formed. In this writer's view, therefore, the kinds of enquiries which have typified analytical jurisprudence even in its broadened modern forms need to be set in (and substantially modified by) a wider theoretical context drawing on social theory. The theoretical study of legal doctrine and legal institutions – if it is to add significantly to the lawyer's perception of doctrine and institutions – needs to be set in the context of a wide theoretically informed view of the nature of societies: of their structure and of the conditions and forms of stability and change in them.[3]

This necessarily involves a rather complex and uneasy relationship between legal theory – which on this view needs to integrate a wide variety of kinds of enquiry within a unified framework of explanation – and claims regarding law as an autonomous discipline. Legal theory is described by William Twining, in the course of a valuable attempt to set out an integrative conception of theory, as 'the theoretical part of law as a discipline',[4] but immediately problems arise with this formulation since everything turns on what is meant by 'law as a discipline'. Twining remarks that law cannot and should not have rigid bounda·ies which segregate it from other disciplines. The study of law is asserted to be 'part of a general intellectual enterprise, the direct end of which is the advancement of knowledge and understanding',[5] and this is surely correct. Nevertheless, he claims that one of the tasks of legal theory is to help to make the discipline of law more coherent and integrated and another is to connect law as a discipline with other disciplines relevant to it.[6] At the same time it is said that the notion of an autonomous discipline or pure science of law 'has, at most, a very limited place'.[7] On the one hand, the idea of law as the basis of a distinct discipline is asserted; on the other, it seems to be substantially denied.

Twining seems to use the term 'discipline' in an extremely loose sense. But what is typically implied by those who talk of the discipline of law is an important element of *uniqueness* and a significant intellectual *autonomy* in lawyers' methods of analysis. Lawyers do plainly engage in quite distinctive forms of practice and it is often very important to professional legal practice to adhere to the idea of an autonomous science of law.[8] But a rigorous legal theory should treat the claims made in favour of 'pure' legal method as part of its subject-matter, as matters to be examined and explained. When law is asserted to be a discipline without an exact specification and elaboration (in comparison with other disciplines, practices and forms of analysis) of what it is which makes legal analysis autonomous or unique in some respects, the assertion has all the flavour of an ideological pronouncement: an assertion that legal questions can be answered by asking other legal questions; that law consists of 'lawyers' issues'; that legal knowledge is somehow self-standing; that the epistemology on which it is founded needs no examination, being expressed satisfactorily in well-understood and taken-for-granted lawyers' traditions of thought and practice. In my view legal theory should not merely replicate legal ideology and its taken-for-granted certainties. It should analyse and explain legal ideology so as to help towards a better understanding of the social significance of legal ideas.[9] Thus it is more appropriate for legal theory to treat law as a *field of experience* than as a discipline; a rather heterogeneous subject of study centred on a variety of types and problems of regulation potentially involving a wide diversity of practices, techniques, modes of thought and forms of knowledge. The boundaries of this subject are, of course, fixed by its focus on the institutions and practices which we choose to specify as legal, a choice which must itself be theoretically justified.

It follows from the postulate that law is a field of experience – of modes of thought and action and of forms of knowledge and practice – that the theoretical problem of identifying the field of law is not that of finding some inherent or natural 'essence' of law, for example in terms of fundamental legal values, principles or concepts; or in terms of a certain logical structure of normative systems; or of distinctive formal patterns of authority. It is that of marking out an intelligible area of empirically analysable social phenomena. Thus the task of conceptualizing 'law' is more like that of defining, say, 'urban problems' in urban sociology, or 'medicine' in medical sociology, or 'transport' in transport economics, or 'the public sector' in public sector economics. Since law, on this view, is an aspect of society, the empirical theory required both to identify it as a field of study and to provide fundamental guidance in understanding the most general features of that field is necessarily social theory. But it is important to stress that identifying a field of experience is not necessarily the same as identifying a 'discipline'.

84

Legal theory can thus best serve the need for better understanding of the nature of law by an agnosticism about law's disciplinary claims. It follows that it can make no commitment to make law more 'coherent' or 'integrated' as a discipline. However, by seeking to explain the conditions shaping the development of contemporary law, it may perhaps suggest how far such aims are feasible. But its sole essential commitment ought to be to better understanding of the nature of law, and this requires that it refuse to ally itself unconditionally with the interests of any particular type of participant in legal processes (lawyer, legislator, judge, policeman, litigant, etc.). Since this commitment involves continually trying to transcend the partial perspectives on law of these various participants, it may, as Professor Twining suggests, help to break down barriers dividing off 'the academic from the applied, theory from practice, the law in books from the law in action'.[10] But it is very important to see this as a possible by-product of legal theory, not as one of its functions, for these barriers are – in a variety of forms in a variety of contexts – part of the world of law which theory should seek above all to understand and explain.

Legal theory cannot ignore or dismiss participants' perspectives. But neither is it very useful to adopt a despairing relativism, assuming that all such perspectives are of equal worth. Some perspectives on law are more comprehensive, better informed and more rigorously thought through than others. They are better able to understand rival perspectives and explain, interpret or incorporate them, revealing their assumptions and limitations. Legal theory should, if it is to be a sustained contribution to the deeper understanding of law, constantly aim for a unifying perspective which incorporates and transcends limited participant perspectives. Even if such an aim may never be realized, to reject it as an aim is to condemn the study of law to the incoherence of a babel of voices drowning out each other; an incoherence which must become more hopeless as the study of law expands its tolerant 'pluralism' to give a hearing to a continually widening range of participant views on law.

This is true no less at the level of what Twining calls 'high theory'[11] than at the level of day-to-day involvement in legal affairs. Of course Rawls and Durkheim, for example, as 'high theorists' of law in society from different intellectual traditions do have something in common, although not nearly as much as, say, Weber and Hayek. But one must surely recognize that radically different kinds of feats are being attempted by different writers in this pantheon of high theory. Some are apparently creating theory to demonstrate the purity of legal discourse, others constructing value systems for Western democracy, others attempting to provide a basis for the systematic study of social behaviour. Still others are trying combinations of these and other aims. An integrative legal theory cannot ultimately be satisfied with collecting all these writers' products somewhat indiscriminately together in an undifferentiated general category as high theory or legal philosophy. A writer's answers to the questions he has set himself cannot be condemned by reference to the findings of another writer concerned with quite different questions. However, all the high theorists of legal theory share a concern with the fundamental question of the nature of law. This common focus may allow us to test the adequacy or significance of the *questions* asked by one theorist by reference to the findings of another theorist of perhaps quite different orientation.

It might be said, for example, that Durkheim makes explicit some of the sociological assumptions on which a theory of justice such as Rawls's ultimately rests; or that Kelsen's pure theory is, in part, an elaboration and rationalization of one particularly important type of legal thought among the several types which Weber links with particular political, social and historical conditions in his massive picture of legal and social history. Such linkings of contrasting theorists are contentious and used here only as tentative illustrations. The point, however, is that an attempt to link such very different kinds of theory by such means may ultimately be necessary to clarify the scope and place of each, to make possible an identification of its limitations and explanatory power by broadening the perspective within which it is considered.

Where do these considerations leave us in determining the utility of legal theory in the analysis of legal doctrine? Theory should aid the lawyer not, it seems to me, by joining with him in his own kind of participation in law; not by helping his rationalization of doctrine by means of improved classifications and definitions. Theory should attempt to put the lawyer's analytical problems into a wider perspective by showing the nature of legal doctrine as it appears in a broader view than that which the lawyer's immediate professional concerns dictate. This broader view comes from the attempt to explain *why* doctrine has a particular form and content at a given time and place, what forces – not just within the legal professional environment but within the social and political environment as a whole – have acted to produce this situation, what consequences follow from it for other aspects of society beyond those to which the lawyer's immediate concerns directly relate, what social forces are acting to bring about doctrinal change, and what directions of doctrinal change appear likely in the light of this analysis. Every one of these enquiries denies the claims of a pure science of law and of law's disciplinary autonomy. They operationalize the assumption that the only real aid to understanding which theory can offer the practising or academic lawyer (or any other legal participant) is a framework of thought in which to extend the necessarily partial perspectives derived from his specific form of involvement with law. In what follows an attempt will be made to apply some of these ideas in discussion of aspects of property law.

ASPECTS OF PROPERTY: PROBLEMS IN THE ORGANIZATION OF LEGAL DOCTRINE

For lawyers, classification of legal doctrine is part of the enterprise of rationalizing legal rules and ideas; organizing the complexity of law as doctrine in ways which make it manageable as a body of knowledge and predictable in its consequences. The classification of a body of law as 'property law' may serve to identify either the legal doctrine relating to a particular area of problems or situations in economic and social life (so-called fact-based classification) or a body of doctrine defining rights or duties or legal arrangements of a kind distinct from those encompassed by other areas of doctrine (a classification founded on the distinctiveness of doctrinal arrangements and devices). Lawyers' doubts about the coherence of property law as a field are founded on uncertainty as to whether either of these

86

modes of classification is presently adequate to provide a basis for rationalizing doctrine. Inevitably the two modes are related. But it is the latter of them which attracts most attention in legal writing.

It is of interest that some American commentators write of the 'death of property'[12] in much the same way that others have heralded the demise of contract.[13] It is suggested that the variety of current usages of the category of property is such that lawyers could dispense with the term 'property' altogether without losing anything in legal analytical clarity.[14] At the heart of this claim is the assertion that the notion of 'thing ownership' – the notion that property rights can be understood as rights against other persons in relation to things – has become incoherent and with it the basis of property itself, since so-called property rights now exist also in relation to benefits far too intangible or diffuse to be considered 'things'.[15]

Charles Reich's much discussed 1964 essay on the 'new property'[16] highlighted the increasing importance of numerous forms of 'wealth' extending beyond the orthodox categories of private property and embodied in franchises, occupational licences, job security, government contracts, social security benefits and numerous other forms of benefit entitlement often dependent on government guarantee. It argued not that these should be recognized as giving rise to rights and duties of the same nature as those associated with traditional forms of private property, but that their modern importance showed the inadequacy of existing legal conceptualizations. It argued that changes in the bases of wealth in modern society had made existing property law thinking too limited in scope to encompass many of the most fundamental modern forms of wealth or entitlement on which most citizens depended, and that, as a result, they lacked adequate legal protection, especially from arbitrary seizure or cancellation by government.

How far can these ideas be applied outside an American context? The context in which Reich's thesis was raised and has subsequently been much discussed includes the 'takings' and 'due process' clauses of the United States Constitution which specifically refer to 'private property' or 'property' and protect it from being 'taken for public use without just compensation'[17] and the owner of property from being deprived of it 'without due process of law'.[18] Debates in American legal literature in recent years on the scope of property and the recognition of 'new property' rights in government largesse naturally reflect the entrenched constitutional significance of the 'property' label which carries particular protections for those rights to which it can be attached. The line between property and non-property is constitutionally important. In at least some of the 'takings' cases it has been drawn by using the 'thing-ownership' conception of property.[19] Yet, it is argued, the concept of property in general legal use has been transformed by pragmatic extensions from a Blackstonian 'physicalist' notion of dominion over 'the external things of the world'[20] to an entirely abstract conception of the protection of value – which can exist in such forms as trademarks, trade secrets or business goodwill. At the same time the nature of these objects of property is such that absolutist concepts of property rights as unfettered dominion have appeared obviously unsuitable in relation to them. Thus it is claimed that while the concept of property has been extended in numerous ways to encompass increasingly significant forms of wealth – and arguments around

The Law of Property and Legal Theory   87

the Reich thesis rage over its further extension – the attribution of property rights
no longer allows reliable predictions of the kind of protection which will be granted
by the law.[21] Hence the term property no longer identifies a coherent field of
legal rights and duties. Property is 'dead' as a result of having been worked to
death in indiscriminate legal application.

In the English context the matter may appear somewhat differently. For one
thing, the constitutional significance of the property label is largely absent.[22]
The thing-ownership conception of property can be treated as perhaps no more
than a dispensable motif in legal analysis. Hohfeld is often credited with firmly
establishing in Anglo-American legal thought the 'bundle-of-rights' conception
of ownership which explicitly displaces legal concern with a relationship between
the individual property-holder and the thing constituting the object of property,
and sees property essentially as a cluster of jural relations between persons by
which entitlements are fixed. Given this viewpoint the object of property, the
'thing' in relation to which rights exist, often ceases to be of much interest in
legal analysis. But viewing matters in a broader comparative perspective of legal
history and development there may be dangers in putting too much emphasis
on the contrast between Blackstone's mid-eighteenth-century pronouncements
on property in terms of 'things' and Hohfeld's twentieth-century 'revolution'
in legal thought as marking fundamental changes in the nature of doctrine or
its interpretation. The Hohfeldian approach can be used to illuminate property
conceptions in extremely diverse legal systems and its relevance is in no way
restricted to modern law.[23] Furthermore it seems clear that English law has for
centuries been thoroughly familiar with the notion that the most abstract of
entitlements can be encompassed by property law. 'The realm of medieval law
is rich with incorporeal things. Any permanent right which is of a transferable
nature, at all events if it has what we may call a territorial ambit, is thought of
as a thing that is very like a piece of land'.[24] The need to think in terms of things
hardly prevented the elaboration of abstractions, so it appears. Throughout much
of English legal history the most concrete of assets – land – has been thought of
in terms of the abstraction of estates; and the notion of incorporeal property has
its roots in ancient and primitive societies.[25] Wolfgang Friedmann notes, in
sharp contrast to the agitated discussion in much of the American literature, that
'as has always been inherent in the common-law concept of property, and as is
increasingly recognized in the civilian legal systems, property is not confined
to the control of "things", but extended to the whole field of legitimate economic
interests and expectations'.[26]

On this view what is of particular interest is to compare the longstanding
flexibility of Anglo-American approaches to property with the struggles of some
civilian systems – particularly the German – to transcend the rigidities of legal
definitions associating property only with corporeal things, and to overcome
problems associated with the inheritance of Roman law notions of *dominion*. And
what is perhaps most salutary for comparative lawyers is the recognition that,
despite widely different doctrinal traditions of common law and civil law systems,
the protection of 'legitimate economic interests and expectations' has been
substantially achieved irrespective of these differences, though the rules providing
this protection may be classified differently (and not necessarily as rules of property

88

law) in different systems.[27] There is a considerable danger in exaggerating the actual practical effects of doctrinal differences between modern legal systems, and also in overestimating the extent, significance or suddenness of changes in legal thought.

In the realm of intellectual property law the legal concept of 'property' itself as applied to this field finds little place in contemporary discussion despite the rapid development and important practical problems of doctrine in the area. It would seem that broad general concepts defining a 'legal essence' of property can be dispensed with in the practical business of constructing protection for a variety of interests out of a range of pragmatically developed bodies of doctrine relating to such as copyright, patents, confidential information and trademarks. A common-sense 'fact-based' classification seems, at least for the present, adequate to define this field. All this is consistent with the pragmatic approach of Anglo-American common law to conceptualization. Where English judges have felt the need to theorize in doctrine about the nature of property in general they have often taken a fairly robust approach, tailoring their view to the circumstances of its application in the instant case and occasionally using a concept fully wide enough to embrace the 'new property' and much more besides. Thus Malins VC remarked in 1869 in *Dixon v. Holden*: 'What is property? One man has property in lands, another in goods, another in a business, another in skill, another in reputation; and whatever may have the effect of destroying property in any one of these things (even in a man's good name) is, in my opinion, destroying property of a most valuable description.'[28]

Where then do the doctrinal difficulties lie? We can identify at least three areas of doctrinal problems which seem of general importance within the property law field at present and, although they are closely related, it is convenient to outline each of them in turn.

Identifying Objects of Property

One area of difficulty arises from the need, despite the flexibility of legal approaches referred to above, to identify clearly in doctrine the assets which modern property law protects. Although there is nothing very new about the 'new property' and nothing new at all about the importance of incorporeal property in law, the range of types of incorporeal property has expanded greatly since the nineteenth century and has assumed greatly increased economic importance. Even the use of the concept of 'thing-ownership' as a mere motif of property law has seemed increasingly unrealistic in legal experience because it seems irrelevant to doctrine relating to forms of wealth which seem to be coming to occupy centre stage in economic life. The name given to the 'bundle of rights' identified in some property claims, for example 'copyright' or 'patent' or 'trademark', is the only name we use to refer to the asset protected, whereas in more traditional property forms we could distinguish, for example, the estate in land from the land itself. But there remains an apparent need – if we are to continue to think in terms of property in these kinds of cases – for a focus of entitlement, an identifiable asset around which rights can crystallize.

The Law of Property and Legal Theory   89

Sometimes it is not easy to see what this can be. According to Anglo-American law, copyright protects not ideas but the form of their expression, yet it may often be hard to separate the latter from the former,[29] or to identify unambiguously the relevant form - as, for example, in protection of computer software.[30] It is often said that it is the labour embodied in the creation which founds the right to protection but English copyright law has tended to provide protection for the commercial entrepreneur rather than the creator as such, given the absence of any clear concept of 'author's right' of the continental type.[31] Thus it seems most appropriate to treat the *result* of the labour as being protected. But what exactly is this? German writers describe it as 'the fabric of the work determined by its substance and form'.[32] The complex nature of creativity and originality has to be explored, since what is actually being protected is the embodiment of ideas.

Certainly, in many cases this causes no problems. Earlier English law found no difficulty in manipulating extremely nebulous property forms. Only when we seek to *generalize* about the nature of property and related areas can serious difficulties arise, for English courts have understandably been reluctant to adopt a general principle that something as hard to define as knowledge itself can be considered property.[33] But as technological or marketing ideas, design innovations and state-of-the-art techniques, trademarks, market information and many kinds of data resources, etc., are recognized as increasingly important forms of *wealth* in contemporary societies - often more important than the material things which have been the traditional focus of property law and which are now increasingly produced by means of, or are dependent on, these modern forms of wealth - the future of property law as a coherent field of doctrine may depend on its capacity to analyse them convincingly as (objects of) 'property'. One problem seems to be to define clearly the proprietary interest protected in such a way as both to facilitate and justify the protection to be provided by law. As will appear, this problem is ultimately not so much a technical-legal one as a social one.

Identifying Rights as Property Rights

A second and closely related area of doctrinal problems concerns the distinction between property rights and other rights. Insofar as property law extends to cover numerous forms of incorporeal property existing merely because the law defines them as identifiable wealth, property means only what the law says it is *in a particular context*. Thus, as Vandevelde points out in relation to American law, we cannot predict the kind of rights which will exist for a property owner merely by virtue of their categorization as *property* rights. They vary extensively with the type of property.[34] The point applies equally to English developments. Of course different kinds of property, such as real and personal, have always been associated with different kinds of rights. But any attempt to assimilate property rights in different fields of property law seems increasingly difficult. Nowadays, the diverse fields of property law - and, again, particularly intellectual property law - show fundamentally differing principles at work determining the nature of property rights. For example, the Plant Varieties and Seeds Act 1964[35] defines

90

the unique rights of an owner of a plant variety at the same time as it creates
this special type of property.

But again it is important to make clear what exactly is new in these developments
and what is not. Just as property law has for centuries protected assets hard to
think of as things, so it has long accepted a great variety of types of property
right. The change that has occurred in relation to property rights as in relation
to property assets is a change in the relative social significance of different property
forms. As more abstract forms of property asset have become of central economic
importance so the diverse kinds of property right associated with them have
assumed increasing importance in legal doctrine. The problem of the diversity
of property rights is moving from being a peripheral problem of property law
doctrine to a central one.

Thus if the categorization of rights as property rights is to be of continuing
value in legal doctrine it is necessary to identify what, if anything, such rights
have in common in modern law. Some literature emphasizes the right of exclusion,
in some sense, as central to the property-holder's position,[36] other writing
explores the position of the property-holder as regards claims by or against third
parties,[37] or the kinds of remedies given by law to protect property.[38] On another
view property rules uniquely create entitlements which can be taken from the
holder only if he agrees and at a price which he negotiates.[39] These possible
identifications of the nature of property rights cannot be discussed here. What
is important is merely to note that the matter remains one of controversy and
is important to the coherence of property law as a field of doctrine.

Use Value and Exchange Value

A third area of problems affecting the coherence of property law doctrine concerns
the relationship between exchange value and use value as matters for protection
by property law. The nature of this relationship has re-emerged as an issue of
great difficulty and importance. It has received more discussion in English writing
on property law than have the two previously mentioned problem areas[40] but,
as will appear, it turns out to be closely related to them.

Typically, modern property law has focused its attention particularly on the
protection of rights to exchange value, that is, on the property-holder's right not
only to use his property asset but also to deal freely with it as a commodity in
legal transactions by which he can exchange it or some part of it for money or
some other commodity. In English land law the simplification of conveyancing
is recognized as the guiding principle behind the 1925 real property legislation.
The legal estates constructed to facilitate the realization of exchange value are
the central pillars of the law around which other interests are arranged. The
importance of the trust for sale and the associated doctrine of conversion; the
doctrine of overreaching in the law of strict settlements; the relationship of legal
and equitable rights under a trust – all these are badges of the centrality of exchange
value among the objects of protection in property law. Rights recognized by law
as mere rights of use without exchange value have, in general, not been treated
as proprietary rights. Although this is a tendency of the law rather than an absolute
principle the general orthodox position is that a proprietary right must be

The Law of Property and Legal Theory 91

'definable, identifiable by third parties, capable in its nature of assumption by third parties, and have some degree of permanence or stability'.[41]

However, recently in numerous contexts assertions have frequently been made before English courts of the need for much more extensive protection of use value alone by means of property rights. The cases have usually involved a conflict between a claimed right of an occupier to remain on land and the claim of exclusive control asserted by the holder of a legal estate in the land. In many recent cases English courts have given protection to the occupier even against a third-party assignee of the legal estate and even though, on orthodox analysis, the occupier possesses no more than a licence to occupy the land.[42] A claim that some years ago would have been recognized as, at best, contractual or involving other rights, founded on reliance in good faith, solely against the original holder of the legal estate, is now increasingly recognized as involving proprietary rights enforceable against third parties. Sometimes the occupier's rights are protected by imposition of a constructive trust on the holder of the legal estate, but a variety of formulations and remedies is used.

These developments should also be seen in the context of an extensive growth, over a longer period, of legislative protection of use value especially through landlord and tenant legislation creating, for example, the 'status of irremovability' of the holder of a statutory tenancy which is non-assignable and therefore lacks exchange value.[43] Also important has been the statutory protection of rights of occupation of the matrimonial home.[44]

Developments such as these create doctrinal uncertainties about the nature of property rights in general and about the legal policy which provides the rationality of their protection. Statutory developments, such as Rent Acts protections, can often be rationalized by property lawyers as the intrusion of public law principles in a private law area. The uncertainties resulting from this intrusion may thus be seen as inevitable and attributable to a familiar and well-understood cause, the clash of social policy and planning considerations and private rights. But the registration of seemingly irreconcilable conflicts between protection of use value and protection of exchange value *within* private law doctrine is harder for many lawyers to accept. In *Williams & Glyn's Bank* v. *Boland* Lord Scarman made the opposing practical considerations in one such instance explicit: on the one hand, the convenience and efficiency of conveyancing promoted by clarity of legal title and the absence of encumbrances on title; on the other, social justice in the protection of a person occupying the land on the faith of a prior agreement or understanding from eviction by a third party obtaining the legal estate.[45] In other cases the problem has been to construct a form of property right primarily to protect use or occupation which would achieve justice without attracting a range of unintended consequences from the applicability of pre-existing property law rules or else undermining those rules.[46]

Finally, it should be noted that the greater attention to rights of use as distinct objects of protection by property rights has emerged in an era when law has increasingly restricted some important use rights of property-holders,[47] for example through planning and pollution controls. In a wider context we can thus speak of a fragmentation, not only of ownership (as orthodox English property law commentary has always asserted), but of the very concept of property right

92

itself. Hence the connection with the more general problem, already discussed, of identifying property rights as such.

THE RELEVANCE OF THEORY

Lawyers require little or no aid from legal theory to produce immediate practical case-by-case solutions to doctrinal difficulties such as those discussed above. Conceptual organization of doctrine of the kind offered by much analytical jurisprudence is likely to be no more than *ex post facto* rationalization of pragmatic legal solutions arrived at in the practical business of deciding cases and legislating to meet immediate perceived regulatory needs. Lawyers' lack of concern for general analysis of the nature of 'property' in the rapid contemporary doctrinal development of intellectual property law illustrates the point. So does the seemingly free and easy approach, noted above, to recognition and specification of rights as 'property rights'. Lawyers systematize and generalize doctrine as seems necessary and possible for the task in hand. Broad concepts give way where necessary to the demands of the moment. And sometimes such concepts seem unhelpful or irrelevant to the solution of pressing doctrinal problems.[48]

How then can theoretical analysis be used in the ways suggested in the earlier sections of this paper to aid understanding of the problems of property law doctrine discussed above? Legal theory can aid the lawyer's understanding by attempting to explain how such doctrinal problems have arisen and what conditions and causes have contributed to them. We should, indeed, as Durkheim suggested, treat *certain* aspects of doctrinal change as an index, a reflection, of wider social change outside the professional milieu of law. But the reflection may, and often will, be distorted in complex ways. Many characteristics of legal doctrine are to be explained in terms of the effects of this narrow professional milieu; and doctrine can, of course, bring about change as well as reflect it. A complex set of interactions between ideas and behaviour is involved.

The problems of contemporary property law which this paper has identified can, when set in a wider context, be arranged in a kind of circle. Property law in capitalist society has been concerned, above all, with identifying and protecting assets which are economically valuable as objects of commerce. The orthodox emphasis on exchange-value protection suggests this but it is reflected more generally in what Charles Donahue has described as the tendency in property law towards the agglomeration in a single legal person of the exclusive right to possess, privilege to use, and power to convey the object of property,[49] an agglomeration which makes possible the unfettered employment of property assets as capital. Thus, at the same time as the law has recognized an ever widening range of commercially valuable assets as objects of property, it has shown a preference for making rights in such assets as complete as possible so as to facilitate economic transactions and the security of capital.

The increasing importance of what we might call knowledge-assets – objects of intellectual property – as wealth has caused serious difficulties for this orthodox approach to property law. The difficulty of recognizing these fully and unambiguously as property-assets and of giving anything like absolute rights in them has been a social rather than a technical-legal difficulty. Insofar as forms of information are to be protected as private property, law is faced with the idea, deeply rooted in contemporary Western societies, that freedom of information is socially valuable. There are fundamental ideological problems in pushing too far the notion that knowledge can be privately owned and controlled. These problems are aggravated by the fact that, unlike the master's secrets which the apprentice of the past took a solemn oath to keep, modern knowledge-assets are typically owned or controlled by large corporations whose moral claims to such assets may seem less obvious than those of the human creator of knowledge derived from personal skills and experience.

In part the proliferation of *limited* property rights, and the more general fragmentation of the concept of 'property right', are a consequence of the problems involved in adapting property law to provide protection for the immense wealth which knowledge-assets represent in contemporary society. The limitation of scope of property rights in these assets has resulted from a *social* judgment that they can constitute property-assets to a strictly limited extent. It may well be, therefore, that the widespread attempts to assert 'new property' rights, and proprietary rights to use or enjoy assets held by others – including those recognized in the English cases and legislation on occupiers' rights – have been strongly, if indirectly, promoted by the disorienting effects on the concept of property which have been brought about by more general changes in the basis of wealth.

Thus property forms appropriate to protect the traditional forms of wealth of the 'haves' – the relatively economically powerful – encounter difficulties as forms of wealth change. As legal forms adapt to protect these new forms of wealth, new claims to property brought by the 'have-nots' (those holding relatively few orthodox property entitlements) seem to become plausible because a claim that, for example, social welfare entitlements or a job may be property[50] is, *prima facie*, no less convincing than that forms of knowledge can be protected as property. It might be argued that in both cases the success of the claim should depend on the degree of security which, according to a judgment of justice or social policy, a private expectation (obtained lawfully by grant or agreement) of income should be given by law when it cannot adequately be protected by contract or other personal rights. Indeed, Bruce Ackerman's analysis of recent developments in American constitutional adjudication on property rights suggests that these developments probably necessitate just such an approach in which the analysis of inherent doctrinal characteristics of 'property' is superseded by adjudication on an explicit policy basis.[51]

But the circle of problems is completed – and revolves without resolution – because any such rationalization and entrenchment in doctrine of this diversity of property forms further prevents the clarity of property rights which capitalist economic activity requires – the first problem in the circle.

The schematic character of the general line of analysis sketched above makes essential the caveat that it is intended merely to indicate directions for further theoretical enquiries. But it suggests that what theory can contribute perhaps most importantly to the lawyer's immediate tasks of analysis of doctrine is an assessment of how fundamentally rooted in wider social changes are the doctrinal tensions which he observes. That in itself may suggest whether piecemeal doctrinal

94

changes are likely to resolve the perceived difficulties or merely to displace them temporarily, or shift them to another area of the law. And, while legal theory as understood in this paper cannot properly dictate moral or political choices, it may, by clarifying the nature of doctrinal problems, indicate where these choices lie and how fundamental in their consequences they may be.

In the teaching of property law these considerations have a special relevance. Land law, perhaps more than any other area of legal doctrine, is frequently taught as an exercise in technicalities.[52] The technical 'rational strength' of doctrine in this area, distilled from the accumulations of legal pragmatism over long centuries, encourages this. But the matters discussed in this paper suggest that particular social/historical conditions lie behind the central technical problems of doctrine. Further, once the sociological factors shaping doctrine and its problems are recognized it becomes possible to understand more clearly the moral and political issues which arise in this broader legal context. Theoretical analysis, by showing law as an aspect of social life, should confront the student of law with the moral choices and dilemmas which 'law-as-technique' and legal ideology disguise or deny. Nevertheless, it is necessary to insist: legal theory exclusively serves no particular constituency. Its perennial responsibility is not primarily to improve legal education, legal practice or legal services. It is simply to promote understanding of the nature of law.

As for the present tasks of theory in this area several related areas of study suggested by the discussion above seem important. One of these concerns the relationship discussed in much of the social scientific, philosophical and historical literature on property[53] between property and *power*. This is a matter which warrants much more analysis. The concept of property in law is a device by which law guarantees relations of power while disguising their nature. In private law, power is not normally recognized directly in legal doctrine as an attribute of an individual which he can wield over another. This is because the fundamental principle of general equality before the law of all citizens is inconsistent with any such general recognition. The property form allows the attributes which give an individual power over another to be *separated* from him in legal doctrine as an asset which he owns. The attributes, facilities, capacities and resources which give some persons power over others become 'things' – objects of property – which can be conceptualized in law as distinct from their holder. In property law, therefore, the situation is not that persons are recognized as having power over others but that power resides in the property which they own – in the things which are conceived by law as distinct from them and to which they are connected by legal rights acquired in various possible ways which, as far as legal doctrine is concerned, are equally available to all. Looking at matters in this way suggests why the problem of defining modern types of property-asset in legally convincing ways may be more than just a minor technical problem for legal doctrine. If the property form provides a particular framework for the exercise of power which is ideologically significant, changes both in the kinds of assets recognized by law and in the kinds of property rights so recognized may have very important consequences for legal ideology.

Closely connected as another area for further enquiry is the relationship between popular lay conceptions of property and lawyers' conceptions. This is something

The Law of Property and Legal Theory   95

which has been extensively considered speculatively in the American literature.[54] But the foregoing discussion of social problems in adapting the property form to secure a convincing legal recognition of knowledge-assets indicates an importance in enquiring into lay conceptions of property which is quite distinct from the considerations involved in the constitutional debates of the American writings. Thus if, as suggested above, the property form disguises and guarantees power by means of the specific relationship established in ideology between the person, on the one hand, and the thing owned, on the other, the thing-ownership conception of property cannot be dismissed as insignificant quite as easily as modern Hohfeldian legal analysis suggests. The conception may be of great social or ideological significance, even if of limited value as an aid to lawyers in solving technical problems in doctrine. Ackerman argues that the thing-ownership conception is, indeed, fundamental to lay conceptions of property.[55] If this is so it may well be that ideology sets important limitations on the scope of legal doctrinal innovation in the property law field.

Analysis of the ideological significance of the property form may help in understanding the persistence of two distinct and apparently competing doctrinal traditions in Western property law: the continental Romanist conception of property as *dominium* over things (single owner having absolute entitlement to a distinct asset) and the common law conception of fragmentation of ownership (no *dominus* but many possible kinds of property entitlement held by different people in relation to a single material source of wealth). It may be suggested that *technically* the common law conception is more appropriate to encompass the changing forms of wealth which have emerged in Western societies since the beginnings of capitalist development, and to provide extremely flexible and sophisticated devices for their deployment and protection. On the other hand, the Romanist conception of *dominium* which serves to crystallize ownership in terms of a distinct, identifiable asset owned (*res*) and a distinct, more or less absolute owner (*dominus*) provides a means of clearly distinguishing property rights from personal rights. In this way it creates the clear separation of owner and owned which, it has been suggested above, is perhaps fundamental to some major *ideological* effects of the property form. That continental systems have sought to modify Romanist tradition in many ways to create considerable flexibility in property conceptions reflects the problem of meeting technical demands on legal doctrine. Equally, the tensions in common law property doctrine identified in this paper suggest that ideological aspects of law may set limits on its technical capabilities.

What lies behind all of these suggestions for further enquiries is the belief that in the area of property doctrine, as in so many other areas of legal thought and analysis, theory can probably achieve most by contributing towards an understanding of the ideological foundations and effects of the law - the wider, taken-for-granted currents of thought and belief in society to which legal ideas are related and to which they contribute. The idea of property has often been associated, not only in a long tradition of political theory but also in popular conceptions, with broad notions of liberty. The orthodox conception of property as the unfettered freedom to do as one will with lawfully held objects of wealth, whatever the social effects of so doing and irrespective of the claims of the

96

property-less to a share in the resources of life, supports a conception of liberty
as the freedom to exercise property-power for the accumulation of profit without
any limits except those created by the opposed property-power of others. One
consequence of the extensive challenges to the orthodox legal conception of
property which this paper has discussed may be a more widespread recognition
that liberty as an ideal in contemporary conditions must mean not the liberty
of property-power but the liberty of *property-security* in which the diffusion of
guaranteed entitlements to the use of resources necessary for personal welfare
is recognized as the basis of genuine freedom. Thus tensions in legal doctrine
in this area may promote ideological change in various ways as well as reflecting it.

NOTES

1 F. H. Lawson, *The Rational Strength of English Law* (1951) p. 79.
2 Generally in this paper I use the term 'lawyers' to refer to both practising and academic
   lawyers. Since the central concern of discussion throughout the paper is with legal
   doctrine and its problems and consequences, this linking of legal practitioners and law
   teachers in a single category is intended in this context to identify a range of legal
   'participants' who have a particular shared professional/intellectual concern with the
   integrity of legal doctrine – its coherence, clarity, rationality and utility as a body of
   knowledge and as a basis of practice. In many other contexts it would, of course, be
   important to distinguish typically different concerns of legal academics and practising
   lawyers, as well as of sub-groups within each of these two broad, ambiguous and
   overlapping categories.
3 The conception of legal theory sketched in the following paragraphs is elaborated in
   Cotterrell, 'English Conceptions of the Role of Theory in Legal Analysis' (1983) 46
   Modern Law Rev. 681; and in *The Sociology of Law: An Introduction* (1984).
4 Twining, 'Evidence and Legal Theory' (chapter 4 above) p. 62.
5 *Id.*, p. 62.
6 *Id.*, p. 64.
7 *Id.*, p. 63. For a response, see below p. 253.
8 See Cotterrell, *The Sociology of Law, op. cit.*, ch. 6.
9 *Id.*, pp. 120 *et seq.*; Cotterrell, 'Legality and Political Legitimacy in the Sociology of
   Max Weber' in *Legality, Ideology and the State* (1983; ed. D. Sugarman) pp. 84 *et seq.*
10 Twining, *op. cit.*, p. 62.
11 *Id.*, p. 64.
12 T. C. Grey, 'The Disintegration of Property' in *Property* (1980; ed. J. R. Pennock
   and J. W. Chapman).
13 G. Gilmore, *The Death of Contract* (1974).
14 Grey, *op. cit.*, p. 73.
15 See e.g. Vandevelde, 'The New Property of the Nineteenth Century: The Development
   of the Modern Concept of Property' (1980) 29 *Buffalo Law Rev.* 325.
16 Reich, 'The New Property' (1964) 73 *Yale Law J* 733. Reich's paper has had very
   considerable influence and its central thesis has been regarded as path-breaking. The
   modern importance of 'new property' rights is, however, stressed by Thurman Arnold
   in his *The Folklore of Capitalism* (1937) pp. 121-2. See also Lynn, 'Legal and Economic
   Implications of the Emergence of Quasi-Public Wealth' (1956) 65 *Yale Law J* 786.
17 US Constitution Amend. V, cl. 4.
18 US Constitution Amend. V, cl. 3; Amend XIV, sec. 1.

The Law of Property and Legal Theory 97

19 *Penn Central Transp. Co.* v. *New York City* (1978) 438 US 104; Grey, *op. cit.*, p. 72.
20 W. Blackstone, *Commentaries on the Laws of England* (15th edn; 1809) vol. II, p. 2.
21 Vandevelde, *op. cit.*
22 Cf. *Belfast Corp.* v. *O. D. Cars Ltd* [1960] AC 490, interpreting the provision regarding the taking of property without compensation under the Government of Ireland Act 1920, s.5(1).
23 Hoebel, 'Fundamental Legal Concepts as Applied in the Study of Primitive Law' (1942) 51 *Yale Law J* 951; Hallowell, 'The Nature and Function of Property as a Social Institution' (1943) 1 *J Legal and Political Sociology* 115.
24 F. Pollock and F. W. Maitland, *The History of English Law* (1968 edn) vol. II, p. 124.
25 Lowie, 'Incorporeal Property in Primitive Society' (1928) 37 *Yale Law J* 551; Hoebel, *op. cit.*
26 W. Friedmann, *Law in a Changing Society* (2nd edn; 1972) p. 117.
27 F. H. Lawson, 'Comparative Conclusion' in *International Encyclopedia of Comparative Law*, vol. VI (1975) ch. 2.
28 (1869) LR 7 Eq. 488 at p. 492.
29 See e.g. the remarks in the American case of *Nichols* v. *Universal Picture Corp.* (1930) 45 F 2d 119 at p. 121.
30 Ulmer and Kolle, 'Copyright Protection in Computer Programs' (1983) 14 *International Rev. Industrial Property and Copyright Law* 161; A. Wilson, 'The Protection of Computer Programs under Common Law - Procedural Aspects and United Kingdom Copyright Law and Trade Secrets' in *The Legal Protection of Computer Software* (1981; ed. H. Brett and L. Perry) pp. 80 *et seq.*
31 W. R. Cornish, *Intellectual Property* (1981) pp. 297-8; Dworkin, 'The Moral Right and English Copyright Law' (1981) 12 *International Rev. Industrial Property and Copyright Law* 476.
32 Ulmer and Kolle, *op. cit.*, p. 181.
33 *Boardman* v. *Phipps* [1967] 2 AC 46; and see Hammond, 'Theft of Information' (1984) 100 *Law Quarterly Rev.* 252; Cornish, *op. cit.*, pp. 289-90 on confidential information as property.
34 Vandevelde, *op. cit.*
35 As amended by the Plant Varieties Act 1983.
36 E.g. M. Cohen, *Law and the Social Order* (1933) p. 46.
37 E.g. Alexander, 'The Concept of Property in Private and Constitutional Law: The Ideology of the Scientific Turn in Legal Analysis' (1982) 82 *Columbia Law Rev.* 1545.
38 Grey, *op. cit.*, p. 72.
39 Calabresi and Melamed, 'Property Rules, Liability Rules, and Inalienability: One View of the Cathedral' (1972) 85 *Harvard Law Rev.* 1089.
40 See e.g. Simmonds, 'The Changing Face of Private Law: Doctrinal Categories and the Regulatory State' (1982) 2 *Legal Studies* 257.
41 Lord Wilberforce in *National Provincial Bank Ltd* v. *Ainsworth* [1965] AC 1175 at p. 1248.
42 See e.g. Moriarty, 'Licences and Land Law: Legal Principles and Public Policies' (1984) 100 *Law Quarterly Rev.* 376.
43 G. C. Cheshire and E. H. Burn, *Modern Law of Real Property* (13th edn; 1982) pp. 455-6.
44 Matrimonial Homes Act 1983.
45 *Williams and Glyn's Bank Ltd* v. *Boland* [1981] AC 487 at pp. 509-10.
46 See e.g. *Binions* v. *Evans* [1972] ch. 359; *Re Sharpe* [1980] 1 WLR 219; *Lyus* v. *Prowsa Developments Ltd* [1982] 1 WLR 1044.
47 See e.g. Friedmann, *op. cit.*, pp. 102 *et seq.*

98

48 See e.g. D. Harris, 'The Concept of Possession in English Law' in *Oxford Essays in Jurisprudence* (1961; ed. A. G. Guest).
49 C. Donahue Jr, 'The Future of the Concept of Property Predicted from its Past' in *Property* (1980; ed. J. R. Pennock and J. W. Chapman).
50 Reich, *op. cit.*
51 B. A. Ackerman, *Private Property and the Constitution* (1977).
52 A laudable attempt to provide a student textbook escaping from this pattern is K. J. Gray and P. D. Symes, *Real Property and Real People* (1981) which in expounding doctrine seeks to look at, *inter alia*, 'the underlying ideology of property law' (p. 7). Despite there being much of value in the book's discussions its theoretical content is inadequate to enable it to do more than scratch the surface of the most fundamental issues surrounding real property doctrine. Thus the models of *Gemeinschaft* and *Gesellschaft* social relations are the fundamental, and almost the sole, tools of theoretical analysis employed. Property law as a whole is seen as expressing social relations of *Gesellschaft*. Such new developments as the decision in *Williams and Glyn's Bank v. Boland* are interpreted as a reaffirmation of *Gemeinschaft* values. All this carries us a little way, but not far. First, it does not explain why such values are being reaffirmed in such a context. Secondly, the concepts of *Gemeinschaft* and *Gesellschaft* are used to epitomize 'the policy motivations which underlie the case law' (p. 364) rather than to provide a basis for understanding the nature of the social relations which law regulates. Hence these snippets of social theory are used only to elaborate the rhetoric of the law, not to pierce it by means of theoretical analysis.
53 Cohen, *op. cit.*; Philbrick, 'Changing Conceptions of Property in Law' (1938) 86 *University of Pennsylvania Law Rev.* 691; K. Renner, *The Institutions of Private Law and their Social Functions* (1949); E. B. Pashukanis, *Law and Marxism: A General Theory* (1978); Reich, *op. cit.*
54 Ackerman, *op. cit.*; Alexander, *op. cit.*
55 Ackerman, *op. cit.*

[13]
Some Sociological Aspects of the Controversy around the Legal Validity of Private Purpose Trusts

In the field of equity, as in other areas of legal doctrine, it is possible to find conceptual problems which, despite very extensive academic discussion, have remained unresolved for many decades. In some such cases legal logic seems to have run into a circle of reiterated, conflicting arguments; doctrinal analysis cannot lift itself beyond the impasse. The student of these problem areas needs to seek explanations for the difficulties beyond the logic of normative legal analysis. Perhaps the problems reflect conditioning circumstances not directly recognised in legal doctrine, nor in the commentary which has tried to clarify and develop it. In such instances a sociological perspective, concerned to interpret and explain structures of legal doctrine in terms of their social (including professional) origins and effects, may be able to help to explain why doctrine fails to resolve the dilemmas it seems to provoke, and why legal commentary and criticism run into a stalemate of well-rehearsed, apparently irreconcilable views. Further, where courts have addressed a particular doctrinal problem over a considerable period, broad patterns of variation in judicial approaches over time may suggest, in an illuminating way, changes in the wider social and intellectual context within which doctrinal problems recur.

The question of the legal validity of (private) purpose trusts, sometimes called unenforceable trusts, honorary trusts or trusts of imperfect obligation, is a particularly interesting topic to consider in this context. Purpose trusts — non-charitable trusts lacking identifiable beneficiaries and whose objects are expressed to be abstract purposes of some kind[1] — have been legally controversial in many common law jurisdictions throughout the twentieth century. Yet the theoretical arguments for and against their recognition as a species of valid trusts have remained largely constant in the same period. These arguments have been restated and elaborated in what is now a very large literature in the common law world. This paper will suggest that the academic debate on the validity of purpose trusts often reflects contrasting and potentially conflicting conceptions of the nature and social functions of trusts. The debate is incapable of resolution to the extent that these conceptions — called here the "moralistic" and the "property-receptacle" conceptions of the trust — are irreconcilable.

In this context, however, it is also necessary to explain what many commentators have seen as a major change in judicial attitudes to purpose trusts during the twentieth century. Nineteenth century cases in England and elsewhere generally do not suggest that purpose trusts must, by their nature, fail. In deed, in various contexts, courts upheld them without any indication that this category of trusts was inherently problematic. The modern view, however, explicitly denies general validity and deals with the older cases primarily as closely limited and even irrational exceptions to a strict requirement that non-charitable trusts must have identifiable beneficiaries. If such a change of judicial view has indeed occurred, why has this happened?

It will be suggested that, while there has been a significant change of judicial outlook, this is not to be seen as symptomatic of any change, in the relevant period, from a moralistic judicial conception of the trust to the property-receptacle conception. There is little evidence in the older

---

1 This paper is not concerned directly with the question of gifts or trusts for unincorporated associations but only with "pure" purpose trusts lacking any identification with a particular group or association of identifiable persons.

304

nineteenth century purpose trust cases that courts were willing to embrace explicitly the general idea of purpose trusts as a significant mechanism for implementing a trust creator's abstract purposes beyond the scope of charity. The purpose trust category, as such, was neither condemned nor approved in these older cases. This paper argues that judicial tolerance of private purpose trusts in nineteenth century cases depended primarily on the generally very limited scope of what settlors or testators sought to achieve through them. Hence they could be allowed as promoting family welfare in various ways, while not fundamentally threatening the property-receptacle conception of trusts which seems to have dominated most doctrinal development in trust law in England and other jurisdictions during the period in which judicial attitudes to purpose trusts evolved. When more ambitious objects of purpose trusts began to appear as a real possibility and to reach the courts in the twentieth century in a significantly changed modern social climate an explicitly hostile judicial view was quickly instituted, possibly because the purpose trust as an institution now appeared much more threatening, than it had previously, to basic trust principles premised on the property-receptacle conception of the trust.

The Nature of the Controversy

There are several established reasons why, in practice, a purpose trust is likely to fail even if, in principle, such a trust is legally possible. These reasons must be identified briefly, since theoretical argument about the general validity of purpose trusts is sometimes closely linked with them. Probably the most important of these ancillary reasons is uncertainty of objects. It may be very difficult to frame an abstract purpose with sufficient clarity to satisfy the test of certainty of objects, even if an abstract purpose can be a valid object of a private trust. Indeed, it may not be easy to predict the degree of clarity which will be judicially acceptable in such a trust. Secondly, purpose trusts may fail as infringing perpetuity rules, unless their duration is expressly or impliedly limited within the relevant perpetuity period. While all private trusts are confronted with complex legal policies with regard to the alienability of trust assets and the establishment and realisation of beneficial entitlements, the issues are, as will appear, especially difficult with regard to purpose trusts. Thirdly, courts have developed the modern doctrine that a trust may fail because its purpose is capricious; in other words, while not illegal, the object is treated judicially as so patently lacking in worth as to require that it be frustrated by invalidation of the trust. Fourthly, a purpose trust may fall foul of the public policy principle that a testator may not, in general, delegate his will-making power: "a man cannot disinherit his heirs by giving away his property unless he really gives it away; he cannot leave it to some one else to make a will for him, nor can he leave it to his trustees to give it for purposes which are to be completely in their discretion, unless these purposes are so indicated as in some sense to confer on a class of beneficiary an interest".[2] Although this last has been said to be "perhaps the strongest ground" for failure[3] the claim seems dubious given that wide powers of appointment have been upheld although they also seem to infringe the principle.[4] In this context the modern non-delegation principle may, perhaps, best be viewed as either the rationale of, or an alternative way of stating, the certainty requirements for a valid testamentary trust.

The central issue here is, however, whether a purpose trust can legally exist at all. Is there a principle denying validity to purpose trusts as such? What, indeed, would validity mean? It is generally agreed that purpose trusts cannot be positively enforced; that is, the trustees cannot legally be required to carry out the trust. Dispute in the literature for nearly a century has been, essentially, only as to whether trustees may act in fulfillment of the trust obligation if they wish.

Against allowing the purpose trust to be fulfilled, it is argued that every valid non-charitable trust must have identifiable beneficiaries. There must

2   *Attorney-General* v. *National Provincial and Union Bank of England* [1924] A.C. 262, 268 (per Viscount Haldane).

3   A. W. Scott, *Law of Trusts* (Boston, 4th ed., by W. F. Fratcher, 1987) vol. 2, p. 232 (para. 123).

4   *Ibid.*; and e.g. A. H. Oosterhoff, *Text, Commentary and Cases on Trusts* (Toronto, 3rd ed., by A. H. Oosterhoff and E. E. Gillese, 1987) 929-30.

306

be some person or persons in whose favour the court can order performance of the trust obligations. Only when beneficiaries' interests are at
stake can there be a final determination of the nature of the equitable
interests which the trustees are obliged to protect. Without beneficiaries
to require performance of a trust it is uncontrollable and ultimately its
obligations are undefined. Hence, a purpose trust arrangement fails by its
very nature. By contrast, in favour of validity it has been argued that,
where trust obligations are imposed on trustees, with certainty of intention, subject-matter and object (that is, purpose) satisfied, and the trustees
are willing to act, there can be no justification for preventing the carrying
into effect of the wishes of the trust's creator. Since the trustee cannot
be compelled to fulfil the trust, his situation may be essentially that of the
holder of a power of appointment. But to give effect to the arrangement
in that way is to promote in a reasonable manner the settlor or testator's
wishes. Adequate means of control are achieved since, even if no one else
is available to enforce,[5] those interested in the property on failure of the
purpose trust can come to court to complain (if only to claim the property)
should the purpose trust not be carried out.

When the most commonly expressed arguments are set out as above
it is apparent that they do not directly confront each other. On the one
side is an argument that purpose "trusts" are not trusts, essentially because
the court cannot provide the supervision and control required to ensure enforcement of a trust. On the other side is an argument that the abstract
purpose of a purpose trust should be allowed to succeed (the most con-

5   Sometimes it is suggested that the settlor, or the representatives of the
     testator's estate, may retain an interest in enforcement which can be asserted:
     see e.g. O. R. Marshall, "The Failure of the Astor Trust" (1953) 6 Current
     Legal Problems 151, 154; H. A. J. Ford and W. A. Lee, *Principles of the Law
     of Trusts* (Sydney, 1st ed., 1983) 171; H. A. J. Ford, "Dispositions for
     Purposes" in P. D. Finn ed., *Essays on Equity* (Sydney, 1985) 176; but the
     idea is rejected in *Re Astor's Settlement Trusts* [1952] Ch. 534. In some
     purpose trusts there may also be the possibility of enforcement by identifiable
     persons indirectly benefited by fulfilment of the purpose as in *Re Denley's
     Trust Deed* [1969] 1 Ch. 373.

venient means of doing so being generally held to be by treating the arrangement as conferring a power of appointment), if there is a designated person or persons willing to put the purpose into effect. It follows that the issues can be expressed in at least two quite different ways: Are purpose trusts a legitimate kind of trust or not? Should purpose trusts be allowed to have any effect or not? Hence, at least four general positions can be adopted from a combination of answers to those questions: (i) purpose trusts represent a legitimate kind of trust but to the extent that they are uncontrollable and unenforceable by the court they can have no effect even if the trustees might wish to implement the trust; (ii) purpose trusts are valid trusts, but insofar as they are unenforceable they take effect only if the trustees are willing to act; (iii) they are not trusts at all, because all (non-charitable) trusts must have identifiable beneficiaries or because they lack means of enforcement and control, and since the settlor or testator's intention was only to create a (non-existent) trust they cannot take effect as anything else (for example, as a power); (iv) they are not trusts (for reasons given in (iii)) but this is no justification for defeating the settlor or testator's underlying purpose if effect can be given to it by letting the arrangement take effect as a power of appointment.

Sometimes it is not easy to see in the literature which of the specific positions above is being advocated. James Barr Ames' 1892 essay on the "Tilden Trust",[6] which began the stream of modern theoretical commentary, argued that there could be no reason in law or policy for a refusal to give effect to the wishes of the trust creator where those wishes expressed a clear and lawful intention, and where trustees were willing and able to put the wishes into effect. Ames recognised the unenforceability of a purpose trust and advocated, as many later writers have, that purpose trusts should take effect as powers. A few years later John Chipman Gray[7] argued, against Ames, that *Morice* v. *Bishop of Durham* in 1804 had laid down what has come to be called in modern times the "beneficiary principle" (the requirement that every non-charitable trust must have an identifiable human or corporate beneficiary or beneficiar-

6   Ames, "The Failure of the 'Tilden Trust'" (1892) 5 Harv. L. R. 389.
7   Gray, "Gifts for a Non-Charitable Purpose" (1902) 15 Harv. L. R. 509.

308

ies). In *Morice* a bequest to the Bishop to be applied by him to "such objects of benevolence and liberality" as he should choose was held void. Sir William Grant M.R. stated:

There can be no trust, over the exercise of which this court will not assume a control; for an uncontrollable power of disposition would be ownership, and not trust. If there be a clear trust, but for uncertain objects, the property that is the subject of the trust is undisposed of and the benefit of such trust must result to those to whom the law gives the ownership in default of disposition by the former owner. But this doctrine does not hold good with regard to trusts for charity. Every other trust must have a definite object. There must be somebody in whose favour the court can decree performance.[8]

In Gray's analysis these words, applied and confirmed by later decisions, conclusively establish the beneficiary principle. It is true that exceptions in cases of testamentary trusts have long been recognised — trusts for the erection or maintenance of tombs or monuments, trusts for the maintenance of specific animals, trusts for the saying of masses for the soul of the testator or his relatives or descendants where such an object was not charitable, the obligation to pay funeral expenses, and — in some old American cases — trusts to take a slave to a free state and to emancipate the slave there. In 1934, in *Re Thompson*,[9] a trust to promote fox-hunting was also held in England to be a valid purpose trust, and a few other isolated cases exist.[10] Writing of those purpose trusts recognised

8   *Morice* v. *Bishop of Durham* (1804) 9 Ves. 399, 404. (Decision affd. (1805) 10 Ves. 522).

9   [1934] Ch. 342.

10 See e.g. *Re Gibbons* [1917] 1 Ir. R. 448 (property to be used by the legatee priests, "to my best spiritual advantage, as conscience and sense of duty may direct"); *Re Will of Ryan* (1925) 60 Ir. L. T. R. 57 (property bequeathed to a priest "to be expended for my spiritual benefit according to his discretion). I leave out of account here cases of "impure" purpose trusts arising from gifts to unincorporated associations.

as of 1902, Gray claimed that no real exceptions to the beneficiary principle existed, most of the lines of case law being ambiguous in effect. Only the payment of funeral expenses and the promotion of charitable objects were indisputably objects for which valid trusts for abstract purposes could exist, the former on narrow grounds of necessity, the latter because of the special public interest involved.

Since the Ames-Gray dispute, numerous commentaries on the legal character of purpose trusts have been published. Given the volume of literature it is striking that the debate has been conducted with little explicit judicial or legislative guidance. In England, for example, it was not until 1952 that the rationale and status of the beneficiary principle was examined in detail in a reported judgment.[11] Since then only a handful of cases has directly addressed the issue. Nevertheless, it seems clear that the beneficiary principle is now generally accepted or assumed in many common law jurisdictions, including those of Canada, Australia and the United States. At the same time, the existence of the tombs, monuments, and animals exceptions is also widely recognised by the courts though generally with little satisfactory explanation of any rationale for these cases. In England the courts seem to have ruled out (again with little detailed analysis of the issues) the possibility of allowing a purpose trust to take effect as a power,[12] a view which, it has been suggested, is likely to be generally followed in Australia.[13] In Canada the power solution has been adopted, apparently without great difficulties, by various provincial statutes,[14] and in the United States this solution has now been adopted in the Restatement.[15]

---

11 Re Astor's Settlement Trusts, supra n. 5.

12 I.R.C. v. Broadway Cottages Trust [1955] Ch. 20, 36 (per Jenkins L.J.); Re Shaw [1957] 1 W.L.R. 729, 746 (per Harman J.); Re Endacott [1960] 232, 246 (per Lord Evershed M.R.).

13 Ford, "Dispositions for Purposes", supra n. 5, at 177.

14 See e.g. Perpetuities Act, R. S. A. 1980, c. P-4, s. 20 (Alberta); Perpetuities Act R. S. O. 1980, c. 374, s. 16 (Ontario); Perpetuities Act R. S. B. C. 1979, c. 321, s. 21 (British Columbia).

15 Restatement 2nd, Trusts, s. 124 (1959).

310

Two Conceptions of the Nature of Trusts

To some extent, the literature of commentary has taken on a life of its own not constrained by the meagre resources of judicial and legislative doctrine. This may suggest that more is at stake here than a few cases on tombs and animals. In general, it would seem that assertion of a beneficiary principle as such amounts to a claim that purpose trusts are not trusts at all; they lack essential private trust characteristics. Thus, it is emphasised that there cannot be a legal interest in the trustee(s) without a beneficial interest in an identifiable beneficiary.[16] A trust duty cannot exist without a correlative right of a beneficiary.[17] The beneficiary principle thus identifies a fundamental characteristic of the trust as an institution. To deny it would "alter one of the basic ideas of the trust".[18]

What, then, is the import of the many contributions to the literature which advocate that purpose trusts should take effect insofar as trustees are willing to implement them? As noted above, such an argument does not *necessarily* commit its advocate to a view on the question of whether purpose trusts are a species of valid trusts. The argument may amount to no more than saying that something (not necessarily to be characterised as a trust) should be salvaged from the settlor or testator's failed trust intention. Thus Scott remarks that "the question is not one of terminology. The question is rather whether and to what extent the desire of the testator

16 Gray, *supra* n. 7, at 513-4.
17 Oosterhoff, *supra* n. 4, at 927.
18 G. G. Bogert and G. T. Bogert, *The Law of Trusts and Trustees* (St. Paul, MI, 1951) para. 166, quoted in Scott, *supra* n. 3, at 243 (para. 124). The revised second edition (1979) notes the argument that a definite beneficiary and enforceability are "inherent characteristics of a private trust" (para. 166). See also D. W. M. Waters, *Law of Trusts in Canada* (Toronto, 1st ed., 1974) 421 ("the whole concept of a trust assumes that there is *somebody* who has a beneficial interest . . ."); C. Sweet, "Restraints on Alienation" (Part 2) (1917) 33 L. Q. R. 342, 357-8 (a purpose trust is "no trust at all" since it lacks "one of the essential characteristics of a trust, that of being enforceable at the suit of some individual").

should be effective".[19] Certainly a wide variety of arguments is employed in the literature to justify allowing purpose trusts to operate in some manner to fulfil the trust creator's intention. But writers who advocate that failed purpose trusts could take effect as if they had been created as powers often appear to put relatively little emphasis on the beneficiary principle as a necessary component of trust law, stressing that a significant amount of case law can be marshalled to raise doubts on this score, and some commentators even deny that the principle contributes fundamentally to defining the nature of private trusts in general.[20] What these writers often emphasise is not the need for beneficiaries, but respect for the trust creator's intention. The essential validity of the arrangement which has been set up is to be defined by the lawful and clear purposes of the trust creator and by the essentially moral necessity for a mechanism to give maximum effect to these purposes.

It might be said that, in this view, the essence of the trust is a moral obligation of conscience, undertaken to fulfil the wishes of the trust creator. While in most trusts the moral obligation is also legally enforced, the absence of legal enforcement in the case of purpose trusts does not, from this standpoint, cancel the moral obligation or remove all legal

---

19 Scott, *supra* n. 3, at 243 (para. 124).

20 See e.g. D. C. Potter, "Trusts for Non-Charitable Purposes" (1949) 13 Conveyancer (n.s.) 418, 424 (purpose trust a valid, though not directly enforceable trust); W. O. Hart, "Some Reflections on the Case of *Re Chardon*" (1937) 53 L. Q. R. 24, 33 (purpose trust may be good even though it lacks ascertained individuals to enforce it); J. W. Harris, "Trust, Power and Duty" (1971) 87 L. Q. R. 31, 56-7 (no single notion of duty applies to all trusts except a duty to hold property for persons or purposes); and n. b. Maitland's definition of trusts (in F. W. Maitland, *Equity* (London, rev. ed., 1936) 44 which includes trusts for purposes. *Cf.* A. K. R. Kiralfy, "'Purpose Trusts', Powers and Conditions" (1950) 14 Conveyancer (n.s.) 374, 374-5 (purpose trusts are not trusts at all but should take effect as powers); and R. E. Megarry, "Note" (1952) 68 L. Q. R. 449, 451 (purpose trust creates "what is in honour a duty but in law only a power of application for the designated purpose").

312

significance from the arrangement which has been created to frame it. The fulfilment of this arrangement by the trustee remains feasible insofar as it has a practical legal form and as long as the trustee himself recognises and accepts the obligation to apply identifiable property to identified purposes, which is the fundamental obligation of any trust. Viewed in this way, the lack of legal enforcement is not an essential defect of a purpose trust, radically distinguishing it from other express trusts: "the defect in the obligatory nature of the trust is not a contradiction in terms, for it is not the obligation but its enforcement which is at fault".[21] The lack of means of enforcement poses merely practical difficulties. It is a matter of fact (not of principle) in each case whether the difficulties can be satisfactorily overcome.

This *moralistic conception* of the trust also explains, to some extent, the apparent lack of concern on the part of many pro-validity writers for the English judicial view that a valid power is not to be spelt out of an invalid trust. Powers and trust obligations are both means of giving effect to the intentions of donors. A logical correlate of the moralistic conception of the trust is that the distinction between trusts and powers is a matter of degree, rather than a rigid separation, since they may embody, often in complex combinations, the legal mechanisms for implementing obligations of varying force and scope. Thus, "there is no fixed dividing line between trust and power".[22] By contrast, those who stress the beneficiary principle tend also, like Gray, to be suspicious of the power solution, hold-

21 L. Leigh, "Trusts of Imperfect Obligation" (1955) 18 Mod. L. R. 120, 137; and see S. Gardner, *An Introduction to the Law of Trusts* (Oxford, 1990) 185 (beneficiary principle a misguided deduction from the principle that trusts must be enforceable).

22 Potter, *supra* n. 20, at 424; J. Hackney, *Understanding Equity and Trusts* (London, 1987) 53; but *cf.* Leigh, *supra* n. 21, at 134 (purpose trusts should be allowed to take effect but argument for a power involves "too great a distortion" of the terms of the original gift). Interestingly, the Ontario legislation (*supra* n. 14) declares both that a purpose trust falling within the terms of the statute "is valid" (presumably as a trust) and "shall be construed as a power".

ing that trusts and powers must be clearly distinguished and applying distinct principles to each, or holding that the power interpretation could not avoid the fundamental legal defects of the purpose trust arrangement.[23]

Since in purpose trust cases application of the beneficiary principle usually leads to the result that the settlor's or testator's purpose will be held to fail, it follows that insistence on this approach normally entails that the notion of the trust as a receptacle for the property entitlements of specified beneficiaries takes clear priority over the idea of the trust as the moral repository of the trust creator's wishes. In terms of this *property-receptacle conception* of trusts the integrity of a workable arrangement for holding legal title to assets of beneficial owners is the primary, if not the sole consideration. A trust creator who has not set up such an arrangement has not created a trust worthy of legal protection. The view entailed here is well expressed as that which holds that (except as regards charitable trusts) "the primary function of the trust . . . [is] the creation of estates or interests".[24]

In general, therefore, the moralistic conception puts primary emphasis on the sanctity of the trust creator's lawful intention, while the property-receptacle conception emphasises the importance of all property being subject to definite beneficial entitlements. An "unattached" fund not beneficially owned is abhorrent to the property-receptacle conception; the defeat of the donor's intentions (even where these involve excluding or restricting the claims of specific beneficiaries to the trust property) is equally abhorrent to the moralistic conception. Ultimately the two conceptions conflict. In the particular field of purpose trusts they are irreconcilable, because the choice between them is an all-or-nothing one. Adoption of one or other conception does not merely modify the scope or effect of a trust; in this context it determines whether or not a certain

---

23   See e.g. E. O. Walford, "Gifts to Non-Charitable Bodies" (1960) 24 Conveyancer (n.s.) 278; Sweet, *supra* n. 18, at 359 n. 3; R. M. Eggleston, "Purpose Trusts" (1940) 2 Res Judicatae 118, 122-4.

24   Ford, "Dispositions for Purposes", *supra* n. 5, at 176. *Cf.* Sweet, *supra* n. 18, at 355.

314

category of trust can exist at all. The choice in favour of giving some effect to purpose trusts, which has been made by many academic commentators, is typically a choice in favour of diversity in using the trust form flexibly for a wide range of desired purposes. In this sense it is compatible with the general assumption that the history of trust law is the story of the adaptation of a fruitful legal device to an ever-increasing range of economic and social purposes. Yet, as will appear, it is not the choice which the courts have generally made throughout the past two centuries.

The Social Context of the Beneficiary Principle

The purpose trust controversy is primarily an ideological dispute — that is, in this context, a dispute about what kinds of devices trusts "really" and "obviously", by their nature, are and should be. It is not fundamentally a dispute on instrumental issues, such as whether or not property owners should be able to dedicate their property for abstract non-charitable purposes. There are many ways in which they can do so, for example by contractual arrangements, such as an *inter vivos* mandate, by transfer to a company limited by guarantee, or perhaps by conferment of a power of appointment. Uncertainties and inconveniences surround some of these methods and they do not necessarily provide the exact benefits sought from a trust arrangement. But means of circumventing practical difficulties arising from application of the beneficiary principle certainly exist.

Undoubtedly, important instrumental issues surround purpose trusts. (Can adequate means of legally controlling or supervising them be found? Is indirect enforcement by residuary legatees, next of kin or people incidentally benefited, or direct enforcement by the settlor or the testator's personal representatives, acceptable or feasible?) But if these issues were the primary ones it might be supposed that they would have been rationally resolved for or against validity or examined as fundamental matters of principle long ago.[25] Unenforceability by the court has, however, been

25 The possibilities are thoughtfully explored in L. McKay, "Trusts for Purposes: Another View" (1973) 27 Conveyancer (n.s.) 420.

seen as a general, major problem only in relatively modern cases, where it often provides a reason for invalidating purpose trusts as a category. In older specific purpose trust cases, while enforcement problems are recognised, they are usually treated pragmatically (often the presence of a residuary legatee who could complain to the court and demand the property if the purpose trustee fails to act, is treated as sufficient to guarantee enforceability and control by the court). Equally, in some jurisdictions the enforcement problem is now treated as a purely practical one not necessarily entailing the invalidity of a purpose trust. Thus, under recently enacted legislation in Bermuda, purpose trusts which are specific, reasonable and possible and not contrary to public policy or unlawful can be created to last for up to 100 years. The trust must be created by a deed or will providing for the appointment of a person to enforce the trust and for the appointment of a successor to such enforcer.[26] In other legal systems, however, the matter is viewed differently. The enforcement issue in modern cases in England and some other jurisdictions is, it seems, the pretext upon which a general negative perspective on purpose trusts can be defended.

Why might the defence of such a general perspective be important to the courts? It is widely recognised that a fundamental theme of the development of Anglo-American property law, at least in the "modernising" era culminating in the late nineteenth or early twentieth century, has been the pressure for the gradual removal of restraints on alienation of property. Undoubtedly, this is a matter of considerable complexity. The concept of inalienability is not unambiguous.[27] Its significance is likely to vary considerably depending on how and to what it is applied and, insofar as legal development has shown a general tendency to promote the free alienability of property, this tendency has hardly been consistent or uni-

---

26 Trusts (Special Provisions) Act 1989. See "New Trust Legislation in Bermuda" (1990) 4 Trust Law and Practice 68.

27 M. J. Radin, "Market-Inalienability" (1987) 100 Harv. L. R. 1849, 1852.

316

form.[28] Nor is it easy to offer any clear overall assessment of the strength
of this tendency in law in particular periods. Nevertheless, it has often
been claimed in the literature of property law that a general legal policy
of facilitating alienation of property has reflected, in essence, a broader
policy of favouring the free development of markets.[29] Some writers have
also emphasised a parallel tendency for rights to the possession, use and
transfer of assets increasingly to cluster or be concentrated in a single
beneficial owner, again with the result that market transactions are sim-
plified and promoted.[30]

  G. S. Alexander has argued, in relation to American developments,
that the broad tendency in legal thought in favour of promoting alienability of property revealed its ambiguities when the need was felt to systematise legal doctrine using this policy as a framework. Especially with
regard to trusts, a particular ambiguity remains as to whether it is a right
of free alienation of the trust creator which should be protected or a
corresponding right of trust beneficiaries to be able to deal effectively with
the trust property to which they are beneficially entitled or, at least, to deal
freely with their beneficial interests under the trust.[31] Alexander attaches
great significance to the development of the specifically American spendthrift trust doctrine and the modification of the *Saunders* v. *Vautier*[32]
principle in the United States[33] as showing that the freedom of the trust
creator to alienate as he wished (and subject to the conditions he chose)

28   *Cf.* M. R. Chesterman, "Family Settlements on Trust: Landowners and the
     Rising Bourgeoisie" in G. R. Rubin and D. Sugarman ed., *Law, Economy
     and Society* (Abingdon, Oxon., 1984) 138-41.
29   See e.g. L. Simes, *Public Policy and the Dead Hand* (Ann Arbor. 1955) 33-
     6; Radin, *supra* n. 27, at 1855.
30   C. Donahue Jr., "The Future of the Concept of Property Predicted From Its
     Past" in J. R. Pennock and J. W. Chapman ed., *Property* (New York, 1980).
31   G. S. Alexander, "The Dead Hand and the Law of Trusts in the Nineteenth
     Century" (1985) 37 Stan. L. R. 1189, at 1231-2.
32   (1841) 4 Beav. 115.
33   *Claflin* v. *Claflin* 149 Mass. 19 (1889).

has sometimes been clearly preferred to the corresponding freedom of beneficiaries. In terms of the trust conceptions used in this paper, the moralistic conception plainly favours the freedom of alienation of the trust creator. The property-receptacle conception, as applied to purpose trusts by means of the beneficiary principle, generally favours the interests of residuary legatees or next of kin. In striking down beneficially "unattached funds" it puts property into their hands promoting their immediate freedom to alienate it.

Thus, either resolution of the purpose trust controversy could appear to be compatible with the tendency towards free alienability of property. More fundamentally, it might be argued that the problem of restraints on alienation does not really arise anyway in this context. Where capital or income are spent on pursuing the particular abstract purpose designated in the trust, property is thereby put into economic circulation. Even where the trust fund is to be accumulated to achieve a certain purpose it might be claimed that the policy in favour of alienability is not necessarily prejudiced. Thus, it has been argued that modern accumulation trusts generally do not run counter to a legal policy favouring the circulation of capital in the market, since trustees are able to invest trust property and so enable capital and accumulating income to play a commercial role.[34] The same argument has been made for purpose trusts: "With respect to the corpus, the trustee is free to buy, sell or exchange for the purposes of the trust investment, subject to such limitations as apply to other trustees in dealing with the trust property".[35] As regards *any specific item of property*, a purpose trust does not necessarily involve a greater problem of inalienability than do other trusts. Despite this, however, it can be suggested that there remains a potential problem of reconciling purpose trusts with a policy favouring free alienability. A purpose trust (like many accumulation trusts), by its nature, creates a structure in which a fund (probably, admittedly, of changeable property) is earmarked for purposes which

34 Simes, *supra* n. 29, at 94-5.
35 B. Smith, "Honorary Trusts and Restraints on Alienation" (1938) 16 Texas L. R. 149, 157.

318

remove the fund, as such, from free economic activity by beneficially entitled persons. The arrangement may well give full recognition to the freedom of a settlor or testator in alienating his property, but only at the expense of introducing significant restrictions on the availability of that property for beneficial use or market exchange. Ultimately full protection of the trust creator's freedom of disposition could be seen to be possible only at the cost of allowing him to "freeze" the assets as he disposes of them.

Alexander's explanation of the two late nineteenth century doctrines (spendthrift trusts and the modification of *Saunders* v. *Vautier*) referred to above as favouring free alienation by the trust creator is interesting in this context. He sees their acceptance as founded significantly on the view that private trusts existed primarily to implement family property settlements, that "a dichotomy between the world of commerce and the world of the family"[36] was accepted in individualist ideology, and that in certain respects trusts could be seen as arrangements "that provided support for the private community" of the family,[37] though their obvious importance in the commercial world as well made their role highly ambiguous. The family protection role of the trust could, however, be invoked to justify certain (exceptional) restrictive arrangements preventing free alienability by beneficiaries of their beneficial interests or, under the *Saunders* v. *Vautier* rule, of the trust capital. These arguments plausibly suggest contextual conditions which may allow the moralistic conception of the trust to prevail in some kinds of case, although it is important to note that "family welfare" considerations can also be used to justify departing from the trust creator's specific intentions, as in rules allowing variation of trusts — often to allow defences against disadvantageous effects of tax laws on trust interests.

However, the important point in the context of this paper is that such considerations will not apply to justify the general validation of purpose trusts as a category on the basis of the moralistic conception. Many

36   Alexander, *supra* n. 31, at 1250.
37   *Ibid.*, at 1252.

purpose trusts would normally be seen as having the effect of *taking property away* from the trust creator's family. Fulfilment of the trust creator's wishes would often appear not as protecting the family as a "haven in a heartless world"[38] but as cheating it of its due.[39] Accordingly, it would seem that purpose trusts as a general category are fated to be judged solely by their largely negative contribution to the free alienability of property in a non-family context. The trust creator's freedom of alienation, expressed in the setting up of a trust for abstract purposes unrelated to the specific interests of family members who survive him, cannot usually be justified as serving any socially useful family purposes (although, as will appear, there may be exceptions). Hence, we should expect, in line with the general tendency of development of property law until recent times, that the property-receptacle conception of the trust, maximising freedom of alienation for identifiable persons beneficially entitled, would inform the general legal treatment of purpose trusts and so encourage the conclusion that they do not constitute a legitimate category of private trusts. In this context it is surely significant that Gray, referred to earlier in this paper as the author of one of the most systematic early defences of the modern beneficiary principle, was also one of the most determined exponents of the idea that a consistent and systematic legal policy maximising freedom of alienation of property properly underlay the development of modern Anglo-American property law.[40]

Nevertheless, parallels were noted above between purpose trusts and accumulation trusts in terms of the policy of promoting alienability. Why should purpose trusts not be acceptable to the extent that accumulation trusts are? Many accumulation trusts can be seen as providing deferred and thereby enhanced benefits to human beneficiaries, typically within families. Again family welfare considerations might justify allowing a temporary withdrawal of funds from the normal conditions of alienability.

---

38   *Cf.* C. Lasch, *Haven in a Heartless World* (New York, 1977) which examines the idea of the family as a kind of buffer between the individual and society.

39   *Cf.* M. Chesterman, *Charities, Trusts and Social Welfare* (London, 1979) 55.

40   J. C. Gray, *Restraints on the Alienation of Property* (Boston, 2nd ed., 1895).

320

More generally, apart from the special needs of family protection, a society of capitalist enterprise certainly makes extensive use of trusts to provide property accumulation devices and stable forms of capital holding, but, assuming the general tendencies of property law indicated earlier, this kind application is likely to be unequivocally recognised only where there are clear economic justifications. Otherwise, the protection of, for example, testamentary freedom to create a purpose trust at the expense of the economic claims of living persons would probably be seen as lending itself merely to sentimental justifications.

However, the particular category of trusts which Lawrence Friedman has termed "dynastic trusts"[41] — set up primarily to perpetuate the trust estate for as long as possible — seems to fit as uneasily as that of purpose trusts into either the family or commercial contexts of trusts. Yet the dynastic trust has been favoured by some aspects of American trust law.[42] Friedman distinguishes dynastic trusts from "caretaker" family trusts precisely because the dynastic trust is not in essence aimed at family welfare and may (as in the case of long term accumulation arrangements) act against it. At the same time, it offends the general economic interest in free alienability of beneficially owned property. If such trusts could be accepted, at least by American courts, why should purpose trusts not be acceptable? Friedman sees the validation of dynastic trusts and spendthrift trusts in the United States in the late nineteenth century as reflecting social unease at economic uncertainties and rapid social and economic change.[43] In such circumstances efforts to use trusts to protect capital by isolating it might not be looked upon with disfavour. If this explanation is correct it suggests that trusts have sometimes been a defence against unwelcome social and economic effects of the general historical tendency towards free alienability of property, and not just in the context of family

41 Friedman, "The Dynastic Trust" (1964) 73 Yale L. J. 547.
42 *Ibid.*, at 550; Simes, *supra* n. 29, at chap. 4 (discussing the development of American attitudes to accumulation trusts).
43 Friedman, *supra* n. 41, at 582-3.

protection.[44] Yet this special role of trusts would still not provide a justification for a general acceptance of purpose trusts, which typically are intended to serve a wide variety of quite different objectives.

Thus, it may be concluded that if the promotion of free alienability of property has been a guiding theme in the development of modern property law in the common law world, and if this tendency has been informed by the wider object of freeing market activity in modernising industrial societies, it would be reasonable to expect that the dominant conception of the trust as applied in judicial practice would reflect these broader trends. Protecting the trust creator's right of free alienation of his property (for example in establishing a purpose trust) at the expense of preventing any persons from obtaining beneficial interests in either capital or income would, it seems, generally be contrary to an underlying policy of promoting alienability of property in a form that would support the development of free economic activity.[45]

In a different ideological climate matters could appear differently. In circumstances where the promotion of free alienability of property (and perhaps the related idea of aggregation of property rights in a clearly identifiable "owner") have given ground significantly to certain other social objectives of property law, the position of purpose trusts might be predicted to become more liberal. In particular, it might be expected that purpose trusts would be treated more sympathetically, or at least more pragmatically, where property law begins (as it may indeed have done recently in some contexts) to emphasise particularly the protection of use-value, as such, in a variety of ways, and the diversity and fragmentation of property rights and even of property as a concept.[46] In such conditions

---

44   See also G. Calabresi and A. D. Melamed, "Property Rules, Liability Rules and Inalienability: One View of the Cathedral" (1972) 85 Harv. L. R. 1089, at 1111.

45   Gardner, *supra* n. 21, at 210-1.

46   R. Cotterrell, "The Law of Property and Legal Theory" in W. Twining ed., *Legal Theory and Common Law* (Oxford, 1986); T. C. Grey, "The Disintegration of Property" in J. R. Pennock and J. W. Chapman ed., *Property* (New York, 1980); J. Singer, "The Reliance Interest in Property" (1988) 40 Stan. L. R. 611.

322

the dedication of property to abstract purposes might not be fatally condemned by its effect in removing assets both from free economic circulation and from availability for family support. It might be seen instead as just one example among numerous forms and circumstances in which the concept of property, and so the rules of property (and trust) law, are available to be applied.

Judicial Development of the Beneficiary Principle

The clear, unwavering assertion of the beneficiary principle in modern English trusts cases seems consistent with the contextual arguments in the previous section of this paper: "In order that a trust may be properly constituted, there must be a beneficiary";[47] "a [non-charitable] trust to be valid must be for the benefit of individuals";[48] "a gift on trust must have a *cestui que trust*";[49] "a trust may be created for the benefit of persons as *cestuis que trust* but not for a purpose [unless charitable]";[50] indeed no principle "perhaps has greater sanction or authority behind it" than the beneficiary principle.[51] On the other hand, it appears that the courts' attitudes to purpose trusts have changed over time and, as has been noted, some kinds of purpose trusts have frequently been held to be valid in the past. How is the development of doctrine in this area to be explained?

It remains very uncertain whether or not Sir William Grant M.R. intended to establish the beneficiary principle, in its presently understood form, in *Morice* v. *Bishop of Durham* in 1804, although many modern cases express no doubt about this. For a long time the statement quoted earlier was treated by English courts only as affirming the need for certainty of objects. This view was expressed soon after *Morice* was

47   *Re Diplock* [1941] Ch. 253, 259 (per Lord Greene M. R.).
48   *Bowman* v. *Secular Society Ltd.* [1917] A.C. 406, 441 (per Lord Parker).
49   *Re Wood* [1949] Ch. 498, 501 (per Harman J.).
50   *Leahy* v. *A.G. for New South Wales* [1959] AC 457, 478 (per Lord Simonds).
51   *Re Endacott* [1960] Ch. 232, 246 (per Lord Evershed M.R.).

decided and in many later nineteenth century cases.[52] These cases generally consider it obvious that in *Morice* "the question was, not whether the trust was illegal, but whether it was sufficiently definite for the court to execute".[53] In many of the nineteenth century decisions the judges emphasise that the vagueness of the trust creator's expressed purposes makes it impossible for the court to enforce the trust. There is no hint that the absence of identifiable beneficiaries is, itself, a problem. Often there is an explicit holding that there is, indeed, a trust, but that it is unenforceable because of the uncertainty of its objects. In *Ommanney* v. *Butcher*, however, there are suggestions that trust obligations the law will recognise must be clearly distinguished from moral duties which are not the concern of a court.[54]

Thus, the beneficiary principle seems to be a late invention. It is by no means apparent that it was established in 1804.[55] It could well be claimed, however, that there was simply no need to express such a principle at that time and for a considerable period thereafter. Any purpose trust, beyond the cases of provision in wills for tombs, monument, masses, animals, and a few other specific purposes which reached the

52 See e.g. *James* v. *Allen* (1817) 3 Mer. 17; *Vezey* v. *Jamson* (1822) 1 Sim. & Stu. 69; *Ommanney* v. *Butcher* (1823) Turn. & R. 260; *Fowler* v. *Garlike* (1830) 1 Russ. & M. 232; *Williams* v. *Kershaw* (1835) 5 Cl. & F. 111; *Ellis* v. *Selby* (1836) 1 My. & Cr. 286; *Hunter* v. *A.G* [1899] A.C. 309, at 323 (per Lord Davey).

53 *Ommanney* v. *Butcher* (1823) Turn. & R. 260, at 271-2 (per Sir Thomas Plumer M.R.).

54 *Ibid.*, at 273.

55 G. W. Keeton claims that Sir William Grant's words refer only to the need for the "three certainties" for a valid trust. See Keeton, *Social Change in the Law of Trusts* (London, 1958) 31; *Modern Developments in the Law of Trusts* (Belfast, 1971) 206; Keeton and L. A. Sheridan, *The Law of Trusts* (London, 10th ed., 1974) 137. The wording of the 11th (1983) edition by Sheridan is weaker, suggesting that it "may be" that the words refer only to the certainty issue. Potter (*supra* n. 20) also views *Morice* as a case on the meaning of uncertainty of objects.

324

courts, would be almost bound to fail for uncertainty. It is easy to see this
with the general pattern of objects expressed in most of the relevant
nineteenth century cases. Many are "extended charity" cases, where
provision is made not only for charitable but also for "public", "benevo-
lent", "philanthropic", or "other purposes" expressed in the most general
terms.[56] In these decisions the issue is whether the vague purposes expressed can be brought within the relaxed certainty rules of charity. In
other cases the purposes are left almost completely open.[57] Broadly
speaking, the only *specific* non-charitable purposes which arise for significant discussion in the English nineteenth century cases are those falling
within the limited ambit of the animals-tombs-monuments-masses range
of objects, or which involve an endowment likely to be caught by the
perpetuity rules.[58]

There seems, therefore, good reason to suppose that purpose trusts
posed few difficulties for the courts for a considerable period after *Morice*
v. *Bishop of Durham* given the way in which abstract non-charitable purposes were usually expressed in the nineteenth century cases. In general
the requirement of certainty of (abstract) objects would be applied and
once it was established that the abstract object was not charitable the trust
would fail because the object was too uncertain to enable the court to
supervise or control its pursuit. The lack of an explicitly asserted beneficiary principle is consistent with the possibility that purpose trusts were
not, in their typical nineteenth century forms, viewed as a threat to the
modern conception of the private trust, as in essence merely a receptacle
for the property of beneficial owners. The trust form was clearly also seen

56 *Vezey* v. *Jamson, Williams* v. *Kershaw* and *Ellis* v. *Selby* (*supra* n. 52); *Re
MacDuff* [1896] 2 Ch. 451.
57 *Kendall* v. *Granger* (1842) 5 Beav. 300 ("undertakings of general utility");
Harris v. *Du Pasquier* (1872) 26 L. T. 689 (deserving objects); *Buckle* v.
Bristow (1864) 11 L. T. 265 (residue to be spent in such manner as executors
should decide); *Fowler* v. *Garlike* (1830) 1 Russ. & M. 232 ("for such
purposes as they should think fit").
58 See e.g. *Thomson* v. *Shakespear* (1860) 1 De G. F. & J. 399; *Re Nottage*
[1895] 2 Ch. 649.

as a most important instrument of philanthropy in the form of public (charitable) trusts. But the courts could police charitable trust purposes, limiting them according to a judicial interpretation of the public good. It would, however, be a different matter to allow testators or donors the freedom to create "unattached" funds for *any* purpose which might occur to them, thus keeping property from rightful heirs and family dependents or out of economic circulation for "eccentric" purposes. The evidence of the cases suggests, however, that, as suggested above, this was not really a problem. The specific purpose trusts, not obviously caught by rules requiring certainty of (abstract) objects or by perpetuity rules, were probably largely limited to the animals, tombs, monuments and masses cases.

Thus it remains to explain the nineteenth century view of these latter cases. Their most obvious general characteristic is that usually the judgments in them devote little space or effort to justifying the upholding of the particular kind of trust as a purpose trust. The judgments are typically short and avoid generalisation beyond the case in hand. Only one of the English cases very obviously does not conform to this pattern. Gray saw this case, *Re Dean*[59] as "really the one important decision in conflict with *Morice* v. *Bishop of Durham*".[60] In it, North J. upheld a trust to maintain the testator's horses and hounds for fifty years, if any of them should so long live. What is striking is that the judgment is expressed in quite general terms: "it is said that the Court will not recognise a trust unless it is capable of being enforced by someone. I do not assent to that view".[61] The cases on monuments and animals are treated not as exceptional but as illustrating the general point that a non-charitable trust does not necessarily require beneficiaries to be valid.

Contrary to the view of Gray and many others, it is reasonable to suggest that *Re Dean* is not in conflict with the doctrine of *Morice*, as the latter case had been generally applied and interpreted throughout the whole period up to the time *Re Dean* was decided. North J.'s expressed

59   (1889) 41 Ch. D. 552.
60   Gray, *supra* n. 7, at 522, 525.
61   *Re Dean, supra* n. 59, at 556.

326

view of the law was probably correct at the time insofar as there was little reliable authority to support a general beneficiary principle. He expressed legal doctrine as it could properly be divined from the explicit pronouncements of earlier cases. Counsel for the residuary legatee had argued for the beneficiary principle, quoting from *Lewin on Trusts*.[62] But the only cases they cited in support, and which *Lewin* relied upon, were ones in which the explicit ground of failure of the trusts was perpetuity.[63]

Nevertheless, in a different sense, North J.'s conclusion was wrong insofar as he failed to appreciate the assumptions underlying, but unstated in, previous purpose trust doctrine. The content of doctrine in this area was explicable on the assumption that, because of the pattern of the abstract purposes for which purpose trusts had *in fact* been created to date, there had been no need for the judges to assert a beneficiary principle. North J.'s judgment did not recognise that circumstances might have changed so that the explicit *denial* of such a principle in general terms would prove counterproductive, given the dominant (property-receptacle) conception of the nature and purpose of trusts in modern society. Indeed, the judgment in *Re Dean* is phrased in terms more compatible with a moralistic conception of trusts.

It is probably impossible, centuries later, to appreciate the climate of thought in which the "anomalous" tombs, animals and other cases first established themselves in English law, but it is reasonable to suppose that the general conception of trusts and of the context of their existence may have been significantly different from that dominant in the law in 1889 when *Re Dean* was decided. We may be able to glimpse this ancient outlook from what seems to be the earliest reported case in which a gift to build a tomb was upheld. In *Masters* v. *Masters*[64] in 1718 the testatrix

---

62 The relevant statement is: "A trust must be for the benefit of some person or persons, and if this ingredient be wanting, as in a trust for keeping up family tombs, the trust is void": 8th ed., p. 106. Later editions accepted, however, that private purpose trusts could be valid.

63 *Rickard* v. *Robson* (1862) 31 Beav. 244; *Lloyd* v. *Lloyd* (1852) 2 Sim. (n.s.) 255.

64 (1718) 1 P. Wms 421. *Cf.* Potter, *supra* n. 20, at 421.

bequeathed £200 "for a monument to her mother". Not only was the gift upheld but it was privileged by the court as against other bequests which had to abate. The personal estate was not sufficient to cover all legacies, but the court decided that, alone among the bequests, that for the tomb should be paid in full. It was a "debt of piety to the memory of her mother, from whom the testatrix received the greatest part of her estate".[65] The words and the outcome of the case strongly suggest the moralistic conception of the trust presupposed and applied in its pre-modern context. Explicitly, the court recognises a moral obligation which constitutes the trust and which is so firm that it takes precedence over substantially any claims of the living to specific benefits from the estate.

Of course, the discourse of a single case is merely suggestive. Maitland noted that, from the beginning of the history of the trust, the main emphasis is not on the formal tie between those we now think of as trust creator and trustee but on the tie between trustee and beneficiary.[66] On the other hand, it is not to be forgotten that in its origins and essentials the putting of property in the trust of another is a moral idea independent of legal definition: "To fulfil such an obligation [of trust] is a moral question of the simplest possible order . . . [its enforcement is] a sacred duty, to compel a party to fulfil so clear a moral obligation".[67] When early cases established certain kinds of purpose trusts they may have done so as particular applications or illustrations of a general moralistic trust conception, not as anomalies or exceptions. But the precedents so established survived into a society ordered by a different world view, in which trusts were part of a structure of property law adapting to the developing demands of commerce and a modern economy. Cases which may originally have merely illustrated the general outlook that equity should fulfil, insofar as practicable, the last wishes of a testator expressed as a moral

---

65   (1718) 1 P. Wms 421, 423 (and see the note appended to the report).

66   "Trust and Corporation" in H. D. Hazeltine, G. Lapsley and P. H. Winfield eds., *Maitland: Selected Essays* (Cambridge, 1936) 162, at 165.

67   A. K. R. Kiralfy ed., *Potter's Historical Introduction to English Law and its Institutions* (London, 4th ed., 1958) 606.

328

obligation, later seemed sentimental, anomalous and archaic decisions at odds with the rationality of modern trust law; a rationality centred on the economic utility of trust arrangements as convenient and efficient devices by which property holdings could be planned and regulated for the benefit of specific persons or categories of persons.

The old cases survived in law firstly, no doubt, because their long continuity as precedents created some deterrent to overruling them, but, perhaps, secondly, and much more importantly, because they appeared as a limited, narrowly circumscribed and, in terms of the overall thrust of modern trust law discussed earlier, very insignificant category. They could, indeed, be seen as operating within the intimate family (as opposed to commercial) arena of trusts. Although they did not benefit living family members, they allowed homage to the family dead or sentimental provision for domestic animals, or (in the old American cases) for faithful slaves. They could be seen as promoting sentimental purposes within "the private community of the family" (to use Alexander's phrase), perhaps fostering its solidarity, reinforcing its traditions or emotional foundations, or merely allowing its living members to pay homage to deceased relatives by indulging the eccentricities or understandable sentiments of these relatives even after their death. At least where comparatively small amounts of property were involved, such trusts would not appear as seriously inimical to a policy of maintaining and promoting the general alienability of property and the facilitation of market activity.

As long as purpose trusts remained within these kinds of category (or else could easily be invalidated for uncertainty or perpetuity) they could, thus, be accepted without need for an explicit beneficiary principle. There are, however, signs that circumstances, or judicial attitudes, or both, may have been changing towards the end of the nineteenth century. For example, cases striking down trusts for specific "capricious purposes" entered the reports in several jurisdictions,[68] suggesting a more active judicial

68 *Brown* v. *Burdett* (1882) 21 Ch. D. 667 (rooms of a house to be sealed up for 20 years); *Board of Commissioners* v. *Scott* 88 Minn. 386 (1903) (direction to destroy property); *M'Caig* v. *University of Glasgow* 1907 S. C. 231 (statues of the testator and towers to be built on his estate); and, generally,

interest in quality control of purposes than the certainty of objects and perpetuity rules alone might allow. Subsequently, early in the twentieth century, in *Bowman* v. *Secular Society*[69] explicit judicial condemnation of private trusts for abstract purposes appears in the form of a clear statement of the modern beneficiary principle. Lord Parker's well known dictum that a trust must be "for the benefit of individuals" or charity was expressed without invoking any prior doctrinal authority and *Morice* was again cited only as authority on the certainty issue. A few years earlier, however, in *Re Davidson*[70] the absence of beneficiaries was mentioned as a general problem for enforcement and an aspect of the certainty issue. Subsequently the beneficiary principle has been forcefully affirmed in a number of English cases.

These cases do not explicitly reveal the reasons for the changed judicial attitudes, though the reports provide some incidental evidence. *Re Astor's Settlement Trusts*[71] in 1952, was the first English case in which the beneficiary principle was justified systematically and in detail in terms of the court's need to be able to supervise, control and enforce trusts. Roxburgh J.'s judgment, which has been widely relied upon in later English cases and in other jurisdictions, contains the revealing statement that purpose trusts pose great difficulties: "In theory, because . . . it is difficult to visualize the growth of equitable obligations which nobody can enforce, and in practice, because it is not possible to contemplate with equanimity the creation of large funds devoted to non-charitable purposes which no court and no department of state can control, or in the case of

---

Scott, *supra* n. 3, at 277-9 (para. 124.7). The vehemence of judicial language ("objects of no utility", "absurd", "eccentric", "rather crazy") in *M'Caig* is notable, and the court does not fail to note that, according to the testator's plan, "this considerable landed estate [is] to be withdrawn from commerce . ." (see pp. 242, 245).

69   *Supra* n. 48, at 441.
70   [1909] 1 Ch. 567; and see *Re Barnett* (1908) 24 T. L. R. 788.
71   [1952] Ch. 534. See generally Marshall, *supra* n. 5.

330

maladministration reform".[72] Much attention is devoted in the case to problems of enforcement or control of purpose trusts, given the absence of beneficiaries. Yet, as has been seen, these problems have not prevented the recognition of purpose trusts as valid in many earlier cases. The suggestion in *Re Astor*, that the logic of these exceptions might be that in general they were cases in which the enforcement problem was solved by the presence of a residuary legatee, is not tenable. Apart from the fact that it is unlikely that all cases have this character, indirect enforcement of this nature should in principle be available to much the same extent in cases without a residuary legatee but where next of kin can claim the property in the event of failure of the trust.[73] While problems of enforcement and control are serious, they are in no way novel and they do not seem to distinguish the validated purpose trusts from the rest; nor do they distinguish the older relaxed attitude to purpose trusts from the post-*Bowman*, modern, explicitly condemnatory attitude.

Roxburgh J.'s reference to the "practical" difficulty with purpose trusts — the possibility of "the creation of large funds" devoted to non-charitable purposes, and outside court or governmental control — may, however, be more telling even though it suggests a matter of policy unrecognised directly in legal rules. In *Re Astor* the trust was of "substantially all the issued shares" of the company owning *The Observer* newspaper. The objects included a range of purposes connected with the promotion of the profession of journalism and a free and independent press. They included the protection of newspapers "from being absorbed or controlled by combines or being tied by finance or otherwise to special or limited views or interests inconsistent with the highest integrity or independence". The trust failed not only through lack of identifiable beneficiaries but also for uncertainty of objects, and undoubtedly some of the Astor objects were expressed in broad terms. On the whole, however, it might be said that this appeared as a carefully drafted trust with its

---

72 *Ibid.*, at 542.
73 See *Re Endacott*, *supra* n. 51, at 246 (per Lord Evershed M.R.). *Cf.* McKay, *supra* n. 25, at 427.

Private Purpose Trusts   331

objects, limited within the perpetuity period, systematically set out. It looked wholly different from most of the nineteenth century purpose trusts. It apparently did involve the creation of a large fund (whereas most of the old "anomalous" cases appear to be concerned with relatively small provisions for sentimental purposes); it may well have suggested that the old weapon of the certainty of objects rule might not always be adequate to strike down sophisticated, professionally devised purpose trusts; and it may have raised the spectre of large amounts of capital being dedicated to purposes which escape both the judicial and administrative policing of private initiatives which is provided by charity law, and the state direction, co-ordination and supervision of public purposes established by the modern welfare state.

This is certainly not to suggest that contemporary law, in England or elsewhere, is intended to prevent such initiatives as those attempted through the Astor trust or in other cases where the beneficiary principle has been affirmed. As noted earlier, means can often be found to pursue them without using the trust form. The question is only whether the dominant conception of the nature and function of trusts will be interpreted as including purpose trusts, especially where the purposes to be achieved have become, in some cases, very much more ambitious than in earlier cases,[74] and where they involve substantial amounts of capital thereby taken out of commercial circulation without being dedicated to accepted family provision purposes. In some cases the purpose might appear controversial or merely eccentric,[75] of dubious social value[76] or de-

74 See e.g. *R.* v. *District Auditor, ex p. West Yorkshire Metropolitan County Council* [1986] R. V. R. 24 (trust set up by the Council to assist economic development in the County of West Yorkshire; to assist bodies there concerned with youth and community problems; to assist and encourage ethnic and minority groups; to inform the public of consequences of the abolition of the Council (proposed by the Government) and of other proposals affecting local government in the County. Held void as a non-charitable purpose trust and as administratively unworkable).

75 E.g. *Re Shaw* [1957] 1 W. L. R. 729 (for research into the utility of a new 40 letter alphabet).

76 E.g. *Public Trustee* v. *Nolan* (1943) 43 S. R. (N. S. W.) 262 (to erect a carrillon near Sydney harbour to welcome overseas liners).

332

terminedly political,[77] but the variety of cases is itself significant.[78] To the extent that the property-receptacle conception of the trust continues to dominate trust law (though, as has been seen, not necessarily academic commentary on it), it seems reasonable to expect that firm assertions of the beneficiary principle will continue because of the existence of these kinds of cases. Such trusts are too distant from what has long been the dominant judicial conception, in a number of jurisdictions, as to what private trusts can do and be.

Conclusion

This paper has argued that the problem of purpose trusts was not really raised, let alone solved, by *Morice* v. *Bishop of Durham* in 1804. Evidence from English law reports suggests that purpose trusts as a category only really became a major problem as the purposes for which they might be used began to seem more ambitious than those considered by the courts in the nineteenth century cases. Most of the latter cases could be controlled adequately by means of the certainty and perpetuity rules. Specific purpose trusts could often be accepted because their purposes were limited

---

77 Among many cases see e.g. *Re Bushnell* [1975] 1 W. L. R. 1596 (promotion of "socialised medicine" in a socialist state); *Bacon* v. *Pianta* (1966) 114 C. L. R. 634 (for purposes of the Communist Party of Australia); *Re Grant's Will Trusts* [1980] 1 W. L. R. 360 (for the purposes of Chertsey Labour Party headquarters).

78 Thus Lord Evershed M.R. in *Re Endacott* states (p. 246) that a failure to insist on the beneficiary principle "would be to validate almost limitless heads of non-charitable trusts". Hackney, *supra* n. 22, at 69, speculates that modern judicial hostility to purpose trusts may reflect the fear that "England might otherwise be like France . . . with a statue of a jumped-up politician in every town square". The general point is that control (presently operating through the medium of the judicial definition of charity) over private promotion of public purposes would be significantly loosened should the beneficiary principle no longer be insisted upon.

to sentimental and economically insignificant objectives, such as the
provision of family tombs, or the care of domestic or estate animals. It
is possible to see these particular instances of purpose trusts as cases
within the broad category of family welfare trusts which would, as such,
be acceptable to the courts even if they made property inalienable in the
market for a limited period. Hence, while judicial acceptance of these
cases is connected with their "sentimental" character, it would be wrong
to see this as an irrational reason for their acceptance. The validation of
these trusts can be rationally explained along the same lines as can the
validation of other kinds of family trust arrangements having the effect of
removing property from the control of identifiable beneficiaries and
significantly restricting its alienability or free utilisation in the market.
Trust law preserved an important role for trusts in the promotion or
maintenance of the private community of the family, alongside their
increasingly extensive role in providing an array of devices for property
arrangements of general economic and commercial utility. However, this
paper has suggested that the scope, variety and ambition of the purposes
in some modern purpose trusts may have been the new state of affairs
which impelled courts to affirm unequivocally and elaborate the modern
beneficiary principle in the twentieth century.

The property-receptacle conception of the trust's nature and functions
has been taken in this paper as underlying the judicial affirmation of the
beneficiary principle. But it would be wrong to see this outlook as
unchangeable or unproblematic. It may well be that trust law is being
influenced by contemporary changes in the perception of property rights
in general and by changes in conceptions of the character[79] and social
functions of property,[80] in a context in which property claims assume
many new forms.[81] The development of the discretionary trust has not
been impeded by old debates about the nature of beneficial interests in

79   See Grey and Singer, *supra* n. 46.
80   C. Reich, "The New Property" (1964) 73 Yale L. J. 733.
81   See Cotterrell, *supra* n. 46.

334

such structures;[82] the development of management trusts such as pension fund trusts has established arrangements in which the fund is intended to be an enduring relatively autonomous capital structure.[83] These and many other developments and circumstances do not indicate a static picture. And we have noted earlier the statutory interpretation of purpose trusts as powers in several jurisdictions, the bold statutory validation of such trusts elsewhere, as well as the continuing stream of academic commentary in favour of a more liberal approach to these kinds of trusts. The legal evolution of the purpose trust is far from over. The aim of this paper has been to suggest that its development reflects social change no less than legal continuity.

82 The English certainty of objects rules for discretionary trusts have been significantly liberalised by *McPhail* v. *Doulton* [1971] A. C. 424. As regards "hybrid" purpose trusts benefiting a class of people, the possibility of enforcement by persons indirectly benefited was opened by *Re Denley* though the scope and long-term influence of the decision remain unclear. In *Re Grant's Will Trusts, supra* n. 77, the Denley trust was held to have been one for a class of individuals and not a purpose trust at all.

83 See e.g. R. Minns, *Pension Funds and British Capitalism: The Ownership and Control of Shareholdings* (London, 1980).

[14]
Trusting in Law:
Legal and Moral Concepts
of Trust

Although the subject to be considered here is theoretical, I hope that
those expecting a discussion of practical issues affecting trusts law
will not be wholly disappointed. It is highly significant for the theme
which I want to develop that the role of trusts in contemporary life
is an increasingly important and pressing issue. It arises, for example,
in financial and commercial contexts, which have recently inspired
new forms or applications of trusts, or their wider use; in essential
social welfare and employment contexts, especially in relation to
pension funds; and in community and philanthropic contexts where
charitable organisations and foundations and voluntary associations
operate with growing centrality and responsibility. This paper is
concerned with developments in these areas but it does not seek to
address specific trusts controversies directly. It portrays some of these
controversies as symptoms or illustrations of more fundamental
theoretical questions about the very nature of trusts and of trusting
relationships in law. These theoretical questions are the focus of this
paper and, to explore them, it relates the legal concept of the trust
to ideas expressed in recent literature in social theory about the nature
of social trust in general. By social trust is meant trust in a broad *moral*
sense: involving reliance, in social relationships, on other people's goodwill, solicitude and competence; or a confidence that general expectations in familiar social circumstances will not be frustrated.

An attempt to relate trusts law to a wider moral notion of trust
as a basis of social relationships is not, I hope, the kind of speculative
legal inquiry that one American lawyer called "a romp through the
clouds".[1] Legal theory should, as one of its main contributions, help

---

[1] L. A. Graglia, "The Constitution, Community, and Liberty" (1985) 8 Harvard
Journal of Law and Public Policy 291.

76

in very concrete ways to explain general patterns of change in legal doctrine. A main concern here is to illustrate that point. The claim is that by putting trusts into a wider theoretical context the nature of controversies surrounding them might be better understood. But legal theory should also be able to contribute to general social theory; it is worth asking, for example, how analysis of the legal concept of trust might contribute to a better understanding of general social or moral notions of trust. Nevertheless, this latter question must be largely left aside on the present occasion. Ideas about moral or social trust are introduced here as elements in an analytical perspective intended to help explain general changes in the nature of the legal device of the trust. I want to suggest that this analytical perspective—which emphasises relationships of power and dependence in the trust and their evolving character over time—offers a useful way of looking at trusts. It stresses the impact of changing social and economic contexts on trusts law and trusting relationships. It may help towards a better understanding of how some current legal problems in the trusts field have emerged and where they may lead.

1. Power and Dependence in Relationships of Trust

The task of exploring, theoretically, connections between the legal idea of trust and broader moral or social conceptions of trust has been largely neglected. Commentary on trusts law typically makes no reference to discussion of the idea of "trust" in moral or social theory. Yet there is now an important literature on that subject.[2] Legal theory also has little to say about the concept of trust. After all, trust is not a concept generalised through law in a manner comparable with ideas such as intention, causation, responsibility or fault. It is generalised in law in the notion of fiduciary relationship, yet although this idea is much discussed[3] it is not among legal theory's central analytical concerns. It remains a relatively open, indefinite,

---

[2] See e.g. N. Luhmann, "Trust" in *Trust and Power: Two Works by Niklas Luhmann* (transl. H. Davies, J. Raffan and K. Rooney) 1979; B. Barber, *The Logic and Limits of Trust* 1983; D. Gambetta (ed), *Trust: Making and Breaking Cooperative Relations* 1988.

[3] See especially P. D. Finn, "The Fiduciary Principle" in T. G. Youdan (ed), *Equity, Fiduciaries and Trusts* 1989; Finn, "Fiduciary Law and the Modern Commercial World" in E. McKendrick (ed), *Commercial Aspects of Trusts and Fiduciary Obligations* 1992.

Trusting in Law 77

even pragmatically applied notion,[4] a gateway in law for a variety of moral evaluations of proper conduct. The concept of trust as a social relationship becomes rigorous and closely defined in English law only as *the trust*, a specific legal device, occupying a relatively specialised corner of legal doctrine. The idea of trusting as a basis of social relationships does not pervade law. Rather, trust is marginalised as a special legal structure, typically delimited in particular forms and categories.[5]

Historically, trusts have been celebrated for their flexibility, for the apparently infinite adaptability and openness of the concept of the trust. But Maitland's famous claims to this effect[6] may mislead. From Lord Nottingham's time, at least, it has seemed important to classify and categorise trusts.[7] In the main period of modern development of trust law much effort was expended on carefully delineating the hallmarks of the trust and distinguishing it clearly from other legal ideas with which it might be confused. One interpretation in recent literature of this activity is that the intensified effort to distinguish trust characteristics was a response to the alien, or at least highly unusual and special character of trust relationships as compared with the arm's length, individualistic relationships familiar in modern common law.[8] Gregory Alexander has suggested that the trust imports into law a certain idea of community or communal norms.[9] It enshrines an important notion of sacrificing one's own interests to those of others, or treating others' interests as one's own. It contains ideas otherwise rare in the doctrine of common law systems, such as that of general positive duties to act in the best interests of others even where no link of legal agreement, no consideration received by the trusted or detriment suffered by those who trust, binds the duty-holder with those for whom he acts.

We might begin to develop a framework for understanding the legal concept of trust in its moral and social context by recognising that trusting as a social or moral relationship raises acute issues of

---

[4] Finn, "Fiduciary Law and the Modern Commercial World", *op. cit.*, p. 8; and see e.g. *Re Coomber* [1911] 1 Ch 723, at pp. 728–9 (per Fletcher-Moulton LJ).

[5] Thus although most developed legal systems find a place for doctrinal recognition of some specific trusting relationships they do so in often radically differing ways and no single legal concept of trust is shared even among Western legal systems.

[6] F. W. Maitland, *Equity: A Course of Lectures*, revised ed. 1936, p. 23.

[7] See e.g. *Cook v Fountain* (1676) 3 Swans. 585 (App.), at pp. 591–2.

[8] See G. S. Alexander, "The Transformation of Trusts as a Legal Category, 1800–1914" (1987) 5 Law and History Review 303.

[9] Ibid, p. 304.

78

power and dependence. To trust someone is to take a relatively open-ended risk[10] of relying on him or her. Trusting involves relying on that person's goodwill in a range of circumstances that usually cannot be comprehensively defined in advance. Thus, as Annette Baier puts it, trust involves "letting other persons . . . take care of something the truster cares about, where such 'caring for' involves some exercise of discretionary powers."[11] The essence of interpersonal trust seems to be not just a belief that defined, agreed benefits (as in a contract) will be supplied. It involves also a belief that the person trusted will exercise discretion, acting in unforeseen circumstances or in relation to new situations, in a manner that protects the interests of the person who trusts. Reliance on another's goodwill makes the person who trusts vulnerable.[12] In social situations of trust, therefore, the person trusted holds power over the one who trusts. Trusting is a way of coping with the impossibility of gaining sufficient knowledge of all aspects of complex circumstances. In trusting, one takes the risk that one's expectations will not be defeated.

How does law affect this social relationship of trust when it guarantees and enforces it in the legal structure of the trust, as between trustees and beneficiaries? Where law effectively and comprehensively guarantees the trustee's personal obligations to the trust beneficiary it *reverses*, to some significant extent, the balance of power and dependence in the trusting relationship. Through this legal intervention it is the person who trusts, the beneficiary, who has power to ensure that the person trusted, the trustee, fulfils the terms of his trust. This power comes from enforceability of the provisions of general trusts law operating to support and supplement the terms of the trust. A person morally dependent on the goodwill of another whom he or she trusts is converted into an (equitable) property owner able to call upon law to control the trustee so as to ensure protection of the beneficiary's assets.[13] Trusts law establishes, for example, theoretically powerful controls to prevent conflicts of duty and interest in trustee behaviour, to prevent trustees profiting from their trust, to remedy and penalise breaches of trust, and to ensure certain standards of prudence in the management of trust affairs. All

---

[10] Luhmann, *op. cit.*, p. 26.
[11] Baier, "Trust and Antitrust" (1986) 96 Ethics 231, at p. 240.
[12] Ibid., p. 235.
[13] R. B. M. Cotterrell, "Power, Property and the Law of Trusts: A Partial Agenda for Critical Legal Scholarship" (1987) 14 Journal of Law and Society 77, at p. 86.

Trusting in Law 79

of these controls are means of reducing the risk involved in a social relationship of trust since they legally reduce or contain the freedom of action of the trustee. Insofar as they are treated as practically significant they allow an important displacement of moral or social trust. To the extent that law controls trustees, the risk of relying on them is reduced and the moral relationship of trust is *displaced from the trustee and attached to law itself*. Thus, law's significance is to reduce the risk of interpersonal trust. Instead of having to put one's moral trust purely in the trustee, one can have confidence in law which guarantees the trustee's proper behaviour.

In relation to trusteeship, therefore, the general effect of trust law has usually been to reduce the power which would otherwise inhere in trustees through the situation of dependence and reliance of others on them. The idea of a reversal by law of the power and dependency relationship of trust is the starting point for an analytical framework, but no more than a starting point. First, if, as noted above, discretion is inherent in all trusting relationships, law cannot remove but can only shape and limit discretions which continue to give trustees power over beneficiaries' affairs in almost all trusts. Beyond this, as will appear, the conditions of many modern trusts often make any significant reversal of the power-dependence relationship especially difficult, partly because of the increased complexity of the structure of these trusts and changes in the role of trusts, and partly because of the changed character of the social relationships of trust which many modern trusts embody.

2. Moral Distance and Trust Relationships

This latter point can be introduced and summarised in two words: "size" and "expertise". The types of trusts that dominate much of contemporary economic and social life might be generically labelled "big trusts", even "megatrusts". They include large pension scheme trusts and other trust arrangements in corporate contexts, unit trusts, major charitable foundations and discretionary trusts with a wide range of potential beneficiaries. They are characterised by large capital holdings administered according to professionally supervised investment policies, or by large numbers of beneficiaries or potential beneficiaries. Often all of these characteristics are present. The efficient, reliable supervision of very large trust funds requires high levels of expertise in financial management and investment practice.

80

Equally, organisational complexity, for example requiring trustees or their agents to deal with the diverse interests of numerous beneficiaries, suggests a need for considerable management expertise. Thus, increased size of funds, increased numbers of beneficiaries and increased reliance on special expertise possessed or controlled by trustees tend to go together.

Big trusts, whatever their nature, are often characterised also by substantial social separation between trustees and beneficiaries. The old image—seemingly underlying much orthodox trust doctrine—of a personal relationship of trust between a paternalistic family trustee and family dependents in whose interests the trustee is required to act may seem very remote indeed from the situation of a large pension trust in which members of the pension scheme as beneficiaries may have no personal contact whatever with the pension scheme trustees, whose essential task is that of efficient, watchful supervisors and co-ordinators of a complex and continually changing job of financial management.[14] In big charitable foundations the trustees' role is often fundamentally similar, requiring the monitoring of practices of income-raising and expenditure from the trust fund in accordance with the terms of the trust. It is unlikely to be one of direct involvement in the use of charitable funds, as in the case of trusteeship in many small charities. Relative remoteness of trustees from beneficiaries typically makes legal or social control of trusteeship harder. It makes it harder for those who benefit or hope or expect to benefit under a trust to evaluate the activity of trustees; it may make it harder for beneficiaries to obtain adequate knowledge to assess realistically the risk of continuing to trust. And where the knowledge held by the trustee is special professional expertise the practical problem of control is intensified.

In a social relationship of trust a judgment that the risk of trusting is too great turns trust into distrust and provokes a withdrawal from the trusting relationship or a radical reshaping of it; in a legal relationship of trust such a judgment may provoke questioning, complaint and perhaps ultimately an action for breach of trust or for an account of profits, or even an application for the replacement of a trustee. But under what conditions can beneficiaries judge the risks of relying on trustees? And where beneficiaries are numerous and dispersed how are they to act collectively? It would seem that the social relationships

[14] Cf. H. Lim and J. Hayes, "Pensions Odyssey 1992" (1992) 6 Trust Law International 44, at p. 45.

Trusting in Law   81

which law must control in big trusts approximate more and more closely to those existing in corporations between management and shareholders. If trusting as a social relationship always involves reliance on goodwill in the exercise of inevitable discretion, the transformation of the exercise of discretion into the application of expert professional judgment typically increases immeasurably the dependence of those who trust and the power of the trusted.

Even the possibility, for those who trust, of making a considered decision that the risks of trusting outweigh the benefits may be increasingly remote. The factors of size and expertise encourage a profound remoteness—a substantial 'moral distance'—between the trusting and the trusted which makes the decision whether or not to retain confidence in the trust relationship increasingly unreal. Conversely, from the viewpoint of trustees as managers, or supervisors of managers of trust assets, the need for even greater moral distance allowing the fullest possible freedom to act, for example in determining investment strategies, appears vital. The pressure, in conditions of intense economic competition and insecurity, and frequently changing tax regimes, is for maximum flexibility in the management of trust funds. The trust increasingly appears as a business enterprise shifting and developing its operations to maintain and enhance its capital value and income producing capacity. This applies no less to big charitable trusts[15] than to unit trusts or giant pension fund operations. The element of discretion inherent in trusting relationships becomes the basis of a realm of management freedom seen as essential to the trust. Traditional controls seem counterproductive and even misguided; the pressure is for much more trustee freedom and flexibility to respond to complex contemporary conditions,[16] a pressure to which courts seem to be responding by canvassing the loosening of traditional controls on trustee powers—for example, with regard to investment of funds and power to borrow—in relation to big trusts.[17]

[15] See e.g. "Charities: A Professional Approach to Investment" Banking World, December 1991, p. 30.

[16] For illustration of the kinds of very wide trustee powers now often professionally recommended for incorporation in trust instruments see the Society of Trust and Estate Practitioners' Standard Provisions 1992. See also on general issues W. A. Lee, "Current Issues for Trustee Legislation" in S. Goldstein (ed), Equity and Contemporary Legal Developments 1992.

[17] Mason v Farbrother [1983] 2 All ER 1078 (a pension trust fund of some £127 million has "something of a public element" which justifies an exceptional widening of trustees' investment powers); Trustees of the British Museum v Att-Gen [1984] 1

82

A focus on power-dependence relationships between trustees and beneficiaries highlights some tensions which changes in the character of trusts seem to provoke. But in any given trust arrangement there are other kinds of reliance to be considered. For example, settlors rely on trustees to carry out their wishes as embodied in the trust. In general, however, law does not redress this particular dependence relationship by giving a settlor rights against trustees according to general trusts law. Beneficiaries, rather than settlors, are in general considered entitled to enforce the trust. Losses caused by trustee failures are assumed to concern the former rather than the latter. The legal protection of settlors is primarily in the law's respect for their trust intentions—a usually settled documentary expression of wishes—though legal modes of varying, terminating and interpreting established trusts put limits even on this protection. In practice, however, settlors in *inter vivos* family trusts have often been able informally to control or influence trustees. The situation in modern big trusts seems, to some extent, comparable. If (debatably) in a company pension trust the employer company can properly be regarded as the primary settlor the company often has a "close nexus" with the pension trustees who are "in so many ways in partnership with the employer"[18] Informal relationships may sometimes exist between trustees of other kinds of trusts and individuals or corporations sponsoring them. An important study of giant American philanthropic foundations notes that founders, in choosing trustees "most frequently named family members, when they were in some rapport with the family, or old business colleagues",[19] preserving a significant intimacy between the trust and its founding sources. Nevertheless the elements of size and expertise which help create moral distance between trustees and beneficiaries in big trusts seem often to have comparable effects as between settlors and trustees. Indeed the distinction between settlors and beneficiaries becomes blurred in trusts (especially, for example, many pension trusts and

WLR 418 (greater flexibility and freedom in investment powers may be appropriate where charitable funds are very large). See, on the general relevance of fund size for trustees' powers, I. Pittaway, "Pension Funds—Is a Separate Branch of Trust Law Evolving?" (1990) 4 Trust Law and Practice 156, at pp. 157–8. On special factors affecting investment decisions in relation to large pension funds see W. A. Lee, "Modern Portfolio Theory and the Investment of Pension Funds" in P. D. Finn (ed), *Equity and Commercial Relationships* 1987.

[18] Lim and Hayes, *op. cit.*, p. 45.

[19] W. A. Nielsen, *The Golden Donors: A New Anatomy of the Great Foundations* 1985, p. 19.

unit trusts) where beneficiaries are also contributors to the trust fund. The big trust, especially, seems to foster a substantial autonomy in relation to all who have an interest in it.

Among other relations of power and dependence in the trust the most generally significant is that between settlor and beneficiaries. In fact this is the one traditionally most discussed in the literature, in terms of public policy, perpetuities and the reach of the "dead hand" of past generations controlling from the grave the property entitlements of the living.[20] It is also the one that seems to show most complexity and variability. The settlor who transfers property for the benefit of trust beneficiaries relies on the carrying into effect of his wishes in relation to the property. The settlor's dependence is on those who obtain access to the property, or who would like to do so, not to seek to upset or undermine the established trust intentions but to allow the property to be used according to the conditions set. Law, insofar as it respects the settlor's wishes, transforms this dependence into a power to determine allocations of property even after the settlor's death and to control beneficiaries (and others) in their use or access to the property given. The familiar idea of the promotion of free alienability of property as a dominant policy of evolving property law in the common law becomes, in this context, unclear in its meaning. As Gregory Alexander has argued,[21] modern common law has operated with an ambiguity as to whether the dominant interest in alienability which is to be legally protected is settlors' freedom of alienation of their property or beneficiaries' freedom to gain access to and deal freely with the substance of their beneficial interests, and, indeed, with the trust assets themselves.

Thus, rules governing variation of trusts, the *Saunders v Vautier*[22] rule, the invalidation of most private purpose trusts,[23] and perpetuity rules are instruments limiting the settlor's power in various respects and enhancing that of beneficiaries, or other persons standing to benefit from the dismantling of restrictive trust arrangements. On the other hand, especially in traditional family trust contexts, trust law allows extensive controls over beneficiaries to be created by settlors,

---

[20] See e.g. L. M. Simes, *Public Policy and the Dead Hand* 1955.
[21] G. S. Alexander, "The Dead Hand and the Law of Trusts in the Nineteenth Century" (1985) 37 Stanford Law Review 1189.
[22] (1841) 4 Beav. 115; affirmed Cr. & Ph. 240.
[23] Cotterrell, "Some Sociological Aspects of the Controversy Around the Legal Validity of Private Purpose Trusts" in Goldstein (ed), *Equity and Contemporary Legal Developments, op. cit.*

84

as in the case of protective trusts, or allows settlors to devise trusts (especially discretionary trusts) that avoid the specification of fixed beneficial property entitlements.

3. Changing Conceptions of The Nature of Trusts

These considerations of power and dependency relations in trusts provide fixed points around which analysis of changing forms and functions of trusts can be analysed. But there is a need for a clearer perspective on change, some means of relating the ideas of power and dependence drawn from general consideration of the moral or social relationship of trusting to a sense of changes in the broad context in which these social relationships exist. In the discussion above, change in the character of trusts has been associated with the development of big trusts. But these trusts are not typical of the whole range of modern express trusts. Indeed, their character as trusts is in certain respects exceptional or controversial, especially where, as in the case of some pension trusts, a contractual nexus defines the position of beneficiaries. We need, therefore, a framework indicating why the most general legal pressures especially associated with big trusts (for example, towards the relaxation of controls on trustees' discretions) seem widely recognisable throughout contemporary trusts law, pointing its development in different directions from that of the trusts law and practice of earlier periods.

Niklas Luhmann's important work on social relations of trust may offer guidance here. Among Luhmann's claims is that trust in modern society has apparently assumed new forms, which do not supersede but are superimposed over the simple form of interpersonal trust in which a person relies on the goodwill of another in personal dealings.[24] These new forms involve confidence not in particular people, considered emotionally, but in *systems*[25] (in Luhmann's view systems of communication). This idea might be applied, for example, to confidence in financial and banking systems, political systems, or economic systems; or to confidence in a particular bank, or business. The removal of the personal nexus of the trusting relationship results in a more abstract form of reliance. Confidence in a relatively abstract and impersonal system is not necessarily positively conferred by the

---

[24] Luhmann, "Familiarity, Confidence, Trust: Problems and Alternatives" in Gambetta (ed), *op. cit.*, at pp. 102–3.
[25] Luhmann, "Trust", *op. cit.*, p. 22.

Trusting in Law   85

person who relies on such a system. The possibility of deciding deliberately whether to give or withdraw trust in impersonal systems may be limited as compared with the situation of interpersonal trust.

Luhmann explains the transformation of trust—its displacement from people on to systems—as a response to the increasing complexity of social and economic life, which is experienced increasingly in terms of ever more numerous, differentiated, extensive and self-sustaining networks of communication.[26] Although Luhmann's discussion of social relationships of trust refers only very briefly to law and makes no reference to the legal device of the trust, the dichotomy between interpersonal trust and system-trust or confidence can be related to the contrast between, on the one hand, the legal image of the traditional family trust emphasising a close personal relationship between trustees and beneficiaries and, on the other, the situation of some big trusts in which trustees supervise or manage a relatively impersonal system of financial relationships and in which the reliance of beneficiaries might be considered much more one of passive confidence than of active conferment of trust.

It would be unwise to draw a rigid dichotomy in trusts corresponding to Luhmann's suggestion of the contrast between a morally rich relationship of personal trust and a relatively passive conferment of confidence on systems which the individual can hardly escape. We might better see most trusts as combining elements of both of these situations. Bernard Barber, influenced by Luhmann, has emphasised two components of trusting which usually exist in combination. These are fiduciary responsibility and expectation of technical competence.[27] Barber discusses tensions between these elements in relation to many social, economic and political contexts of trusting relationships. If we relate them, however, to the legal device of the trust it can be suggested that as moral distance in trusts increases, especially with the elements of size and special expertise, the moralistic notion of fiduciary responsibility, suggesting a personal obligation of care and concern owed to identifiable individual beneficiaries, is likely to recede. Correspondingly, the element of technical competence, implying the need for freedom and initiative to apply expertise, assumes increased prominence. The fiduciary emphasis in the trusts context implies strongly moralistic, strict policing of trustees' duties; the technical competence emphasis suggests relaxed

[26] Ibid., ch 7.
[27] Barber, op cit., ch 2.

86

rules on activities of expert professionals as trustees, especially with regard to investment, business management and profit-making activities as long as these activities relate to the efficient management of the trust as a fund or as a system of financial relationships.

Elsewhere, independently of Barber's and Luhmann's concepts, an attempt has been made to distinguished a related dichotomy between a moralistic idea of the trust, in which interpersonal fiduciary relationships or legally-guaranteed moral ties appear paramount, and a more modern idea of the trust as essentially a property-receptacle, a device for specifying property entitlements in legally reliable, sophisticated and flexible ways.[28] Each of these varied analyses seems to imply a deep ambiguity in the idea of trust and various tensions between, on the one hand, a moralistic personal relationship of trust, emphasising fiduciary obligation, and, on the other, a more mechanistic, system-notion of trust, emphasising efficiency, stability of expectations, and technical competence.

I shall combine the moralistic/property-receptacle dichotomy, Luhmann's interpersonal trust/system-confidence dichotomy and Barber's stress on the contrasting elements of fiduciary relationship and reliance on technical competence to suggest that the modern history of trusts can be understood in terms of a tension between three different kinds of trust ethos, one of which is gradually coming to dominate. These three kinds of ethos do not represent an evolutionary scheme. They are rather fundamentally different conceptions of the nature and function of trusts in general; Weberian ideal or "pure" types which might be reflected in important aspects of dominant approaches in particular periods, but not in any unchallenged or unambiguous form. I shall retain the term moralistic for the first of these types, but divide what I have earlier called the property-receptacle conception of trusts into two types, which can be called an individual property type and a capital management type. Thus three trust conceptions—moralistic, individual property and capital management—can be distinguished.

The *moralistic* type treats the trust as a legally guaranteed structure of essentially moral relationships between persons. While the personal relationship of trustee and beneficiary is vital here, the moral obligation created by the trust also involves a moral obligation to give effect to the trust creator's lawful wishes to the fullest extent. Guiding

---

[28] Cotterrell, "Sociological Aspects. . .", *op. cit.*

Trusting in Law   87

principles within such a moralistic conception will include strict respect for the settlor's intentions (if necessary at the expense of immediate utility to beneficiaries); significant subordination of any policy of promoting alienability of property to an overriding respect for trust purposes; respect for dynastic or family protection aims of settlors, even at the expense of indulging eccentricities or allowing property to be kept out of commercial circulation for significant periods. A moralistic conception might also inspire a relatively paternalistic approach[29] in trust law to the welfare of beneficiaries (perhaps glimpsed in the old treatment of restraints on anticipation),[30] rather than a rigorous definition and efficient servicing of their property interests as such.

This pure type was no doubt never closely mirrored in actual legal doctrine, even in the early periods of legal development. Yet, reflecting a simple idea of trust as an interpersonal moral relationship, it may, as an abstract conception, unify fragments of doctrine from past and present trusts law. I have argued elsewhere that the advocacy, in an extensive literature of academic commentary, in favour of the legal validity of private purpose trusts has often presupposed such a moralistic approach to trusts and that such a moralistic approach can perhaps be glimpsed in the earliest of private purpose trust cases.[31]

D. E. C. Yale notes, in relation to the period of Lord Nottingham's Chancellorship, an important shift of emphasis in trusts law from "the dominance of the notion of confidence reposed in the feoffee by the beneficiary" towards a more modern emphasis on "the beneficiary's interest with its increasingly proprietary tinge"; a shift "from the relationship to the equitable right".[32] With the movement away from an idea of personal obligation it became possible for corporate bodies to be trustees since, as Nottingham put it, "the whole power of the Chancery doth not rest merely in a personal coercion, as the old books speak".[33]

We need not try to identify any specific historical transition but

---

[29] See Alexander, "Transformation of Trusts. . .", *op. cit.*, p. 321.

[30] W. G. Hart, "The Origin of the Restraint upon Anticipation" (1924) 40 Law Quarterly Review 221.

[31] Cotterrell, "Sociological Aspects. . .", *op. cit.*, pp. 310–4, 326–8.

[32] D. E. C. Yale (ed), *Lord Nottingham's Chancery Cases Vol. 2*. Selden Society Vol. 79, 1961, "Introduction" p. 90.

[33] Report of *Sterling v Wilford* (1676) in Yale (ed), *Lord Nottingham's Chancery Cases Vol. 2, op. cit.*, p. 447 (Case 579).

88

merely recognise that gradually in trust doctrine, and in a variety of ways, a conception of trust strongly contrasting with the moralistic conception begins to flourish. The trust comes to be seen as a receptacle for property in which clear rights of ownership exist, recognised in equity. This property-receptacle conception of the trust initially centres on the recognition and clear definition of rights of beneficiaries as individual property owners. The move towards an emphasis on clearly fixed proprietary rights in the trust may be related to a general trend in modern equity towards assimilation of trusts law doctrines to common law rules of property.[34] Whatever the forces at work in promoting this *individual property* conception of the trust its effect is to remove the legal idea of the trust further away from the simple moral idea of interpersonal trust with its diverse discretions and diffuse dependencies and obligations.

The property emphasis in trusts is expressed in the affirmation of the policy of free alienability applicable both to trust assets and trust interests. This operates to maximise the accessibility of trust property to beneficiaries, for example through the *Saunders* v *Vautier* rule, and to entrench the general principle that they can deal freely with their interests under the trust. It is reflected in rules preventing perpetuities and controlling accumulations, as well as in the beneficiary principle requiring that, in general, property not be held in a private trust unless for ascertained or ascertainable human beneficiaries. The replacement of the moralistic conception by a property-receptacle conception is reflected also in some lessening of respect for the trust creator's intentions, shown in the invalidation of capricious and pure purpose trusts, and increased possibilities for varying trusts to improve their utility or efficiency in the interests of beneficiaries.

Historically there is no simple transition between these conceptions of the trust. If they are plausible as pure or ideal types they help organise aspects of legal doctrine in most periods of development of trusts law in complex combinations and never as fully or uniformly applied conceptions in practice. But these conceptions or types are useful as a means of suggesting how trusts law separates itself, because of the emphasis on the trust as a property-receptacle, from the powerful moral idea of interpersonal trust sketched earlier in this paper. Trusts law reduces the diffuse dependence of beneficiaries on

---

[34] Alexander, "Transformation of Trusts. . .", *op. cit.*, especially pp. 322ff.

Trusting in Law   89

trustees by creating *property* interests enforceable against trustees
and other persons. In this way it partially reverses the relations of
power and dependence inherent in trusting as an interpersonal moral
relationship. It does this, above all, by developing the idea of equitable
property which serves as a stable focus for rights and duties.

Much recent debate around trusts law implies, however, that this
transition has not run its course; that the movement of trusts law is
from moralistic and individual property conceptions of the trust
towards a third conception, a further extension of the idea of the
trust as a property-receptacle, and one which is especially clearly
reflected in the characteristics of what I have been calling big
trusts. Among striking recent developments in trusts law in various
jurisdictions can be noted the following: a significant relaxation
of rules relating to perpetuities and accumulations; an increased
willingness to validate private purpose trusts, even to deny their
problematic character; the continuing development and wide use of
discretionary trusts; the return to some blurring of the distinction
between trusts and powers—which previously could have been
regarded as an important element in the clarification of the nature
of property rights under trusts;[35] and the adoption of extremely
wide, and ever widening, powers of management and of relatively
uncontrolled discretions for trustees. All of these developments go
along with, but are not necessarily directly inspired by the proliferation of big trusts.

I believe that these developments relate in various ways to a further
move away from the moralistic conception of the trust. But what are
they a move towards? If the moralistic conception for the trust mirrors
the simple moral idea of trusting as an interpersonal relationship in
social life, the move away from this is, I think, ultimately towards a
conception of the trust that mirrors ever more directly Luhmann's
image of trust or confidence in impersonal systems.

This third conception or type of the trust, then, is that of a *capital
management* system. In a society dominated by monopoly capital the
trust has tended to become simply a structure of capital holding.
Alienability of property may be less important as a matter of policy
in such circumstances than the need for means of holding property
securely in stable funds, even on a semi-permanent basis. Equally,
individual beneficial interests may assume less importance. In many

[35] Cf. ibid., pp. 333–6.

90

trusts, especially big trusts as has been noted, beneficiaries may be numerous, constituting a fluctuating population of claimants, and trust management may be more a matter of control of standardised inputs and outputs from the fund than stewardship of specific, individual beneficial interests in trust property. Thus the line between trust obligations and powers may blur as emphasis attaches to flexible, variable strategies of trust supervision. Ability to accumulate and to hold funds dedicated to abstract purposes rather than defined by reference to individual or collective beneficial entitlements may also seem increasingly important. And around all of this there is typically an overriding concern to use maximum freedom in trust management to minimise tax liability, by switching investments, restructuring or relocating, dividing or amalgamating funds and even, where appropriate, altering trust terms beyond anything the settlor originally envisaged. Hence the pressure is for ever greater freedom for trustees in managing the trust fund.

4. The Politics of Trusting

These competing conceptions of the nature of trusts will not be further elaborated here. My intention on this occasion is only to sketch a framework for interpreting current dilemmas surrounding the idea of the trust. What I want to suggest, however, is a kind of conceptual movement, reflected in complex, ambiguous and sometimes contradictory ways in legal doctrine, from a moralistic conception of the trust towards the idea of the trust as a property-receptacle, an idea which is itself subject to development. The trust as property-receptacle is defined initially in terms of beneficiaries' proprietary rights recognised in equity and protected by analogy with common law protections for property. The further course of this conceptual movement is towards an idea of trusts as almost disembodied capital funds, in which the moralistic linkage between individuals involved in trusting relationships becomes further weakened or subordinated to the exigencies of capital management. While this picture is highly schematic it allows striking connections to be made with the most important modern discussions in non-legal literature of the changing nature of trusting relationships in social life as a whole, and of the tensions inherent in relationships of trust.

Thus, the sharp contrast between moralistic and capital management views of the trust can be compared with Luhmann's contrast

Trusting in Law   91

between interpersonal trust relationships, on the one hand, and
relatively passive reliance on impersonal systems, on the other.
Luhmann's claim is that the giving and accepting of interpersonal
trust involves a definite moral bond, and often a positive conferment
of trust by the truster on the trusted, a decision to take the risk of
relying on the other. But he notes that having confidence in impersonal
systems, for example, banking and financial systems, is often not a
matter in which the individual who trusts in these systems has much
choice, or can make any reliable calculation of the risks involved.[36]

Adapting these ideas to the situation of trusts, the moralistic
conception of the trust stresses the need to protect a close personal
bond between truster and trusted. It emphasises the fiduciary character
of the trust relationship and implies the importance of policing this
strictly. But the very means by which law has attempted to do this,
reversing the usual power-dependence relations in interpersonal trust,
leads away from the moralistic emphasis and towards the idea of the
trust not as a personal relationship but as a property-receptacle.
Law's protection of trust thus seems to set a path towards the
development of impersonal system characteristics in trusts. Ultimately
it appears to lead towards the capital management conception of the
trust. And the consequence of this seems to be that elements of
technical competence assume ever greater significance—reflecting the
need for efficient management of the trust as a system—while
fiduciary aspects of the trust relationship become vaguer, more
diffuse, and significantly harder to protect. The balance between
emphases on technical competence and fiduciary relationship, the twin
elements which, as noted earlier, have been considered fundamental to
trusting relationships,[37] has moved significantly in favour of the
former, seemingly at the expense of the latter.

Evidence of this is not hard to find. It has been noted that
increasingly "trust instruments contain a provision exonerating or
indemnifying a trustee for failing to act with care, skill, prudence or
diligence".[38] This does not mean, of course, that trustees are to be
excused for failing to show these qualities; the opposite is true and
the demands of efficiency upon them may be higher than ever. It
means that their specific accountability to individual beneficiaries for
the use of particular professional or other skills is reduced on the

---

[36] Luhmann, "Trust", *op cit.*, pp. 50–1.
[37] Barber, *op. cit.*
[38] Lee, "Current Issues for Trustee Legislation" *op. cit.*, p. 248.

92

assumption that they must be free to exercise discretion in trust management or supervision. General trust law still contains moralistic biases inspiring strict judgments of trustee actions. But trust instruments, framed with a view to increasingly significant imperatives affecting the trust as an ongoing capital system, seek to exclude moralistic limitations on trusteeship. Sometimes the tension between moralistic and capital management concerns appears to be defused by separating trusteeship from routine trust management (as in the case of unit trusts[39]). But whether this really aids, rather than reducing even further, the maintenance of meaningful fiduciary elements in trustee-beneficiary relations remains unclear.

In general, if technical competence has tended to become an increasingly important consideration in trusts, the conditions that have provoked this increased emphasis make strengthened fiduciary obligations equally necessary. Fiduciary obligations should be stronger because people who trust are generally less able to calculate the risks of trusting where moral distance is increased in the trust relationship, and less able to judge how and when to seek help from law to protect their interests. But, as has been seen, important pressures exist to reduce or contain fiduciary obligation. The need for freedom in management of big trusts in contemporary conditions is invoked as a reason for relaxing some rules regulating fiduciary conduct. And a further tendency seems apparent: the increased prominence of contract analysis in trust contexts. Examples are the use of contract principles in determining entitlements to assets of unincorporated associations;[40] the blend of contractual and proprietary rights associated with pensions entitlements;[41] and the increased involvement of charities in contractual relationships as a means of securing funds and fulfilling charitable purposes.[42] The use of contract principles further tends to reduce emphasis on fiduciary bonds[43] in trust analysis, and blurs the nature of trust relationships. But the conception of trusts as capital management structures may

[39] For an outline of the relationship of duties between trustee and manager see J. W. Vaughan, *The Regulation of Unit Trusts* 1990, pp. 33–8.

[40] *Re Recher's Will Trusts* [1972] Ch. 526.

[41] Pittaway, *op. cit.*, pp. 160–3.

[42] See e.g. J. Warburton and D. Morris, "Charities and the Contract Culture" (1991) Conveyancer 419.

[43] Cf. the use of contractual clauses modifying fiduciary obligations in financial services relationships. See *Fiduciary Duties and Regulatory Rules*, Law Commission Consultation Paper No 124, 1992, Part 3 "Contractual Techniques for Managing Conflicts".

Trusting in Law 93

well encourage emphasis on a diversity of contractual rights arranged around capital funds rather than a traditional emphasis on specific equitable proprietary interests demanding a range of diffuse fiduciary protections.

It is not possible here to explore the question of how inevitable the "conceptual movement" described here in relation to trusts really is and what lessons the experience of trust law may teach about the possibilities for protecting and institutionalising relationships of trust generally in social life. I want only to draw a few specific themes from the discussion above which may provide pointers towards further consideration of these matters.

First, we have noted that law's primary device for supporting trust relationships has been essentially that of reversing the positions of power and dependence as between the person who trusts and the person trusted. Yet even in the simplest trust where the degree of moral distance between truster and trusted may be at its smallest, where personal relationships of trust are at their most intimate and where there are only a small number of beneficiaries so that their beneficial entitlements can be clearly identified and relatively easily protected, law cannot wholly reverse the power-dependence relationship entailed in interpersonal trust. It cannot do this because, as Baier stresses,[44] every trusting relationship involves the exercise of discretion by the person trusted. The trustee necessarily holds discretionary power. However much, therefore, the beneficiary's trust in the trustee is displaced on to law—that is, however much it becomes merely confidence in the protections which the law of trusts provides—a significant degree of personal trust in the trustee, and so dependence on the trustee remains. Law cannot, therefore, ultimately substitute for the personal, essentially moral responsibility that a person who accepts another's trust necessarily owes to that other.

Nevertheless, secondly, we have also noted that trusts are not only relationships between trustees and beneficiaries involving dependence of the latter on the former. They are networks of *interdependence*, involving elements of *mutual reliance*—between settlor and trustees, settlor and beneficiaries, trustees and beneficiaries. This is a point that is likely to be too easily forgotten in considering modern trusts, especially big trusts, as systems in which people have confidence, in Luhmann's sense. The temptation, into which Luhmann himself

---

[44] Baier, *op. cit.*, pp. 237–8.

94

seems at times to fall, is to see reliance on systems as almost wholly passive, as if the individual who trusts the system really has little choice but to do so.[45] It is as though banking systems, political systems, economic and financial systems have a life of their own in relation to which individuals must somehow orientate themselves. Similarly in big trusts the emphasis on technical competence and efficiency, in place of a sustained emphasis on moral obligations owed to those who trust, implies that huge "system" trusts such as those of giant pension schemes have an autonomous existence almost irrespective of the specific individual moral claims of those who put their trust in them.

But here too trusts are systems of mutual reliance. A trust arrangement may not only attract but also depend upon the confidence and respect of those for whom it exists. If this confidence or respect is seriously lacking various possibilities may arise. A familiar one in traditional trusts scholarship is the attempt by beneficiaries and others to subvert trust intentions, to destroy the scheme which the settlor sought to establish. Large modern trusts may seem less vulnerable to these threats, especially from dispersed and numerous beneficiaries. Nevertheless, if moral purposes for which trust relationships exist are not fully understood and respected, efforts at subversion may come from a range of sources, not excluding, as the Maxwell pensions affair shows, those who have access to or influence over the use of trust funds. However, a more likely effect of insufficient emphasis on moral foundations of trust relationships in big trusts and, more generally, in the systems which Luhmann sees as pervading social, economic and political life is that, where possible, people vote with their feet, so to speak. They avoid reliance wherever possible on structures or systems that they no longer trust. In relation to different kinds of systems this can take a variety of forms: the withdrawing of funds, the cashing in of investments, or more broadly, an opting out of involvement and concern,[46] or the use of alternative (sometimes illegitimate) methods of protecting one's interests, acting perhaps on the basis of distrust rather than trust. Where avoidance is impossible

[45] Cf. Luhmann, "Trust", *op. cit.*, pp. 50–1 57; although he offers complex and somewhat ambiguous analyses of relations between interpersonal trust and confidence in systems: see "Familiarity, Confidence, Trust. . .", *op. cit.*, pp. 99, 102–3.

[46] For example, donors who settle property on charitable trusts often rely on a well-founded expectation that particular items given will be held subject to the trust in perpetuity. Subsequent sale of these items (e.g. land or works of art) might be assumed to have a deterrent effect on other potential charitable donors.

Trusting in Law   95

the likelihood is simply that systems will slow down; the pace of economic, financial life, for example, slows as individuals calculate more carefully and more reluctantly whether and when to involve themselves in relationships of reliance which appear to them increasingly insecure.

This connects with, and presupposes, a third point. Trust or confidence in impersonal systems does not exist independently of interpersonal trust but is closely related to it. Luhmann's emphasis on a movement from interpersonal trust to confidence in impersonal systems is illuminating. But it should not mislead us into believing that somehow the need for moral bonds of interpersonal trust has become less or that systems can somehow dispense with trusting relationships between individuals. Ultimately, systems (including systems of communication) depend significantly on the individuals who communicate within those systems.

How far law can reinforce moral relationships of interpersonal trust effectively in contemporary conditions may be a question that can only be answered after taking a general theoretical view as to whether the individualistic outlook of contemporary Western law is really capable of being adapted in some way to recognise fully "communal norms"[47] of trusting in contemporary conditions. There is no doubt that a sustained consideration of the possibilities for this is now imperative. The prevailing emphasis on efficiency and technical competence in modern debates around trusts law merely obscures this pressing need. It is also a need which extends far beyond the somewhat rarefied field of trusts law. In this paper, however, trusts law has provided a concrete focus for approaching some problems in the analysis of trusting relationships that may go to the heart of legal and social theory.

---

[47] Cf. Alexander, "Transformation of Trusts. . .", op. cit., p. 304.

[15]
Some Aspects of the Communication of Constitutional Authority

Constitutions provide and define authority for the principal organs of government in a political society or other collectivity. This is assumed to be the fundamental reason for their existence.[1] Where comparisons are made between constitutions it is usually on the basis of the form in which they express this authority, the kind of allocation of governmental powers for which they provide and the legal limits that they impose on government action. This chapter argues, however, that constitutions not only 'constitute' government for particular societies, mapping structures of authority and normative relationships between various arms and agencies of government, as well as their specific powers, responsibilities and jurisdictional limits. They also typically contribute to 'constitute', in a certain sense, *the governed society* itself, and this contribution is one of their most important aspects.

My argument is that, in order to provide authority for government in a political society, constitutional thought evokes, reinforces or proclaims certain cultural characteristics of that society which are favourable to the establishment and maintenance of political authority. Specifically, constitutional ideas help to affirm the identity of the political society that is made up of those from whom the constitution demands allegiance.[2] In so far as constitutions are themselves considered authoritative this is because they construct, focus, organize or affirm in certain ways plausible images of the general nature of the society comprised of those whose allegiance to the constitution is required.

How is this evocation of images of society achieved? In many so-called 'programmatic' national constitutions[3] the appeal to symbols of the nation is

130 *Law as Communication*

blatant. Descriptions in constitutional provisions of the symbolic meaning of the colours of the national flag[4] or the design of the national emblem, evocations of the political history, values and aspirations of the nation,[5] or perhaps specifications of the national language or languages or even of the music to be recognized as the national anthem[6] appeal to or are calculated to influence a collective national consciousness. But symbolic aspects of constitutional communication are not limited to these easily recognized forms. Constitutional symbols can be regarded as all those features or objects of constitutional discourse and constitutional practice that are powerfully (if often ambiguously) evocative in some way of assumed fundamental characteristics of the political society as a whole.

Symbolic aspects of constitutions are recognized in British constitutional law texts but are usually firmly marginalized. The predominant conception of a constitution in British legal literature is that of a set of rules about government, comparable in form with legislative rules.[7] Nevertheless what constitutions communicate about the nature of the political society in which they exist may or may not be conveyed through the medium of rules or legal principles. Hence symbolic aspects of constitutional communication tend to appear in legal reasoning and legal theory as peripheral in so far as they are not understandable in terms of the typical substance and forms of legal doctrine. They appear as matters of rhetoric rather than constitutional substance of concern to lawyers.

An aim of this chapter, which focuses specifically on comparisons between British and US constitutional structures, is to suggest that this view is too narrow. The particular legal form of constitutional ideas (including the manner in which and even the extent to which they are expressed in constitutional documents) may be much less significant than the communicated ideas themselves. And the significance of what is communicated may often lie in its ambiguity rather than in the kind of interpretive clarity which lawyers try to find in law. Indeed constitutional communication may be impossible to confine within specific modern legal forms with which lawyers typically feel at ease. The attempt to so confine it may account for some enduring dilemmas of contemporary constitutional interpretation.

In American literature the idea of the constitution as symbolically constituting society is much more familiar and widely discussed than in British writing.[8] According to some recent commentators, the US Constitution's role is that of 'the "constituent agent" of our identity as Americans';[9] the constitutional document 'assumes the identity of the nation itself';[10] it represents 'the lifeblood of the American nation, its supreme symbol and manifestation ... so intimately welded with the national existence itself that the two have become inseparable'.[11] The American legal scholar Sanford Levinson quotes the following statement: 'To be an American means to be a member of the "covenanting community" in which the commitment to freedom under law, having transcended the "natural" bonds of race, religion and class, itself takes on transcendent importance', and he adds that the 'central "covenant" of the community, from this perspective, is the Constitution'.[12] A major recent study of US constitutional law begins with the declaration that 'Americans revere their Constitution',[13] often treating it as sacred.[14] The frequent suggestion is that in some sense Americans are 'made' by it; it creates their identity as members of the political society. They recognize themselves as citizens, seeing their image as members of society through a kind of double mirror effect[15] reflecting the image of the society which the constitution and associated instruments of symbolic power – such as the flag and the Declaration of Independence – help to shape and sustain.[16]

Constitutions both convey authority and require authority. Janus-like, they face two ways – towards the *cultural sources* that provide their moral and political authority and stability, and that in certain ways they represent symbolically, and towards the *agencies of government* for which they provide legal authority. A constitution can hardly provide authority for government unless it attracts authority and respect to itself. The bases of the authority of constitutions may differ in different political societies. An argument to be pursued in this chapter is that the fundamentally different, though historically related, bases of authority of the British and US Constitutions are reflected in the different kinds of authority that these Constitutions provide for government. These differences register also in the contrasting ways that the British and American Constitutions contribute towards the symbolic representation of the nature of the societies in which they exist.

I have argued elsewhere that modern legal thought, at least in Britain and the USA, contains presuppositions about the regulatory structure of the society to which it relates: that is, legal discourse expresses or assumes certain very general images of the structure of the regulated population. In broad terms, two kinds of images of the regulated society seem identifiable in modern legal thought in the Anglo-American context. One is an image of *imperium*, essentially an image of hierarchical political organization and of individuals as subjects of centralized political authority. The other is an image of *community*, essentially the image of a social group whose members are linked in voluntary association as autonomous political actors by their allegiance to shared group values.[17] Contrasts in legal philosophy and judicial rhetoric[18] and in certain patterns of judicial decision making[19] can be understood, to some extent, in the light of the power of these contrasting images of the regulatory or normative character of society. It seems reasonable to suggest that these images may also be reflected and presented, in part, through the symbolism of constitutions. In other words, in so far as the

132   *Law as Communication*

British and American Constitutions do more than map and guarantee the authority of government – in so far as they contribute towards constituting the idea of the political society as such – they might be supposed to do this in ways that are understandable in terms of these images of community and imperium.

The different authority bases of the British and American Constitutions ultimately determine the different ways in which constitutions in these countries provide authority for government. And identifying the differences has practical significance. Indeed a comparison of these authority bases may cast light on possibilities for constitutional change in Britain in a situation in which British public lawyers have increasingly 'come to doubt the stability and adequacy of our constitutional heritage'.[20]

THE NATURE OF CONSTITUTIONAL SYMBOLISM

Before developing this comparison it is important to recognize some important general problems of the analysis of constitutional symbolism. The increasing attention attached to the study of symbol and myth[21] in law is, in part, a response to gaps or inadequacies in the established paradigms of sociological inquiry about the social significance of legal ideas. The study of legal ideology has been an important means of recognizing this social significance, especially in terms of the tendency of cognitive ideas and values associated with legal doctrine to become organized in social consciousness in relatively closed systems of understanding and evaluation.[22] These systems, in so far as they can be accepted as comprehensive and closed in this sense, exert a certain power to define social reality – the taken-for-granted understandings and evaluations of the general character of social life – and to exclude the possibility of accepting other definitions.

Nevertheless the emphasis on ideological closure – on the idea of ideology as a total perspective, a comprehensive viewpoint abolishing ambiguity and uncertainty for the ideological thinker and replacing it with a conviction of the natural, commonsensical, absolute, 'truth' of what is represented in ideological thought – may seem insufficient for a sociological presentation of the range of mechanisms of influence of legal ideas. For example, law operates not merely through the calculated attempt (especially in legislative enactments and judicial discourse) to establish legal understanding as a field of authoritative certainties but also through the creation of *infinitely suggestive ambiguities* which defy closure of cognitive meaning or value relevance and seem by their nature open to an indefinite range of levels of interpretation[23] and to serve as a focus or stimulus for a myriad of cultural references, understandings and emotions.[24]

Communication of Constitutional Authority 133

Symbolism in law presents ambiguities of meaning (an openness to contrasting interpretations of what is being communicated) the sociological significance of which is recognized in functional analysis.[25] Yet the functional analysis of legal symbolism typically rationalizes the significance of symbols according to postulated functional needs or a theoretical deduction of the social effects of symbolic communication. It confines and 'tames' symbolic ambiguity or indeterminacy by specifying its functional place in a rationally explained social order. By contrast, many recent inquiries about symbolism in law are concerned to recognize the indefinitely wide ramifications of the ambiguity of symbols, and to emphasize the rich overlay of symbolic references that provide the 'irrational', contradictory or mystificatory foundations of modern legal rationality.[26]

This route is worth following, but the cost of following it needs emphasizing. The overlap of symbolic references that spill out from and beyond legal texts creates a dense texture of signification in which possibilities of meaning and interpretation are potentially almost unlimited and yet narrowly local in origin. The 'forest of symbols'[27] envelops those who inhabit it, so that the difficulty of gaining a broad perspective on the terrain of symbolic communication is acute and the temptation is to give up systematic attempts to do so. A failing of many studies of ideology may be the assumption that (to extend the metaphor) it is possible somehow to climb above the forest of symbols to open, higher ground from which the contours and shape of the forest can be 'externally' observed and conclusively mapped. But interpretations of symbolic meaning necessarily remain indeterminate and are permanently controversial.[28] To let light into the 'darkness' of the symbolic forest it may be necessary to provide guidance for these interpretations from the conceptual frameworks for understanding legal communication that are suggested by studies of legal ideology. At the same time it can be recognized that the significance to be attached to symbols is not exhausted by whatever significance is established in terms of these frameworks. For example, it may be especially useful to analyse the ways in which ambiguous symbols are interpreted in popular and legal professional consciousness so as to reinforce the assumed certainties of ideological thought. Emblematic institutions, elements of ritual, or certain ideas and references presented in or associated with constitutional doctrines may be analysed in terms of the ways in which they are understood by citizens so as to reinforce and complete ideological representations or images of the 'essential' nature of the political society to which these symbols relate.

The quest is therefore still for a sociology of legal symbolism; for a mode of understanding law's symbolic significance in the generalizing context of empirical social theory. We need, at least, to climb the highest branches in the forest of symbols so as to try to see from an appropriate theoretical

134   *Law as Communication*

vantage point patterns of symbolic representation and to interpret these in relation to a larger, more general project of social understanding. As Durkheim noted, 'one must know how to go underneath the symbol to the reality which it represents and which gives it its meaning'.[29] But this is always a matter of studying symbols for *particular* sociological purposes, *conceptualizing* the represented 'reality' sociologically and hence *choosing* the symbolic meanings that are to be considered significant.

The problems of interpreting symbols parallel problems of interpreting the legal nature of constitutions. It is said that 'the defining feature of legal modernity lies in the attempt to make law self-founding.'[30] The peculiarity of law as a normative system, according to Hans Kelsen, is that it regulates its own creation;[31] it can be portrayed as a self-reproducing rule-system.[32] Whatever the general problems of this understanding of law, there are serious problems in applying it to constitutional law. Constitutions may indeed regulate their own creation or inhabit a self-reproducing legal system in the limited sense of providing procedures for modification of their own documentary provisions, or even for replacement of their entire written text. But, in the graphic Kelsenian image, the (historically first) constitution provides the legal foundation of the legal system as a whole. As such, however, it is necessarily only ambiguously legal in quality itself, for its norms – at least according to Kelsen's instructive analysis – are derived not by imputation from other legal norms but from the fabric of *cultural elements* expressed for the limited purposes of legal theory in the fictional idea of the basic norm.[33] Indeed, whether or not anything like the Kelsenian perspective is adopted, the specifically *legal* character of constitutions remains difficult to define because constitutions significantly defy the project of making law 'self-founding'. They are the conduit by which elements of social authority (attributed, for example, to a social contract, popular will or the political virtues of the Rule of Law) or transcendental authority (attributed, for example, to notions of natural law, divine right or religious origins of government or society) are carried into law and legal interpretation as the basis of its legitimacy.

Much follows from this. Constitutions are not to be seen as bounded by the orthodox forms of positive law but extend through and beyond these legal forms. Their character as simultaneously legal, moral and political institutions and as bridges or conduits between the cultural conditions of existence of the political society, on the one hand, and positive legal doctrine, on the other, suggests that their scope is never confined to the contents of constitutional *documents*. On the one hand, they are expressed in familiar forms of enacted positive law (statements of rules, rights and duties, principles or procedures, or formal definitions and authorizations of governmental structures, set out in a constitutional document or documents). On the other, they include elements of signification not necessarily conveyed or conveyable in familiar legal forms, and certainly not constrained in meaning by such forms. In particular, these elements of signification may include symbolic representations of the culture of the regulated political society in so far as that culture provides the identity of the society to which the constitution as a foundation of governmental authority appeals and from which it is considered to draw its own authority.

These representations might be identified through the analysis of a wide range of phenomena: for example, constitutional documents themselves; judicial decisions and pronouncements and other professional and lay commentary on particular constitutional issues; established practices and traditions in the conduct of government and public affairs; the literature of constitutional theory and constitutional history, including popular (non-specialist) writings; lay opinion about the constitution and about questions of government; and public rituals, procedures, ceremonies and celebrations linked with matters of governmental continuity and authority. Thus symbolic elements of the constitution are identifiable in both its 'written' (documentary) and 'unwritten' components.

POPULAR SOVEREIGNTY AND FUNDAMENTAL LAW

The aim in what follows is to illustrate two (apart from many other) different ways in which constitutional thought can contribute to 'constitute' the society in which it exists; in other words, two different ways in which constitutions reinforce cultural sources of their authority through symbolic representations that help to establish a particular image of the nature of the regulated society. For this purpose the focus is limited to some crucial distinctions between the bases of constitutional authority in the UK and the USA.

In a classic essay of 1928, Edward Corwin remarked: 'It is customary nowadays to ascribe the *legality* as well as the *supremacy* of the [United States] Constitution – the one is, in truth, but the obverse of the other – exclusively to the fact that, in its own phraseology, it was "ordained" by "the people of the United States".' Corwin notes that two important ideas are thereby brought into play. 'One is the so-called "positive" conception of law as a general expression merely for the particular commands of a human lawgiver, as a series of acts of human will; the other is that the highest possible source of such commands, because the highest possible embodiment of human will, is "the people".'[34]

Corwin appropriately pinpoints the essential intellectual development that enabled a specific constitutional document, or small group of documents, to

136   *Law as Communication*

achieve recognition as fundamental law, superior to all other law, in the United States. To be law in the modern positivist conception that was becoming established in the common law world in the late eighteenth and nineteenth centuries, especially as a result of Jeremy Bentham's and John Austin's ideas, the Constitution had to be seen as 'posited' by a human legislator, and no such legislator could have greater lawmaking authority than 'the people', treated as a political unity. Thus the theory of the Constitution as a superior positive legal creation of 'the people' simultaneously established the centrality of the popularly enacted constitutional document in the idea of the Constitution and enabled the Constitution, understood in this sense, to dominate all other law conceived in similarly positive terms. 'The people' is thus the image of the regulated population which underpins constitutional authority and is promoted in constitutional thought.

The idea of a special popular authority of some kind underlying the Constitution is carried through to the most recent debates about American constitutional law. Bruce Ackerman's analysis[15] of what he calls America's dualist democracy distinguishes between, on the one hand, the authority of ordinary legislation conferred by the popular mandate to govern given to legislators by periodic elections and, on the other, the popular foundations of the Constitution. These foundations consist in the notion that the Constitution was established by a convention of the people and can be altered by decisions of the American people as a whole (rather than their elected representatives) registered in ways (formal or informal) outside the mundane political processes of representative democracy. Thus amendments to the Constitution are no ordinary acts of legislation. They are expressions of a popular authority distinct from that which authorizes legislators to develop law through everyday processes of legislative amendment. Ackerman declares: 'Americans have not been "born equal" through some miraculous act of immaculate conception. To the extent that we have gained equality, we have won it through energetic debate, popular decision and constitutional creativity.'[36] The message is that the values and structure of the Constitution are popularly defined and capable of being changed or developed by popular will. For Ackerman, 'the people' refers to individuals who can through collective action bring about constitutional change.

The idea of popular sovereignty, focused on the image of a polity of active citizens, is strongly present also in the resurgence of the idea, in the American context, of deliberative democracy.[37] This involves the advocacy of a kind of informed and dynamic conversation among the populace at large about the fundamentals and directions of the polity, as well as the closely related insistence that determination of the meaning of the Constitution is not to be treated as a monopoly of judicial wisdom.[38] Indeed the debate over who should have authority to interpret the Constitution acquires a prominence comparable to, and explicitly compared with, theological disputes as to who should have the authority to interpret holy scripture. The tradition of popular sovereignty sometimes seems to inform the drawing of analogies between judges and priests as interpreters and to inspire a 'protestant' suspicion of both in so far as they claim unique authority, through their access to an 'expert' tradition of doctrine that supplements the words of the written text, to fix the meaning of ideas that should belong to the whole people.[39]

But in what way, specifically, can 'the people' act except through legislative representatives? If they act through such representatives it seems appropriate to speak of legislative supremacy rather than popular sovereignty, and the idea of the superiority of a constitution, founded on popular sovereignty, over mere legislative majorities becomes incoherent. However, James Fishkin's recent analysis of mechanisms of deliberative democracy[40] is an attempt to demonstrate how even in a large, complex polity such as the USA certain procedures can be created to allow democratic deliberation as a form of action by the people as a whole. Some other modern writers, too, are concerned to ask hard questions about the mechanisms through which 'the people' can act, but in much literature the possibilities remain startlingly unclear. How, for example, is 'protestant' interpretation of the Constitution by ordinary citizens able to compete with judicial interpretation? Is it in the end unimportant unless it creates civil disturbance or revolt? Again, adopting Ackerman's own question about America's dualist democracy, how can a process be organized to mark out 'the rare occasions' when a political movement is to be recognized as acting in the name of the people as a whole?[41]

Such problems of popular or direct democracy are familiar in the history of political thought. How is popular government possible except through representatives? One way to avoid this practical cul-de-sac is simply to ignore the implication in the idea of popular sovereignty that the question requires an answer. Thus, while the popular basis of government is treated as fundamental, it can be assumed to be adequately safeguarded through the ordinary processes of representative democracy. Ackerman asserts that this kind of denial of dualist democracy has in fact become 'dominant among serious constitutionalists over the course of the last century'.[42] The consequence of such a denial, however, is that the idea of the Constitution as fundamental law, superior to ordinary legislation, has to be sought in some source other than that of popular sovereignty.

American constitutional history shows that such other sources have always seemed to be available. Many writers have traced the origins of American constitutional thought in ideas of natural law and natural rights, in general traditions and principles associated with English common law, and in documentary sources such as Magna Carta. It has been claimed that the

138   *Law as Communication*

USA has always had an unwritten constitution existing alongside the written one;[43] that the Framers of the documentary Constitution assumed that the unwritten elements of constitutional thought and tradition would continue to coexist with the constitutional document which they now saw as invested with popular authority[44] and that the documentary Constitution presupposed these unwritten elements as necessary to the completion of its meaning. On this view the idea of popular sovereignty was never the sole basis of the Constitution's authority. On the other hand, the unwritten elements of the Constitution are organized around and given coherence and focus through the existence and status of the constitutional document, which gains its special authority as the creation of 'the people'.

The recognition of the continuing significance of non-documentary components of the Constitution, located in ideology, inherited values and legal and cultural traditions, raises, in itself, interesting questions about the possibility of popular interpretation of the Constitution. On one view, since the words of the constitutional document cannot be understood without reference to a tradition of values, interpretations and understandings external to the document itself, it must be accepted that constitutional interpretation is necessarily the monopoly of experts (such as judges of a specialist constitutional court) who are learned in that tradition. On the other hand, this 'catholic' view[45] of the necessary qualifications to be an interpreter is not inevitable. Ronald Dworkin, for example, asserts that there is no reason why ordinary citizens should not be able to involve themselves in the process of interpretation of the underlying value structures of the Constitution.[46] In general, however, as a matter of practicality, judges monopolize constitutional interpretation. The idea of popular sovereignty accommodates this situation in so far as the judiciary can be seen as guardians of and spokespersons for the values and traditions that unite 'the people' as a political community, and that complete the meaning of the popularly created documentary Constitution.

The above discussion indicates that the idea of popular sovereignty may be interpreted in various ways, and that it is not necessary to treat it as the sole basis of current constitutional authority in the USA. Nevertheless it remains the distinguishing idea that makes possible the special character of the written US Constitution as fundamental law. Because of this, the question remains: in what way and by what means do 'the people' give authority to the Constitution? In answering this question the nature of 'the people' presupposed in the idea of popular sovereignty is of the greatest importance. As has been noted, 'the people' is not a democratic majority. It is rather the entire nation viewed as a single community. Much literature suggests that 'the people' is not necessarily restricted to the citizens existing at any particular moment but refers also to the continuity of the political society through time.

Communication of Constitutional Authority   139

How then can 'the people' be conceptualized as a historical actor? At the most mundane level it can be treated as the electorate, but acting through special procedures (those which the Constitution provides for its own amendment), distinguished from the procedures that give popular sanction to ordinary legislation. The amendment process preserves a separation between expressions of popular authority for the creation of constitutional provisions, on the one hand, and of ordinary legislation, on the other. But this conceptualization of 'the people' as an actor is relatively weak. 'The people' appear primarily as the legislative representatives of the electorate acting through exceptional procedures.[47]

Much more powerful conceptualizations of 'the people' are rooted in the 'exceptional process'[48] of the Constitution's creation. 'The people' are symbolized most significantly in constitutional history by the Framers, the few dozen delegates of the 13 states, whose deliberations at Philadelphia leading to the signing of the Constitution in 1787 are evoked and analysed in an immense popular and scholarly literature. Creators of a constitutional agreement based on principled deliberation, easily treated as symbolizing a social contract on which the nation was founded, the Framers – 'superb democratic politicians'[49] – are seen by some historians as heroic, having had the infinite wisdom to craft 'a perfect and complete political theory, adequate to all our future needs'.[50]

Charles Beard's thesis of the economic origins of the Constitution[51] 'appeared to demonstrate irrefutably and with all the paraphernalia of scientific scholarship'[52] the unrepresentative character of the Framers in relation to the populations of the states and the extent to which they had framed the Constitution in pursuit of their personal economic interests. But the issue of how far the Framers represented – in any sense of formal political representation – the diversity of the actual populations of the states seems unimportant. In one sense, the Framers are not legislative representatives of an electorate at all; their representative status is cultural, not political. They *symbolize* in constitutional thought the nation as a diverse but unified cultural entity. But the symbol is ambiguous. The Framers are also seen as political representatives of the 13 existing states; that is, they represented as historical actors political societies already established and agreeing together a 'compact' for a government to unite them, this unity being recognized as essential to remedy major crises of government arising in relationships between the states.[53] In negotiating this compact the Framers are seen as having established the basis of a new political society.

'The people' is thus ambiguously represented as a community based on free agreement and shared values. The status of the Constitution as fundamental law remains dependent on the coherence of the idea of popular sovereignty; constitutional thought and tradition reinforce the image of the

140   *Law as Communication*

people as sovereign. But constitutional thought, lay and professional, helps to constitute 'the people', partly through symbolic representations derived from traditions of the Constitution's origins. It imagines the nation as a *community*, a morally cohesive association of politically autonomous people, related through natural, spontaneous or freely chosen association on the basis of values held in common.[54] It might be suggested that the need for the constitutional promotion of the image of the people has increased as the Constitution has itself required stronger authority, gradually becoming recognized less as the consequence of a limited compact between small states and more clearly as the sole guarantor of legal authority for an increasingly powerful central government[55] directing economic and social policy in a huge, complex and perhaps – given its ethnic and other diversity – potentially disunified nation.

PARLIAMENTARY SOVEREIGNTY AND FUNDAMENTAL LAW

By contrast to American constitutional thought the British Constitution is characterized by an almost total absence of the idea of popular sovereignty. The British Constitution, however defined, represents symbolically the nature of the political society in which it exists in radically different ways from those typical of American constitutional thought. In what follows the concern is not with constitutional history as such but with identifying the dominant image of British society represented in constitutional thought and some of the symbolic means of this representation.

Many writers have remarked on 'the United Kingdom's attachment to *ad hoc* solutions and its lack of interest in general constitutional issues'.[56] The Constitution does not occupy the place in popular consciousness that the US Constitution seems to have. A sophisticated and ironic passivity infuses the notion that, lacking a supreme constitutional document, the UK has no Constitution. Foreign observers are struck by the 'failure of politicians and civil servants to think constitutionally'.[57] Ultimately, this constitutional passivity is rooted in the cultural acceptance of legislative supremacy, associated with the idea of parliamentary sovereignty. If parliamentary sovereignty means what it says, writes Terence Daintith, 'there is certainly no room for any constitutional principles, since the maintenance of any rule, principle or body of practice is wholly contingent upon parliamentary abstinence from its alteration'.[58] Parliamentary sovereignty, and thus legislative supremacy, *is* the Constitution, according to this view. For many constitutional commentators this situation has become the central theoretical problem of government in Britain. The solution is generally seen in constructing, either through constitutional enactments or judicial activity, principles to limit or modify parliamentary sovereignty. An object is to devise means of controlling the governmental power of transient political majorities, which may represent only social minorities, given the limitations of electoral arrangements.

But a prerequisite for understanding possibilities for engrafting new constitutional principle on an unprincipled Constitution is to understand the basis of authority of the Constitution. As Dicey correctly noted, the British Constitution is firmly rooted in the tradition of common law thought. One of the most striking consequences of this is that constitutional documents which, in other circumstances, might have become established as fundamental law have often been treated as expressions of already existing common law principle. In the English context common law thought provided both a folk and a professional legal philosophy that eventually became the only significant potential source of fundamental law. Magna Carta for a time, especially in the fourteenth century, assumed immense status as a fundamental basis of English legal freedoms,[59] but when revived as such by Edward Coke in the seventeenth century as 'fountain of all the fundamental laws of the realm',[60] its significance was as declaratory of the unchanging heritage of common law freedoms.

As J.G.A. Pocock has shown,[61] the doctrine of the 'ancient constitution' in the seventeenth century presented, in an important tradition of English legal and political thought, the common law as immemorial and unchanging, except through processes of elaboration reflecting the timeless wisdom of the community – a wisdom entrusted to the professional common lawyers and necessarily expressed as the 'artificial reason' of the law. The doctrine of the ancient constitution was a powerful weapon against royal power since, according to Pocock, it enabled the common lawyers to argue that all political authority in the realm derived from unimaginably ancient cultural sources, still present in an unbroken legal tradition; indeed a tradition unbroken by any political change, including that of the Norman Conquest itself.

The assumed supremacy of the common law tradition, graphically illustrated in the doctrine of the ancient constitution, is most dramatically presented in Coke's assertion, especially in the context of *Bonham's Case*, of the common law's authority to control Acts of Parliament and declare them void 'as against common right and reason, or repugnant, or impossible to be performed'.[62] Natural law enters the discourse of English law, if only briefly and impractically,[63] as the substance of common law principle. But of greater importance is the example of common law method available to be used, with no such dramatic rhetoric, in everyday judicial decision making, not necessarily opposed to political lawmaking but usually allied with it. The tradition of common law thought enabled courts to attach the authority of the supposed immemorial wisdom of the community to principle fash-

142   *Law as Communication*

ioned for the moment and consciously shaped by the judges.[64] It allowed
them also to recognize that legislation could be accepted as an expression of
the common law tradition. A common law judge, writes Pocock, elaborating
the implications of his original thesis, 'was not in the least precluded from
thinking of law as decreed by the king's authority in the king's courts, from
discerning the affinity between what he was doing and the sovereign reason
by which the king-in-parliament made statutes binding on him and the
whole nation ...'.[65] Behind such reasoning, however, is the idea that the
common law gives authority to all who professionally or officially interpret
or develop law, whether courts or legislators, and no other source of ultimate authority is available to do this.[66]

These ideas suggest that common law principle should remain, at least, a
subordinate source of constitutional principle, as in the USA, where it is
treated by exponents of the 'unwritten constitution' as supplementing the
documentary Constitution positively established on the basis of popular
sovereignty. A fundamental difference between the British and American
contexts, however, is that in the former no doctrine of popular sovereignty –
no image of 'the people' as an active lawmaking collectivity – was available
to become attached to the contents of a specific *document* as fundamental
constitutional law and become an enduring reference point in constitutional
thought. Thus the common law tradition subsumed specific enactments
within itself as exemplifications of common law principle while validating
the processes of parliamentary legislation.

Undoubtedly something more was necessary to provide an intellectual
foundation of parliamentary sovereignty as long as the authority of the
political legislator was treated as located in the superior authority of common law. John Figgis's classic thesis on the transition from religious to
modern secular understandings of ultimate political authority describes processes by which mystical ideas of the 'sacredness' of monarchical authority
provided a climate of thought which paved the way for the acceptance of
modern theories of sovereignty.[67] In England, especially in the seventeenth
century, a tradition of religious ideas about authority was transformed into a
secular conception of political sovereignty, which in its early development,
at least, could receive aid from the common law's ambivalence about the
appropriate location of authority in the state and its convenient emphasis on
communal sources of all regulatory power.

As parliamentary processes acquired an independent political legitimacy,
they inevitably freed themselves of all elements of common law tutelage.
On the basis of Figgis's arguments, it can be suggested that the concept of
parliamentary sovereignty succeeded to similar assumptions about government (as a hierarchical, 'top–down' relationship of superiors and subordinates) to those surrounding earlier ideas of monarchical authority. Further,

the vague authority base of common law in the idea of immemorial communal wisdom – accessible only to lawyers – could hardly compete with that of a parliament not only having established lawmaking power but also gradually coming to possess some democratic credentials. In the USA, elements of common law principle, together with many other value elements derived from a variety of ideological sources, could find a focus for constitutional relevance as part of an 'unwritten constitution' given secure existence by its connection with the documentary Constitution founded by political acts of 'the people'. In Britain, such elements could acquire no relevance in constitutional interpretation, since no independent constitutional focus to compete with a legislative sovereignty aspiring to democratic legitimation had been established. In the absence of such a focus, common law could not impose limitations of principle on parliamentary legislation.

Thus it may, indeed, be said that parliamentary sovereignty and the associated idea of legislative supremacy, in the British context, amount to the Constitution. The authority of the Constitution, once given by the common law tradition, is now found in representative democracy. And common law is revealed as lacking any authority to limit parliamentary legislative activity. Legislative supremacy founded in parliamentary sovereignty seems constitutionally unchallengeable.

As has been seen, American constitutional thought portrays 'the people' as a unified creator of law, though the problems of this idea lead to contrasting emphases and formulations. British constitutional thought portrays the regulated population symbolically in a quite different way. Certainly classical common law, as typified by the seventeenth-century writings of Matthew Hale and Coke, embodied an image of the regulated population as a community linked by shared values, history and traditions.[68] The mythical ancient constitution was understood as the national heritage of the English people, whose cultural unity and homogeneity had defied all political disturbances that might have threatened it. Yet this premodern image of community is very different from the image of the active law-creating community of American constitutional thought. The community of classical common law thought coexists with royal power and its law confers authority on the King's courts and the King-in-Parliament. The symbolic representation of the regulated population in classical common law thought is not that of an active law-creating community but that of a unified nation of loyal English subjects, content with the legal structures which they have inherited from a shared past and with which they collectively identify.[69] Hence the terms 'community', 'nation' and 'realm' are interchangeable. The popular will or reason of the community does not make law. Law is the 'artificial reason' of professional lawyers given force by the institutions of the monarchical state.

144   *Law as Communication*

Hence, as common law sustains and ultimately subordinates itself to parliamentary sovereignty in English history, citizens are not recognizable in legal thought as part of a unified lawmaking community but are either individual *objects* of regulation (since Parliament, not citizens, creates law) or individual electors who choose their parliamentary representatives and so put their legal sovereign in place. In either case they are passive in their specific relation to law: delegating to others the creation of regulation, or submitting themselves to it. The image of society that the British constitution implies is thus one of *imperium*: of individual subjects of a superior political authority.[70] Certainly this authority may be conceived in abstract terms. It may, for example, be taken to be the authority of law itself, as in the idea of the Rule of Law. But nothing in the constitution suggests the idea of a unified lawmaking community. The democratic foundation of parliamentary sovereignty does not require symbolization in terms of a population actively involved in the shaping of its law.

Anachronistic as the claim may seem, in this light the central constitutional symbol at present in the Constitution of the United Kingdom might appropriately be considered to be that of the monarch. Walter Bagehot, one of the few classic writers on the Constitution to have attached due significance to its purely symbolic – or, as he termed them, 'dignified' – elements, suggested as much.[71] The monarch and the monarch's family represent many aspects of the political society in the ambiguous manner characteristic of constitutional symbols. The image of hierarchy and of the relation of sovereign and subject, underlying and preceding the idea of a democratic polity of free citizens, is coupled with that of the universal family and its cycle of births, marriages and deaths as the foundation of social life.[72] Again monarchy symbolizes the divisive elements of privilege and class deeply rooted in society, yet also the authority that renders all members of society equal in their subjection. Bagehot thought that, in a political society whose unity centred on common adherence of subjects to a sovereign authority, the monarchy provided an easily intelligible focus of allegiance. A constitutional partnership of church and state is also evoked in coronation rituals and other events and in the official allegiance of the monarch to a declared religious faith. In a regulated population represented constitutionally as a society of onlookers who do not participate in government but, as in classical common law thought, 'identify' with it, the monarch and the royal family are symbols of the minimal social structure (individuals within families) and, as such, easily seen as a microcosm and exemplification of the nation's moral character, its strengths and weaknesses. Monarchy, finally, symbolizes in its dynastic continuity the historical continuity of the political society and the endlessly self-renewing character of authority. Yet nothing is fixed and unchanging: as political and social conditions change, so the significance and power of all of these symbols may change too.

CONSTITUTIONAL SYMBOLISM AND LEGAL ANALYSIS

Two examples of constitutional symbolism – the symbolism of the Framers in American constitutional thought and that of the institution of monarchy in modern British constitutional thought – have been emphasized above. Many other constitutional symbols could be considered. As noted earlier, a central problem for this kind of analysis is that the interpretation of symbols remains indeterminate and unlimited because of their inherent ambiguity and uncontrollable proliferation. For this reason it requires guidance and control within a theoretically structured inquiry.

If such an inquiry is about *law*, we must ask: how, specifically, does the identification and interpretation of constitutional symbols help in understanding legal communication and in structuring the problems addressed by constitutional lawyers? Consider first the idea of the Framers as a symbolic representation of the people as makers of the United States Constitution. In constitutional interpretation the concentration on the Framers' intentions as the basis of the Constitution's meaning is explicable once it is understood that the Framers are the symbolic representation of the fundamental authority of the constitutional document. A recent writer such as Ronald Dworkin might insist that the fiction of seeking the Framers' intention should be replaced by an overt recognition that constitutional lawyers, like other lawyers, are engaged in the task of interpreting the political and moral meaning of the legal order as a whole.[73] But if we recognize that such interpretation must often become a political battle about deeply controversial values, a battle that continually threatens to burst beyond the constraints of constitutional discourse and challenge the idea of a constitutional (legal) framework for politics,[74] the appeal to Framers' intentions may be the most plausible claim to a constitutional authority founded on shared values or legal traditions.[75] It presents itself as an appeal to the powerful symbols of a popular agreement whose controversial origins are blurred by history. It avoids the difficult question of who 'the people' currently are and in what way the Constitution continues to express 'their' values as a unified collectivity.

Consider also the symbolic significance of monarchy in the British context. Orthodox constitutional analysis typically treats the monarchy as a relatively insignificant element in the constitutional structure. Legal discussions focus on conventions and legal powers associated with the monarch's role in relation to government.[76] But it seems important to consider evidence of transformations of monarchy's symbolic significance as well as its role as

146   *Law as Communication*

a specific agent in decision making within the state structure or in organizing the exercise of governmental and especially lawmaking powers. A focus
on constitutional symbolism might locate monarchy, for reasons noted
earlier, close to the heart of constitutional concerns because of its symbolic
importance as part of the constitution's evocation of an image of the regulatory structure of society which, in turn, underpins the authority which the
Constitution provides for government. Legal provisions that link the institution of monarchy with governmental processes harness to these processes
the complex symbolic representations of authority that monarchy provides.
Since constitutional interpretation is concerned with locating and defining
authority for government action it cannot realistically ignore symbolic forms
as conduits of that authority. Specifically, therefore, an analysis of the legal
significance to be attached to monarchy must include a recognition of
symbolic elements that help to infuse the 'constitution as hard law'[77] with a
wider culture of constitutional thought.

   Again, the significance of bills of rights should be seen, not only in terms
of their utility as positive law available for invocation by citizens, but also in
terms of symbolic aspects. The United States Bill of Rights can be considered to express not only a set of rights available for enforcement through the
courts but also a powerful symbol of the centrality of the idea of individual
autonomy in the structure of the American polity. The Bill of Rights helps to
evoke the idea of the political society as one of individuals joined in civil
society on the basis of free mutual agreement. It adds further symbolism to
the idea of 'the people' as an association of autonomous citizens, whose
rights as such are fundamental to the entire structure of political authority.

   As discussion earlier in this chapter has suggested, constitutional symbolism contributes to reinforce images of the nature of the political society,
which, in turn, can be seen as informing the constitution and defining the
nature of its authority as fundamental law. Constitutional symbolism must,
therefore, to this extent be consistent with the cultural basis of authority at
the heart of the constitutional structure. In the British context we have noted
the absence of a culture of popular sovereignty independent of parliamentary sovereignty. For this reason there is no easy answer to the question
raised in much recent discussion of constitutional reform in Britain as to
how elements of a written (documentary) constitution or bill of rights might
be entrenched as fundamental law, even if such constitutional innovations
were thought desirable.[78] In the US context the authority of the people
provides the essential *independent* authority of the written Constitution
which makes it supreme over all other legal authority, including that of
legislation produced by democratic majorities. Interestingly, the Preamble
of a recent elaborate draft written constitution for Britain[79] begins with the
declaration that 'We the People of the United Kingdom ...' affirm and

respect certain principles of government and social justice, which are to inform the constitution. The need to protect these principles justifies constitutional limitations on ordinary legislative activity and the requirement that all agencies of the state conform to the requirements of a bill of rights set out in Chapter 2 of the draft. But the American idea of 'We the People' is alien to British constitutional thought. Without the appeal to popular sovereignty, or some equivalent foundational authority, the problem of the legal impossibility of entrenchment arises.

No claim is being made here that the image of community – of popular sovereignty arising from free association of citizens establishing some kind of morally unified collectivity – is essential as the image of society which *any* documentary constitution must somehow appeal to in order to secure its status as fundamental law. As a substitute for 'the people' one might envisage the charismatic 'saviour' who gives law, probably in time of emergency and danger, to bring order and justice to the polity. The image of a society structured by the inspiration of such a charismatic figure or figures, perhaps charismatic only because of the circumstances of the times, is likely to be an imperium image of some kind. It might well found the authority of a documentary constitution, perhaps through the kind of process which Max Weber described as the routinization of charisma.[80] In modern times this process might be seen in the establishment of constitutions at the beginnings of the independent existence of nations or after periods of crisis or war. Again the idea of 'the past as present' – the timelessness of tradition – might found the authority of a documentary constitution, although the best illustration of the constitutional appropriation of this authority would seem to lie in the idea of the 'unwritten' ancient constitution of common law.

We have noted, however, how the imagery of the regulated society in British constitutional thought reinforces the specific form of constitutional authority embodied in parliamentary sovereignty. It seems that common law cannot easily be invoked to provide principles that could limit or challenge parliamentary sovereignty, since this sovereignty is itself given legitimacy by the common law. The image of society symbolized in British constitutional thought encompasses the idea of the Rule of Law (of law, once created, having authority over all within the realm) but envisages the citizen as passive in relation to the processes of law creation.

The symbolic significance of components of the British Constitution is most obvious and consistent when viewed in connection with the image of imperium – the image of a hierarchically ordered society of individuals united only in their allegiance to superior authority. It might be appropriate to conclude with two further instances of this powerful symbolism. The survival of the House of Lords as a second chamber can undoubtedly be

148	*Law as Communication*

explained or defended on functional grounds, in terms of what Bagehot called 'efficient' elements of the Constitution, yet in its present form its main constitutional significance – more central than its specific legislative or governmental powers – might be considered to be the permanent symbolic rejection at the very heart of the constitutional structure of the idea of popular sovereignty, of the image of society as a free association of autonomous citizens agreeing together on the nature of their (self-) government. Hereditary peers do not sit as representatives within the Lords but are the traditional elite class of the realm incorporated *directly* in Parliament. Their constitutional importance is primarily as a symbol of imperium: of a society founded on hierarchy, deference and distant, unchallenged political authority.

Again, the legal necessity for the recording of the monarch's assent to legislation is regarded as a matter of pure formality in most discussions of British constitutional law. Yet the symbolism of the requirement for the monarch's assent to legislation as the final element in the parliamentary legislative process insists – again at the very heart of the constitutional process of law creation – that royal power (and thus established hierarchical structures of political society, immune from democratic modification and carrying the weight of ancient privilege) is necessary in order to confer final authority as law on anything proposed through democratic processes. In practice the conferring of this authority will not be refused.[81] But the provision for its formal conferment reinforces in every democratic legislative act the symbolism of hierarchy and subjection, evoking the image of imperium implicit in law, and the cultural source from which the Constitution continues to draw its ultimate authority.

NOTES

1	See, for example, S. De Smith and R. Brazier, *Constitutional and Administrative Law*, 7th edn, London, Penguin, 1994, p.7.
2	Cf. B. Thompson, *Textbook on Constitutional and Administrative Law*, 2nd edn, London, Blackstone, 1995, pp.13–14.
3	Cf. De Smith and Brazier, *op. cit.*, note 1 above, p.4.
4	See, for example, Constitution of Angola, 1975 (revised 1980) Part 4; also Thompson, *op. cit.*, note 2 above, p.13.
5	See Constitution of Algeria, Preamble; cf. Thompson, *op. cit.*, note 2 above, pp.14–15.
6	On the significance of national anthems in symbolizing the nature of the political society, see K.A. Cerulo, 'Sociopolitical Control and the Structure of National Symbols: An Empirical Analysis of National Anthems', 1989, *Social Forces*, **68**, 76.
7	See, for example, C. Munro, 'What is a Constitution?', 1983, *Public Law*, 567.
8	For early discussions, see E.S. Corwin, 'The Constitution as Instrument and as Symbol', 1936, *American Political Science Review*, **30**, 1071; M. Lerner, 'Constitution and Court as Symbols', 1937, *Yale Law Journal*, **46**, 1290.

9   S. Levinson, *Constitutional Faith*, Princeton NJ, Princeton University Press, 1988, p.5.

10   M. Foley, *The Silence of Constitutions*, London, Routledge, 1989, p.37.

11   H. Kohn, quoted in Foley, *op. cit.*, note 10 above, p.37.

12   Levinson, *op cit.*, note 9 above, p.5.

13   C. Sunstein, *The Partial Constitution*, Cambridge, MA, Harvard University Press, 1993, p.v.

14   E.S. Corwin, 'The Worship of the Constitution', in R. Loss (ed.), *Corwin on the Constitution*, Ithaca NY, Cornell University Press, 1981, pp.47–55; T.C. Grey, 'The Constitution as Scripture', 1984, *Stanford Law Review*, **37**, 21–5; Levinson, *op. cit.*, note 9 above, ch.1.

15   Cf. L. Althusser, 'Ideology and Ideological State Apparatuses', in *Essays in Ideology*, London, Verso, 1984, p.54.

16   Cf. Levinson, *op. cit.*, note 9 above. p.11.

17   R. Cotterrell, *Law's Community: Legal Theory in Sociological Perspective*, Oxford, Clarendon Press, 1995, ch.11.

18   Ibid., pp.222–40.

19   R. Cotterrell, 'Judicial Review and Legal Theory', in G. Richardson and H. Genn (eds), *Administrative Law and Government Action: The Courts and Alternative Mechanisms of Review*, Oxford, Clarendon Press, 1994.

20   N. Walker, 'The Middle Ground in Public Law', in W. Finnie, C.M.G. Himsworth and N. Walker (eds), *Edinburgh Essays in Public Law*, Edinburgh, Edinburgh University Press, 1991, p.57.

21   See especially P. Fitzpatrick, *The Mythology of Modern Law*, London, Routledge, 1992.

22   R. Cotterrell, 'Sociological Perspectives on Legal Closure', in A. Norrie (ed.), *Closure or Critique: New Directions in Legal Theory*, Edinburgh, Edinburgh University Press, 1993.

23   Cf. V. Turner, *The Forest of Symbols: Aspects of Ndembu Ritual*, Ithaca NY, Cornell University Press, 1967, p.44.

24   See E. Sapir, 'Symbols', in E.R.A. Seligman (ed.), *Encyclopedia of the Social Sciences*, Vol. 14, New York, Macmillan, 1934, p.493.

25   For a sample from a large literature, see, for example, T. Arnold, *The Symbols of Government*, New Haven, Yale University Press, 1935, *The Folklore of Capitalism*, New Haven, Yale University Press, 1937; J. Cohen, 'The Value of Value Symbols in Law, 1952, *Columbia Law Review*, **52**, 893; M. Edelman, *The Symbolic Uses of Politics*, Urbana, University of Illinois Press, 1964; V. Aubert, 'Some Social Functions of Legislation', 1966, *Acta Sociologica*, **10**, 98; C.D. Elder and R.W. Cobb, *The Political Uses of Symbols*, New York, Longman, 1983; H. Gunnlaugsson and J.F. Galliher, 'Prohibition of Beer in Iceland', 1986, *Law and Society Review*, **20**, 335; and, generally, R. Cotterrell, *Sociology of Law*, 2nd edn, London, Butterworths, 1992, pp.102–6.

26   See, for example, Fitzpatrick, *op. cit.*, note 21 above.

27   Cf. Turner, *op. cit.*, note 23 above.

28   Cf. Carl Jung's statement that 'a symbol is always the best possible expression of a relatively *unknown* fact, a fact, however, which is none the less recognised or postulated as existing' (quoted in Turner, *op. cit.*, note 23 above, p.26).

29   E. Durkheim, *The Elementary Forms of the Religious Life*, 2nd edn, London: Allen & Unwin, 1976, p.2.

30   P. Goodrich, 'Fate as Seduction: The Other Scene of Legal Judgment', in Norrie (ed.), *op. cit.*, note 22 above., p.116.

150   *Law as Communication*

31   H. Kelsen, *The Pure Theory of Law*, Berkeley, University of California Press, 1967, pp.71, 221.
32   H.L.A. Hart, *The Concept of Law*, Oxford, Clarendon Press, 1961.
33   H. Kelsen, 'The Function of a Constitution', in R. Tur and W. Twining (eds), *Essays on Kelsen*, Oxford, Clarendon Press, 1986.
34   E.S. Corwin, 'The "Higher Law" Background of American Constitutional Law', 1928, *Harvard Law Review*, **62**, 151.
35   B. Ackerman, *We the People. Volume 1: Foundations*, Cambridge MA, Harvard University Press, 1991.
36   Ibid., p.27.
37   See especially J.S. Fishkin, *Democracy and Deliberation: New Directions for Democratic Reform*, New Haven, Yale University Press, 1991.
38   Sunstein, *op. cit.*, note 13 above; R. Dworkin, *Taking Rights Seriously*, London, Duckworth, 1977, ch. 8.
39   Levinson, *op. cit.*, note 9 above, pp.27–8; cf. Grey, *loc cit.*, note 14 above.
40   Fishkin, *op. cit.*, note 37 above.
41   Ackerman, *op. cit.*, note 35 above, p.7.
42   Ibid., p.3.
43   T.C. Grey, 'Do We Have an Unwritten Constitution?', 1975, *Stanford Law Review*, **27**, 703; 'The Origins of the Unwritten Constitution: Fundamental Law in American Revolutionary Thought', 1978, *Stanford Law Review*, **30**, 843.
44   S. Sherry, 'The Founders' Unwritten Constitution', 1987, *University of Chicago Law Review*, **54**, 1127.
45   Levinson, *op. cit.*, note 9 above, p.27; Grey, 'Constitution as Scripture', note 14 above.
46   Dworkin, *op. cit.*, note 38 above, ch. 8.
47   United States Constitution, Article V.
48   Munro, *op. cit.*, note 7 above, p.656.
49   J.P. Roche, 'The Convention as a Case Study in Democratic Politics', in L.W. Levy (ed.), *Essays on the Making of the Constitution*, 2nd edn, New York, Oxford University Press, 1987, p.179.
50   Daniel Boorstin, quoted in Foley, *op. cit.*, note 10 above, p.37.
51   C.A. Beard, *An Economic Interpretation of the Constitution of the United States*, New York, Macmillan, 1913.
52   L.W. Levy (ed.), *op. cit.*, note 49 above, p.3.
53   See Levy, 'Introduction: The Making of the Constitution, 1776–1789', in Levy (ed.), *op. cit.*, note 49 above.
54   Cf. Cotterrell, *Law's Community*, *op. cit.*, note 17 above, pp.222–3.
55   Cf. L.H. Tribe, *Constitutional Choices*, Cambridge MA, Harvard University Press, 1985, ch.9.
56   Gillian Peele, quoted in Foley, *op. cit.*, note 10 above, p.97.
57   J. Cornford, quoted in Foley, *op. cit.*, note 10 above, p.126.
58   T.C. Daintith, 'Political Programmes and the Content of the Constitution', in Finnie *et al.* (eds), *op. cit.*, note 20 above, p.46.
59   Corwin, '"Higher Law" Background', *op. cit.*, note 34 above, p.178.
60   1 Co. Inst. 81.
61   J.G.A. Pocock, *The Ancient Constitution and the Feudal Law*, extended edn, Cambridge, Cambridge University Press, 1987.
62   8 Co. 118a (1610).
63   See J.W. Gough, *Fundamental Law in English Constitutional History*, Oxford, Oxford University Press, 1955.

64 Pocock, *op. cit.*, note 61 above, pp.268–9.
65 Ibid., p.269.
66 Ibid., pp.269–71.
67 J.N. Figgis, *The Divine Right of Kings*, 2nd edn, Cambridge, Cambridge University Press, 1913.
68 See, for example, G.J. Postema, *Bentham and the Common Law Tradition*, Oxford, Clarendon Press, 1986, p.73.
69 Ibid., pp.73–4.
70 Cotterrell, *Law's Community*, *op. cit.*, note 17 above, p.223; 'Judicial Review and Legal Theory', *op. cit.*, note 19 above.
71 W. Bagehot, *The English Constitution*, London, Collins, 1963 edn, ch. 2: 'The use of the Queen, in a dignified capacity, is incalculable. Without her in England, the present English government would fail and pass away' (p.82). See, further, T. Nairn, *The Enchanted Glass: Britain and its Monarchy*, London, Radius, 1988 and, for recognition of the symbolic significance of monarchy in recent discussion of constitutional law, De Smith and Brazier *op. cit.*, note 1 above, p.121.
72 Bagehot, *op. cit.*, note 71 above, pp.85–6.
73 R. Dworkin *Law's Empire*, London, Fontana, 1986.
74 See, for example, Tribe, *op. cit.*, note 55 above, ch. 1.
75 R. Post, 'Theories of Constitutional Interpretation' in Post (ed.), *Law and the Order of Culture*, Berkeley, University of California Press, 1991, p.21, discussing the claim that 'the Constitution is the fundamental will of the people; that is why it is the fundamental law' and arguing that the most common form of this claim 'regards the intentions of the Framers as the best evidence of the agreement represented by the Constitution'.
76 See, for example, G. Marshall, *Constitutional Conventions*, Oxford, Clarendon Press, 1984, ch. 2.
77 Cf. Post *loc cit.*, note 75 above, p.19.
78 Cf. J. Jaconelli, *Enacting a Bill of Rights: the Legal Problems*, Oxford, Clarendon Press, 1980.
79 Institute for Public Policy Research, *The Constitution of the United Kingdom*, London, IPPR, 1991.
80 M. Weber, *Economy and Society*, Berkeley, University of California Press, 1968, pp.246ff.
81 See, for example, Marshall, *op. cit.*, note 76 above, pp.21–3.

[16]
Comparative Law
and Legal Culture

I. Introduction

An interest in understanding law in its various cultural settings might be thought to underlie all imaginative comparative law scholarship. In the past this has often been merely implicit. However, since the early 1990s, an explicit concern with law's relation to culture, and especially with the concept of legal culture, has become much more prominent in comparative legal scholarship. In particular, the idea of legal culture has had an important place in major recent debates about the nature and aims of comparative law. Indeed, it has been taken up by some comparatists as a tool to try to reorient the entire field of comparative legal studies.

The idea of legal culture entails that law (as rules, practices, institutions, doctrine, etc.) should be treated as embedded in a broader culture of some kind. This culture may, but need not necessarily, be seen as wider than the lawyer's or lawmaker's professional realm of law. Certainly, elements that make up the 'official' world of law (for example, lawyers' and lawmakers' practices, traditions and professional understandings) may be seen as themselves comprising a culture—some kind of complex totality of meaning and experience. Often, however, conceptions of legal culture encompass much more than this professional juristic realm. They refer to a more general consciousness or experience of law that is widely shared by those who inhabit a particular legal environment, for example a particular region, nation, or group of nations.

Whatever approach to fixing the scope of legal culture is taken, the basic message which the use of the concept of legal culture gives is clear: much more than legal rules needs to be subjected to comparison, even if advocates of cultural approaches to comparative law may disagree about what exactly the additional elements are. In emphasizing legal culture, these advocates often suggest that much of previous, mainstream (especially positivist or functionalist) comparative legal scholarship has been wrongly focused; that it has studied only limited or surface aspects of legal reality.

Thus, for comparatists who emphasize culture, a positivist focus on legal rules alone misses much that—while not expressed in rule-form—is important about law and should be taken into account in any worthwhile comparison of legal phenomena. Such non-rule elements might include underlying values or principles of a legal system, as well as traditions, shared beliefs, common ways of thinking, constellations of interests or patterns of allegiances of lawyers, lawmakers, and citizens.

Functionalist approaches, identifying criteria of comparison in terms not of rules but of problems, tasks, or societal needs to be met by law, are usually held by cultural comparatists to be no less deficient.[1] Functionalist approaches are seen as

---

[1] Pierre Legrand, 'The Same and the Different', in Pierre Legrand and Roderick Munday (eds), *Comparative Legal Studies: Traditions and Transitions* (2003), 240, 292; Vivian Grosswald

failing to recognize that purposes and tasks of law are inevitably defined using the terms of reference provided by particular cultures, and cannot be satisfactorily generalized or abstracted from these.

Culture, therefore, appears fundamental—a kind of lens through which all aspects of law must be perceived, or a gateway of understanding through which every comparatist must pass so as to have any genuine access to the meaning of foreign law.

II. LAW INSIDE CULTURE

The concept of legal culture has been invoked for a wide range of purposes in comparative legal studies. Prominent among recent advocates of a cultural focus have been scholars who argue that comparative legal studies should devote much more attention to exploring and appreciating differences, rather than similarities, between legal ideas, legal systems, and legal traditions. For Vivian Curran, for example, 'different categories [of thought] undergird each legal culture'.[2] Culture marks important cognitive boundaries. A recognition that law inhabits different cultures must, in Pierre Legrand's view, require the comparatist to develop an 'empathy for alterity',[3] an interest in and appreciation of differences in legal experience in different cultural environments—a shift away from the comparatist's more traditional focus on trying to remove legal differences and disagreements between jurisdictions.

If law is embedded in culture it may be that the study of law can be undertaken realistically only by adopting the standpoint of someone 'inside' a culture, by a kind of 'immersion'[4] in it. According to this approach, the comparatist must understand law in the same way that people who participate in its culture do. Such a study must recognize the integrity, identity, or coherence of the culture in which law exists, and the interwoven characteristics that make that culture unique and distinguish it from others. To understand law, the scholar will try to operate, as far as possible, in the thought patterns of that law's particular culture.

Law cocooned inside a culture, it might be claimed, is *necessarily* different from law that exists in another culture. If each culture has its own identity, it will be different from all others. This radical differentiation of cultures entails the radical

---

Curran, 'Cultural Immersion, Difference and Categories in U.S. Comparative Law', (1998) 46 *AJCL* 43, 66, 71.

[2] Curran, (1998) 46 *AJCL* 43, 45.   [3] Pierre Legrand, *Fragments on Law-as-Culture* (1999), 11.
[4] Curran, (1998) 46 *AJCL* 43 ff.

712

differentiation of the laws that exist within them. So, an attempt to compare the law embedded in one culture with the law embedded in a different one (even if the legal rules appear to be the same) might pose particular difficulties. The reason is that, as suggested earlier, legal rules alone can never tell us all we need to know. The meaning of the law may not be revealed 'on its face', in the letter of the law. Deeper inquiries may be needed to discover this meaning—inquiries about established practices, traditions, implicit assumptions or preconceptions that will colour the way rules are understood and applied—in short, inquiries about aspects of the law's cultural setting. The claim of most of the leading advocates of a cultural approach is that the letter of the law can *only* be read in the cultural context that gives it meaning. Read in a different cultural context it will simply be different law.

In the view of many cultural comparatists comparative law has devoted too much attention to seeking similarity between the legal phenomena (usually rules) that it sets out to compare. Its overwhelming focus has been on harmonization or unification of law between jurisdictions, and this has tended to be a superficial, technical focus, rather than an effort to understand law in depth. An appreciation of difference may be more intellectually justifiable than a search for similarities, where the latter relies on finding a sort of 'lowest common denominator' of legal doctrine in different systems. Sometimes the claim is that, for moral or political reasons, it is imperative to celebrate legal differences rather than to minimize them. On this view, promoting legal harmonization or unification between different legal systems or doctrines may be far from a self-evidently good thing, although comparatists have usually thought of it in this way. For many cultural comparatists there are important virtues in 'sustainable diversity' in law.[5]

Thus, behind the efforts of at least some cultural comparatists a powerful agenda can often be seen: comparative law must become a more useful enterprise than it has been in the past; a more effective agent for promoting mutual understanding; a voice against the undermining, ignoring or domination of cultures. It must not just tolerate but appreciate legal difference, no less urgently than it seeks similarity between the laws of different systems. This outlook easily connects with wider political or reformist positions. As will appear, these include positions on multiculturalism, European legal integration, and globalization.

Often explicit among cultural comparatists generally, and particularly those who stress 'difference', is a claim that mainstream or traditional comparative law scholarship has simply lost its way. It suffers from a deep 'malaise',[6] having failed to link with wider currents of non-legal scholarship (especially in philosophy and history) and having set its goals in too limited a manner. Most fundamentally, the claim is made that, because of its narrow conception of law and its consequent

---

[5] cf H. Patrick Glenn, *Legal Traditions of the World: Sustainable Diversity in Law* (2nd edn, 2004).
[6] See, especially, William Ewald, 'Comparative Jurisprudence I: What was it Like to Try a Rat?', (1995) 143 *University of Pennsylvania LR* 1889, 1961–65.

misunderstanding of what legal comparisons involve, mainstream comparative law has undermined its intellectual promise as a field of social inquiry as well as its practical promise to promote effective communication between lawyers and lawmakers in different nations and cultures.

While the focus on 'difference' has been prominent among some leading cultural comparatists, it is important to stress that legal culture has also been an important idea in other contributions to comparative legal scholarship that do not have this focus and seem motivated by completely different concerns. In what follows, I shall look first at these other developments involving the concept of legal culture, and at some general considerations about its use, before returning to consider the multi-faceted argument that, above all, comparatists 'must learn to detect, to understand, to value, indeed, to cherish difference'.[7]

III. Cultures as Fields of Similarity

If invoking legal culture has appealed to some scholars as a basis for emphasizing 'difference' in law, other uses of the concept have been in a seemingly opposite cause: to promote or celebrate a growing harmony in law across large cultural spaces. Using an idea of legal culture, one can look *outwards* at other cultures, perhaps stressing cultural difference and the need to respect it. But one can also look *inwards*, at the common experience within a culture, the shared points of reference that culture gives to those who inhabit it. A cultural approach might show that seemingly similar rules are actually different when understood in the context of their different cultural settings. But, conversely, recognition of law's roots in culture might make it possible to show profound *unities* between the laws of different legal systems that inhabit a common legal culture even where legal rules differ between these systems.

1. European Legal Culture

For example, if it can be shown that a common European legal culture exists, linking the different national legal experiences of Europe, it may be possible to recognize deep links between, say, French and Italian law, or even between English common law and German civil law; links that are important despite differences between legal

---

[7] Legrand (n 3), 10–11.

rules in those systems, or even despite differences in legal styles that comparatists associate with contrasting 'families' of law (such as common law and civil law).

Thus, in contrast to cultural approaches that emphasize legal difference, there can certainly be cultural approaches that stress similarity and seem to offer bases on which legal harmonization or unification might be extended and enriched in a certain cultural area. The most important example of such a postulated cultural area in recent comparative legal studies is, indeed, 'Europe'. The idea of a European legal culture, with deep roots in partly common, and partly parallel, legal histories of the major Western European nations, has provided both an inspiration and a kind of template for recent efforts towards harmonizing European private law.

Franz Wieacker's identification of elements of European legal culture has been influential here. He emphasizes three elements that may together indicate the essence of this culture.[8] Thus, 'Personalism' refers to the 'primacy of the individual as subject, end, and intellectual point of reference in the idea of law', but it implies also a balance and tension between individual freedom and social duty, and an emphasis on both liberty (of individuals and groups) and sovereignty (of state, monarch, or people). 'Legalism' indicates decision-making through general rules of law not dependent for validity or acceptance on some moral, social, or political value or purpose. It points to a positivistic separation of law and morals, and of law and politics; and ultimately (by expressing collective social responsibility in statutory form) to the legal framework of a welfare state. Finally, 'intellectualism' indicates a general, intellectually orderly, systematic way of thinking about law that, for Wieacker, strains towards 'thematization, conceptualization and contradiction-free consistency'.

Presented at such a level of abstraction ('a first draft' of 'a synopsis') these markers take us only a short distance. The paleness of their generalizations is a reminder that culture is primarily something lived in and experienced. It does not lend itself to neat summary but needs complex description, evocation, and exploration 'from within', from 'the centre or root of the system'.[9] Wieacker himself offers this, from one perspective, in his own rich historical narrative of European private law.[10]

Cultural comparatists have noted that intellectual inspirations for this kind of exploration can be traced to Johann Gottfried Herder's late eighteenth-century romantic nationalism which emphasizes the particularity of cultures as a source of meaning and as a framework for common history.[11] Links can also be made particularly with Friedrich Carl von Savigny's early nineteenth-century romantic

---

[8] Franz Wieacker, 'Foundations of European Legal Culture', (1990) 38 *AJCL* 1, 20–5.
[9] Giorgio Del Vecchio, 'The Crisis of the Science of Law' (1933), in Ralph A. Newman (ed), *Man and Nature: Selected Essays by Giorgio Del Vecchio* (1969), 171, 180.
[10] Franz Wieacker, *A History of Private Law in Europe* (trans Tony Weir, 1995).
[11] Ewald (n 6), 2004–12; Legrand (n 1), 266–71.

nationalist view of law as tied to culture rather than to political organization,[12] so that, for him, it could make good sense to consider the evolution and internal coherence of a distinctively German law founded on inherited Roman sources, even in the absence of a unified German polity. In other words, culture could be envisaged as unifying and giving meaning to law, and perhaps inspiring its future development in ways that would be justified by the sense of a cultural heritage in which changing positive law finds secure moral and emotional foundations.

It is not surprising, then, that Reinhard Zimmermann calls for the development, in a Europe-wide context, of what Savigny called an 'organically progressive' legal science, and for the reconstitution of Savigny's German historical school of jurisprudence on a European level.[13] Implicit in this is the idea that legal culture itself cannot be codified but has to grow from diffuse sources, hard to define or categorize. If, in reality, a European legal culture hardly exists as a strong feature of contemporary legal experience, or exists only sketchily in history, tradition, emotional allegiances, and certain complex beliefs and values that resist final specification in neat formulae, the idea of such a culture might nevertheless provide inspiration and direction for legal integration, and a promise of an ultimate harmonization of law. This kind of argument is now familiar among many European comparatists.

2. Components of Culture

Yet, because the components of culture are hard to specify, or at least to agree on, much controversy is likely to accompany any attempt to claim the existence or explain the nature of cultural unities. Social scientists, who use the concept of legal culture in empirical research and have produced a large literature on the subject, often demand unambiguous specification of its components.

On this basis, the German legal sociologist Volkmar Gessner, noting Wieacker's claims, declares bluntly that no common European legal culture exists. 'As long as patterns of interpretation (values, attitudes) and behavioural routines with respect to law as well as social institutions which form part of the legal implementation process are not integrated, a common or even similar legal practice cannot be expected.'[14] For Gessner, 'important indicators for a comparison of European legal cultures are goal attainment of public administrations, degree of legalization of state activities, frequency of illegal (corrupt) behaviour of public officials, knowledge of law in the general population, attitudes towards state regulation,

---

[12] Friedrich Carl von Savigny, *Of the Vocation of Our Age for Legislation and Jurisprudence* (trans Abraham Hayward, 1831).

[13] Reinhard Zimmermann, 'Savigny's Legacy: Legal History, Comparative Law and the Emergence of a European Legal Science', (1996) 112 *LQR* 576 ff.

[14] Volkmar Gessner, 'Global Legal Interaction and Legal Cultures', (1994) 7 *Ratio Juris* 132, 134, 135-6.

preferences for formal vs. informal dispute resolution and the ideological position of judges'.[15] What is at issue here is not the hardly fathomable working of a diffuse cultural force like Savigny's postulated 'national spirit' (*Volksgeist*) in law but a set of concrete behavioural and attitudinal indicators, detectable in the activities and opinions of lawyers and other citizens.

James Gibson and Gregory Caldeira, following a similar kind of approach, predict, on the basis of a survey of popular attitudes to law among European citizens, that 'differences in legal cultures [within Europe] will play an even greater role in the ways in which EC law gets implemented within each of the member states'.[16] Studies of this kind at least illustrate that legal culture can mean many things. For some scholars, especially comparatists, it exists primarily in the outlook and practices of legal professionals. For other scholars, including many social scientists, it exists, most significantly, in wider, probably very varied, popular attitudes to and experiences of law.

Some social scientific approaches, such as those of Gessner and Gibson and Caldeira, adopt a very different way of studying legal culture from that of many cultural comparatists. The cultural comparatist, using 'a capacity for imaginative projection',[17] may try to see legal culture through the 'habits of thought'[18] of those (especially lawyers) who inhabit it. This is not a matter of using social scientific indicators but of 'feeling oneself into' the experience characteristic of a particular culture.[19]

Perhaps these kinds of approaches that advocate an immersion in culture, an empathetic exploration of the meaning it has for those who participate in it, will tend to emphasize the irreducibility of cultural differences to a greater extent than approaches that focus on identifying precise cultural indicators. The close definition of such indicators to make them usable in cross-cultural research allows them to act as foci for broad generalization or abstraction from experience. Indicators select particular points of comparison, suggesting common reference points—in a sense, meeting-points between the particularities of environments, histories, or lives. But immersion in culture, as a kind of hermeneutical method, is likely to emphasize the irreducible uniqueness of the experience of that culture and the inevitable strangeness and 'otherness' of what lies outside it.

Those invocations of legal culture that have accompanied the most sweeping claims about growing uniformity or harmonization of law between legal systems have usually focused on specific indicators of legal convergence or uniform traits of law.

Thus, the American legal sociologist Lawrence Friedman sees a vast '*modern*

---

[15] Gessner, (1994) 7 *Ratio Juris* 135.

[16] James L. Gibson and Gregory A. Caldeira, 'The Legal Cultures of Europe', (1996) 30 *Law and Society Review* 55, 80.

[17] Legrand (n 3), 64.   [18] Ewald (n 6), 2045.   [19] cf Ewald (n 6), 1942.

legal culture: the legal culture of modern, industrial, "advanced" societies' as being in process of formation.[20] Modern law in general, as Friedman sees it, is characterized by rapid change. It is 'dense and ubiquitous', notable for the increasing bulk of legal doctrine and law's pervasiveness in more and more areas of life. It is instrumental—a mere tool for achieving social and economic aims—but is also expected to be an expression of human rights. What links these instrumental and expressive aspects of law is legal individualism, with the idea of 'right' or 'entitlement' at its heart. Modern law 'presupposes a society of free-standing, autonomous individuals'. Finally, modern law exists in the shadow of economic globalization and so tends towards convergence, harmonization, and the elimination of differences between legal systems and national legal cultures; towards 'a certain melting together of world cultures' that finds expression in law.[21]

No less ambitiously than Friedman, the sociologist Philip Selznick refers to a broad 'rule of law culture' founded in 'the Western legal tradition' and an emerging 'post-modern legal culture' that promises to extend the rule of law 'to all spheres in which power is exercised and may be abused'.[22] A focus on legal culture can thus inspire a search for increasing similarity and convergence in law no less than an appreciation of difference.

3. Who Defines Culture?

No doubt, the canvas on which images of law can be painted is greatly enlarged when culture is brought into the discussion, but there is always a danger of reading into legal culture what one wishes to see. Friedman finds rights and entitlements fundamental to his, admittedly tentatively sketched, overarching modern legal culture. Wieacker, however, emphasizes a balance of freedom and responsibility—a different conception of individualism in a specifically European context.

The primary difficulties, which affect all uses of the concept of legal culture, are twofold. First, how are components of legal culture to be identified in an acceptable way? (Whose acceptance matters? Those who see themselves as inhabiting the culture? Those who observe it as outsiders?) Second, how are the boundaries of legal culture to be recognized? Friedman is prepared to recognize innumerable legal cultures, overlapping and interacting. For comparatists who start from an idea of national legal cultures, the presumption will be of common legal experience within nation states and different experiences between them. But a recognition

---

[20] Lawrence M. Friedman, 'Is There a Modern Legal Culture?', (1994) 7 *Ratio Juris* 117, 119. Emphasis in original.

[21] Friedman, (1994) 7 *Ratio Juris* 125, 126.

[22] Philip Selznick, 'Legal Cultures and the Rule of Law', in Martin Krygier and Adam Czarnota (eds), *The Rule of Law after Communism: Problems and Prospects in East-Central Europe* (1999), 21, 26, 29, 34.

of European, Western, modern, or post-modern legal cultures (and many other possible varieties) will indicate other boundaries, other parameters, determining when and where similarity, on the one hand, or difference, on the other, will be the governing presumption about legal experience.

It can, at least, be said that to invoke legal culture is *always* to imply both similarity (within) and difference (between) cultures. Culture is invariably invoked *against* something, however much it is used to emphasize the common interests, beliefs, values, traditions, or allegiances of those who share the culture. Vivian Curran has noted that the European *émigrés* who became leading figures in developing comparative law in the United States after World War II tended to seek legal similarity—the unification or harmonization of law between nations as the objective of comparative legal scholarship—although many of them naturally and unostentatiously informed their legal studies with a broad awareness of the diverse cultural roots of law, grounded in their own cosmopolitan experience.[23] She sees some of these pioneer modern comparatists as subscribing to a vision of a single humanity and of a law that could express universal human attributes—in short, a Natural law. Yet this vision is set up, she plausibly suggests, at least partly in reaction against the Nazi *inhumanity* which many of them fled.

Somewhat similarly, the Italian legal philosopher Giorgio Del Vecchio, writing soon after World War II, saw the 'unity of the human mind' as a basis for comparative law, so that this field is 'as large as that of the history of man' and 'the greater part of legal principles and institutions form a common inheritance of humanity at all times'.[24] For Del Vecchio, the best way for the comparatist to treat 'barbaric forms' of law that 'sometimes reappear among so-called civilized countries' is to see them as regressions to a historical phase already past.[25] Thus, in this case, the 'other' against which a common humanity is set is its own past—a different (more primitive) culture.

IV. Legal Culture and Legal Change

One very influential body of recent work in comparative law relies heavily on an idea of legal culture but does not initially seem to fit into the picture so far sketched. Alan Watson's work does not focus directly on either similarity or

---

[23] Curran, (1998) 46 *AJCL* 43 ff.
[24] Giorgio Del Vecchio, 'The Unity of the Human Mind as a Basis for Comparative Legal Study', (1950), in Newman (n 9), 31, 32, 33.
[25] Del Vecchio (n 24), 35–6.

difference between legal ideas, systems, or traditions. Instead, it treats culture as a filter for legal change or development. A consequence of Watson's researches, he remarks, has been 'my appreciation of the enormous power of the legal culture in determining the timing, the extent, and the nature of legal change'.[26]

Perhaps surprisingly, Watson's view of the nature and effects of legal culture is much closer to Lawrence Friedman's than to that of most contemporary cultural comparatists. Like Friedman, Watson sees culture as an *agent*, a major cause of legal change or legal inertia. He is less concerned to explore, evoke, and describe cultures as ways of thinking about, practising, and experiencing law, than to ask how culture works on law, sometimes impelling its development, sometimes slowing or preventing it, but always shaping it. This is also Friedman's concern.

But Watson the comparatist and Friedman the legal sociologist disagree strikingly about the location of the power of legal culture. Friedman distinguishes 'internal' (or mandarin) legal culture (the culture of lawyers and those who professionally manage, maintain, and develop the legal system) from 'external' (lay or popular) legal culture—the law-related attitudes and beliefs of citizens at large. He sees external legal culture as ultimately much more powerful than internal culture; the latter will adapt to the former.[27] Watson, by contrast, is almost entirely concerned with internal legal culture in Friedman's sense. The occupational culture of lawyers and lawmakers is crucial and, in Watson's view, operates largely autonomously of 'external' social forces in shaping legal change.

This is not the place to attempt a detailed evaluation of Watson's claims about the causal power of legal culture,[28] which he sees primarily as the outlook, traditions, values, and interests of legal elites. But it is important to note that Watson's approach raises the same kind of serious problems of proving cause and effect, and determining the boundaries and content of legal culture, that have been identified in relation to Friedman's use of the concept.[29] If culture is a variable in explaining legal change, it is essential to be able to define this variable precisely—that is, to identify the exact components of legal culture and their relative weight in influencing change in law.

Watson is better placed than Friedman in that his conception of legal culture as an effective cause is narrower and more focused than Friedman's. Watson is almost entirely concerned with the effects of identifiable legal elites. For Friedman, by contrast, significant legal cultures of many different kinds are found anywhere and everywhere in society. Nevertheless, a focus on the effects of legal elites demands

---

[26] Alan Watson, 'Legal Change: Sources of Law and Legal Culture', (1983) 131 *University of Pennsylvania LR* 1121, 1154; *idem*, 'From Legal Transplants to Legal Formants', (1995) 43 *AJCL* 469, 470.

[27] See especially Lawrence M. Friedman, *The Legal System: A Social Science Perspective* (1975).

[28] For a recent evaluation see Roger Cotterrell, 'Is There a Logic of Legal Transplants?', in David Nelken and Johannes Feest (eds), *Adapting Legal Cultures* (2001), 71 ff.

[29] Roger Cotterrell, 'The Concept of Legal Culture', in David Nelken (ed), *Comparing Legal Cultures* (1997), 13 ff.

empirical study of those elites and an identification of which cultural components, from among their interests, values, beliefs, traditions, and allegiances, are more or less important in producing effects on law.

Without such a study, Watson's appeal to legal culture explains very little. It does not enable us to predict *how* legal elites will shape law in any particular context or period. It would allow us to say only that, *whatever* change occurs or fails to occur in law, the (main) cause will always be (in some unknown way, and to some unknown extent) legal culture. Watson's work points inescapably to a need for sociological inquiries about the forces that shape law. It should direct him to the terrain that Friedman occupies—that of sociology of law. But Watson's use of the concept of legal culture is a sociologically oriented one—without any sociology.

In fact, what is most intriguing about the way Watson's ideas on legal culture have been applied in some recent comparative legal studies is the effort, based on them, to *marginalize* the contribution of sociological and anthropological studies to comparative law, and to argue for the centrality of philosophy and history in the comparatist's enterprise.[30] Legal culture is seen not only as fundamental in determining most legal change but as something that develops with a kind of inner dynamic and a substantial autonomy from 'external' social forces.

In the understandings of Watson and his sympathetic interpreter William Ewald, legal culture is to be understood historically (as a matter of the shaping by legal elites of their practices and traditions over time) and philosophically (as a matter of the shaping by these elites of the ideas and values that inform law). Yet given the focus of this approach on culture's causal significance in explaining legal change, there is still a need—seemingly unrecognized by Watson and Ewald—to examine how and under what conditions general philosophical currents influence legal elites (or are transformed by them) and what social forces in history are significant in shaping the experience of legal elites. Social scientific inquiries addressing these matters cannot realistically be excluded; they should be central to the Watson–Ewald use of the concept of legal culture.

This unjustified (and rare) attempt explicitly to marginalize sociological or anthropological perspectives in comparative law is intriguing because it shows that ultimately Watson's and Ewald's invocation of legal culture is indeed, like all other uses of the concept by comparatists, closely associated with the similarity-difference axis. In this case, legal culture is a means of differentiating the culture of legal elites—often 'distant from social reality'[31]—from the social world at large. *Similarity* exists, for Watson, between the practices and experiences of legal elites: indeed, to 'a considerable degree, the lawmakers of one society share the same legal culture with the lawmakers of other societies'.[32] *Difference*, however, exists in the

---

[30] Ewald (n 6); William Ewald, 'Comparative Jurisprudence II: The Logic of Legal Transplants', (1995) 43 *AJCL* 489 ff.

[31] Watson, (1995) 43 *AJCL* 469.   [32] Watson, (1983) 131 *Univ Pennsylvania LR* 1157.

form of a clear distinction between the typical power of these elites to shape legal change and the typical powerlessness of society at large to do so. Crudely, we might say, it is a postulated (but entirely undemonstrated) almost absolute difference between the world of jurists and the world of sociologists. Thus, Watson's view of legal culture celebrates both similarity and difference, in a strikingly different way from that of most cultural comparatists.

V. IDENTIFYING AND INTERPRETING LEGAL CULTURES

We have noted that legal culture can mean various things in its different uses in comparative legal studies. And it can be understood in different ways—from the 'inside', by trying to appreciate the thought processes and experience of participants in a culture, and from the 'outside', as observable indicators of culture. Either of these approaches (or a combination of them) could be congenial to comparatists. An immersion in the legal experience of a foreign legal system is likely to involve many of the interpretive techniques that lawyers use in relation to their own legal systems. Equally, identifying various indicators of legal culture might be close to lawyers' everyday positivistic identification of sources of law and of valid legal rules in their own legal system. In either case, however, it may be natural for lawyers— concerned with law as ideas embodied in practices—to focus on cultures as ways of thinking, on the one hand, and traditions of practice, on the other.

For Pierre Legrand, culture is 'the framework of intangibles within which an interpretive community operates' and it refers to 'ways of organising one's place in the moral universe through commitments to standards of reference and rationality'.[33] Legal culture is a matter of *mentalité*, an entire distinctive way of thinking about law and legal experience, 'a particular epistemological framework'.[34] It is a cognitive structure that allows individuals to make sense of the legal world in which they exist.

What are the boundaries of any particular *mentalité*, or legal culture? The answer is not clear but often the assumption is that national legal systems have their distinctive cultures. Beyond that, the common law tradition has its *mentalité*, as does that of the civil law. For Legrand, however, delineating boundaries is not important, except, as will appear, when he addresses particular issues about the

---

[33] Legrand (n 3), 19, 27.
[34] Pierre Legrand, 'What "Legal Transplants"?', in Nelken and Feest (n 28), 55, 65.

transferability or influences of legal ideas, especially in the European context. What counts—the fundamental message of cultural comparison—is that those who participate in law, especially lawyers, look out at the world from inside a legal culture that shapes all their legal perceptions and differentiates these from the perceptions of people who are not a part of the same culture. Legrand very often couples references to legal tradition with references to legal culture but he discusses culture mainly as ways of thought and modes of understanding, rather than traditions of practice. William Ewald has a similar view of legal culture: 'what we need to understand is neither law in books nor law in action but law in *minds*'.[35] Watson adopts the view that 'the essential core of culture consists of traditional (i.e. historically derived and selected) ideas and especially their attached values'.[36]

Some of these formulations (perhaps especially Legrand's and Ewald's) are reminiscent of much older appeals to the 'spirit' of legal systems, and a lineage of ideas traceable from Montesquieu, via Vico, Herder, and others,[37] through to the preferences of legal philosophers such as Del Vecchio for 'the intrinsic spirit of the [legal] system', extending far beyond the 'almost invariably imperfect' letter of particular rules.[38]

The claim of the cultural comparatists is typically that comparative law fails to understand the nature and meaning of foreign law unless it can appreciate legal culture conceptualized in some such way.[39] Unless comparatists understand the culture which foreign law inhabits they are fated to misinterpret or underestimate this law. Even when foreign legal rules seem familiar, easily intelligible in terms of comparatists' experience of their own legal system, problems of translation remain. These may be problems of translation in the most obvious sense—the language of foreign law may itself be foreign to the comparatist. But there may be more profound problems of translation in so far as language is only one aspect of culture. Thus, between, say, English law and American law, sharing the same language, it is easy to fail to recognize important differences of legal outlook that, even when not unambiguously signalled on the face of rules, reside in deeper differences in, for example, patterns of values and beliefs, historical experience, and national outlook. These kinds of influences colour law and provide its 'self-understood';[40] its unstated, taken-for-granted, yet vital elements.

---

[35] Ewald (n 6), 2111. Emphasis added.
[36] Watson, (1983) 131 *University of Pennsylvania LR* 1152–3.
[37] See eg James Q. Whitman, 'The Neo-Romantic Turn', in Legrand and Munday (n 1), 312, 315–26.
[38] Del Vecchio (n 9), 179, 180.
[39] The same claim can be made with regard to legal historians' efforts to understand the law of distant eras; on this, see Ewald (n 6), discussing medieval trials of animals.
[40] David Daube, 'The Self-Understood in Legal History', (1973) 18 *Juridical Review* 126 ff. The important idea here is that law relies on understandings (including specific rules) that are not expressed in legal doctrine because they are generally self-evident to both the regulators and the regulated. Sacco's notion of 'cryptotypes' or non-verbalized rules seems closely related. See Rodolfo

We might say that the primary warning which many cultural comparatists seek to give by emphasizing legal culture is: prolong your puzzlement!—do not jump to easy or convenient conclusions about the nature of foreign law and those who use it; and never try to explain foreign laws and societies using criteria that reflect only your own cultural experience.

How, then, is legal culture as ideas, ways of thinking, an epistemological framework, to be grasped by the comparatist? One might say, defensively, that the cultural comparatist's warning is unnecessary; that immersion in the whole context of foreign law is what a good comparatist will obviously seek. Curran asks American comparatists 'to beware of avoiding truths and the complexities of truths, of losing the gist of attributes of other legal cultures by overlooking the untranslatables'.[41] The comparatist should understand not merely rules but also underlying principles. Curran gives, as an example, the principle of the binding character of contractual obligation in German contract law.[42] That such an exhortation needs to be made seems odd, but some cultural comparatists might see the necessity as arising from a legacy of a narrowly technical positivism and functionalism in comparative legal studies.

If we look for more incisive and elaborate statements of what is needed to engage with culture in comparative law the literature seems disappointing. Legrand often refers to a need for 'thick or deep understanding', a formula reminiscent of Clifford Geertz's method of thick description[43] in anthropology, the detailed recording and in-depth empathetic interpretation of experience in the culture being studied. While Curran uses the term 'cultural immersion', it is not clear how deep this immersion need be. 'It contemplates a slow pushing against cultural barriers towards an ideal of mutual comprehension . . . and a recognition that some distances will remain.'[44] Legrand rejects the idea of 'immersion' because, for him, it suggests trying to be a part of the foreign culture, which he thinks impossible: 'one cannot "be" the other'; any interpretation will be an 'intervention' with the comparatist maintaining 'critical distance'.[45] For Nora Demleitner, more than

Sacco, 'Legal Formants: A Dynamic Approach to Comparative Law II', (1991) 39 *AJCL* 343, 384–6. A legal system that cannot rely on an extensive 'self-understood', in this sense, will presumably be wracked by uncertainties and interpretive difficulties and will often have the appearance of arbitrariness.

[41] Curran, (1998) 46 *AJCL* 43, 85.   [42] Curran, (1998) 46 *AJCL* 43, 78–83.
[43] Clifford Geertz, 'Thick Description: Toward an Interpretive Theory of Culture', in *idem, The Interpretation of Cultures* (1973), 3 ff. Geertz writes that the comparative study of law should be 'an attempt . . . to formulate the presuppositions, the preoccupations, and the frames of action characteristic of one sort of legal sensibility in terms of those characteristic of another. Or, slightly more practically, to bring off this hermeneutical *grand jeté* with respect to some more focused problem . . .': see Geertz, 'Local Knowledge: Fact and Law in Comparative Perspective', in *idem, Local Knowledge* (1993), 167, 218–19.
[44] Curran, (1998) 46 *AJCL* 43, 91.   [45] Legrand (n 1), 251–2, 253.

724

tolerance of the unfamiliar is required; there must be 'a commitment to find common ground and to put our most deeply held beliefs at risk'.[46]

Apart from a degree of vagueness at the level of general methodological pre-scription, there seem to be differences of emphasis in these views. For Legrand, it would take something comparable to a religious conversion to be able to think in terms of a different *mentalité*. A common lawyer, for example, can never think like a civil lawyer, and vice versa.[47] On the whole, Legrand's emphasis is on the formid-able difficulties of cultural translation. For Curran, Ewald, and Demleitner, by contrast, there is much emphasis on communication and the need to increase and improve it between cultures, even though there will always be 'distortion', and 'perfect comparison' is impossible.[48]

While these variations in expression should not be exaggerated, their import-ance may be primarily as a reflection of differences in political uses of the concept of legal culture in recent comparative legal scholarship. A relatively negative focus on the difficulties of understanding another culture in anything like its own terms may be particularly important for a writer, such as Legrand, who has argued for the importance of protecting the separate integrity of legal cultures (eg the legal culture of English common law in Europe) against what he sees as a process of undesirable homogenization. By contrast, a positive, even optimistic, emphasis on the possibility of overcoming inter-cultural interpretive difficulties and extending communicative possibilities between cultures might be especially significant for writers, such as Curran and Demleitner, worried by a perceived parochialism in aspects of their own American national legal culture and seeking means to overcome it. The positive emphasis might also be significant for efforts to equip comparative law to deal sensitively and progressively with differences between local cultures *within* the nation state, and so to link with movements in legal and social theory that are already engaging with pressing problems of multicultural communication.

How should the analytical significance of the concept of legal culture (as con-trasted with its possible political usefulness) be judged? When we ask how far the concept of legal culture helps comparatists *directly* in obtaining reliable knowledge of foreign legal systems and especially in making comparisons between them, the answers are not necessarily encouraging. The same is true when we ask how useful the concept of legal culture is in unambiguously identifying and organizing objects of study in comparative law.

It has often been claimed that, as Geoffrey Samuel puts it, culture 'is too weak a concept to act as an epistemological model in itself'.[49] It seems impossible to

---

[46] Nora V. Demleitner, 'Challenge, Opportunity and Risk: An Era of Change in Comparative Law' (1998) 46 *AJCL* 647, 655.

[47] Legrand (n 3), 77.   [48] Curran, (1998) 46 *AJCL* 43, 45, 49.

[49] Geoffrey Samuel, *Epistemology and Method in Law* (2003), 50.

specify the content, scope, or power of legal culture with clarity. Samuel asks: if (as Legrand implies) an Italian lawyer cannot think like an English lawyer, why should it be assumed that a lawyer from Welsh-speaking North Wales can think like an English lawyer born and bred in London? If, however, these can indeed be considered to share a legal culture, do lawyers in parts of Belgium and France also share one? What are the important boundaries and essential elements of culture for purposes of comparison?

There is no problem as long as culture is used without any implication that it refers to a *bounded unity* of some kind which can be distinguished absolutely from others. There is no difficulty as long as culture remains just a portmanteau term for a more or less arbitrarily assembled aggregate of phenomena, and a means of referring provisionally to a compendium of bits of social experience whose interrelations are not yet known. Used in this way culture is a highly convenient idea: like a box in which a miscellany of objects can be kept safe and together, until at some later time they can be examined, sorted, and stored individually.

There may, indeed, be no problem as long as culture is not seen as a unified *cause* of legal or social effects: for example, as long as it is not seen as an impediment to or facilitator of legal harmonization or legal change. To have any prospect of evaluating such causal claims it would be necessary to know what 'it' is. But that would involve disaggregating culture—breaking it up into precisely defined components that can be linked to specific consequences. How it might be possible to disaggregate culture is a matter to return to later, but it is hard to see that much would be lost if we were to speak only about the various disaggregated elements; for example about such matters as inherited traditions and customs, shared beliefs and values, common allegiances and emotional attachments, or convergent interests and projects. The main loss would be the convenience of an evocative and familiar idea that links in fuzzy, indeterminate fashion many features of life and law that seem important.

This negative view of legal culture's usefulness is not the final conclusion I want to reach. A far more positive evaluation of the concept is possible. And it is no slight to cultural comparatists to suggest that the most powerful impact of the idea of legal cultures is a political or even a moral one. The demand that cultures be understood from 'the inside' can, indeed, produce inquiries that, to some extent, avoid the intellectual difficulties just mentioned. This is possible when these inquiries entirely avoid issues about the boundaries or unity of legal cultures, their exact delineation from other cultures or their causal significance; instead, they set out to explore the meaningfulness, emotional power, and everyday appropriateness of cultures for those who inhabit them and find identity in them.

These kinds of inquiries (and the advocacy of them by cultural comparatists) can have powerful *political* significance by suggesting the *moral* legitimacy of different ways of life and law, and the corresponding illegitimacy of efforts to eliminate or undermine these without recognizing and respecting the security and

identity that they can give to those who share participation in a culture that they
regard as their own.

VI. CELEBRATING DIFFERENCE

How far does the literature of comparative law emphasize these moral-political
aspects of the use of the concept of legal culture? Certainly, there are efforts to give
the prioritization of difference an intellectual rather than a moral-political basis.
Thus Legrand sees a logical necessity for this priority: 'How, ultimately, could
the self exist if the other were reconcilable with it? . . . Only the existence of
non-identity allows identity to exist as identity . . . identity owes its existence to
non-identity . . . it takes its being from non-identity or difference.'[50] Difference,
he thinks, is more fundamental than similarity; it is the foundational concept. 'To
accord difference priority is the only way for comparative law to take cognisance of
what is the case'; comparatists should 'privilege alterity at all times'.[51]

Curran takes a more moderate and defensible position. For her, 'difference . . . is
equally as foundational a concept as identity'; Western thought has erred in treating difference as a derivative concept 'such that one can say that two things are
different only if one can say that they are not the same'.[52] Both Legrand and Curran
cite Jacques Derrida's work, which would seem to support Curran's position that
each concept (similarity and difference) must presuppose the other, its excluded
opposite. But Legrand's apparent claim for some kind of philosophically necessary
priority of difference seems merely an effort to disguise the essentially moral and
political character of the argument that comparatists have been too concerned
with seeking harmonization and unification of laws and too little with appreciating
law's cultural foundations and the benefits of cultural diversity. Curran's disagreement with Legrand is clear: she states that her 'aim is not to promote a search for
differences', nor to reverse functionalist emphases 'by presuming difference. Rather,
I am anxious for comparatists to beware of avoiding truths and the complexities
of truths, of losing the gist of attributes of other legal cultures by overlooking the
untranslatables.'[53] The message is exhortatory: look more deeply, avoid conclusions based only on the doctrinal surface of the law; discover the common-sense
assumptions and shared understandings that do not need to be expressed in legal
rules but colour all understanding of them.

---

[50] Legrand (n 1), 245, 263.   [51] Legrand (n 1), 279; *idem* (n 34), 67.
[52] Curran, (1998) 46 *AJCL* 43, 46. Emphasis added.   [53] Curran, (1998) 46 *AJCL* 43, 85.

1. Multiculturalism and Legal Pluralism

Once the claim to some logically necessary priority of difference over similarity is rejected, it becomes possible to concentrate on moral-political reasons for advocating special attention to legal difference in comparative law. These include a call 'for the voice of the other and, specifically, for the voice of the other-in-the-law to be allowed to be heard above the chatter seeking to silence it'.[54] Legrand's terminology here calls to mind feminism's demand that 'different voices' of women's experience be heard, as well as efforts to raise the voices of (eg ethnic, racial, sexual, or religious) minorities in and through law. Cultural comparatists who emphasize difference often contrast what they see as the moribund state of comparative law as a critical discipline with vital recent critical movements in legal and social theory. Among these movements they cite feminism, critical legal studies, critical race theory, legal semiotics, and economic analysis of law.[55]

A focus on celebrating cultural difference is a way of trying to link comparative law with a recent but well established 'jurisprudence of difference'[56] which questions in a host of ways the focus of much mainstream legal theory. Traditionally, mainstream legal theory has set out to demonstrate unity or system in legal doctrine and legal thought, and to portray legal regimes as relatively comprehensive, unified, and integrated normative structures. The new jurisprudence of difference emphasizes the significance of different understandings of law among law's various professional interpretive communities in so far as these are linked to different social constituencies. The prioritizing of difference in comparative law is potentially allied with this jurisprudence of difference in legal theory in so far as both of these aim to highlight the diversity of the *social*—that is, the social environment in which law exists and from which it receives its meaning and moral force. The plea to celebrate diversity wholeheartedly is, in one of its aspects, a plea to rethink radically law's relation to the social, and to recognize that legal analysis can no longer take the social for granted, leaving it to social scientists to study.

In particular, legal analysis can no longer treat the social as made up only of interchangeable 'abstract individuals', 'citizens', or 'subjects'—persons uniformly addressed by law, owing allegiance to it, and 'owning' law jointly and severally through democratic processes. The question of what law means in different parts of the social, among different population groups, and in the context of different cultures is one that needs to be addressed in legal thought. Curran suggests that comparatists may need to reject an old assumption that recognizing difference

---

[54] Legrand (n 1), 250.

[55] Legrand (n 3), 20; Curran, (1998) 46 *AJCL* 43, 84; Nora V. Demleitner, 'Combating Legal Ethnocentrism: Comparative Law Sets Boundaries', (1999) 31 *Arizona State LJ* 737, 738.

[56] Roger Cotterrell, *The Politics of Jurisprudence: A Critical Introduction to Legal Philosophy* (2nd edn, 2003), ch 8.

728

necessarily goes along with social exclusion of the 'differentiated'.[57] Perhaps, when twentieth-century European *émigré* comparatists in the United States favoured seeking similarity over appreciating difference in law, they were indirectly reflecting their cultural assumption that *assimilation* of minorities was the only way to minimize the threat of repression of these minorities by the majority.[58] Now, assimilation (as opposed to integration) is no longer perceived to be desired by many minorities, nor necessarily by majorities who value the cultural richness and inventiveness that diversity can offer. In general, the often brief and undeveloped references by cultural comparatists to countering ethnocentricity, responding to the challenges of multiculturalism, and recognizing legal pluralism[59] (the idea of a diversity of official and unofficial legal regimes negotiating their coexistence in a single social environment), all point to a need to bring comparative legal studies into areas of debate that have become familiar and fundamental in contemporary legal theory.

It might be thought that some of these concerns are far removed from comparative law, with its familiar focus on the study of foreign legal systems. After all, multiculturalism is primarily a challenge *within* legal systems. And legal pluralism, in so far as it focuses on various kinds of unofficial 'law' which many lawyers might not recognize as law at all, is a special concern of legal sociologists and legal anthropologists rather than comparative lawyers. But the appeal in comparative law to ideas of culture and legal culture directs attention far beyond the boundaries of legal positivism's view of law. As noted earlier, the cultural approach understands legal phenomena as including much more than positive law. Even Watson's relatively narrow view of legal culture at least recognizes the existence of a popular (non-lawyers') legal culture, although it puts almost exclusive emphasis on the cultures of legal elites. As we have seen, one of its deficiencies is its failure to understand those elites sociologically and so to see the continuities between lawyers' legal cultures and popular legal cultures.

Thus, the appeal to culture in comparative law denies any strict limitation of comparative law's concerns to the positive law of nation states. It makes possible a recognition that different legal cultures can exist inside the boundaries of a single nation state,[60] and that legal cultures may transcend these boundaries—as in the idea of European, Western, or 'modern' legal cultures. To this extent, the idea of legal culture (whatever problems there are in making it analytically rigorous) points clearly to a far wider and more flexible view of law than the one that positivist lawyers typically adopt. Hence the work of cultural comparatists has the

---

[57] Vivian Grosswald Curran, 'Dealing in Difference: Comparative Law's Potential for Broadening Legal Perspectives', (1998) 46 *AJCL* 657, 665–7.

[58] See Curran, (1998) 46 *AJCL* 43, 66–78.

[59] Demleitner, (1999) 31 *Arizona State LJ* 737 ff, offers one of the fullest discussions of these matters.

[60] See eg Prakash Shah, *Legal Pluralism in Conflict: Coping with Cultural Diversity in Law* (2005).

potential to move comparative legal studies towards a legal pluralist understanding of the scope of law that is close to that of many legal sociologists and legal anthropologists. While legal pluralism is far from universally accepted in sociology of law or legal anthropology, it is nevertheless a familiar, much discussed idea in these fields and has been since their modern beginnings.[61]

2. European Legal Integration

In a very different field, that of European legal integration, the politics of legal culture and of difference in comparative law seem no less significant. Pierre Legrand has argued, in many publications, against a general harmonization of European private law—a process of legal change that is, however, well under way and has been gathering pace. He writes that 'Europe's cultural heterogeneity' must not be jettisoned 'in the name of an instrumental re-invention of Europeanism dictated by the ethos of capital and technology'.[62] He opposes the 'frenetic and hasty search' for common doctrinal roots of European law in various fields as 'irresponsible simplification'[63] and sees a tendency by Continental civil lawyers to minimize the real differences between English common law and Continental civil law. In fact, Legrand insists, each of these 'must be seen as a discrete epistemological construct' and 'such difference is irreducible so that is not possible for a civilian to think like a common lawyer' or vice versa.[64] A civil lawyer might see English common law's 'casuistic nature', 'bizarre traditionality', and 'peculiar interlocking' of law and equity,[65] while English lawyers see not casuistry but practicality and flexibility, not traditionality but secure rootedness in aspects of national culture, and a conceptual separation of (but intimate interaction between) law and equity as natural and productive.

Legrand is concerned at what he sees as a bowdlerization of Continental civil law in pragmatic, patronizing, and culturally myopic technical expositions for English audiences. But his main fear is of misunderstandings from the other direction, and a politics of European legal integration that makes them dangerous. Thus, in Europe, 'the common law is being squeezed out of significant existence'[66] and 'the civilian must resist the urge to dismiss the common law as unsophisticated or primitive'.[67] Common law is not a deviation from the civilian tradition which will be reabsorbed into it; rather it represents a separate legal culture that reflects distinctive national traditions, a culture formed from a collective will to express a unique and complex historical and social experience in law.

---

[61] For a convenient survey see Jørgen Dalberg-Larsen, *The Unity of Law: An Illusion? On Legal Pluralism in Theory and Practice* (2000).

[62] Legrand (n 1), 294.   [63] Pierre Legrand, 'Book Review', (1999) 58 *Cambridge LJ* 439, 442.

[64] Legrand (n 3), 64.   [65] Zimmermann, (1996) 112 *LQR* 587.

[66] Legrand (n 1), 311 (quoting Tony Weir).   [67] Legrand (n 3), 79.

730

These positions have much merit in insisting on the positive benefits of a sensitive recognition of Europe's legal and cultural richness and diversity. But the controversial political impulsions behind them are shown by the extremes to which Legrand takes his arguments. It seems that, for him, *any* significant moves towards a convergence between common law and civil law in Europe are misguided (despite much evidence that they are happening and producing effects). Legal transplants— the carrying of legal ideas, rules, or institutions—from one legal system to another are, in his view, not merely difficult but *impossible*[68] because any legal import (eg the Continental notion of 'good faith' in contracts, carried into English law by European Directive) will be transformed into something different from what it was in the legal system from which it was imported. It will therefore not be a 'transplant' but something new and perhaps unpredictable.[69]

Legrand's outlook has been termed 'naïve epistemological pessimism'[70] because of its seemingly dogmatic negativity, which nevertheless is motivated by a passionate commitment to protect the autonomy of cultures. The flaw in his thinking that leads to his extremes of view is his reification of legal culture, his tendency to assume that cultures are integrated, well-bounded, and homogeneous totalities, either immune from external influence (so that it will be futile to try to exert it) or vulnerable to disruption from it (in which case it must be prevented or resisted). Legrand's writings remain ambiguous as to which of these two conditions of legal culture he accepts.[71] Either of them, however, provides a superficial, but ultimately insecure, basis for arguing against efforts to integrate or unify European private law.

No less extreme arguments can be found for the opposite position (ie that legal convergence in Europe is easy and painless). Thus, Alan Watson sees the creation of a European code of private law as mainly a matter of technical problems, which concern only lawyers and can be dealt with by having them talk things out together as professionals. No profound difficulties stand in the way since to 'a considerable degree' lawmakers in different European societies all share the same legal culture.[72]

But, if we recognize law as having roots in beliefs, ultimate values, national sensibilities and traditions of thought, this view is no less simplistic than 'naïve epistemological pessimism' (and not unrelated to the kind of narrowly technical thinking that surely contributed to the débâcle of the European draft constitution

---

[68] Legrand (n 34).

[69] See Gunther Teubner, 'Legal Irritants: Good Faith in British Law or How Unifying Law Ends Up in New Divergences', (1998) 61 *Modern LR* 11 ff.

[70] Mark Van Hoecke, *Deep Level Comparative Law* (2002), 8.

[71] David Nelken, 'Towards a Sociology of Legal Adaptation', in *idem* and Feest (n 28), 7, 37–8.

[72] Alan Watson, 'Legal Transplants and European Private Law', (2000) 4 *Electronic Journal of Comparative Law*, no. 4 <http://www.ejcl.org/44/art44-2.html>; *idem* (1983) 131 *University of Pennsylvania LR* 1157.

in 2005). To be able to say how much legal convergence in Europe is possible it is necessary to ask: *which aspects of culture, including legal culture, favour convergence and which aspects hamper it?* Culture needs to be disaggregated to examine how its different facets relate (perhaps in contrasting ways) to law. This is a matter to be addressed in the final part of this chapter.

3. Globalization and Legal Parochialism

A broader but related expression of the politics of difference among cultural comparatists is in arguments about globalization. Homogenizing tendencies of economic and cultural globalization (eg through the internationalization of trade and mass media, and the worldwide extension of communication and travel) may make 'cultural difference' specially relevant and attractive as a rallying cry. Nora Demleitner writes that: 'The on-going globalization of all aspects of life has led to increasing cultural penetration': populations move more extensively than in the past and 'the same geographical space is inhabited and shared by groups with diverse cultural and legal backgrounds'. Thus, 'new identities of hybridity' have replaced national identities. But 'there is reluctance to recognize, let alone accept, such changes politically, economically, socially and legally'.[73] It may be doubted how far actual replacements of national identity have taken place. Much more important is an ongoing, gradual reshaping of these identities, as a result of the interplay of internal and external cultural influences, as well as external pressures for national economic reforms or transnational economic harmonization.

In this situation, the issue of celebrating cultural difference can easily become one of protecting an assumed *integrity* of cultures—by, on the one hand, denying the need for a thoroughgoing cultural assimilation within nation state populations that contain cultural minorities (protecting cultural difference within the nation state); and, on the other, by resisting cultural influences from abroad that seem hostile to cherished aspects of existing national culture (protecting the cultures of the nation state from external colonization). The enemy in both cases is seen as bland cultural homogenization or, worse, the substantial repression of some cultures in favour of others. Here the politics of difference becomes a politics of resistance to standardization and a fierce assertion of identity: 'the other refuses to disappear: it subsists, it persists; it is the hard bone on which reason breaks its teeth'.[74]

Is this politics, then, one of *unreason?* One might see it as a politics that opposes merely *instrumental* reason. It notices something far more important in culture than that which can be reduced to efficiency requirements. I mean by efficiency

---

[73] Demleitner, (1999) 31 *Arizona State LJ* 737, 745.
[74] Antonio Machado, quoted in Legrand (n 1), 301.

732

requirements, on the one hand, the perceived requirements of optimal economic performance, including the effective organization of an emerging global economic order (with its legal supports); and, on the other, the perceived requirements of governmental control and of a national (and transnational) rule of law that demands similarity (legal uniformity) as a bureaucratic convenience, rather than purely as a support for personal and group freedoms and for autonomous ways of life.

Matters such as these clearly provoke much passion. The Hungarian legal scholar Csaba Varga has described bitterly some mechanisms by which legal similarity as a servant of globalizing efficiency has been pursued in Central and Eastern Europe. Since the fall of communism, 'an army of dandies, arrivists, fantasizers, dreamers and easy experts of international agencies' has 'flooded the region to give hope for remedy' by 'hammering in magic [legal] words. . . . [U]nknown "civilisators" . . . arrive uninformed of the region with a few weeks' commission and leave still uninformed, without having even learnt about its varied historic past and culture, customs and potentialities.' After the local translation 'of laws taken out of their pockets' they 'return home with the epoch-making news: "By giving them a (New) World I acted as their transformation's Madison!"' [75]

Appreciating difference here, therefore, means bothering to learn about foreign 'others'; respecting them and taking them seriously as people with *different*, no less valid, understandings, expectations, ambitions, allegiances, and memories. But it should be remembered that these 'unknown civilisators' do not arrive uninvited. They are either Watson's law-creating legal elites, or are brought in to cooperate with these elites. For those who see cultural realities as primarily a matter of modernization and reform according to more or less uniform economic and governmental templates, the conversation of legal elites alone may be adequate to address all important relationships of law and culture. But, for others, harmonization or reform in ignorance of the 'varied historic past and culture, customs and potentialities' is a moral and political affront. They are likely to see it as a recipe for disaster unless cultural conditions, ignored by the harmonizers or reformers, are eventually addressed.

This kind of outlook in the politics of difference in comparative law suggests a close connection between charges of insensitivity in the pursuit (perhaps, the engineering) of legal similarity between countries, and charges of *parochialism* in the outlook of some comparatists—complaints that they judge foreign legal experience through the criteria provided by their own local legal culture. The charge of parochialism has been made especially in relation to recent American comparative legal scholarship.[76] Curran associates a retreat to parochialism with

---

[75] Csaba Varga, 'Comparative Legal Cultures: Attempts at Conceptualization' (1997) 38 *Acta Juridica Hungarica* 53, 58.

[76] Ugo Mattei, 'Why the Wind Changed: Intellectual Leadership in Western Law', (1994) 42 *AJCL* 195 ff.

the passing of the old generation of Continental European *émigré* comparatists in the United States and a relative lack of foreign language competence among more recent American comparatists.[77] Demleitner claims that, increasingly, 'American society and academia have become inward looking even though much lip service is being paid to the global society and the internationalization of markets and societies'.[78] The more general point is that parochialism, wherever found, tends to go along with an assumption that similarity is more desirable than difference.

In a sense, perhaps, appreciating difference, in law and culture, requires more effort than assuming or seeking similarity. One's 'home' culture is almost inevitably privileged through familiarity and the reinforcement of comfortable myths. Demleitner makes the powerful point that, because of this, comparisons with foreign cultures will frequently be to their disadvantage; 'the reality of the "other" will be disappointing, open to criticism and even rejection while the domestic system and its values will provide (unsubstantiated and undeserved) cause for celebration and even glorification'.[79] Comparative study, as part of legal education, can do something to counter this tendency, but only where legal cultures, not just rules of law, are compared.

VII. DISAGGREGATING CULTURE

One does not need to accept the various positions that have been taken, in the politics of difference in comparative law, to recognize that the call to appreciate difference has the capacity to reinvigorate aspects of comparative legal scholarship, merely by emphasizing aspects of culture that raise issues about non-instrumental objectives of legal comparison. The dominant trend in modern comparative law scholarship has been to assume that unification or harmonization of law is a primary objective of comparative legal studies. While many reasons for valuing the search for similarity in law have been given, the main one has surely been to foster trade and transnational commerce, and more generally to facilitate international legal communication and cooperation—a more effective use of law in regulating relations between individuals and corporations in different jurisdictions. Thus, a primary focus has been on law's role in regulating instrumental relations, the relations of people engaged in convergent or common projects.

The emphasis on legal culture in recent comparative law can be understood as,

---

[77] Curran, (1998) 46 *AJCL* 43, 54–9.   [78] Demleitner, (1998) 46 *AJCL* 647, 648–9.
[79] Demleitner, (1999) 31 *Arizona State LJ* 737, 761.

734

in part, an effort to bring into sharp focus law's contributions to many other kinds of relations apart from instrumental ones. Law is not merely valuable as a facilitator of contractual, commercial, and corporate relations. It is also a protector and shaper of traditions, an expression of shared beliefs and ultimate values, and—in much less definable ways—an expression of national expectations, allegiances, and emotions. Savigny tried to grasp this elusive aspect of law in the *Volksgeist* idea, which threatens always to slide into a dangerous mysticism. Nevertheless, the suggestion that law has an important role in expressing or recognizing aspects of emotional experience in personal or collective life is not absurd. While at one level this focus on affective relations is extremely abstract—for example, on the nation, or even on 'Europe' or the 'West'—at another it is found in everyday aspects of the regulation of domestic, fiduciary, or caring relations at interpersonal level.

As regards law's relation to tradition we should not just think in terms of custom as a source of law, or of the contradictory relations between law and time—for example, law enshrining in normative form accepted practices of the past until they are changed by new positive law, but able also to delegitimize those practices instantaneously in an essentially political process by a stroke of the lawmaker's pen. We should think rather of a very diverse set of links between law and tradition—including the protection of national heritage in the form of architecture, national monuments, historic sites, and cultural artefacts; the protection of historical memory (eg in laws that criminalize denials of the historical reality of the Holocaust); attempts to protect by law various aspects of national language, or to promote and preserve minority languages; and laws to protect the natural environment, as well as the conditions of everyday neighbourly relations. One aspect of the legal expression of culture is the promotion by law of all of these diverse aspects of tradition—understood as the inherited environment of coexistence. Legal action in these areas—essentially *conservation* action—is very different from law's involvement with the promotion and guarantee of commercial or other projects, in which people are engaged in activities which they understand as instrumental in a direct and obvious sense: producing or building things, trading or negotiating to increase wealth, or developing economic networks.

The linking of law and culture also emphasizes law's relation to beliefs and ultimate values. But here it highlights some of the most elusive of law's regulatory contributions. Ultimate values are easily recognized, for example as 'liberty', 'human dignity', 'equality', or 'justice'. Yet, clarifying them poses difficult philosophical problems. In a given cultural environment certain values or beliefs may be familiar and seen as generally accepted, yet their interpretation may vary significantly among participants in the culture. Nevertheless, it is not a pointless exercise to try to understand common beliefs and shared ultimate values that animate a culture. Thus, James Whitman has tried to contrast a Continental European ultimate value of 'human dignity', with a fundamental American value of 'liberty'.[80] By their nature, however, the exact meaning of these values in a culture will be hard for outsiders to appreciate.

Even more difficult will be any attempts to link conclusively particular legal *rules* with ultimate values or beliefs, so that the former can be considered to express the latter. Because of the ambiguity and complexity of these values and beliefs, they will rarely be expressed in any simple way in law. Often they will not be directly expressed at all, merely taken for granted as part of the 'self-understood', the unstated intellectual context in which legal rules are given meaning and purpose. All of these matters of value-invocation or value-expression resist conclusive interpretation. It will be difficult for the comparatist to talk about them without stirring fierce controversy.[81] By contrast, law's link to instrumental social relations may seem relatively straightforward: a matter of technical drafting and precise specification of appropriate legal frameworks for social relations that are relatively limited in scope. Law's relation to values and beliefs poses much harder problems since, while law reflects values and beliefs, it rarely tries to codify them and almost always runs into problems if it tries to do so.

The primary importance of the legal culture literature in recent comparative law is that it reminds us of law's significance in addressing social relations shaped by tradition (in the sense referred to above), ultimate values and beliefs, and elusive affectual or emotional elements. Cultural comparatists' critique of mainstream comparative law's strong focus on legal harmonization or unification may be driven by a wish to emphasize non-instrumental or expressive aspects of law, and by a desire to focus attention on aspects of culture that go beyond economic or other instrumental social relations.

Patterns of instrumental social relations are certainly a part of culture. Anthropologists speak of *material* culture in discussing such matters as the level of technological or economic development of a society. But material culture alone is a thin, limited indicator of culture. Social relations based solely on instrumental benefits (utility) to the participants are typically weak social relations, lasting only as long as the convergent or common projects continue. Nevertheless, the law that expresses and guarantees these relations is often relatively strong (ie it produces the main regulatory results intended), and it may be unusually well-defined and precise in its aims. This is because it addresses relatively well-defined, limited social relations. Because they are typically limited or 'thin', compared to social relations based on affection, shared beliefs, or common ultimate values, instrumental social

---

[80] James Q. Whitman, 'The Two Western Cultures of Privacy: Dignity Versus Liberty', (2004) 113 *Yale LJ* 1151 ff.

[81] See eg Gerald L. Neuman, 'On Fascist Honour and Human Dignity: A Sceptical Response', in Christian Joerges and Navraj Singh Ghaleigh (eds), *Darker Legacies of Law in Europe: The Shadow of National Socialism and Fascism over Europe and its Legal Traditions* (2003), 267 ff, rejecting (as unfounded or too ambiguous to assess) Whitman's controversial claims about the contribution of Nazi policies and 'old norms of social honour' to modern European conceptions of human dignity.

736

relations lend themselves to relatively precise technical regulation, and perhaps to regulation that can be more or less the same in many different societies where these social relations exist. Much of the basic law relating to traditional relations has some similar characteristics. Hence it may be unsurprising that an emphasis on unification or harmonization of law has often been typical of private law comparatists who focus attention on such fields as contract and tort/delict that can be considered basic to instrumental and traditional social relations, respectively.

The analytical separation of instrumental, traditional, affective, and belief-based social relations is a first step towards *disaggregating culture*, and so towards understanding more precisely law's relations to culture.[82] As this chapter has sought to show, culture and legal culture are full of problems, as concepts used to designate a distinct component of the social. Yet the appeal to ideas of legal culture in recent comparative law remains important and valuable. It emphasizes moral imperatives to recognize and understand the integrity of the 'other', and political imperatives to accept the legitimacy of diversity and conflict in beliefs, ultimate values, traditions, national allegiances, and worldviews. Culture should be understood not merely in terms of indicators that can be proposed (controversially) at a relatively abstract level, but also as far as possible in terms of its intimate meaning for those who participate in it. That is, culture should be seen as the basis of participants' moral and cognitive experience. Because of this, the appeal to culture, despite its problems, has a moral and political force that may vitalize comparative legal studies as an agent of good in a contemporary world wracked by dangerous misunderstandings, suspicions, and intolerances.

BIBLIOGRAPHY

Csaba Varga (ed), *Comparative Legal Cultures* (1992)
Clifford Geertz, 'Local Knowledge: Fact and Law in Comparative Perspective', in *idem,
Local Knowledge* (1993) 167 ff
William Ewald, 'Comparative Jurisprudence I: What was it Like to Try a Rat?', (1995) 143
University of Pennsylvania LR 1889 ff
William Ewald, 'Comparative Jurisprudence II: The Logic of Legal Transplants', (1995) 43
AJCL 489 ff
Antoine Garapon, 'French Legal Culture and the Shock of "Globalization" ' (1995) 4 *Social
and Legal Studies* 493 ff
David Nelken, 'Disclosing/Invoking Legal Culture: An Introduction', (1995) 4 *Social and
Legal Studies* 435 ff
Pierre Legrand, 'European Legal Systems are not Converging', (1996) 45 *ICLQ* 52 ff
David Nelken (ed), *Comparing Legal Cultures* (1997)

[82] For further discussion see, generally, Roger Cotterrell, *Law, Culture and Society: Legal Ideas in the Mirror of Social Theory* (2006).

Vivian Grosswald Curran, 'Cultural Immersion, Difference and Categories in U.S. Comparative Law', (1998) 46 *AJCL* 43 ff

Gunther Teubner, 'Legal Irritants: Good Faith in British Law or How Unifying Law Ends Up in New Divergences', (1998) 61 *Modern LR* 11 ff

Nora V. Demleitner, 'Combating Legal Ethnocentrism: Comparative Law Sets Boundaries', (1999) 31 *Arizona State LJ* 737 ff

Pierre Legrand, *Fragments on Law-as-Culture* (1999)

David Nelken and Johannes Feest (eds), *Adapting Legal Cultures* (2001)

Pierre Legrand, 'The Same and the Different', in Pierre Legrand and Roderick Munday (eds), *Comparative Legal Studies: Traditions and Transitions* (2003), 240 ff

Roger Cotterrell, *Law, Culture and Society: Legal Ideas in the Mirror of Social Theory* (2006)

PART FOUR

LAW, MORALITY, COMMUNITY

[17]
Common Law Approaches to the Relationship between Law and Morality

ABSTRACT. How are general relations of law and morality typically conceived in an environment of Anglo-saxon common law? This paper considers some classical common law methods and traditions as these have confronted and been overlaid with modern ideas of legal positivism. While classical common law treated a community and its morality as the cultural foundation of law, legal positivism's analytical separation of law and morals, allied with liberal approaches to legal regulation, have made the relationship of legal and moral principles more complex and contested. Using ideas from Durkheim's and Weber's sociology, I argue that the traditional common law emphasis on an inductive, empirical treatment of moral practices has continuing merit, but in contemporary conditions the vague idea of community embedded in classical common law thought must be replaced with a much more precise conceptualisation of coexisting communities, whose moral bonds are diverse and require a corresponding diversity of forms of legal recognition or protection.

KEY WORDS: common law, community, Durkheim, law and morality, legal positivism, Weber

This paper is concerned with aspects of the relations of law and morality, seen from a common law perspective. In other words, it adopts a perspective informed by English legal traditions and practices and their reception and development in other legal systems regarded as part of the 'family' of common law systems. My approach is primarily that of a legal sociologist. I ask how law as a *practice* of public regulation tends to approach moral issues in a common law context. How does law address changing tensions in or changing patterns of popular moral convictions? In answering this question some frameworks of analysis offered by the classical sociology of Émile Durkheim, on the one hand, and Max Weber, on the other, are used. Durkheim's ideas about general relationships between law and morality as social phenomena offer a partial theoretical framework for discussing common law practice. By contrast, Weberian sources underpin ideas, in the paper's final part, about the nature of moral communities. I argue that these ideas may help, at least in a common law environment, in understanding the complexity of law's relationship to morality in contemporary conditions, and perhaps the complexity of the idea of morality itself as a concern of law.

10

1. MORALITY AND COMMON LAW PRACTICE

We can begin with Weber (though initially to criticise him). He characterised common law, by contrast with continental European civil law, as a practice of 'empirical law-finding' (Weber, 1978, pp.87, 889ff). He saw common law as essentially pragmatic and, above all, empirical; firmly focused on the particular facts of cases and seeking solutions that appear intuitively just in relation to these facts. Common law is, for Weber, a kind of 'kadi justice', a form of legal practice that is, in his specific sense, irrational, not capable of being reduced to systematically organised rules (Weber, 1978, p. 976). Developed by lawyers serving private client interests, rather than by university jurists or national reformers, common law lacked the abstract, systematising legal rationality that allowed continental civil law eventually to serve as an instrument of rational bureaucracy, tailored to political and organisational purposes.

Weber's ideal-typical description is interesting in portraying common law as a kind of legal practice that failed to develop the specific kind of formal rationality that, elsewhere in the modern world, encouraged an explicit effort to separate law and morality for analytical purposes. But this portrayal greatly underemphasises the search for principle that drives common law practice. Very broadly, it can be said that traditional common law method emphasises inductive approaches to the development of legal principle and a certain resistance to systematisation and generalisation (especially in the form of rational codification). According to a familiar view, common law technique is 'devoted to the careful and realistic discussion of live problems' and more ready 'to deal in concrete and historical terms than to think systematically or in the abstract' (Zweigert and Kötz, 1998, p. 181). A Scottish judge (reflecting both common law and civil law experience) starkly contrasts the two: 'The civilian naturally reasons from principles to instances, the common lawyer from instances to principles. The civilian puts his faith in syllogisms, the common lawyer in precedents; the first silently asking himself as each new problem arises, "What should we do this time?" and the second asking aloud in the same situation, "What did we do last time?" . . .. The instinct of a civilian is to systematise. The working rule of the common lawyer is *solvitur ambulando* ' (Lord Cooper, quoted *ibid* 259).

While common law method does not necessarily encourage logical systematisation of law beyond the needs of practical decision making, it strongly encourages what might be called *cultural* systematisation. In other words, it allows moral and other ideas developed in diverse practical contexts to receive extensive elaboration and relatively precise, yet always provisional, formulation. It allows them to be linked in complex, continually developing and reforming networks of legal doctrine. Every so often the precedents must be put in order; the anomalies must be pruned away; underlying principle must be brought to light; the direction of legal development must be sensed and made explicit. This is part of the common law judicial task. Nevertheless, legal doctrine is hard to codify definitively because of the assumption that law's principles receive their weight and significance in the context of specific cases. Hence each new case has the potential to alter the meaning of legal doctrine to some extent. The net of law does not break precisely because of its flexibility and resilience and because many links in it are continually being replaced or repaired.

The inductive methods of common law privilege the position of the judge. As a recent writer notes: 'English common law had no significant tradition of distrust of the judiciary, at least since the time of [Edward] Coke. Thus it placed no particular emphasis on restricting the judicial function. To the contrary, judicial decisions were the principal means of developing the law . . .' (Herman, 1981, p. 177). In classic seventeenth century English common law writings (Coke, Matthew Hale), the judge was, in some sense, treated as spokesperson for the community (Postema, 1986). But 'community' remained (conveniently) an undefined notion, often synonymous in these old writings with the nation or realm but importing an idea of cultural or social rather than political unity which could apply ambiguously to an indefinite range of groups or contexts. The judge, according to the classical common law conception, expresses the essence of the community's moral experience, distilling it in the form of 'wise' decisions.

Wisdom here does not refer specifically to capability in the logical elaboration of concepts. It is rather a matter of being able to reflect accurately popular moral intuitions and draw from them general principles to provide reliable, coherently elaborated, and, above all, practical guidance for the future as well as a meaningful interpretation of the concrete case to be decided. The wise decision would be one that would satisfy the popular sense of justice of the community, and would be capable of being understood as rational, principled and consistent in the light of prior decisions and predictable future cases. Thus, ideally, cases wisely decided would not accumulate into a chaos of unrelated decisions, but nor would they lose touch with the moral intuitions, experiences and felt needs of the litigants, reflecting the diverse contexts in which disputes arose or wrongs were done. They would, above all, be workable, intelligible guides to conduct. In these guides lawyers could find bases for predictions,

12

especially about the security of future transactions or established entitlements, and informed citizens could find some common sense meaning, even if overlaid with heavy shrouds of technicality.

On the other hand, lawyers' need (at least for the purposes of their collective work) to create standardised procedures, to produce communicable guidance on legal practice, to turn experience into intelligible rules, and, not least, to bolster legal expertise as a special professional knowledge naturally pulled law away from the moral experience of the 'community' and made it what Coke famously termed an 'artificial reason', available only to those who had learnt law and practised it professionally. Common law's claim to reflect and distil moral experience thus refers simultaneously to a practice, an ideal and an ideology. It affirms the traditional idea that law finds its ultimate authority in its reflection of community morality, even though the political authority of the judges is obviously guaranteed by the state. It de-emphasises the idea of the judge as mouthpiece of state policy in favour of that of the judge as interpreter of communal experience. Common law practice is thus a legal practice founded on a particular, partial perspective on the social and political situation and role of the judge.

In understanding this approach, Durkheim's interpretation of the relation of law and morality, and also his sociological view of morality itself is helpful (Cotterrell, 1999). Although he wrote in France, his ideas here seem compatible with underlying assumptions of common law practice. That is, they seem to mirror in certain respects the view of the nature of law and morality that is presupposed in common law. Thus, for Durkheim, law necessarily seeks to provide relatively generalised, universal structures of normative regulation. It tends towards these structures as a consequence of the very act of declaring norms in some public manner as general norms of society. Law must be understood as having the function of reflecting and expressing society's most prominent unifying moral norms. But moral practices are, Durkheim notes, often unsystematic, not deduced from general philosophical principles. Rather, they relate to concrete circumstances in which, taking account of all relevant facts, moral judgments must be made.[1]

Morality is thus, on this view, empirical and historical, validated by requirements of social solidarity as understood in particular times and in relation to particular social conditions. Specific moral practices or moral needs in various contexts yield principle; they inspire general statements of values, which can be rationalised as value systems. For example, in

---

[1]Durkheim, 1975, pp. 267–8 (morality as 'a very great number of particular precepts'); Durkheim, 1973, p. 25. See generally, Cotterrell, 1999, ch. 4.

COMMON LAW APPROACHES TO THE RELATIONSHIP   13

modern society, these practices and needs yield a value system focused, according to Durkheim (1970), on the moral worth of each individual human being. Thus, insofar as morality is to be incorporated or recognised in law, it might be assumed that some degree of tension can certainly exist between the effort, on the one hand, to create law as an objective system of general application, and, on the other, to reflect the relative specificity of moral practices and judgments, which nevertheless suggest enduring general patterns of cultural values.

Traditional common law method might be thought of as taking as its task, in part, that of translating the particularity of community moral experience into legal form. Thus the judge is the primary forger of links between law and morality in the common law conception because the essential task of common law practice is to create legal principle out of diverse moral and social experience, reflected in the unpredictability and never-ending variety of the cases that come before the court. Historically, the jury perhaps had some role in this process too with its obligation and entitlement to give its 'verdict according to conscience' (Green, 1985). However weakened this role may be, certainly in Britain, American judicial rhetoric still refers to the jury as expressing community values and speaking for its community (Cotterrell, 1995, pp. 235–6).

The adversary system of trial, typical of common law systems, can be partially understood as an institution that implicitly recognises, for legal purposes, the plurality and relativity to context not only of moral experience but also of truth itself.[2] The common law trial court does not set out to find the ultimate truth of the case before it but to choose the most plausible of rival accounts presented by opposing litigants through their counsel.[3] And often it seeks to affirm legally not an absolute but only a relative right. The title to land, for example, that a court will recognise and protect as 'good title' is ultimately the best title available (the best that can be proved) rather than a necessarily absolute title. The judges of an appellate court usually give their separate, independent and often conflicting judgments on the case before them. All of these judgments will typically be printed in law reports. Lawyers will study and compare the judgments, attempting to draw legal principle from them. Law is thus created by the negotiation and interpretation of a diversity of meanings. Not all the meanings reflect

---

[2] A situation which can, of course, be regarded as inherently unstable, so that it can easily lead to lawyers seeing their role as that of arguing their client's case without any serious responsibility for contributing towards a consensual 'best' view of truth and law as related to the case at hand (the so-called 'hired gun' syndrome).

[3] Cf. Garapon, 1995, contrasting this with a French civil law outlook.

14

moral issues or perceptions. But the process can be seen as one in which a process of deliberation –which continues in lawyers' commentaries after the court has decided – attempts to distil principle out of the chaos and diversity of social experience (Collins, 1986; cf. Cotterrell, 1999, ch. 11). As regards the tension, therefore, between sensitivity to the particular, on the one hand, and aspirations towards universality and generality, on the other, common law practice sets the balance between these – and between concrete and abstract, unsystematic and systematic, flexibility and fixity – closer to the former than the latter in each case.

Common law method, portrayed in this way, represents only a certain slanted, idealised view of modern legal practice, and a certain style colouring practice. The old common law image of law distilled from community experience and morality, brought to the court in litigation, has to co-exist with the modern – and, in many ways, much more powerful – image of enacted positive law, handed down 'from above', in the form of statutes and other law produced from non-judicial sources. Certain fields of law in common law systems are now extensively systematised in code-like form, though with a continuing emphasis on the piecemeal detailing of technicalities. Much judicial practice is a practice of statutory interpretation. The old conception of common law as having moral experience fed into it 'from below' – that is, brought through litigants' claims and experiences to the attention of a court, co-exists with a modern conception of law as legislated 'from above', superimposed on diverse moral claims and experiences. Whereas in the old conception judicial choices on moral issues could often be disguised as the recognition of practice or precedent, now in the newer conception they can often be presented merely as the faithful interpretation of statutory words.

It is important to recognise the considerable tension between the modern concept of enacted positive law and the older idea of common law as found by judges. English law has seen a long 'cold war' between these two conceptions, in which common law thought has fought a lengthy rearguard action in a battle of ideas with modern legal positivism. The stakes were set historically by the seventeenth century controversy between Coke, Hale and Thomas Hobbes on the balance between custom, reason and sovereign authority in law, by Jeremy Bentham's vitriolic attack on common law methods and his (unsuccessful) advocacy of rational codification, and by the polemical portrayal by Bentham's follower John Austin of common law in the mid-nineteenth century as an 'empire of chaos and darkness' to be contrasted with the 'order and light' represented by modern Romanist legal traditions (Postema, 1986; Austin, 1885, p. 58).

Legislated positive law typically proclaims its analytical separation from morality in a way that is much harder for judge-made common law to do.

Positive law imports the idea of law deliberately 'laid down' in the form of rules; law enacted by political (legislative) authorities, or affirmed by politically authorised agencies, such as courts. Positive law provides, according to prevailing liberal thought, the rules of the game that allow diverse private moralities to co-exist (see e g. Bobbio, 1987, p. 156). But common law, according to the old, classical understandings of its nature, may be best thought of not even as rules at all [4] but rather as flexible principles which gain their meaning in practical interpretation in specific contexts. They need a context of cultural understandings – including prevailing moral ideas – to bring them to life.

Yet the modern 'positivisation' of law (the idea of law as enacted) has invaded and colonised common law thought, so that in the English context *all* law, including judge-made common law, is typically thought of as self-evidently a matter of rules set in place (Hart, 1994).

Corresponding to this process, morality itself has been 'positivised', as seen from the standpoint of law's modern regulatory concerns. In the prevailing view of jurists and politicians, law's concern with morality, insofar as law is considered to have any such concern, is with 'public morality' (Cotterrell, 1995, pp. 238–40). Law does not address, on this view, private morality, a matter of personal ethical choices, intuitions, practices or decisions grounded purely in conscience. Public morality seems to refer, at least in English legal discourse, to morality that can be expressed in the form of rules of general application, rationally justifiable in abstract terms, legislated by public opinion and, in practice, relatively easy to translate into legal rules. It has required a determined critical effort (more successful in the American than the contemporary English context) to restore, even to serious debate, the old idea that context-dependent principles rather than rules can be treated as the dominant resources in judicial lawmaking in common law systems (Dworkin, 1978, ch. 2; 1986). Interestingly, contemporary European law seems to be influencing English law towards greater concern with legal principles. But it has been suggested that the effect will be to renew traditional common law emphases on principle which are otherwise more familiar in modern American rather than modern English common law practice (Levitsky, 1994; Teubner, 1998).

Certainly, a tension is apparent throughout the literature of modern Anglo-American legal philosophy between an image of law as produced

---

[4]Simpson 1986. Cf. Watson, 1985, p. 102 ('the judge is not expected to set out the legal rules by which he judges; they are for subsequent judges to determine').

16

in some way by or in the name of 'the community' (perhaps mainly through the medium of courts) and of law as politically created by a sovereign (whether or not democratically elected) for its subjects. The images compete with each other in practice in the enduring problem of relating law's need for political authority to its parallel need for moral authority (Cotterrell, 1995, chs. 11 and 15).

2. The Climate of Legal Positivism

How do these frameworks for relating law to morality in a common law context bear on contemporary moral issues? Clearly there are many benefits in the analytical separation of law from morality, strongly associated with legal positivism. Law *tolerates* moral diversity and moral complexity, without explicitly celebrating or facilitating them. Contemporary law in advanced Western societies typically makes no judgment on many aspects of personal lifestyles. In Durkheimian terms it purports to affirm a central, unifying value of individual freedom and dignity but does not go beyond this. For Durkheim, the sole universal moral stance which law appropriately makes in the conditions of modern complex societies is an insistence on universal recognition of the personal worth of each individual (Cotterrell, 1999, ch. 7).

One can doubt how far such a value system is, in fact, consistently expressed in any legal system. Perhaps the value system of individualism is best reflected, in standard Anglo-saxon legal philosophy, in John Stuart Mill's assertion that the coercive power of criminal law may legitimately be used only to prevent 'harm' to individuals other than the perpetrator, and not to protect moral or other sentiments, to protect people from their own errors of judgment, or to guard against offence to beliefs (Mill, 1993).

Mill's concern was undoubtedly to require appreciation of the dignity and moral integrity of other individuals as autonomous actors. Yet it seems that this approach is often seen not as an affirmation of moral principle – a morality of individual dignity and respect such as Durkheim associates with modern society generally. Rather, it is often treated as an exclusion from law of specifically moral concerns, which are largely viewed as matters purely of individual conscience (Hart, 1963). Utilitarian ideas, which have since the nineteenth century, become established as the (usually implicit) common sense basis of much practical legislative activity in Britain, have similarly tended to be seen as embodying not a moral stance but simple governmental practicality or economic rationality. Consequently, when occasional reassertions of overtly moralistic arguments[5] about the functions of law have been raised,

---

[5]'See e. g. Stephen, 1873; Devlin, 1965; *Shaw v DPP* [1962] AC 220.

either in academic writing or judicial pronouncements, they have tended to appear as authoritarian, and hence highly controversial.

Few English jurists today make any important aspects of the old, classical outlook of the common law a basis of theoretical ideas on the contemporary relations of law and morality. Modern legal positivism, as the dominant outlook on law and morals, usually adopts an agnostic view on the question of the significance of moral influences on or from law, but insists that the validity of law (or, in stronger versions of positivism, law's interpretation) can be understood without recourse to discussions of morality. John Finnis' (1980) sophisticated argument for an essential moral basis of contemporary law seeks, very unusually in the modern British context, to revive a version of natural law theory. Interestingly, however, Finnis' approach does not challenge the claims of legal positivists about the non-moral bases of law's practical validity. Rather it seeks to add another dimension to thinking about law, supplementing, rather than attacking legal positivism.

In the American context, however, classical common law thought is still reflected, to some extent, in legal philosophy. This can be seen in the work, in the first half of the twentieth century, of Roscoe Pound which celebrates methods of common law lawmaking (Cotterrell, 1989, ch. 6). Pound emphasises the idea of law as a balancing of interests. Yet this is not a purely utilitarian balance though Pound speaks of law's supervision of this process as justified by the need to avoid 'friction and waste' in social life. He sees law's balancing process as governed by and, at the same time, yielding principles simultaneously moral and legal (the jural postulates of the time and place). Consistently with classical common law thought, the judge is presented as the key actor in law's balancing processes. Pound's work now has little influence, perhaps mainly because it pays little attention to the reasoning processes by which law's balancing of interests and application and development of values is to be accomplished.

From one point of view, Pound's mantle has been assumed by Ronald Dworkin whose work (using very different methods from Pound) has come to focus ever more specifically on law as a process or activity of interpretation of values, as expressed in rules and principles (Dworkin, 1986). Dworkin's work is, in part, a modern theorisation of classical common law practice. He invokes the old common law idea of law 'working itself pure' by the process of reasoning from case to case,[6] developing principle out of the

---

[6]See *Omychund v Barker* (1744) 1 Atk 21 at p. 33 (argument of Solicitor-General Murray, Ist Lord Mansfield). Cf. Dworkin, 1986, p. 400; and, on this aspect of Dworkin's work, see Cotterrell 1989, ch. 6.

18

particularities of moral experience. If classical common law thought recognised the place of legislation only grudgingly, Dworkin, like any modern jurist, must make an important place for it in his picture of law. Hence it was necessary for him to distinguish principle, with its overtones of moral meaning, from policy, which guides political input into law, usually expressed in legislation. As in the classical common law outlook, however, the judge's role is seen, in Dworkinian terms, primarily as one of applying and developing principle. The elaboration of policy through law is in essence a matter for legislators. Judges encounter policy not directly but, in general, only as embodied in established law. Consistently with the classical common law outlook, the judge is at the heart of Dworkinian law, and is seen not as a servant of the state but as the trustee of the community's values, which are continually restated and imperceptibly reformed in the endless process of judicial interpretation of cases, and in the infusion of principle into the rule structures created by legislation.

One other American theorist, unjustly eclipsed at present, but equally insistent on the inseparability of law and morality, in a common law context, requires mention here. The work of Lon Fuller may be most important for its serious attempt to delineate the different realms of lawmaking, adjudication and dispute resolution and to explore the moral dimensions or presuppositions of each. Thus law's 'internal morality', for Fuller is a procedural morality of lawmaking, especially relevant to legislation. It expresses the moral dimensions of what should be a relationship of reciprocity, trust or 'fidelity' between legislative sovereign and subject. It insists on clarity, non-contradiction, effective promulgation, non-retroactivity, constancy, generality of application and other matters as moral virtues to be pursued in lawmaking (Fuller, 1969). Thus Fuller insists on a morality of legislation. But much of his work affirms the outlook of a common lawyer concerned with the moral reason that case law can and should provide. Rather than merely celebrating the judge's role as decision-maker, however, as so much common law thought does, Fuller tries to specify the 'forms and limits of adjudication' and the 'forms and functions of mediation'; assessing these practices purposively, with an eye to the moral or other expectations surrounding them (Fuller, 1981).

In the contemporary English (and more broadly United Kingdom) context, however, such theorisations of common law practice can relate only to subsidiary matters, a kind of undertow or residue of common law thinking. This thinking is now heavily overlaid with a modern positivism that assumes legislation to be the overwhelmingly dominant source of new law and that law's relations with morality are set predominantly not by judicial attitudes and practices but by political lobbying and the content of legislation. Where judges make decisions or pronouncements considered morally unacceptable in public opinion the assumption is often that it is for Parliament to put matters right.

The centrality of the judge in the negotiation of law's relations with morality is much harder to maintain in the legal environment of Britain than in that of the United States. In the latter context a supreme court has ultimate authority to interpret a written constitution and bill of rights which are, themselves, seen as the repository of political and moral values. The introduction of a bill of rights in the United Kingdom may move judges closer to the centre of attention in matters of the morality of law. But the idea of the centrality of legislative and administrative agencies of the state to law creation is at least as firmly dominant in the British context as it is in many continental European contexts. Indeed, a typical implication of modern legal positivism is that 'ethics is foreign to the judge's judgment' and 'is assigned consequently to the theory of legislation'; that is, 'to the private citizen, expressing himself through [democratic processes that lead to] legislation' (Northrop, 1959, pp. 247–8). But the efficacy of that legislative expression as a statement of popular moral convictions may be doubted. Law's affirmation (such as it is) of the value system of individualism is perceived in positivist terms not as a distillation of the values of a legal community but as made 'from on high', so to speak, as a political programme or professional construct, and as a legal and moral abstraction, requiring practical elaboration in specific contexts but essentially set in the form of 'public policy'. Policy and principle are thus impossible to separate as a practical matter.

3. COMMON LAW AND COMMUNITY

What, despite the problems discussed above, can be retained from the heritage of common law thought as a fundamental basis for theorising contemporary relations between law and morality? Common law assumes an idea of community as the basis of both law and morality. Yet the tradition of common law thought from Coke and Hale to Pound and Dworkin ignores sociological questions about the structure of a community which creates law, the way its values arc formed and what the experience of being a member of such a community is. Nevertheless, common law traditions might be harnessed to meet contemporary conditions by rethinking the idea of community embedded in them. This rethinking involves recognising that law cannot realistically be regarded today as relating to a single morally unified community. Rather, it relates to different kinds of moral community reflecting different types of social relationships that bind people together.

20

A few illustrations may clarify the point. One of the most famous cases on civil liability in English law[7] concerns the duty of care of a manufacturer to the consumer with regard to the product supplied, in the absence of a contractual relationship. Lord Atkin, in *Donoghue* v *Stevenson*,[8] drew legal principle directly from moral principle, deliberately modifying the latter to the requirements of the former. If morality decrees that I should love my neighbour, declares Atkin, law rewrites this to require that I must not injure my neighbour. And neighbours are, in law, all persons so closely and directly affected by my act that I should take account of them in considering my actions.[9] There is thus a type of abstract community created by mere proximity; by being in the same environment or area, or happening to be caught up in shared experiences, events or circumstances. It arises more from happenstance or custom, circumstances that happen to throw people together, than from any positive engagement in relations with others. So it can be called *traditional community*, by analogy with Weber's ideal type of traditional action – action that is motivated subjectively merely by the fact that things are done in a certain way, or always have been (Weber, 1978, p. 25). Manufacturer and consumer have, for most purposes, no real relationship. They just happen to co-exist in the same environment. But that is enough to require that the manufacturer take some account of the consumer's existence; not affirmatively to promote the welfare of consumers, but at least to take care not to hurt them. Much of criminal and tort law (the law of delict) addresses the general requirement that one's 'neighbours' are not to be injured.

This kind of social relationship can easily be contrasted with others that often seem much more active and involved. For example, relationships may be based on common adherence to beliefs or values, a positive sharing of moral, spiritual, ideological or intellectual commitments. Or they may be based on affective ties (love or friendship). Finally, they may be purely instrumental: the relationships of people linked together to achieve common or convergent purposes, especially economic purposes.

Viewed from their regulatory aspect, social relationships may be considered in terms of these four pure types of community – *traditional community, community of belief, affective community* and *instrumental community* (Cotterrell, 1997). Any actual social relationship is likely to combine these types. A business relationship is not necessarily purely instrumental. An actual family is not necessarily even a partial embodiment

---

[7]And Scots law. The case in fact arose in a Scottish court.
[8][1932] AC 562.
[9]*Ibid.*, p. 580.

of affective community; even where it is, the affective character of family relationships may co-exist with, for example, instrumental or merely traditional aspects, or may be sustained by common beliefs or values. So these types of community are ideal types in Weber's sense. They derive from Weber's four pure types of social action – traditional, affective, instrumentally rational (*zweckrational*) and value rational (*wertrational*) (Weber, 1978, pp. 24–26). They make it possible to think of law as relating to four entirely different general kinds of relationships that link people together and thus require legal regulation or recognition. Because these relationships are of different kinds, not only will the principles of their regulation differ but law may have quite different tasks, capacities and limitations in its involvement with them.

For this reason law's relations with morality, and, indeed, the meaning of 'morality' as a concern of law may appear exceptionally complex. Where only traditional community is the focus, law's moral demands are scaled down, it seems, to requiring that one keep out of other people's way and not interfere with them. But if Durkheim is to be believed, it may be that modern society is also to some extent a *community of belief* – belief in the dignity and worth of the individual. This would require more than keeping out of others' way. It would require not just that I can assert my own dignity and autonomy but that 1 should actively promote other people's dignity and autonomy as being as important as my own. Much ambiguity remains in this. Does it involve, for example, absolute protection of the life of others (even when they are embryos, when illness has reduced the quality of their life to zero, or when they refuse to act in a way consistent with the dignity that law seeks to protect)? Nevertheless, this value of individualism seems at least partly enshrined in the idea of human rights. The aspiration to carry human rights to an ever greater level of universality is, seen from this viewpoint, an effort to build a community of belief that is appropriate to contemporary social complexity and can co-exist with it.

But this community of belief may be fully appropriate only to complex, diverse, industrially advanced and secular societies. In other words, as Durkheim argued, it may have particular sociological conditions of existence. In other contemporary environments, it might not be appropriate to the same extent, or in the same way. Apart from this essential community of belief or values, focused on individualism, in contemporary Western societies, a recognition in law of the need to protect or respect community of belief means a recognition of diversity of beliefs and values. Here, classical common law's ambiguity about the meaning and extent of 'community' is significant and even useful. In a nation as large as the United

22

States, for example, 'contemporary community standards' in defining obscenity might well, as the United States Supreme Court once decided, have to be considered in relation to a variety of overlapping communities, whose standards differ radically.[10]

Because of limitations of space, 1 shall say little about the relevance of *affective community*, except to suggest that because affective relationships – of love or friendship – are open-ended and diffuse, the moral expectations and intuitions linked with them are particularly hard to codify or generalise and these relationships are hard to interpret legally in any comprehensive way. English law has only recently recognised that a husband can be convicted of raping his wife (Kennedy, 1992, pp. 130–4). The increasing willingness to intrude into domestic relations to give (still far from adequate) legal protection to women abused in intolerable relationships shows a long overdue recognition that while the family for some legal purposes will be treated as an affective community not to be regulated by rigid rules, this will not be allowed to deny the basic protections that derive from being a citizen or the entitlements that derive being a subject of human rights. Yet the perennial problem in the law of rape, as applied in English courts, of proving the intentions of the parties involved – and, in particular, lack of consent to sexual intercourse – may be some indication of the sheer difficulty law faces in interpreting the meaning of relationships and actions that can be linked to the concept of affective community.

It is tempting to see the principles underlying *instrumental community* as those of what Durkheim termed egoism, as opposed to individualism. Law's relation to instrumental community is one of promoting efficiency, reliability and predictability; facilitating the rational pursuit by each contracting party of his or her self-interest. In the common law world, at least, the moral foundations of contract law are usually traced to the idea of promise and the obligations it creates (Atiyah, 1981; Fried, 1981). But it is easy to see law in this area as concerned primarily not with morality in any usual sense but with managing in orderly, predictable fashion the compromise of individual wills or interests asserted by the parties. English law does not, for example, enforce a morality of reciprocity (a mere nominal consideration given by one party is usually enough to allow that party to enforce the binding contractual promise of the other). Equally, law will sometimes remake the parties' promises, adding to or subtracting from them. Instrumental community (like the other types of community) depends on mutual trust between the parties involved. But this may be merely a

---

[10]See *Miller v Califiornia*, 413 US 15 (1973), noting (at p. 32) that 'our nation is too big and too diverse' for a single national standard to apply.

trust that the other party will perform obligations reliably according to the
settled terms of the bargain made. The task of contract law is to guarantee
performance or else compensation for its failure. The law makes possible
a secure, confident assertion of individual will. It provides technical means
by which a person may plan and realise projects, pursuing self-interest.
And it requires that I respect the self-interest of others, but only within the
specific terms of the bargain I have made with them.

In one sense the contrasting of such different kinds of relations between
law and community, taken in the abstract, ideal-typical senses sketched
above, is no more than an affirmation of the insight of Weber and others
about the radical incomparability of 'value-spheres' in modern life
(Weber, 1948). Different contexts are governed by different structures
of values. But here the emphasis is on different types of social relations,
and hence on different conditions of trust and understanding that enable
them to exist; hence, also, on different regulatory characteristics which
these types of social relationship have. Finally, it is vital to recognise
that these types of community interrelate in complex ways in any actual
pattern of social relations that may exist. Perhaps then, it is difficult to
talk about a single relationship between law and morality, but rather a
diversity of relationships between law and value systems reflecting the
social conditions of different types of community co-existing in any
modern society. Seeing matters in this way, morality might be redefined
as the common understandings about obligation and entitlement that make
possible and foster mutual interpersonal trust in these various, contrasting
kinds of community.

Common law method, in its classic, traditional form, assumed that the
experience of 'community' could be translated into normative form; that
the judge could distil law out of social experience, presented to the court
in the testimony, complaints, defences and excuses of litigants; that law
could be shaped in a never-ending process of incremental adjustment to
changing circumstances. Perhaps in complex modern societies there is
still much to be said for an idea of drawing law from experience –though
not for the idolisation of judges that accompanies it in common law
thought. Distrust of the state as a distant, morally-remote imposer of
solutions has long been familiar. But common law thought often treated
judges as *separate* from the rest of the state, and somehow able to keep
it out of the life of the citizen. Common law thinking has never really
resolved an incoherence at its heart: that the judge as agent of the state
could be trusted to speak for the community and its members, if necessary
against the state. The reason is that it has tended to ignore the problem
of reconciling, or at least relating, law's dual sources of authority: moral,

24

on the one hand; and political, on the other. By contrast, legal positivism has tended to dismiss entirely the question of law's moral or cultural authority; seeing only a need for political authority.

1 think that common law methods, despite their problems, offer some advantages in confronting contemporary moral issues because of their empiricism and particularity – their focus on the specific context and consequently their ability (in theory at least) to adapt law almost imperceptibly to the changing complexities of moral judgment and moral practices. An empirical, case-by-case method can recognise the diversity of value spheres, and not necessarily be confounded by contradictions between them. The ambiguities of the common law idea of community can be exploited. Law should be seen as the law of different types of communities that interrelate in complex, varied ways. Different groups or patterns of social relations embody combinations of the different types of community (traditional, belief-based, instrumental and affective) mentioned earlier. The empiricism of common law method might also help us to reject the idea of uniform moral 'truth' – codified and timeless – without lapsing into a disabling relativism. This is because common law thought treats morality (insofar as it must inform legal regulation) as culturally rooted: 'Knowledge, or wisdom [including moral knowledge or wisdom], on this view, is essentially a collective product and a collective possession' (Postema, 1986, p. 66).

Nevertheless, problems in realising these theoretical advantages seem inherent in common law practice. Extreme manifestations of the adversarial system hamper efforts to make law reflect contemporary moral experience through consensual principle. They encourage a view of law as always a compromise of (mainly) private interests (as Weber characterised modern law in general). Furthermore, few judges approach the Herculean wisdom that common law thought and its philosophical rationalisers see as the ideal to aspire to.

Again, an inherent disadvantage of common law as a carrier of morality is its relative inability (the consequence of its specificity and empiricism) to make abstract declarations that can be a powerful symbolic expression of societal values. In many common law jurisdictions, this disadvantage is addressed by enacting bills of rights, which give values highly visible, public expression. Since such documents typically express these values in terms of *individual rights*, they enshrine to some extent the key values Durkheim associated with the individualism of complex modern societies. But the idea of such an abstract legal declaration is ultimately at odds with common law empiricism. In a bill of rights, values are enshrined as fundamental in legally definitive form, but the common law tradition treats them as evolving, fluid, subject to variable expression in specific contexts and acquiring their meaning always in relation to changing, variously interpreted social experience.

REFERENCES

Atiyah, P.S., *Promises, Morals, and Law*. Oxford: Oxford University Press, 1981.
Austin, L., *Lectures on Jurisprudence or the Philosophy of Positive Law*, 5th edn. London: John Murray, 1885.
Bobbio, N., *The Future of Democracy: A Defence of the Rules of the Game*, transl. by R. Griffin. Cambridge: Polity, 1987.
Collins, H., Democracy and Adjudication, in N. MacCormick and P. Birks (eds.), *The Legal Mind: Essays for Tony Honoré*. Oxford: Oxford University Press, 1986, pp. 67–82.
Cotterrell, R., *The Politics of Jurisprudence: A Critical Introduction to Legal Philosophy*. London: Butterworths, 1989.
Cotterrell, R., *Law's Community: Legal Theory in Sociological Perspective*. Oxford: Clarendon Press, 1995.
Cotterrell, R., A Legal Concept of Community, *Canadian Journal of Law and Society*, 12 (1997), pp 75–91.
Cotterrell, R., *Émile Durkheim: Law in a Moral Domain*. Edinburgh: Edinburgh University Press/ Stanford: Stanford University Press, 1999.
Devlin, P., *The Enforcement of Morals*. Oxford: Oxford University Press, 1965.
Durkheim, É., L'individualisme et les intellectuels, in Durkheim, *La science sociale et l'action*, ed. by L-C. Filloux. Paris: Presses Universitaires de France, 1970, pp. 261–78.
Durkheim, É., *Moral Education*, transl. by E. K. Wilson and H. Schnurer. New York: Free Press, 1973.
Durkheim, É., *Textes 2. Religion, morale, anomie*, ed. by V. Karady. Paris: Les Éditions de Minuit, 1975.
Dworkin, R.M., *Taking Rights Seriously*, revised edn. London: Duckworth, 1978.
Dworkin, R.M., *Law's Empire*. London: Fontana, 1986.
Finnis, L., *Natural Law and Natural Rights*. Oxford: Clarendon Press, 1980.
Fried, C., *Contract as Promise: A Theory of Contractual Obligation*. Cambridge, Mass.: Harvard University Press, 1981.
Fuller, L.L., *The Morality of Law*, revised edn. New Haven: Yale University Press, 1969.
Fuller, L.L., *The Principles of Social Order*, ed. by K. I. Winston. Durham NC: Duke University Press, 1981.
Garapon, A., French Legal Culture and the Shock of 'Globalization', *Social and Legal Studies*, 4 (1995), pp. 493–506.
Green, T.A., *Verdict According to Conscience: Perspectives on the English Criminal Trial Jury*, 1200–1800. Chicago: University of Chicago Press, 1985.
Hart, H.L.A., *Law, Liberty and Morality*. Oxford: Oxford University Press, 1963.
Hart, H.L.A., *The Concept of Law*, 2nd edn. Oxford: Clarendon Press, 1994.
Herman, S., Quot judices tot sententiae: A Study of the English Reaction to Continental Interpretive Techniques, *Legal Studies*, 1 (1981), pp. 165–89.

26

Kennedy, H., *Eve Was Framed: Women and British Justice*. London: Vintage, 1992.

Levitsky, L, The Europeanisation of the British Legal Style, *American Journal of Comparative Law*, 42 (1994), pp. 368–78.

Mill, J.S., *Utilitarianism, On Liberty, Considerations on Representative Government*, ed. by G. G. Williams. London: J.M. Dent, 1993.

Northrop, F.S.C., *The Complexity of Legal and Ethical Experience*. Boston: Little, Brown, 1959.

Postema, G.L, *Bentham and the Common Law Tradition*. Oxford: Clarendon Press, 1986.

Simpson, A.W.B., The Common Law and Legal Theory, in W. Twining (ed.), *Legal Theory and Common Law*. Oxford: Blackwell, 1986, pp. 8–25.

Stephen, J.F., *Liberty, Equality, Fraternity*. London: Smith, Elgard, 1873.

Teubner, G., Legal Irritants: Good Faith in British Law or How Unifying Law Ends Up in New Divergences, *Modern Law Review*, 61 (1998), pp. 11–32.

Watson, A., *Sources of Law, Legal Change and Ambiguity*. Edinburgh: Scottish Academic Press, 1985.

Weber, M., Religious Rejections of the World and Their Directions, in H.H. Gerth and C.W. Mills (eds.and transl.), *From Max Weber: Essays in Sociology*. London: Routledge and Kegan Paul, 1948, pp. 323–59.

Weber, M., *Economy and Society: An Outline of Interpretive Sociology*, transl. by E. Fischoff et al. Berkeley: University of California Press, 1978.

Zweigert, K. and Kötz, H., *Introduction to Comparative Law*, 3rd edn., transl. by T. Weir. Vol. 1. Oxford: Clarendon Press, 1998.

Faculty of Laws
Queen Mary and Westfield College
University of London
London E1 4NS
UK

[18]
Legal Effects and Moral Meanings: A Comment on Recent Debates on Approaches to Legislation

The theoretical discussions that have taken place among Dutch scholars in recent years on the nature and effects of legislation have often been explicitly related to important legislative policy issues in the Netherlands. But it is clear that the significance of these debates is not limited to their Dutch setting. They raise general issues about the character and tasks of legislation: fundamental questions that should be asked in the context of any complex modern representative democracy. For this reason I welcome the opportunity, as an outsider to the Dutch context but an admirer of much that I know of it, to comment on these debates so as to try to relate themes in them directly to theoretical concerns developed from a different legal and social experience. This paper considers these debates (i) from the standpoint of someone steeped in the English common law tradition, with its particular view of relations between judicial lawmaking and legislation and (ii) in relation to a law-and-community approach to socio-legal questions, informed especially by aspects of the sociology of both Emile Durkheim and Max Weber.

340

1

The themes this chapter takes up are drawn mainly from writings by Professor
John Griffiths on the social working approach to legislation[1] and by Professor
Willem Witteveen and Dr. Bart van Klink on the communicative approach to legislation.[2] Initially, reading this literature, I found myself in the strange position of
agreeing with much – in fact, from one perspective, almost all – of what I was
reading from both sides of the Griffiths–Witteveen debate while being aware that
these writers see themselves as disagreeing profoundly, in important respects, with
each other.

   Are symbolic effects of legislation to be regarded as real effects, matters of
significance, so that in some circumstances they might even represent a fulfilment
of legislation's most important social tasks? Or does the idea of legislative symbolism merely cloak the reality of frequent legislative ineffectiveness judged in instrumental terms, and represent more fundamentally a failure to recognise the social
processes by which legislation produces effects and the limitations and necessary
conditions under which it is capable of doing so?

   I agree that a space should be found for 'soft law'[3] (law containing open concepts or provisions awaiting and, indeed, inviting interpretation in specific contexts)
in conceptions of legislation. It seems right to do this – within the terms of the
analysis of legislative purpose that Professor Witteveen develops – so as to recognise
that the ideal working of legislation and the aspirations attached to legislative craft
may properly be very different from the command model of legislative direction
that is often assumed. The communicative approach suggests that legislation is
not (or not just) a tool of behavioural influence but a part of broad communication
structures that make social co-existence possible and fulfilling. This approach enriches theoretical understanding of legislation as an enterprise.

   On the other hand, I agree with the social working approach's strictures on the
crude model of instrumentalism and its insistence that if legislation's working is

---

1   Especially Griffiths (1995; 1999a; 1999b).
2   Especially Witteveen (1999); Witteveen and Van Klink (1999).
3   Witteveen and Van Klink (1999).

to be understood realistically it is important to consider empirically the particular local conditions under which legislative communication takes place. Too much juristic speculation about law has ignored empirical evidence of its significance (or lack of significance) in social life. In this light, the working of legislation must not be seen through a fog of illusions. Legislation rarely works in the way legislators intend. Legislative meaning is filtered through media of communication. In this filtering process, those addressed by law may influence legislation's practical meaning as much, if not more, than those who draft it. But soft law might merely serve to make the message even more confused, ambiguous or unpredictable. It might be impossible to understand precisely what the message is and, therefore, impossible to begin to examine how, if at all, it is received. Then the task of understanding how, in practice, legislative provisions might work – in the sense of having some effect on conduct – becomes even harder.

From my point of view, a productive way to begin to make sense of my agreement with most of the substance of two approaches that are often presented as in conflict with each other is to note that: (i) ideals for legislation (what it might or should be, envisaged philosophically) are not necessarily invalidated, or rendered trivial by the record of legislation's failures in producing specific intended behavioural effects; (ii) legislation may have very varied aims and does not need to take the same form in pursuing all of them; (iii) law's social working can be a matter of its capacity to express cultural phenomena – shared values, understandings, interests or attachments, and inherited traditions of various kinds – no less than its ability to affect conduct, and this expressiveness may be important even though it cannot be measured as an effect of law; (iv) the study of the nature of particular social contexts of legislative activity is a different enterprise from the elaboration of a general theory of the nature of legislation; but (v) any theory of legislation should take careful account of what empirical research can explain about how law influences social conditions. The reason for this final point is not that talk about legislative ideals is empty unless reduced to social science; it is rather that the practical should, if possible, be distinguished from the utopian, and empirical sociological study may give at least some guidance on (even if it cannot determine) how to draw this distinction in fixing legislative aims.

342

Professor Griffiths wants to produce reliable findings and powerful theory in sociology of law. The social working approach he advocates involves looking at law not as an instrument but as a contribution of normative doctrine (essentially rules), which may or may not be received into the semi-autonomous social fields that make up social life. To understand law's social working is to appreciate local conditions in these social fields which sometimes lead to legislative precepts being rejected or ignored, and almost always result in them being understood in different ways from those the lawmakers envisaged. This approach is explicitly sociological. The objective is to make the theory of legislation a product and achievement of sociology of law – sociology of law being understood as concerned with the study of behavioural aspects of law. The social working approach, in Griffiths' view, may at last fulfil sociology of law's promise to produce a distinctive social knowledge of law. But perhaps, also, it can be tentatively suggested that an ideal or an over-riding value underlies this project. To see law not as a grand instrumental failure but, potentially at least, as a modest 'social working' success is to suggest a model of how law might best be evaluated: not as a political directive but as a component of negotiated communal social relations.

Professor Witteveen is directly concerned with legal philosophy – in this context, a philosophy of legislation: key issues are what legislation ideally should be, how it can realise certain legal values, and how those values should be defined. Witteveen is interested in law's destiny as a moral phenomenon, involving reciprocity between rulers and ruled, the affirmation by law of societal values, the legal establishment of normative structures in which social communication is fostered, and the responsiveness of law to social needs and demands. Significantly, Lon Fuller's mature legal philosophy, on which Witteveen draws in developing some of these themes[4] (and which Griffiths sometimes cites), is highly sensitive to sociology: Fuller's reliance on the work of the sociologists Talcott Parsons and Georg Simmel is especially notable (Fuller shared the teaching of Harvard seminars on law with Parsons).[5] Also significant as cited sources of ideas about responsive law

---

4   And see Witteveen (1999b).
5   See Summers (1984), p. 13.

– ideas which underlie much of the Witteveen–Griffiths debate, influencing both sides in it – are writings of Philip Selznick.[6] Selznick might be seen as, in disciplinary terms, a kind of mirror-image of Fuller. If Fuller's legal philosophy reaches out strongly to sociology, Selznick's sociology is powerfully shaped by legal-philosophical concerns, especially the explorations of the nature of legality in Fuller's work.

Taking account of these orientations and influences, where do differences and convergences in these debates lie? If it is to be assumed that a debate exists, rather than just two sides talking past each other, it must also be assumed that the debaters are talking about the same thing: the same phenomenon (legislation) or the same problem (how to make legislation effective for its purposes). I think the main *differences* in the parts of the legislation debates with which this paper is concerned derive from differences of disciplinary perspective applied to the same phenomenon, legislation, and the same problem of legislative effectiveness. A self-consciously sociological perspective might direct inquiry towards studies of behaviour in particular social fields. A self-consciously philosophical perspective might focus on the aims, ideals and conditions of legislative craftsmanship. Possibilities for *convergence* arise when each side is prepared to look beyond assumed disciplinary boundaries, or insofar as the literature of the legislation debates can be read in a way that denies sharp boundaries between legal philosophy and legal sociology.

Because I want to deny these boundaries, perhaps it is natural for me to stress convergences rather than oppositions in these debates. My strongest intellectual allegiance is to legal sociology, but I think the sociological study of law is an unfulfilled enterprise if it cannot contribute theoretically to unravelling moral puzzles about law and explaining its doctrinal character.

---

6   Nonet and Selznick (2001); Selznick (1992), pp. 463-76.

344

2

This kind of viewpoint is squarely in the Durkheimian tradition. Durkheim advocated a sociology of morals as valuable in its own right, but also as an essential underpinning of sociology of law.[7] A sociology of morals does not explain morality away sociologically but explains the conditions in which moral issues arise, their parameters in particular historical experience, the sociological reasons why moral debates take certain forms in certain times and places. Durkheim's sociology of morals was inadequate primarily because he tried to read the nature of morality from a grand theory of the nature of societies. Today, after a barrage of postmodernist critiques, the risks of relying on master narratives and grand theories[8] are well known. It seems wise now to trust only modest sociological theories that recognise the great variety, contingency and unpredictability of much of social life.

But if, as I think, legal philosophy needs sociology's aid in considering law's ideals and its potential, this is because legal philosophy must understand the social constraints under which law is made, interpreted and applied. If those constraints are not appreciated, moral critiques of law become unfocussed because it is impossible to know the parameters in which critique can be 'realistic' – that is, have any chance of altering the legal system and its contexts of operation. A sociology of law and morals does not explain away moral issues or debunk legal ideals. It seeks to explain the social conditions under which these issues and ideals become meaningful: relevant to the time and place in which they are being considered.

The communicative approach to legislation may be strongest when understood as an exhortation to recognise fully law's potential: that is, when it is seen as a moral critique of impoverished views of what legislation is for and can achieve. If I feel specially close to its concerns, stated in this way, it is because I have come to think that all legal study should be concerned with law's moral meanings – its doctrinal reason and principle rooted in social experience. When law seems to have

---

7   Cotterrell (1999a), ch. 4.
8   Cf. Lyotard (1984).

no such meanings, it is mere words on paper or sheer coercive power; to use Durkheim's striking metaphor, it has lost its soul.[9]

Ultimately, on this view, law's effectiveness becomes a moral question, and law's effects can be conceptualised only in terms of moral assessments. In representative democracies, where the use of violence to enforce regulation is subject to many cultural limitations (which would not be abandoned willingly by most citizens), law's *effectiveness* depends significantly on perceptions of its *moral worth* – its nature as a principled, reasonable, normative framework of social relations. This is an important reason why the moral concerns of legal philosophy and the behavioural concerns of legal sociology should be brought into close interrelation and, if not fused, at least regarded as separated only by differences of emphasis.

In a thoughtful early essay,[10] Fuller described judge-made common law as combining fiat and reason: that is, on the one hand, authoritative command supported by coercion and, on the other, cohesive doctrinal principle supported by persuasive rationality. Law without coercive power is not regulation but advice, but law without principled rationality (i.e. moral meaning) is not fully law. For Fuller, it may ultimately lack the indicia of legality, breaking the covenant of reciprocity between rulers and ruled. Franz Neumann made a related distinction between *voluntas* and *ratio*[11] as components of law: law is a matter both of the imposed will of lawmakers and the integrity of doctrinal reason revealed in interpretation. Certainly the element of will and power must not be neglected: hence Robert Cover's dictum that 'legal interpretation takes place in a field of pain and death'.[12]

The point is that, from a legal-philosophical standpoint, it is important not to become so concerned with law's interpretation and the elaboration of its moral meanings that its sheer coercive force is underemphasised. From the standpoint of sociology of law, it is important not to focus so heavily on the nature and practice of law's interpretative communities, that its instrumental force is too little emphasised. On this view, we should not abandon concern with law as instrument,

---

9   Cotterrell (1999a), p. 5.
10 Fuller (1946).
11 Neumann (1986). Cf. Cotterrell (1995), pp. 317-20.
12 Cover (1986), at p. 1601.

346

or with the power of lawmakers to *impose* their will directly on regulated populations: law can surely be very effective if enough terror supports it. But in such
circumstances it may lose the attributes that democratic societies value and assume
necessary: *ratio*, substantive rationality, consistent principle, moral meaningfulness.

3

Professor Griffiths has long been an eloquent advocate of legal pluralism in sociology of law. He sees this argument as now won.[13] But even if that is so, legal
pluralism still has little purchase among lawyers and jurists, at least in my country.
I wish that it were otherwise. A legal-pluralist perspective is vital to indicate that
law's authority is never a given but always a matter of negotiation and sometimes
conflict (even in the most peaceful, stable legal systems).

It has been said that lawyers must always ultimately assume only one meaning
of law, a single legislative voice.[14] In fact, however, legal meaning is often not
finally resolved and one unambiguous legislative voice is not necessarily heard.
Different agencies of the state, perhaps representing different constituencies, may
not agree on the meaning of regulation and no final authoritative ruling may ever
be secured. Different state agencies, in practice, may be legally authoritative in
different contexts (for example, relatively unsupervised police on the streets; courts
whose decisions are in practice rarely appealed; enforcement agencies that negotiate
practical regulation strategies with the enterprises they regulate; bureaucracies that
develop their own internal interpretations of law governing their operations).

It is this point – rather than arguments about the social mechanisms that mediate
law's effects – which may undermine most profoundly the crude instrumentalist
paradigm of lawmaking and its consequences. It may often be not so much that
law's messages inevitably become obscured, altered or rejected in transmission as
that *mixed* messages emerge from the agencies of the legal system. Law is pluralistic

13 Griffiths (1995), pp. 201-2.
14 Van Roermund (1999), at p. 112.

in its official doctrinal structures as much as in its social sources. Hence legal pluralism ought to be a major concern for lawyers no less than legal sociologists. In the specific context of the legislation debates, this seems important because, potentially, it greatly complicates analysis of what legislation (or other law) seeks to communicate to the regulated population.

The legal pluralism of the social working approach emphasises the vast plurality of social sources in which social norms are produced.[15] So it seems very different from my pluralist emphasis above, although I think that plural meanings of state law and a plurality of competing sources of state legal authority often do reflect the existence of different social sources, in the sense of distinct social constituencies to which different parts of the state and the official legal system are linked in various informal ways. Griffiths' key concept of pluralism, that of semi-autonomous social fields (SASFs), borrowed from Sally Falk Moore,[16] very usefully highlights the infinity of different settings and sources of social regulation outside state law and of different kinds of interaction of social regulation with juristic norms.

But is it possible to develop a general theory of legislation and its working, faced with the immense variety of SASFs and having declared the concept of SASF central to such a theory? If legal philosophy seeks a general view of legislation's nature and potential, is this quest rendered hopeless by the infinite variety of SASFs which now are said to hold the key to legislation's working? The theory of law's social working might claim that that is a problem only for legal philosophers, but it is surely a problem for *any* general theory of law and legislation (as contrasted with a theory of the characteristics of SASFs). The question becomes: is the theory of law's social working really a theory of *law* (which could therefore engage with the communicative approach to legislation which certainly seeks to theorise about the nature of law) or is it a theory solely about the nature of law's social contexts?

The point of these comments is to keep firmly in mind that the proclaimed objective on both sides of the legislation debates is to develop a general theory of legislation and its working. It is surely significant that, in her original essay on

---

15 Griffiths (1995), pp. 207-8.
16 Griffiths (1999a), pp. 92-3.

SASFs, Moore used, to exemplify them, two relatively well-defined and well-structured social fields: a section of the New York garment industry and the tribal life of the Chagga people of Tanzania. She describes SASFs mainly as groups or networks of groups[17] that are *social actors* in the sense that they 'can generate rules and coerce or induce compliance to them'.[18] Griffiths notes that SASFs maintain their own norms 'and resist the penetration of competing external norms' and some 'more or less totally control the flow of legal information to their members'.[19]

My worry is that although this represents some very important social phenomena accurately it may not adequately characterise the social in general; that is, the general social environment which law or legislation seeks to address. It makes SASFs sufficiently concrete and sharply defined to be perceived as collective actors responding to state law. The concept of SASF seems analytically useful to the extent that it emphasises this concreteness. But this may not adequately represent the fluidity of social relations that contemporary law addresses and much contemporary social thought highlights[20] and hence also the variety of law's theoretical relationships with the social.

What seems to be needed is an approach to conceptualising law's place in social life which could (i) retain the powerful emphasis on the diversity of the social which the social working approach offers and (ii) respond to the call, which the communicative approach to legislation makes, to recognise *for the purposes of general legal theory* different ways in which law addresses the social (sometimes instrumentally, sometimes expressively, and sometimes to indicate normative frameworks for further constructive interpretation to develop new rules or shared understandings). Legal theory cannot realistically be expected to characterise – and differentiate comprehensively within – the almost infinite variety of groups, networks and relationships that can make up the social.[21] It needs abstract or formal rather than

---

17 See also Van Schooten (1999), at pp. 202-7, essentially treating SASFs as groups.
18 Moore (1978), p. 57.
19 Griffiths (1999a), pp. 93, 94.
20 See, e.g., Beck and Beck-Gernsheim (2002).
21 This point was made long ago by Carleton Kemp Allen in castigating Eugen Ehrlich's classical sociology of law as 'megalomaniac jurisprudence' – that is, a legal theory of potentially infinite scope – because it sought to encompass and characterise the practical regulation of every social association of whatever kind; see Allen (1964), p. 32. In fact, the concept of SASF,

empirical concepts as its components, but abstract concepts that can still recognise the fact of the vast differentiation of the social.

4

Elsewhere I have tried to argue that 'community' can serve as such an abstract or formal concept and that, following and adapting Max Weber's four ideal types of basic forms of social action, it is possible to identify just four pure, basic types of social relations of community. These are *instrumental* relations (often economic) focussed on the pursuit of common or convergent projects; *value-based* relations (in which relations of community are based on common adherence to certain beliefs or ultimate values); *affective* relations (based on purely emotional ties); and *traditional* relations (focussed on the fact of co-existence in an inherited environment – for example, geographical locality, common language, shared customs, history or experience).[22] In actual social networks, these ideal types of community are superimposed on each other, combined in an infinity of ways. In this understanding, then, 'community' is not a thing but a quality, or a set of qualities that can colour social relations. For the purposes of this paper it is important to stress only that, while law can be considered pluralistically as a regulation of these different types of community and their interrelations in networks of community, it is very unlikely to relate in the same way to each of the four types of community.

Law's relation to instrumental social relations (for example, commercial and contractual relations) may be relatively straightforward in many contexts. But, as the communicative approach to legislation implies, law's links to social relations

---

considered in its broadest application, seems remarkably close to Ehrlich's concept of 'social association' and suffers from the same problem of being intended to encompass in a single idea an infinite diversity of actually existing social networks and groups; see Ehrlich (2002), p. 39. In practice, Ehrlich's identification of social associations was governed by his juristic focus on those associations he saw as having direct relevance for lawyers' concerns with the categories, concepts and interpretive problems of state law. But it is not clear that a focus on SASFs is intended to be so limited.

22 For elaborations and applications of this typology, see Cotterrell (1997; 1999b; 2000; 2001, pp. 71-92, especially at pp. 82-90; 2002; forthcoming).

built on shared values or beliefs may be more complex and enigmatic and might properly give rise to symbolic soft law. And much that bears on the regulation of affective social relations of community might require complex legislative strategies. As Professor Witteveen says, the act of legislation is an act that 'produces meaning'.[23] But what kind of meaning is appropriate and likely to be understood will depend on what kind of social relations of community are to be regulated. So it seems right to argue that a variety of forms and approaches to legislation may be appropriate.

Instrumental legislation may often be appropriate, especially to support or guide instrumental relations of community. Law may seek, with varying success, merely to add its incentives and deterrents into the calculations of instrumental action that relate to the common or convergent projects at the centre of communal relations. It seeks to send a clear message that relates directly to the participants' pursuit of their projects.[24] A somewhat similar direct strategy may often be appropriate where law is concerned merely to support basic, minimal conditions of neighbourly co-existence (a form of traditional community), through criminal law[25] or the law of torts (delicts). But Witteveen persuasively suggests that a different (symbolic) kind of law might be appropriate where 'the audience of ... [the] laws forms a community that incorporates a morality'.[26] This seems close to what I have characterised as a community of values or belief. Even harder regulatory tasks may arise when legislation seeks to influence affectual (emotion-based) relations in which the parties' motivations and reasons for action may be difficult to interpret or influence legally.

From my point of view, it would be productive to draw more detailed parallels between, on the one hand, arguments about law's diverse links to different types of community and, on the other, the illuminating ideas developed by writers on the communicative approach to legislation about the diversity of legislative styles

---

23 Witteveen (1999a), p. 27.
24 Cf. id., pp. 30-4.
25 Id., pp. 31-2.
26 Id., p. 35.

and strategies and the conditions under which they are appropriate. To do so, however, would stray too far from the purpose of this chapter as a commentary.

What seems, however, important here is to emphasise that the use of ideal types of community offers a route towards making 'community' a *legal* concept, rather than solely a sociological one, and hence may contribute towards developing a legal theory that can nevertheless recognise the vast diversity of the social (represented in this theory as networks of community which are combinations, intersections and interrelations of the four Weberian pure types of community). In this way, a concept of community can help towards drawing important projects of legal philosophy and legal sociology closer together. Community can be a legal concept because it remains an abstract or formal, rather than an empirical concept: it does not describe actually existing social relations but refers only to pure types of social relations (instrumental, affective, value-based, traditional). So it provides a framework for classifying and analysing the regulatory aspects of actual social relations. To this extent, the concept of community functions in the way that most other legal concepts do, generally portraying social relations in formal, rather than empirical terms. Law necessarily abstracts from the infinite complexity of social life, analysing social relations in terms of its own abstract doctrinal classifications and typifications (contract, obligation, responsibility, liability, causation, ownership, possession, fiduciary relationship, etc.).

Community as a legal concept embracing four distinct types of community is a framework for characterising for regulatory purposes the diversity of social life: this diversity arises from the combination and interaction of types of community. The important point is that some of these combinations and interactions are relatively strong and enduring (as the model of semi-autonomous social fields suggests); some may be stable groups or social networks with a relatively strong identity. Others may be transient, vague, shifting, sometimes vibrant but sometimes very faint and weak. Using the typology of community, however, legal theory can recognise the sheer diversity of social life – the shop-floor contexts of regulation, as Professor Griffiths sees them – without being overwhelmed by this diversity and unable systematically to relate it to law.

352

5

I have tried to emphasise links between law's moral meanings and its social effects. To take discussion of this matter further in the specific context of legislative activity it is surely necessary to clarify what, if any, special character legislation has as a type of law. How far is legislation distinct from other kinds of law? The social working approach seems to apply to any kind of law, not just legislation in the form of statutes. Nothing in this approach suggests that legislation's social working is necessarily different in character from that of any other kind of law. Correspondingly, the communicative approach to legislation emphasises mainly not the special processes of *creating* legislation but its *reception* in interpretive communities – an idea which previously has been most prominent in relation to Ronald Dworkin's theory of the mainly professional search for 'best' readings of legal doctrine as an integrated whole.[27] The communicative approach shifts emphasis from the idea of legislation as a one-way message to that of law as a collaborative product of meaning construction; from the issuing of legal commands to, ultimately, a kind of 'law symphony'[28] as a complex, rich collective social product. As a result, much that in *common sense perceptions* seems distinctive about legislation is sidelined: it becomes just a (perhaps specially extensive and sophisticated) source of norms to be interpreted.

What are these common sense perceptions?[29] First, legislation is often thought of as *deliberate production of law* (in contrast to judicial or other interpretation or application of existing legal norms). In common law terminology, legislation is law that is made, not found. So legislation usually presents *new* legal norms. But obviously this is not always so. Legislation may consolidate, codify or restate existing norms: it may order or systematise existing law. A related perception is that legislation is proactive (identifying problems and addressing them) whereas judicial decisions are reactive (dependent on problems being brought forward for decision).

---

27 Dworkin (2000).
28 Witteveen (1999a), p. 64.
29 I am aware that the way they are described in what follows is necessarily coloured by a
    particular English experience of common law.

Yet legislative action may be no less reactive than judicial decision-making: legislatures may be pressured into providing legal solutions to emergent social problems. Conversely, common law courts, at least, sometimes seize the opportunity given by a case to develop legal doctrine in a more far-reaching way than the need for a ruling on the dispute might justify.

Secondly, legislation is often seen, in contrast to other lawmaking, as an explicitly *political process*: that is, governed by overt political conflict or debate. The law that results typically embodies policy: in Dworkin's formulation, defined collective goals.[30] But judicial decisions can, of course, also be policy-oriented while legislation may (as the communicative approach emphasises) be concerned to define general principles and standards, or parameters of social interaction.

In attacking the assumption that legislation is to be judged solely in terms of instrumental (directive, policy-implementing) achievements or objectives, it seems that the various sides in the legislation debates agree in challenging all of the doubtful specifications, above, of legislation's essential character that set it apart from other law.

A third common sense perception is that primary legislation is distinguished from other law by the *greater moral distance*[31] of its processes of production from the contexts in which it is to be applied. Judicial decision-making, after all, takes place in relation to a specific case: a particular, concrete fact situation to which the court's decision is supposed to relate directly. Legislation may address the regulated population only in relatively abstract terms and perhaps with little awareness of specific contexts. This is clearly a major theme of the legislation debates. The social working approach, stressing the contexts of legislation, seems to acknowledge moral distance as inevitable, so that state law is always an external intervention in SASFs, an intrusion in fields that seek self-regulation. By contrast, the communicative approach to legislation seems not content to treat moral distance as inevitable: this can, it seems, be overcome by making the legislative process part of an inclusive, interpretive social process.

---

30 Dworkin (1978), pp. 22-3.
31 See Cotterrell (1995), p. 305.

Durkheim's fragmentary writings on legislation may be useful here.[32] Durkheim sees the legislative process not as a political struggle of opposed interests, leading to a victory or compromise enshrined in the form of enacted rules. He sees it rather as a process of *deliberation* ('analogous to thought in the individual')[33] in which the state works out regulatory ideas for the benefit of society as a whole. Thus, no sharp distinction exists between legislative and judicial development of law, though legislatures may have access to better information about social conditions in general than do judges. So the legislative process may often be better fitted to lay down rules of general application. Presumably, however, the judicial process, addressing the particular circumstances of cases, may be better able than would a more remote legislator to adapt its rulings to those circumstances. Apart from these differences, legislative enactments and judicial decisions should rely on similar processes of disinterested deliberation.

Of course, it can be objected that the legislative process is, in fact, rarely if ever disinterested and that Durkheim's view of it misleads in treating it as a search for collective understandings to be expressed in regulatory form (the state as the 'brain' of society, thinking on its behalf). But, if this is so, the idea of an interpretive community professionally determining the meaning of legal ideas may be no less misleading if it fails to take account of the conflicts of interest that often actually drive interpretive disputes. If ultimately, legislative and judicial (and other law-producing processes) are, from a certain viewpoint, not dissimilar in nature, the problem of moral distance is not a special problem of legislation but one that potentially applies to all forms of lawmaking. It may be a problem of inadequate knowledge of conditions to be regulated (knowledge available to the lawmakers or legal interpreters and informing their deliberation) or of inadequate representation of interests at stake in processes of lawmaking of legal interpretation.

One final common sense view of the distinctiveness of legislation can be mentioned. Legislation might be thought of as a process aiming at a certain finality, a *conclusive clarity* in legal expression. This is a view at odds with some features

---

32 Cotterrell (1999a), chs. 10 and 11.
33 Durkheim (1957), p. 80.

of legislation which the communicative approach seeks to emphasise. In the perspective of the communicative approach there may be considerable virtues in 'open texture' and suggestive if indefinite legislative wording. This may encourage further interpretive activity in appropriate contexts to fix legal meanings for those contexts, or to keep open ongoing processes of legal development. Nevertheless, especially from an English common law perspective, judge-made law may seem provisional in a way that legislation is not: it can be regarded as a 'work in progress', in which the court edges towards general statements of rules or principles but these remain to be modified or restated in new ways as new applications or contexts for them arise serendipitously in future cases. Case law is always being restated in updated form, so that it is often possible to expound the law adequately in a given field solely by reference to cases decided over the course of just a few recent decades. By contrast, legislation may aim at a conclusive definition of relevant concepts, and even code-like comprehensiveness.

6

One of the great virtues of the writings, from the legislation debates, considered here, is that they emphasise that this last-mentioned attempt to present legislation as relatively distinctive from other kinds of statements of law fails no less dramatically than the earlier-mentioned ones. The modern domination of legislation as a legal source has arisen in parallel with the intellectual domination of legal positivism in legal thought. And positivism's model of legal certainty has often been misleading. For a long time it sidelined questions of legal interpretation, encouraging jurists to think of them as problems of logical technique (rather than moral evaluation) or as non-legal processes (exercises of political discretion).[34]

Both the social working approach and the communicative approach emphasise the importance of interpretation and evaluation of legal ideas in specific social contexts. The idea of interpretive communities is treated, in the communicative

---

34 Hart (1994), ch. 7.

356

approach, as central to understanding how the meanings of legislation are established. The question of the clarity and comprehensiveness of law is approached in new ways that are far more illuminating and sensitive to law's social contexts than legal positivism's traditional analyses. Producing clarity and comprehensiveness in the meaning of law is shown to be a responsibility not just of law-drafters and judges but of the entire membership of the communities addressed by law. In this way the very meaning of law is seen as the product of community life rather than as a matter only of juristic prescription. One of the most appealing aspects of the legislation debates, from this commentator's perspective, is the effort, in a sense, to return law to the communities in which it must exist and to which – if it is to have any significance – it must convey its moral meanings.

I certainly do not mean to deny that, in practice, legislation as a process is often very different from, for example, the stating of law in judicial decisions. But the common sense differentiations, discussed above, of legislation from other law have often had a pernicious effect on legal and social thought. In general they have been distinctions that put legislation at a disadvantage: encouraging emphasis on its remoteness (in the assumption of greater moral distance), its controversial character (as the product of political struggles or political domination), its interfering nature (the result of its proactiveness), its inflexibility (when its propositions aim at legal finality). To show (as the legislation debates seem to do in many different ways) legislation's basic similarity to other law, despite differences in its practice in many particular contexts, is to remove easy prejudices against legislation as a source of law. As Jeremy Waldron has noted, 'there is sense in legal philosophy that legislation lacks some of the *dignity* associated with the venerable institution we call law'.[35] There is, he suggests, an embarrassment about legislation and a lack of attention in much contemporary legal theory to its prominence in developed legal systems.[36] By making analysis of the nature of legislation central to theoretical analysis of legal communication in general, the legislation debates properly re-emphasise legislation's dignity and importance.

---

35 Waldron (1999), p. 10.
36 Id., pp. 1, 16.

A further appealing aspect of these debates, from this commentator's point of view, was implied at the beginning of this paper. The legislation debates seem to open up the prospect of a real collaboration, or even a partial integration, of legal philosophy and sociology of law. To emphasise that interpretation is fundamental to law and to see legal interpretive processes as social processes, not confined to certain limited juristic contexts, is to require that legal philosophy draw explicitly on the resources of social science to understand better the nature of law's interpretive communities. Correspondingly, to assert that sociology of law can contribute to a theory of legislation requires, ultimately, a recognition that legal sociology must engage with the task of developing concepts appropriate to a theory of the nature of law as institutionalised doctrine.[37] To do this surely requires collaboration with legal philosophy. For these reasons, quite apart from the merits of the particular claims of particular writers, the existence of the current legislation debates is very important. It points to a future in which legal scholarship may, at last, no longer be hamstrung by the arbitrary limitations of rigid disciplinary allegiances.

REFERENCES

Allen, C.K., *Law in the Making*, 7th edn. (Oxford: Oxford University Press, 1964).

Beck, U., and E. Beck-Gernsheim, *Individualization: Institutionalized Individualism and Its Social and Political Consequences* (London: Sage, 2002).

Cotterrell, R., *Law's Community: Legal Theory in Sociological Perspective* (Oxford: Clarendon Press, 1995).

Cotterrell, R., 'A Legal Concept of Community', *Canadian Journal of Law and Society*, 12 (1997), pp. 75-91.

Cotterrell, R., *Emile Durkheim: Law in a Moral Domain* (Stanford: Stanford University Press, 1999a).

Cotterrell, R., 'Transparency, Mass Media, Ideology and Community', *Cultural Values*, 3 (1999b), pp. 414-26.

Cotterrell, R., 'Common Law Approaches to the Relationship between Law and Morality', *Ethical Theory and Moral Practice*, 3 (2000), pp. 9-26.

Cotterrell, R., 'Is There a Logic of Legal Transplants?', in D. Nelken and J. Feest (eds.), *Adapting Legal Cultures* (Oxford: Hart, 2001).

Cotterrell, R., 'Seeking Similarity, Appreciating Difference', in A. Harding and E. Örücü (eds.), *Comparative Law in the 21st Century* (London: Kluwer, 2002), pp. 35-54.

---

37 Cf. Cotterrell (1995), ch. 1.

358

Cotterrell, R., 'Law in Culture', forthcoming in *Ratio juris*.

Cover, R.M., 'Violence and the Word', *Yale Law Journal*, 95 (1986), pp. 1601-29.

Durkheim, E., *Professional Ethics and Civic Morals*, transl. C. Brookfield (London: Routledge & Kegan Paul, 1957).

Dworkin, R., *Taking Rights Seriously* (London: Duckworth, 1978).

Dworkin, R., *Law's Empire* (repr. Oxford: Hart, 2000).

Ehrlich, E., *Fundamental Principles of the Sociology of Law* (New Brunswick: Transaction, 2002).

Fuller, L.L., 'Reason and Fiat in Case Law', *Harvard Law Review*, 59 (1946), pp. 376-95.

Griffiths, J., 'Legal Pluralism and the Theory of Legislation', in H. Petersen and H. Zahle (eds.), *Legal Polycentricity: Consequences of Pluralism in Law* (Aldershot: Dartmouth, 1995), pp. 201-34.

Griffiths, J., 'Legal Knowledge and the Social Working of Law: The Case of Euthanasia', in H. van Schooten (ed.), *Semiotics and Legislation: Jurisprudential, Institutional and Sociological Perspectives* (Liverpool: Deborah Charles, 1999a), pp. 81-108.

Griffiths, J., 'The Social Working of Anti-Discrimination Law', in T. Loenen and P.R. Rodrigues (eds.), *Non-Discrimination Law: Comparative Perspectives* (The Hague: Kluwer, 1999b), pp. 313-30.

Hart, H.L.A., *The Concept of Law*, 2nd edn. (Oxford: Clarendon Press, 1994).

Lyotard, J.-F., *The Postmodern Condition: A Report on Knowledge*, transl. G. Bennington and B. Massumi (Manchester: Manchester University Press, 1984).

Moore, S.F., *Law as Process: An Anthropological Approach* (London: Routledge & Kegan Paul, 1978).

Neumann, F.L., *The Rule of Law: Political Theory and the Legal System in Modern Society* (Leamington Spa: Berg, 1986), pp. 45-6.

Nonet, P., and P. Selznick, *Law and Society in Transition: Toward Responsive Law* (New Brunswick, N.J.: Transaction, 2001).

Selznick, P., *The Moral Commonwealth: Social Theory and the Promise of Community* (Berkeley: University of California Press, 1992).

Summers, R.S., *Lon L. Fuller* (London: Edward Arnold, 1984).

Van Roermund, B., 'Legislative Voices: A Rousseauist Note on Legal Pluralism', in H. van Schooten (ed.), *Semiotics and Legislation: Jurisprudential, Institutional and Sociological Perspectives* (Liverpool: Deborah Charles, 1999), pp. 109-21.

Van Schooten, H., 'Instrumental Legislation and Communication Theories', in H. van Schooten (ed.), *Semiotics and Legislation: Jurisprudential, Institutional and Sociological Perspectives* (Liverpool: Deborah Charles, 1999), pp. 185-211.

Waldron, J., *The Dignity of Legislation* (Cambridge: Cambridge University Press, 1999).

Witteveen, W.J., 'Significant, Symbolic and Symphonic Laws: Communication through Legislation', in H. van Schooten (ed.), *Semiotics and Legislation: Jurisprudential, Institutional and Sociological Perspectives* (Liverpool: Deborah Charles, 1999a), pp. 27-70.

Witteveen, W.J., 'Laws of Lawmaking', in W.J. Witteveen and W. van der Burg (eds.), *Rediscovering Fuller: Essays on Implicit Law and Institutional Design* (Amsterdam: Amsterdam University Press, 1999b), pp. 312-45.

Witteveen, W.J., and B.M.J. van Klink, 'Why Is Soft Law really Law? A Communicative Approach to Legislation', *RegelMaat*, 14, 3 (1999), pp. 126-40.

[19]
Ideals and Values in Law:
A Comment on
The Importance of Ideals

The essay collection, *The Importance of Ideals*,[1] is a clarion call from a group of leading Dutch legal scholars and legal and political theorists to take ideals seriously in legal studies and political philosophy. As the editors, Wibren van der Burg and Sanne Taekema, put it: attention to ideals 'may help us to understand social reality better'. In particular, they argue that 'ideal-oriented theory' must be a part of legal studies.[2] The eleven authors are part of a larger group of scholars who cooperated at Tilburg University between 1997 and 2002 in a research programme on 'The Importance of Ideals in Law, Morality and Politics'. Clearly, the resulting book is the outcome of extensive collaborative work.

Although the project's intellectual foundations and motivation are not fully explained in the text, some sources are clear. One is the anti-positivist legal philosophy of Lon Fuller, focussed on exploring the value of legality and the moral foundations of various kinds of legal practice and institutions.[3] Another more general influence is the American pragmatist tradition, especially as represented in Philip Selznick's sociolegal work. But as van der Burg and Taekema stress, the book's contributors share a perspective, not a theory. The aim is to assert that ideals are worth studying as values embedded in social practices.[4] Ideals matter, they make a difference.

Surely that is right. But, to preface the commentary that will follow, some admissions are needed. Initially, the title 'The Importance of Ideals' conjured up for me the ghosts of old apprehensions and antagonisms. I should like to

---

1 W. van der Burg & S. Taekema (eds) The Importance of Ideals: Debating Their Relevance in Law, Morality, and Politics [hereafter IofI], Brussels: Peter Lang 2004.
2 Ibid., p. 13, 30.
3 See further W. J. Witteveen & W. van der Burg, Rediscovering Fuller: Essays on Implicit Law and Institutional Design, Amsterdam: Amsterdam University Press 1999.
4 IofI, p. 39.

take a few moments to explain why, because this will also explain the perspective from which I approach this rich, stimulating book.

I

As an undergraduate law student, I found appeals by my teachers to ultimate values in legal analysis infuriating. These values (and practical models of the good, derived from them, as ideals)[5] seemed to resist analysis or
to require none. The most abstract values, invoked in legal studies, often
gave a vague sense of the rightness of legal rules or decisions, so that inquiries about the precise social effects of law were unnecessary. How could one
argue against the rule of law, sanctity of property, or freedom of contract as
indispensable foundations of legal thought and practice? Secure in a kind of
fuzzy comprehensiveness, these ideas allowed such phenomena as administrative discretion, planning law or consumer protection to be presented
as exceptional and peripheral to the great value-centres of law. It seemed
that legal rules and decisions could often be judged conclusively – but sometimes in unpredictable, ad hoc ways – by applying values. So these values
were *inside* law. Yet they were largely *outside its study* except sometimes in
legal philosophy, which was widely considered to have no bearing on legal
practice. Constitutional law, the only course that (briefly) mentioned the
rule of law, presented A.V. Dicey, its British prophet, as an ancient guru
whom it was not necessary to read. If he misunderstood legal responses to
the growth of the modern administrative state, this in no way impugned his
classic status. Values were not subject to empirical critique.

Yet some of them directly coloured practical legal understanding and informed professional ideals: among these, for example, were reverence for precedent (embodying particular values of order and authority); an ideal of
judicial wisdom as imaginative incrementalism (the work of the best common law judges was often contrasted with the poor quality of legislation);
the separation of law from politics; the superiority of private over public
law; the model of the 'reasonable man';[6] and an ideal of morally neutral
legal technicality, combining social conservatism with intellectual ingenuity. Professional legal practice was hard to understand except by referring to

---

5   Roscoe Pound, in his The Ideal Element in Law, Indianapolis: Liberty Fund reprint 2002, p. 7,
    defines an ideal (in legal contexts) as 'a mental picture of what one is doing or why, to what
    end or purpose, he is doing it'. Pound's book (based on lectures delivered in 1948) is not mentioned
    in Iofl, but he too argues forcefully that legal ideals should be given 'the same thoroughgoing
    analytical study' that rules receive in legal study (p. 9).
6   See e.g. M. Moran, Rethinking the Reasonable Person: An Egalitarian Reconstruction of the
    Objective Standard, Oxford: Oxford University Press 2003.

such ideas. Yet insofar as practice embodied or seemed to follow ideals, the ideal elements were usually taken for granted, as though separable and immune from the criticism that practice itself might attract.

If ideal-oriented discourse in this context seemed complacent, social science offered a way to address this complacency. It held out the prospect that ultimate values as elements of practice could be examined empirically and, especially, historically. It might become possible to see (i) how the dominance of some particular value had come about; (ii) whose interests it served or disadvantaged; (iii) what the effects (political, economic, social, cultural) of its influence on practice were, now and in the past; (iv) under what conditions certain values were widely accepted or came to seem problematic; and (v) whether other values might appear more meaningful if conditions changed.

This approach did not reject values or ideals: quite the opposite, it affirmed their importance. But it contextualised them by studying their conditions of existence. Since a commitment to ultimate values often seems strongly resistant to challenge from the evidence of experience, this commitment could easily be understood as ideological, entailing adherence to whole systems of valuation and understanding offering *comprehensive* interpretations of the world or some aspect of it. The linking of ideas to interests, stressed in Marxist conceptions of ideology, was also a promising approach – although not if it involved claiming that the attractiveness of ideas made sense *only* in terms of economic interests they might promote.

Overall, it seemed (and still seems to me) helpful to approach the study of legal values and ideals from the standpoint of a sociology of legal doctrine (i.e. rules, principles, concepts and values, and modes of reasoning with these in the various settings in which they are institutionalised). This is not just a sociology of *lawyers'* ideas and practices because legal understanding and experience is not the monopoly of lawyers.[7] Empirical studies of the ways legal values are invoked outside lawyers' practice are therefore of great value. And because values are part of legal doctrine, a sociology of morals (i.e. socially recognised values) must surely accompany a sociology of law. Emile Durkheim's sociology is very important in this context. More than any of the other great social theorists, he emphasises the ultimate inseparability of law and moral values – law being identifiable from the wider realm of morality because its judgments are organised rather than

---

7   See e.g. P. Ewick & S.S. Silbey, The Common Place of Law: Stories from Everyday Life, Chicago: University of Chicago Press 1998.

diffuse:[8] law is thus normative doctrine institutionalised in organised processes.[9]

Of course, the problem of values and ideals cannot be simply subsumed into sociology. Sociologically-oriented study of law is itself guided by values and ideals. But I think this study can and must examine systematically and empirically the social contexts in which ultimate values and ideals gain their meaning – including those that inform its own scholarly practices. Hence the need for an endlessly reflexive approach which finds values embedded in practices, and recognises that provisional interpretations of experience are central to any claims about 'truth'. This begins to sound a little like pragmatism – at least, enough so to provide a lead into discussing *The Importance of Ideals* which, in part, is strongly informed by pragmatist views of the treatment of ideals in law.

II

Queries will be raised later about some aspects of the pragmatist outlook that informs parts of *The Importance of Ideals*, but there is much in the book as a whole that appeals very strongly to this commentator. For example, the important point that the ambiguity of ultimate values may not impair but sometimes enhance their power to structure legal discourse (the 'fuzzy comprehensiveness' I mentioned earlier) is strongly brought out in Willem Witteveen's study of the *Pikmeer* case which established a significant immunity of Dutch municipal authorities from criminal liability, at least with regard to environmental controls.[10] Witteveen shows different kinds of appeal to the rule of law (or legality) in judicial and juristic practice. Legality, he says, can be best seen as a cluster of ideals, often in tension. Their significance is apparent when they are invoked in practice: on the one hand, strategically as devices of government and legal control and, on the other, as aspirational reference points in political and legal debate. Invoking legal ideals is never innocent. It presupposes particular objectives of debate and regulatory strategies.

He also notes 'large differences in local understandings of the rule of law',[11] a point that ties in with efforts to study ultimate legal values not only as promulgated 'officially' in the legal agencies and institutions of the state

8 R. Cotterrell, Emile Durkheim: Law in a Moral Domain, Edinburgh/Stanford: Edinburgh University Press/Stanford University Press 1999, p. 60.
9 See also W. van der Burg, An Interactionist View on the Relation between Law and Morality, in: IofI, at p. 212 (law's distinctiveness has its primary basis in its institutional dimension).
10 W.J. Witteveen, Realist Idealism and the Rule of Law, in: IofI.
11 Ibid., p. 119.

but also as these values are understood by different social groups and in different regions of society. Marc Hertogh, introducing the valuable idea of the 'living *Rechtsstaat*', examines the views of local population groups in Zwolle about acceptable standards in regulatory practices.[12] Empirically studying legal values as they exist in popular understandings, his paper links with a substantial body of legal sociological research on law and popular consciousness. The key point is that legal values, like all aspects of law, are not the monopoly of lawyers, judges and jurists. Their centre of gravity (to adapt Eugen Ehrlich's idiom) lies not in the activity of the state but in society itself.[13] The role of legal values can be appreciated only by seeing how they inform the practices and understandings of lay citizens as well as legal professionals. Caroline Raat's essay[14] on *Rechtsstaat* values in private organisations extends the point, following Selznick's lead in recognising that legal values do not only concern the state legal system and the regulation of public life. They can apply also to private rule systems, as Selznick showed in studying legality as a value in industrial relations.

Yet it is right to criticise (as Hertogh and, by implication, Raat do) mechanical applications of official values (those recognised by officials in the state legal system) in local social contexts. What is needed is a pluralistic sociological view of values. The implication goes beyond legal studies to political philosophy: there is no Archimedean point,[15] 'perspective of eternity' or 'view from nowhere' which makes it possible to see values in a single perspective and thus theorise them in some absolute way irrespective of context. This is Bert van den Brink's point in advocating a 'hermeneutical perspectivism'.[16] Such an approach accepts that there is always a particular standpoint from which values are conceptualised and embedded in practice. We should ask what values bearing on regulation are accepted in different social settings and populations. What diverse practical models of the good (ideals) do these promote?

But serious analytical problems arise for any study of ideals that seeks to combine sociological sensitivity and philosophical rigour. First, there is the general problem of perspectivism (how to communicate across the divide of

---

12 M. Hertogh, The Living Rechtsstaat: A Bottom-Up Approach to Legal Ideals and Social Reality, in: IofI.
13 E. Ehrlich, Fundamental Principles of the Sociology of Law, transl. W. L. Moll, New Brunswick, NJ: Transaction repr. 2002, p. 390.
14 C. Raat, Stories and Ideals, in: IofI.
15 Cf. R. Dworkin, Hart's Postscript and the Character of Political Philosophy, (2004) 24 Oxford Journal of Legal Studies 1 (rejecting 'Archimedeanism' in legal studies).
16 B. van den Brink, Ideals of Doing Political Philosophy: From the Perspective of Eternity to Hermeneutical Perspectivism, in: IofI.

different perspectives). Van den Brink suggests solving this through an overarching ethos of civility[17] but that seems to me merely to introduce another value which (viewed from one perspective or another) may or may not be accepted. Secondly, even if the perspective of just a single sociolegal observer is considered, legality may appear not as a single value but several in potential tension (as in Witteveen's study of the *Pikmeer* case). What relation then can or should exist between these values? What is to be made of a value such as legality if, as empirical studies show, it means different things in different contexts and to different population groups? Surely 'value' and 'ideal' as objects of inquiry need clarifying, and further questions remain to be asked as to how values, in all their vagueness and indeterminate plurality, are to be studied.

How far does this book answer these questions? Ideals, as values embedded in social practices, are seen by the editors as a third category of normative standards, alongside rules and principles. What I call their vagueness is termed by Van der Burg and Taekema a 'surplus of meaning'.[18] So ideals are usually too indefinite to control legal decisions but can influence long term legal development.[19] They stimulate the imagination and aid debate, sometimes providing a framework which opposing arguments can share, or identifying fundamentally opposed reference points. Van der Burg and Taekema properly note that idealism has led to disasters and that adherence to ideals can be a recipe for irreconcilable conflict. But they stress that attention to ideals can also show common presuppositions behind a plurality of viewpoints and so facilitate understanding. A focus on ideals might clarify conceptual disagreements.

This is the aspect of the ideal-oriented approach that attracts Roland Pierik in considering debates between liberal egalitarians and multiculturalists in political philosophy.[20] The ideal of equality may be shared by both sides but they differ as to what endowments of individuals are natural, what choices are meaningful for them and how culture relates to these matters. Pierik quotes Will Kymlicka's critique of liberals' 'idealised model of the polis in which fellow citizens share a common descent, language and culture'.[21] But many liberals, for their part, see a multiculturalist focus on groups as undermining the equal protection of individuals. Pierik claims that, given the common focus of both positions on equality, there need be no intrinsic

17 Ibid., p. 159.
18 IofI, p. 21.
19 Ibid., p. 17-18.
20 R. Pierik, The Ideal of Equality in Political Philosophy, in: IofI.
21 Ibid., p. 180-181.

incompatibility between the two approaches.[22] What seems important, extending his argument, is to examine different contexts of interpretation of the equality ideal, and its meaningfulness in the experiences of different social groups. Philosophical deadlock points to a need for empirical social inquiry guided by a focus on ideals.

This suggests partial answers to the problem of perspectivism noted earlier. Sociological inquiries can clarify the contexts in which values are interpreted and given significance. If values are inherently vague, the 'surplus' of meaning is, to some extent, controlled in specific practices that can be empirically studied.[23] Practices are informed by values, values acquire practical meaning (as ideals). What is entailed is an endless reflexivity uniting philosophy and social science, evaluation and experience. Does this involve combining fact and value, and seeing knowledge as validated by practice? That, of course, would be to move close to the postulates of pragmatist philosophy, and it is to the use of pragmatism in *The Importance of Ideals* that we need to turn now.

III

A main attraction of pragmatism is that it treats ideals and values as 'rooted in reality' in 'the concrete situation', to use Sanne Taekema's words.[24] Ideals, understood pragmatically, are 'part of problem-solving', not some external criterion of evaluation added on to practice. They exist objectively 'in the constraints provided by the way the world is' and subjectively as creatively imagined desirable possibilities.[25] So they are part of practice and something with which empirical social science can concern itself (as in Selznick's value-oriented sociology). Yet they remain also aspirational, available to inspire debate, indicate progress and aid communication. Perhaps most importantly, they need not be seen as distant or abstract. The first intuitive knowledge of an ideal comes from experience. It presents itself as a hypothesis: the ideal will be judged by the factual consequences of adhering to it.[26] Fact and value are intertwined, 'aspects of the same reality which can be distinguished, though not separated.'[27]

---

22 Ibid., p. 182.
23 But not always, according to some essays in IofI. Peter Blok's study of the ideal of privacy in data processing law suggests that its use has created 'a turn to abstraction' obscuring empirical differences in the contexts of practice. By contrast, Jonathan Verschuuren and Timon Oudenaarden, studying environmental law and policy, see relevant ideals as too indefinite to provide any real guide for practice in this area.
24 S. Taekema, What Ideals Are: Ontological and Epistemological Issues, in: IofI, p. 40- 41.
25 Ibid., p. 39, 45; and Van der Burg & Taekema, Introduction, in: IofI, p. 15.
26 Taekema, What Ideals Are, p. 51-52.
27 Ibid., p. 54.

Wouter de Been, discussing pragmatism and sociolegal studies,[28] sees
pragmatist social scientists as actively engaged with society's concerns.
Pragmatism frees science from positivist illusions: social science must choose its goals, hence it cannot avoid values and commitments; it cannot be
neutral. There can be no absolutes to found its scientific protocols but only
the 'partial concepts and contingent scientific procedures inherited from
earlier generations to frame the best possible solutions for the problems
thrown up by an ever-changing world'.[29] Unlike some postmodernist
thought, pragmatism does not discard science as an illusion. But neither
does it hope to find foundations for scientific inquiry (or for judgments of
'truth') beyond what accumulated experience has made methodologically
plausible for the time being: it offers a 'bootstraps' theory of knowledge
(and of ideals and values) for a world all too aware of contingency and instability.

Durkheim, comparing pragmatism's outlook on knowledge with that of his
sociology, termed it logical utilitarianism.[30] He meant that, while utilitarianism judges values and policies consequentially in terms of their practical
results for individuals, pragmatism assesses the validity of knowledge in
similar terms. Hans Joas criticises Durkheim for failing to recognise that
pragmatism does not leave individuals to make such assessments of consequences. Instead, it locates these assessments in collective social experience
and history.[31] Thus, Joas sees very close parallels between pragmatism and
Durkheim's sociology: both aim to address philosophical issues empirically,[32] both see truth as a *social* product in some sense, but both need to find
new justifications for the universality of knowledge.[33] I think this is a fair
assessment and, in the rest of this comment, I want to explore its implications for sociolegal studies of values and ideals, such as those included in
The Importance of Ideals.

The issue of how the *usefulness* of ideals, values or forms of knowledge is to
be judged remains a serious problem for pragmatism. What makes a value

---

28 W. de Been, Pragmatism and Ideal-Oriented Socio-Legal Study, in: IofI.
29 Ibid., p. 64.
30 E. Durkheim, Pragmatism and Sociology, transl. J.C. Whitehouse, Cambridge: Cambridge
    University Press 1983, p. 72-74.
31 H. Joas, Pragmatism and Social Theory, Chicago: University of Chicago Press 1993, p. 59-60.
32 Joas (ibid., p. 57) claims that both tend to treat philosophy's key questions ('what can be known
    as true and what is morally good') 'in a manner which is saturated in empirical evidence and
    which draws on historically and culturally variable forms of morality and worldviews'. In my
    view, this empirical orientation characterises Durkheim's sociology, but how far pragmatism
    as *philosophy* actively seeks such broad materials remains in doubt.
33 Ibid., p. 57-58.

useful? Who must it be useful for? If it emerges out of problem-solving, how are problems defined or identified? What if they appear differently to different people, so that relevant ideals embedded in them also appear differently (contrasting meanings of legality might be an example)? What kind of collective experience provides sufficient validation of knowledge or values and why, for example, should my individual experience not be, for me, a better validation than any collective one? Does pragmatism lead, as Durkheim insisted, to a disabling relativism? Pragmatism may claim that relativism is irrelevant once it is accepted that absolutes are in practice unattainable;[34] yet we need means of assessing competing claims about knowledge or values.

Undoubtedly, to some extent, an immersion in practice (or a close empirical study of practice, which is near to the same thing) does make it possible to gain a new perspective on conflicts in knowledge-claims made at an abstract level. So Wibren van der Burg argues illuminatingly[35] that conflicts between natural law theory and legal positivism over the separation of law and morals can be better understood and even avoided by focusing on the practice of law, rather than on the idea of law as product (i.e. as finished knowledge or doctrine). But practice itself (like experience) can be interpreted in different ways. Whose interpretations count? What makes them count, so that we can use them to identify plausible knowledge claims (and coherent values and ideals)? These problems remain.

Ultimately most of them come down to the difficult idea of values as useful, and what this can mean. Ronald Dworkin argues that pragmatism 'self-destructs wherever it appears'.[36] The pragmatist might say, for example, that knowledge is successful practice. But if lawyers or scientists find it useful to treat knowledge *not* as successful practice but as an understanding of the way things are (what the law in force is; what the characteristics and mechanisms of the natural world are), where is the advantage in utility-talk? To know that scientific knowledge (or law, or legal values) is 'actually' a matter of successful practice would not help that practice. It still leaves open many questions as to how judgments about knowledge are (and should be) made in order to engage in successful practice, and how to judge success. Unless it becomes a demand that knowledge be judged ceaselessly against an ever-widening diversity of experience, pragmatism may encou-

---

34 W. James, Essays in Pragmatism, New York: Hafner 1948, p. 170-171.
35 W. van der Burg, Interactionist View, loc. cit. in: IofI.
36 R. Dworkin, Pragmatism, Right Answers and True Banality, in: M. Brint & W. Weaver (eds.), Pragmatism in Law and Society, Boulder, Colorado: Westview 1991, p. 361.

rage complacency, as in a ready acceptance of its own homely 'banality'[37] or a tendency to mock ambitious, comparative social explanation as 'fancy theory'.

A way forward is perhaps, first, to emphasise forcefully the role of a *reflexive, permanently self-critical social science* in broadening perspectives on practice: the aim of such a science should be to overcome parochialism as far as possible by endlessly comparing the contexts and meanings of practices. Secondly, it might be helpful to distinguish, more precisely, different kinds of values that need to be understood in relation to practice.

As regards the first of these matters, *The Importance of Ideals* says relatively little about empirically-oriented social theories (theories of social change and social stability and of the nature of societies, social groups and social relations in general). Certainly, such theories offer no more than a perspective, but at their best they aim to embrace a wide swathe of empirical description of social life. At the same time, the best social theory attempts to remain sensitive to the detail of social practice. Social theory remains essential to put interpretations of social practices into the widest possible contexts and so to revise provisional judgments of social 'truth'. The effort continually to broaden perspectives entails that particular experience is always to be confronted with other, different experience, especially beyond our own era, society and culture; in other words, with experience that continually, relentlessly *challenges* what we know and what we value.

As regards the second suggestion made above – to differentiate kinds of values or ideals – pragmatist approaches seem to me to be relatively unconcerned with this. Nevertheless, the old dissatisfactions I felt with appeals to values when I first studied law were linked to the apparently endless fluidity and imprecision of legal ideals, invoked at many levels of generality and encompassing a vast array of valuations. I felt that these were of different kinds, yet very hard to classify and so to analyse.

In considering values and ideals surely we should distinguish different moral criteria (social valuations) applicable to different kinds of social relations. This is a prerequisite for judging the sociological significance of ideals and values (locating them in the contexts that fix the parameters of their practical meaning for actors). Using such an approach it might be possible to see more clearly how such basic resources as 'trust' and 'morality', needed

---

37 Cf. R. Rorty, The Banality of Pragmatism and the Poetry of Justice, in: Brint & Weaver, op. cit; James, Essays, op. cit. p. 146.

to structure social life, require very different meanings (and legal expressions) in different social contexts – for example, in instrumental relations between contracting parties, or relations based on a shared common environment, or on emotional responses or affection, or on commitment to some abstract ultimate value, such as liberty, human dignity or equality.

Durkheim's main disagreement with pragmatism was around its understanding of the nature of truth. He condemned its relativism: for him, the social world gives truth, a truth 'out there' that bears on us and which we need to discover so as to orient ourselves to our environment. Pragmatists claim that whether truth is 'out there' in any absolute sense or not makes no difference since our only access to truth is through experience. Perhaps the issue comes down to how intensive, wide-ranging and ambitious the search for truth about the social world should be. Ronald Dworkin adds another perspective. For him, political values are 'real', not dependent on anyone's 'invention, or belief or decision'. So legality as an ideal has a significance not reducible to its existence as an aspect of practice or problems, yet that significance is discoverable only in endless interpretation and debate.[38] Religious believers have a different view of truth again. Ultimate truth is beyond human cognition, but faith affirms its existence; the truth that can never be finally known is, indeed, the most important truth of all. Faith is the only means of connecting with it; faith puts into perspective human beings' feeble efforts at understanding.

Do claims about the existence of (an unreachable) ultimate truth matter? I think they do. The idea that perspectives are to be broadened towards some ultimate understanding, and not merely juxtaposed with each other, is what makes the ongoing, ungrounded philosophical conversation[39] worthwhile. It may persuade us, finally, why civility in that conversation matters, and why reflexivity and endless self-criticism in social inquiry are necessary. If truth cannot finally be *validated* in experience, neither can ideals. They can, however, be clarified philosophically, and social science can help us to say what the consequences of adhering to them will be. In that way it becomes possible to establish empirically the parameters in which values seem meaningful in practical contexts.

---

38 Dworkin, Hart's Postscript, loc. cit., p. 12, 23-26.
39 R. Rorty, Philosophy and the Mirror of Nature, Oxford: Blackwell 1980.

[20]
Culture, Comparison, Community*

Abstract

This article proposes a response to legal scholarship's recent concerns with the complexity of law's relations with culture, looked at from a sociolegal point of view. It argues that legal studies today must have a comparative dimension, and that they should contribute to an understanding of law in relation to culture, or as a cultural phenomenon. But there are problems with culture as a legal concept (or a social scientific one). Also, many long-established sociolegal ideas about 'law and society' are becoming obsolete. A way forward is to relate law to four pure types of community that interact in complex ways in social life and, together, embrace the various dimensions of culture. The article claims that a law-and-community approach to legal study clarifies law's relation to culture, and provides a framework for comparative studies of law.

1. Culture

What can an English legal scholar, with an almost entirely European social and legal experience, hope to contribute to a realistic discussion of legal studies in a country with a profoundly different culture – for example, India? The challenge is to try to find a way of bridging cultures through legal and social theory, legal and sociological scholarship. It is also to find a way of talking about culture that is neither vague and merely impressionistic (like a tourist), nor misleadingly dogmatic so that complex communal ways of life are labelled 'cultures' as if they were monolithic and uniform, and irreducibly different from other cultures. On the one hand, there is a danger in using the concept of culture in a way that assumes an inevitable similarity between people who are different in important ways. On the other, the danger is in assuming an irreducible difference between the 'other' and 'us', when in fact much may be shared and bridges of understanding can be built that make culture highly 'porous' – open to cross-influence, mutual learning, recognition of commonalities, and inter-group translation of experience, beliefs, aspirations and attachments.

This article's aim is to outline a theoretical framework that might be helpful in addressing some of the complexities of culture in social studies of law. It presents ideas about culture, comparison and community in law at a fairly high level of abstraction. But my hope is that the ideas are broad enough and sensitive enough to have some local resonance, and that they may be criticised and tested to explore their applicability for legal studies in specific contexts. Certainly, they are grounded in traditions of social theory that are almost entirely western. Although the ideas in this article reflect a strong interest in comparative legal studies and legal history, I know that they cannot entirely escape the predominantly English common law experience that has shaped their author.

All of us inhabit cultures that, in part, we are aware of. But, in part, insofar as culture forms us and makes us who we are, we are not conscious of it. To understand culture it is necessary somehow to step outside ourselves, observing ourselves participating in life, and up to a point this is possible. Observation and participation cannot ultimately be separated. We necessarily observe the situation

---

* This article is adapted from a paper given at the National Law School of India University, Bangalore, India on 11 August 2005.

2 |

in which we participate, while we participate in it (like a lawyer who, arguing a case in court, watches the judge and other participants and gains useful knowledge from observing their behaviour). And we often participate in order to observe. This may be a virtual participation (as in the empathetic understanding that a Weberian sociologist needs in studying social action) or it may be actual participant observation, which all of us do all the time if we are curious about social life.

The point is that cultural translation is very difficult, but not impossible. In getting to grips with culture (which, this article will argue, is a crucial aspect of legal studies today), there is no sharp line to be drawn between observation and participation, insiders and outsiders, internal and external viewpoints. The concept of culture becomes dangerous when it is used to draw those lines of demarcation, presenting them as fixed rather than infinitely fluid and dependent on standpoint and perspective. In other words, culture must not be treated positivistically, as a 'thing', a 'social fact' in Emile Durkheim's (1982) sense. One of the hardest challenges for legal studies today is to decide how to deal with the idea of culture, integrating it into legal thinking but avoiding the kind of reification that treats culture as monolithic, a causal factor in itself, or an explanation of legally relevant behaviour (as, for example, in the use of 'cultural defences' in criminal law and other legal fields: see Renteln, 2004). Later in this article some suggestions will be made as to how this problem can be avoided.

But is culture really important in legal studies? Legal positivists have long assumed that it is not. Law, in their view, may derive both coercive power and legitimacy from its link to the state (or, in the Austinian version, the sovereign), and the question of state authority is seen as one for political theory; otherwise law is to be understood as a system of norms of rules that regulate their own creation (Hart, Kelsen) – law is portrayed as normatively autonomous and self-standing. If culture relates to law it is, on the legal positivist view, a professional culture: the culture (in this case the values, traditions, allegiances or interests) of legal 'officials' who accept a rule of recognition, or the existence of a basic norm. But even in western countries, where an assumption of law's isolation from culture has long had currency, this assumption is becoming increasingly untenable. Law is now seen, even in lawyers' doctrinal writings (not just the writings of legal sociologists or legal anthropologists), as related to culture in many ways.

The following are a few examples. Comparative lawyers invoke the concept of legal culture in referring to the fact that it is not only rules that must be compared between legal systems but also ways of 'doing' law, practising, invoking and developing it. If law is changing more quickly than ever before in many countries, the forces behind legal change need to be understood. Culture may be a good concept to use in addressing these matters. The study of rules alone may give little real assistance in understanding law in flux.

At the same time, literature on globalisation often suggests that law moves easily from country to country, and across national boundaries. Law is seen as the 'camp follower' of transnational economic and financial development.[1] Law is often assumed to be straightforwardly instrumental in character; a mere technical device. In this context, ideas of legal culture (for example, relating to the organisation of transnational professional legal practice)[2] are sometimes convenient in referring to sociolegal conditions that facilitate globalisation. But legal culture can also refer to local ways of practising, using and thinking about law that operate as factors of resistance to globalising trends and harmonisation of law (see, e.g., Legrand, 1999).

Culture is important also, in western countries, as a legally relevant idea in considering the legal challenges and possibilities of multiculturalism, in issues such as the recognition of

---

1   Cf. Barber (1993, p. 119): 'Law has always been the destitute camp follower of the itinerant armies of transnationalism.'

2   See especially Dezalay and Garth (1996).

polygamous marriages in monogamous cultures (e.g., Shah, 2005, Ch. 5); varied practices of marriage and divorce (e.g., Murphy ed., 2000, Chs. 4 and 5); the legal recognition of minority religious or traditional practices (e.g., Shadid and Van Koningsveld, 2005; Freeman, 1995); the use of 'cultural defences' against criminal and civil liability, as mentioned earlier; and the protection of 'cultural heritage'.[3]

I have not defined 'culture' here. The examples given earlier suggest many different meanings of the term – and that is this article's first major theme. *Culture does not refer to a single idea that is analytically useful in legal studies.* This does not mean that culture is unimportant – quite the opposite. It is vitally important as a matter for legal scholars to take into account. But it refers to many disparate elements – different kinds of social bonds and experiences. They need to be separated analytically. Otherwise, in talking about culture we are sometimes talking about religion or other belief systems; sometimes about traditions and customs that may be entirely secular; sometimes about material culture (levels of economic well-being and technological development); and sometimes about emotional ties (for example, to nation, to kinship group, to communal goods such as music and other arts, to shared memories, etc.) as well as emotional hostilities (to 'other' nations, races, religions, ethnic groups, etc.). It is impossible to make much progress in relating law and culture systematically without separating these different elements that may pull against, as much as reinforce, each other.

2. Comparison

Before considering how this separation of elements of culture might be achieved, it is important to say more about changes in legal studies in general that are making the relation of law and culture increasingly significant. One important consequence of these changes is, I think, that comparative legal studies are becoming much more central to legal scholarship. Comparative law as a scholarly field has served many functions,[4] but its dominant practical roles in western countries have been as a technical aid to improve national law, and as a servant of efforts to unify or harmonise law between nations, or to aid legal communication between them, especially in the interests of facilitating commerce. The dominant idea in much comparative legal scholarship seems to have been to seek similarity in law, to get rid of obstacles of legal difference that hamper legal interaction between modern nation states. Alan Watson's influential writing on legal transplants relates, in part, to this orientation. For him, comparative law is concerned with studying how particular legal systems develop by borrowing legal ideas from other systems (Watson, 1993). The focus is on integrating legal ideas in unified legal systems, not on recognising differences between laws in different systems.

Some recent writers such as Pierre Legrand (1999) and Vivian Curran (1998) have, however, advocated that comparative law should recognise, respect and even protect difference.[5] What kind of difference? There seems no obvious reason to celebrate difference in positive law as such. For the new 'comparatists of difference', the focus is on recognising, even celebrating *cultural difference*, focused on law. Thus, legal culture becomes, in this kind of comparative legal study, a central idea – referring vaguely to the entirety of ways of practising and thinking about law in a certain environment. It seems to point to the range of values, traditions, allegiances and collective interests that surround and inform law in a particular time and place. Legrand, however, talks of legal culture in terms of

3   For fuller discussion and other examples, see Cotterrell (2004).

4   For an indicative summary, see Cotterrell (2003a).

5   In Jacques Vanderlinden's (2002, p. 166) view, the task of comparatists is to 'try to "understand" the Other, in space and time, as deeply as they possibly can'.

4|

mentalités – outlooks, ways of thought, legal world-views – a notion that seems to retain the usual imprecision of the term culture, but may not indicate the full range of matters which, as seen earlier, this term can address.

Why is comparative law becoming central to legal scholarship? First, globalisation (if hard to define uncontroversially) is a reality affecting law in many countries. Even if law is merely a technical instrument, a camp follower of globalisation, the building of globalised technical law and the adapting of local legal variation to transnational demands for uniformity require comparative legal expertise. But the links already suggested between law and culture show that law is more than mere technology. Globalisation creates situations where law is an object of struggle, a prize to be fought for in cultural wars around globalisation. Multinational corporations, nation states and the 'itinerant armies of transnationalism' in commerce, finance, intellectual property and other fields, devote much attention to ensuring a favourable legal climate for the pursuit of their projects abroad. For the foreseeable future, that involves drawing on certain kinds of comparative legal expertise. And, as population flows make ethnic and religious diversity commonplace in nations that once thought themselves unproblematically homogeneous, the need to think of law and culture pluralistically makes comparative legal studies important (Demleitner, 1999). In legal theory, feminism, critical race theory and other developments symbolise the fact that the professional interpretive communities of lawyers are becoming much more diverse, especially in countries such as Britain and the United States.

What all of these indications add up to is the recognition that neither legal systems nor societies can be thought of as unified and integrated in the way that western legal thought has often assumed. A comparative legal perspective is no more than the systematic recognition that law is always fluid, pluralistic, contested and subject to often contradictory pressures and influences from both inside and outside its jurisdiction; that it reflects an always unstable diversity of traditions, interests, allegiances, and ultimate values and beliefs. If the comparative perspective on law was once a view of the exotic legal 'other', or of the 'external relations' of one's own law with the law of other peoples in other lands, now it is a view of transnational legal patterns and of the cultural complexities of law at home. We live in conditions where the law of the nation state must respond to a great plurality of demands from different population groups within its jurisdiction. At the same time, it must respond to powerful external pressures. Legal thought in national contexts is being fragmented *from within* in a new 'jurisprudence of difference' (Cotterrell, 2003b, Chs. 8 and 9), and globalised *from without* in demands for transnational harmonisation or uniformity.

Comparative law today is thus concerned both with seeking similarity (legal harmonisation, or unification) and appreciating difference (between legal ideas, practices, systems and experiences). Similarity is often sought on the level of positive law and with the assumption that law is an easily transferable or changeable technical instrument. The problem of adaptation is seen as essentially a technical, juristic one. But this assumption is mistaken. It applies only to those problems of regulation that are essentially instrumental in character, yet constitute only part of the responsibilities of regulation. Legal positivist or functionalist approaches, which have dominated unification or harmonisation movements among comparatists, are appropriate mainly to those kinds of law that are essentially concerned with instrumental relations (e.g., contract, commercial law). They lack the resources to address regulatory problems that bear on some other aspects of culture.

On the other hand, when comparative law seeks to appreciate legal difference – usually explicitly invoking ideas of culture or legal culture to do so – it runs up against the problem that this article has already identified: that culture is not a single thing, that it is a vague term referring to an indefinite range of aspects of the social. It lacks analytical utility and rigour. So, there is no alternative but to break culture down in some way into elements that can be treated rigorously for the purposes of legal analysis and sociolegal inquiry.

3. Community

In December 2004, in Britain's second largest city, Birmingham, a play staged at its main theatre caused riots. The Asian playwright Ash Kotak wrote

> '*Behzti* (meaning *Dishonour* in Punjabi), the play that caused violent clashes between Sikh protesters and police in Birmingham at the weekend, was closed yesterday. With its scenes of rape and murder taking place within a Sikh gurdwara (or temple), Gurpreet Kaur Bhatti's play offended a vocal conservative group within the [Sikh] community...The playwright should only have to answer to his or her conscience...But the play comes at a particularly sensitive time when religious people from all quarters feel threatened – both by what they perceive as the moral breakdown of society and by others' accusations of religious funda-mentalism.'   (Kotak, 2004)

The writer of the play, a British Sikh herself, critical of aspects of life among Sikhs in the UK, especially those affecting women, was forced into hiding by death threats after the play's opening. The issue of respect for religion was prominent in public discussion of the play and its consequences. So also was freedom of speech, treated as a fundamental value of British society as a whole. Reports dwelt on the sensitivities of minority groups, and also on tensions between different generations of the British Sikh community and between conservative/traditional and progressive/modern sections of it. Meetings were organised between community leaders and concerned artists to discuss freedom of expression. Leading theatres across Britain backed proposals to host readings of the script to demonstrate support for the author's right of artistic expression (Dodd et al., 2004).

One feature of the public debates around this painful episode is particularly relevant to this article: the very weak identification of the various *constituencies* or communities involved. There was much talk of the Sikh community, but also a hazy recognition of fundamental divisions within it. There was, in the debates, the implication of a national community united in support for the value of free speech, as well as a more professionally concerned theatrical community. There was the hint of a feminist constituency, perhaps within the Sikh community but perhaps including some Sikh women along with others of different faiths or none. Ash Kotak's report, quoted above, implies the existence of a community of religious people, from all quarters, with a stake in society's moral well-being; and also the idea of society itself (unspecified in nature or scope) which may or may not be threatened with moral breakdown. Is 'community', which is invoked so often in these debates, no less opaque, vague and slippery a concept than 'culture'?

Used in this way, the answer is clearly yes. It is unsurprising that nothing conclusive arose from all the newspaper coverage and discussion between various groups after the Birmingham distur-bances. Not merely did the constituencies remain undefined, but (partly as a result) the issues remained not clearly distinguished so that they could not be addressed systematically. Some issues were about values and beliefs (the integrity of the Sikh religion, the value of free speech); but there were also questions about gender relations (raised by the play) and about traditional allegiances and customary ways (the changing character of the Sikh minority; the place of minority groups generally in British society). In addition, there were economic and professional interests at stake (the concerns of theatres, actors and playwrights to be able to pursue their work profitably). No doubt other matters could easily be identified.

But, with significant adaptation, the concept of community could be used in a more rigorous way, separating the various kinds of issues and groups indicated. Just as a culture should not be thought of as a 'thing' in positivist fashion, neither should a community. Community indicates a web of understandings about the nature of social relations. It 'exists as something for people to think with' (Cohen, 1985, p. 19) in making sense of social relations and their place in them. But these

6 |

understandings are part of social relations themselves, not separate from them. They constitute social relations in different ways. Community entails that social relations have positive meaning for the participants in them, so that people experience a sense of bonding and mutual interpersonal trust of some kind. Social relations of community have some continuity and intelligibility for those who participate in them, and this ongoing character of the relationships can be identified also by other people who are outside them.

Some sociolegal theorists, notably Georges Gurvitch, have gone to great lengths in categorising numerous kinds of social relations of community (he calls them forms of sociality) expressed through law or addressed by law (Gurvitch, 1947, Ch. 2). But legal theory needs to classify only a *minimal* number of types of community. These can then be considered practically in the contingent ways they combine in actual social life. Isolating this small number of irreducible types of community enables us to ask whether each of them has some special features that law necessarily addresses differently. Do different types of community entail different types of legal regulation, or different challenges for law? In general, I think the answer is yes.

Following this approach, it is possible to distinguish just four abstract types of community: instrumental community, community of belief or values, traditional community and affective community (Cotterrell, 1997). The Birmingham Sikh protests case revealed a *community of belief* among the religious believers involved, as well as among others united by their common commitment to ultimate, overriding values of free speech. It also showed the power of *tradition* which, in some respects, united the Sikh minority, but in other respects divided it generationally. Traditional community refers to social relations based on common experience, environment, history, language or customs. *Instrumental* community is the community formed by people engaged in common or convergent projects or purposes, often economic but not necessarily so. In the Sikh case it is represented in part by the common concerns of those engaged in theatrical work to be able to present plays and perform them. *Affective* community is community based on purely emotional ties (or, sometimes, hostilities). Negatively, it may be a type of community based on dislike or hatred of others. Positively, it is based on affection for those with whom one identifies.

A warrant for separating these four types of community lies in a direct adaptation of Max Weber's sociology. Weber (1978, pp. 24–26) identifies four basic types of social action,[6] irreducibly distinct from each other and comprehensive; he claims that they underlie all social patterns, structures and institutions. The four types of community directly reflect Weber's types of action. Like them, they are ideal types. That is, the types of community are not found in pure form in reality, but are combined in many ways in the patterns of social association in which people live. These combinations can be called networks of community.

How can this idea of community help practical legal inquiry? First, a law-and-community approach frees sociolegal inquiries from the old paradigms of 'law and society' or 'law in society'. Unfortunately, for lawyers and most sociologists, 'society' has come to mean mainly the politically organised society of the nation state. But transnational law, now developing in many forms, must relate to social environments (networks of community) that extend beyond or across nation state boundaries. Equally, pluralistic views of law and culture, discussed earlier, suggest that law needs to be related systematically to diverse social groups and networks in national societies. These groups and networks are linked by aspects of common culture, but by using the typology of community it becomes possible to break down the elements of culture into bonds of shared beliefs or values, bonds formed around common projects, bonds of shared history, customs or experience, and bonds of emotional allegiance. The webs of culture are woven from these distinct and sometimes conflicting elements.

---

6   Weber's types of social action are 'instrumentally rational', 'value-rational', 'affectual' and 'traditional'.

Thinking in terms of law and community is not inevitably conservative or reactionary. Instrumental community almost always looks towards change, achievement and development. It aims at building something new. Traditional community, by contrast, looks towards roots, stability, the familiar, the tried and tested, the customary or the habitual. Affective community, based on pure feelings of attraction or repulsion, is often volatile (Weber thought purely affectual social action was not susceptible to rational interpretation). Community of belief or values can be revolutionary or reactionary, evangelical or fundamentalist, open or dogmatic, tolerant or censorious, stable or unstable. This variety combined in different ways in the types of community also suggests that regulatory problems of community are likely to vary considerably from one type to another. It also suggests that networks of community (combining these types) will often show contradictory regulatory requirements or demands.

Much more work would be needed to identify in a theoretically adequate way the different regulatory challenges posed by these different abstract types of community.[7] Nevertheless, it is possible to make tentative suggestions – exploratory or indicative rather than comprehensive – about relations between modern state law and the four types of community.

There seem good grounds for suggesting that, of these four types, *instrumental community* is usually the easiest to regulate legally. Law regulating common or convergent projects – for example, business enterprises and transactions, trade and financial institutions and other economic networks is usually itself instrumental in character. It often addresses narrowly defined social relations, limited in scope (focused only on the project, deal or enterprise). Sometimes these relations are strictly limited in duration too, lasting only until the project is completed or the deal is fulfilled. Law in this setting may well be the 'camp follower' of globalisation: seen as relatively unproblematic and effective because strictly limited in social aim and scope. Comparatists usually see commercial or contract laws as the types of law easiest to harmonise or unify (Bonell, 1995) or transplant (e.g., Levy, 1950).

On the other hand, systems of values or beliefs are notoriously difficult to define conclusively and so to make the object of direct legal regulation. Thus, *community of belief* is legally problematic. The integrity of religious doctrine is, for example, always at risk from diverse interpretations, schisms or heresies. It can be conclusively defined only when it has authority structures at least as strong, and probably stronger than those of state law (for example, expressed in terms of the 'infallibility' of certain religious leaders in making rulings or issuing interpretations or edicts). State law, as such, can only make rules that *imply* ultimate values; that is, it can create structures of rules that can be plausibly interpreted as collectively expressing these values. But there will usually be room for debate and, because the debates focus on beliefs or values that are objects of commitment, disagreements may become bitter or violent. Even if almost everyone, for example, supports the sanctity of human life as an ultimate value, people may disagree as to whether an unborn foetus is such a life, or whether there is a point at which this value no longer holds when quality of life has deteriorated beyond a certain point (as in cases of patients in a permanent vegetative condition).

This does not mean that state law can or should have no concern with supporting certain values or beliefs. The problem is to recognise the limits in which it can do this and the wisdom of avoiding legal pronouncements on some value controversies. At the same time, it is necessary that, in complex, pluralistic modern societies, law should, on the one hand, firmly defend the right of communities of belief to exist and flourish and, on the other, no less firmly defend as 'universal' the values of personal dignity and autonomy that are essential for all individuals of whatever creed (or none) to co-exist peacefully and with mutual respect.[8] Human rights law is especially relevant,

---

7   For some exploratory studies see Cotterrell (forthcoming, 2006).

8   On this theme, see Selznick (1992, Ch. 4).

8 |

today, to these kinds of legal tasks. But the types of community do not correlate neatly with juristic classifications of law.

Traditional community was associated above with a focus on roots, custom, and familiar ways. Boaventura De Sousa Santos (2002, pp. 177, 296) speaks of 'rights to roots' as well as 'rights to options' as being demanded in the contemporary world. Globalisation makes some people and organisations more mobile than ever; they may be established in one country or several, invest in other countries, and own property or trade in yet others. For these actors, rights to options (unfettered movement) are a priority. But many people – the majority of the world's population – are not easily mobile in this way. Law is faced with demands to protect conditions of co-existence in which people find themselves living, whether by choice or not: traditional locales, practices, languages, physical and social environments. Law's most basic task in this context (performed usually mainly by criminal and tort law) is to prevent the frictions that arise as a result of mere proximity to others.

In some respects this is relatively simple law. Like law protecting and promoting instrumental community, law protecting basic conditions of co-existence has a limited, narrowly defined, even straightforward social task. It is surely no surprise that the most basic aims of criminal and tort (delict) law are not strange to most citizens in many countries. On the other hand, legal conditions of basic co-existence are becoming increasingly complex and contested: local communities seek to defend their local environment against the ravages of commercial exploitation or pollution from outside. Conversely, global environmental concerns (for example, about rain forests or endangered animal species) are pitted against local needs to exploit natural resources in order to provide a means of livelihood or to increase local prosperity. The specific dilemma for law in relation to traditional community is not so much how to devise means to protect rights in this community as how to define the *arenas* of co-existence. In one sense, these arenas are enlarging with globalisation – people are increasingly aware of world-wide common concerns with physical security and with the ecological health of the planet. At the same time, distinctive local environments seem more precious as global forces foster a bland uniformity in the conditions in which people live.

Of all the types of community, *affective community* may be hardest to regulate by state law. Social relations based purely on emotional attachment (or rejection) are very difficult to analyse in legal terms, since law requires precise rules and binding definitions of the meanings of actions and situations. For example, lines between consensual sexual intercourse and rape, between invited intimacy and assault, between attraction and repulsion, are clear in theory, but in practice may be established and moved in ways that law is powerless to rationalise. Law directed against racism or religious intolerance may be faced with levels of bigotry that it simply cannot counter with reason or with normal sanctions. In regulating social relations powerfully shaped by emotion, law seems often to work by indirection, addressing not the unfathomable relationship itself but action resulting from it or demonstrable conditions of domination or vulnerability created through it.

4. Conclusion

A law-and-community approach gives basic theoretical resources for analysing law in social context today. The social universe to which law relates cannot be thought of simply as 'society', a unified, monolithic, politically organised society whose boundaries are those of the nation state. Law now is called on to express the aspirations and provide the security of nation states; of nations within states; of states and nations within larger unions (for example, the European Union); of transnational networks of business and finance; of ethnic groups, adherents of particular religions, carriers of endangered traditions and ways of life, populations in threatened environments, globally mobile entrepreneurs, social movements of many kinds; and of slowly emerging global communities united in concern for the future of the world. Such demands, in total, are beyond the capacity of any currently existing legal order to bear. Nevertheless, they form what will be an agenda for legal studies on a global scale in future.

This article has tried to suggest that culture is fundamentally important to law. In large part this is because invoking the idea of culture hints at many of these agenda items. Comparative study of law is the means by which legal scholarship must gradually expand its horizons to come closer to accepting this agenda. But, despite the legal significance of culture, culture cannot become a legal concept adequate to the theoretical tasks involved. A law-and-community approach, as sketched here, may be a necessary means of working towards theory that can help in distinguishing the regulatory tasks that the future agenda of legal studies will have to address.

References

BARBER, Benjamin R. (1993) 'Global Democracy or Global Law: Which Comes First?', *Indiana Journal of Global Legal Studies* 1: 119.

BONELL, Michael Joachim (1995) 'The UNIDROIT Principles of International Commercial Contracts' in R. Cotterrell (ed.) *Process and Substance: Butterworth Lectures on Comparative Law 1994*. London: Butterworths.

COHEN, Anthony P. (1985) *The Symbolic Construction of Community*. London: Routledge.

COTTERRELL, Roger (1997) 'A Legal Concept of Community', *Canadian Journal of Law and Society* 12: 75.

COTTERRELL, Roger (2003a) 'Comparatists and Sociology' in P. Legrand and R. Munday (eds.) *Comparative Legal Studies: Traditions and Transitions*. Cambridge: Cambridge University Press.

COTTERRELL, Roger (2003b) *The Politics of Jurisprudence: A Critical Introduction to Legal Philosophy*, 2nd edn. London: LexisNexis/Oxford University Press.

COTTERRELL, Roger (2004) 'Law in Culture', *Ratio Juris* 17: 1.

COTTERRELL, Roger (forthcoming 2006) *Law, Culture and Society: Legal Ideas in the Mirror of Social Theory*. Aldershot: Ashgate.

CURRAN, Vivian Grosswald (1998) 'Cultural Immersion, Difference and Categories in US Comparative Law', *American Journal of Comparative Law* 46: 43.

DEMLEITNER, Nora V. (1999) 'Combating Legal Ethnocentrism: Comparative Law Sets Boundaries', *Arizona State Law Journal* 31: 737.

DEZALAY, Yves and GARTH, Bryant G. (1996) *Dealing in Virtue: International Commercial Arbitration and the Construction of a Transnational Legal Order*. Chicago: University of Chicago Press.

DODD, Vikram, BRANIGAN, Tania and HIGGINS, Charlotte (2004) 'Arts and community leaders to discuss freedom of expression' *Guardian* newspaper (London) 22 December.

DURKHEIM, Émile (1982) *The Rules of Sociological Method and Selected Texts on Sociology and its Method* (transl. W. D. Halls). London: Macmillan.

FREEMAN, Michael (1995) 'The Morality of Cultural Pluralism', *International Journal of Children's Rights* 3: 1.

GURVITCH, Georges (1947) *Sociology of Law*. London: Routledge & Kegan Paul.

KOTAK, Ash (2004) 'Not in our gurdwaras: My generation of Asian writers has reason to provoke' *Guardian* newspaper (London) 21 December.

LEGRAND, Pierre (1999) *Fragments on Law-as-Culture*. Deventer: W. E. J. Tjeenk Willink.

LEVY, Ernst (1950) 'The Reception of Highly Developed Legal Systems by Peoples of Different Cultures', *Washington Law Review* 25: 233.

MURPHY, John (ed.) (2000) *Ethnic Minorities, Their Families and the Law*. Oxford: Hart.

RENTELN, Alison Dundes (2004) *The Cultural Defense*. NY: Oxford University Press.

SANTOS, Boaventura de Sousa (2002) *Toward a New Legal Common Sense: Law, Globalization and Emancipation*, 2nd edn. London: Butterworths.

SELZNICK, Philip (1992) *The Moral Commonwealth: Social Theory and the Promise of Community*. Berkeley: University of California Press.

10 |

SHADID, W. and VAN KONINGSVELD, P. S. (2005) 'Muslim Dress in Europe: Debates on the Headscarf', (2005) *Journal of Islamic Studies* 16: 35.

SHAH, Prakash (2005) *Legal Pluralism in Conflict: Coping with Cultural Diversity in Law.* London: Glass House Press.

VANDERLINDEN, Jacques (2002) 'Religious Laws as Systems of Laws: A Comparatist's View' in A. Huxley (ed.) *Religion, Law and Tradition: Comparative Studies in Religious Law.* London: Routledge Curzon.

WATSON, Alan (1993) *Legal Transplants*, 2nd edn. Athens, Georgia: University of Georgia Press.

WEBER, Max (1978) *Economy and Society: An Outline of Interpretive Sociology* (transl. E. Fischoff et al.). Berkeley: University of California Press.

[21]
Lawyers and the Building
of Communities*

When the editors of the *Student Bar Review* asked me to write a special comment for this issue I was delighted to accept. But very soon (I think it was on the plane flying back to London from Mumbai), the obvious, awful question struck me. What can an English professor who has visited India only once (for the 'Enculturing Law' conference at NLSIU Bangalore in August 2005) say that could be relevant in an Indian context? There are important links between our countries and their law – links that made it a huge, never to be forgotten pleasure for me to come to India. But I was afraid of sounding like too many people in the West who, from a position of profound ignorance, try to tell others around the globe what to think or do.

The conference I participated in focused on law's roots in culture and the possibilities and responsibilities of legal education. The paper I wrote for it emphasised the increasing significance of comparative legal studies in the world today and the difficulty – but necessity – of discussing culture as an idea in legal [26] studies. Writing the paper beforehand, at home in London, I knew I would learn far more from visiting India than I could hope to contribute through my visit. That paper, like this comment, had to be concerned with communicating across cultural boundaries while focusing on themes that transcend those boundaries.

A key argument of my conference paper was that 'culture' is complex and elusive (a mix of traditions, values or beliefs, economic activity and conditions, and emotional ties), but it is often unanalysed and taken for granted as long as we stay in what we think of as our own culture. Yet lawyers are increasingly forced to recognise the legal relevance of culture in some sense as they experience an intermingling or confrontation of cultural traditions and values. In Britain this is now very obvious. London, today, is one of the world's most culturally diverse cities. UK law is having to work out its stance on, for example, marriages contracted and ended in different ways in different cultures, diverse adoption practices and patterns of family life, the possibility

* Originally published in (2006) 18 *Student Bar Review* (National Law School of India University), no 1, pp. 25–30. Original pagination is marked in the text.

of 'cultural' defences to legal claims, and the protection of diverse religious practices and sensibilities.[1] Culture – however defined – must be addressed in legal studies, if lawyers are to be sensitive to major social changes, especially those brought about by population movements and the world-wide spread of ideas.

At the same time, globalisation has its impact. While cultural issues are often associated with a demand that *difference* be legally recognised (different religions, customs, languages, lifestyles, values, traditions, aspirations), globalisation is usually associated with *homogenisation* or *harmonisation* (in law, trade practice, etc). World-wide changes drive both globalisation and localisation – or glocalisation, as some have called it. In some ways, the pressure is to lessen differences between countries and legal systems (promoting, for example, the transnational operation of commercial, financial, intellectual property, information technology and human rights law). In other ways, it is towards recognising the value of a diversity of ways of using and thinking about law, and of the responsibilities that attach to legislators and courts to make law a living, valued and respected institution in their particular countries and cultures.

Is the job of being a lawyer something that cuts across all these complexities? Despite all the changes occurring, is there something that stays constant in lawyers' **[27]** responsibilities? It would be nice to think so. But law has been portrayed as a 'destitute camp follower' of globalisation's 'itinerant armies';[2] in other words, law and lawyers' practice are seen as meekly adapting to serve a new transnational economic order. So, one might think, law now is merely *instrumental*, endlessly adaptable to whatever environment lawyers happen to find themselves in. We must be honest and admit that this is what law often is: just a technical means of achieving whatever ends are set for it: the lawyer's job is to be a skilled and reliable *technician*.

A more ambitious role might be that of the lawyer as *political actor*. The role is still instrumental – to get things done – but here it is in the service of goals or values that lawyers may choose for themselves: for example, to help prevent an environmentally catastrophic dam being built; to get compensation for the victims of a man-made disaster; to campaign for better conditions for the poor

---

1   See e.g. S. Poulter, *Ethnicity, Law and Human Rights: The English Experience* (Oxford, 1998); J. Murphy ed., *Ethnic Minorities, Their Families and the Law* (Oxford, 2000); W.F. Menski, 'Muslim Law in Britain' (2001) 62 *Journal of Asian and African Studies* 127; A. Phillips, 'When Culture Means Gender: Issues of Cultural Defence in English Courts' (2003) 66 *Modern Law Review* 510.

2   Cf. B.R. Barber, 'Global Democracy or Global Law: Which Comes First?' (1993) 1 *Indiana Journal of Global Legal Studies* 119: 'Law has always been the destitute camp follower of the itinerant armies of transnationalism.'

by asserting rights on their behalf; to get prisoners out of Guantanamo Bay, or off death row; or to use law to help to undermine caste, class, race, religious, sexual-orientation or gender discrimination.

I would like to go beyond these expressions of lawyers' roles and responsibilities, very important though they are. I think the lawyer's central role is to contribute to the building and strengthening of communities. This may seem a strange idea because a dominant view is that lawyers primarily serve *individual* clients (including corporations). But lawyers get a bad press because of the instability of their focus on individual clients: they serve clients by serving the legal system, but they try to make the legal system serve the client. There is a potential contradiction there. Where, as in the US legal system, the client-focus is often very strong, the image of the lawyer can be that of a 'hired gun'. The hired-gun role is basically the technician role, but added to the neutral idea of technicality is an aggressive, confrontational, sociopathic, gunfighter image. No-one who cares about law as a profession can fail to note that something has gone badly wrong when lawyers are thought of in this way.

If, on the other hand, we think of the lawyer's role as being to serve the community, it is possible to stabilise the difficult balance of responsibility to the individual client and responsibility to the legal system. What is a legal system? Surely it is nothing if not the regulatory structure of a community of some kind – the rules needed to guarantee a minimum of stability and order in communal life and to define social relations of community. The lawyer's responsibility to **[28]** individual clients is to protect their place in the structures of community (but also to inform them of their legal responsibilities to the community and to help them fulfil those responsibilities).

What links us (you, if you are a law student, and me, a law professor) is, most directly, legal education. I have taught law for more than thirty years; you are (or perhaps were) a consumer of legal education. We are, I hope, jointly interested in asking: what kind of lawyers does legal education produce and what sort should it produce? In a book store in Kerala last August I found Gandhi's writings about lawyers.[3] I confess that I had not read them before. He wrote passionately about the importance of the lawyer's role in ending disputes – if possible, by negotiating settlements, bringing the parties together and showing them an honourable way out of their conflict. On this view, litigation and the need for a court decision may often be, for the lawyer, an admission of social failure.

A few years ago, before encountering Gandhi's thoughts on lawyers, I wrote an article about the primacy of the lawyer's role in what I called the 'routine

---

3   M.K. Gandhi, *The Law and the Lawyers* (S.B. Kher ed.) (Ahmedabad, 1962).

structuring' of relationships, transactions, institutions and organisations.[4] Lawyers get a bad press because many members of the public (certainly in Britain) associate them mainly with litigation and with criminal prosecution and defence; in other words with things going wrong in society, rather than going right. Lawyers are widely seen as parasitic on social pathology. Yet empirical sociolegal research highlights the pervasive role of lawyers in setting up deals and negotiating understandings (contracts, corporate structures, etc.), defining lines of authority (constitutions, regulations, etc.), making provision for future contingencies (wills, trusts, contracts, etc.), limiting risks, facilitating projects, encouraging trust, and so on. In other words, it shows them helping to build networks of community and co-operation. What lawyers do in this way is often what Gandhi thought they should do. Often it involves great technical skill, bluff, tact, foresight, psychological insight, hard-headed practicality and the carefully calculated use of legal pressures to make the parties see a way to peace.

Routine structuring is not just another aspect of lawyers' instrumental role (getting things done, making the wheels turn). It also has a moral aspect. Lawyers should be *moral entrepreneurs*, and this is what I really mean by building community. In our contemporary multicultural societies, different religions somehow have to co-exist. So must different customs and traditions, allegiances [29] and affections, aspirations and projects. And all these have to confront often rapid economic change. Law has to serve many different networks of community including commercial and financial networks and enterprises; ethnic, kinship, religious or linguistic groups; urban populations and rural populations; cities, towns and villages. The nation is made up of all of these, and the nation itself is sometimes seen as a network of community, though often with a fluctuating, unstable basis – as an economic commonwealth, a focus of emotional patriotism, the haven of certain values or beliefs, or just a territory given identity by geography or the shared historical experience of its population.

All networks of community ultimately depend on interpersonal trust among their members for their survival, and trust can be of different kinds for different types of communal bonds. Business communities no doubt need honesty, fair dealing and good faith to some degree among their members to be secure; local communities thrive on the courtesy and mutual consideration of neighbours; religious communities rely on their members' integrity, sincerity of belief and mutual identification. Families and friendship groups flourish where there is empathy, and mutual care and concern. The law of the state, of course, plays a variable and sometimes only very limited role in supporting these and other

---

4 R. Cotterrell, 'Subverting Orthodoxy, Making Law Central: A View of Sociolegal Studies' (2002) 29, *Journal of Law and Society* 632.

moral bases of community. It does so often in a negative way, by fixing limits of conduct beyond which individuals must not go; limits which are needed to prevent the most blatant contraventions of community morality. Lawyers' efforts towards routine structuring, properly understood, are, however, a *contribution* in this direction. At least, they should be, if lawyers are to be true to the moral responsibilities of their social status.

When I studied law a long time ago as an undergraduate, no ideas such as the above figured anywhere in my legal education. Law was just a matter of rules to be learned in positivist fashion – as given data from law reports, legislation or statutory instruments. I quickly felt dissatisfied. But it took me a long time to see that if the moral elements of law were to be understood in a realistic way – not as a kind of natural law valid for all times and places (which I did not believe could be discovered) but as a set of legal values appropriate to the time and place – legal studies needed social science. Often, empirical sociolegal studies, on the one hand, and philosophical studies of law's relation to morality, on the other, are regarded as two entirely unconnected fields. But they should be intimately connected.

Sociological ideas – for example about the nature of communities in contemporary societies – are essential for understanding what kinds of moral responsibilities law (and lawyers) can properly be expected to fulfil in any particular society. My favourite sociologist, Emile Durkheim, taught that societies require not just individual economic activity to make them stable and strong, but [30] also solidarity – a commitment of citizens to their society.[5] He thought solidarity was a simple idea. But, in fact, societies like India or the United Kingdom are far too complex to have any single key to solidarity. Their innumerable, complex networks of community require solidarity of many different kinds. Law is needed to support and encourage this solidarity, even if it cannot create it. But social science is required to reveal to lawyers and lawmakers the nature of the networks of community and therefore the kinds of solidarity (or moral bonds) possible in them and the conditions for encouraging these.

Perhaps all this sounds too abstract. While travelling in auto-rickshaws around Bangalore, I often mentally compared this with driving in London traffic. Maybe in both cities you sometimes feel you are taking your life in your hands sitting in the back of a taxi. You can marvel at the way the drivers negotiate seemingly impossible hazards, as traffic swarms around their vehicle (with you in the back of it). There are rules, of course, different in the two cities and probably hard for a newcomer to understand – for example, whether and how to use your horn, when to give way, when and where to pass, how

---

5   E. Durkheim, *The Division of Labour in Society* (W.D. Halls, transl.) (London, 1984).

to calculate a fare. Some of the rules are informal, others official (legal). We could call them all 'law' in a sense, legal frameworks of community. We could also call them aspects of culture. To me, auto-rickshaws are part of the exotic, fascinating culture of Bangalore which I have only recently encountered. Red double-decker buses and black taxis are widely regarded as part of London's culture.

What point am I making? We should not draw any absolute line between law and culture, or between law and community. Law is a continuum of regulation that reaches deep into culture. It is also the regulatory framework of many different kinds of community life. As lawyers, we have a responsibility to be aware of these roots of law and draw on social science to explain their character.

I look back on my narrow, old-fashioned undergraduate legal education as dry and rather barren. Law comes alive when we recognise what Durkheim thought of as its moral 'soul' – its nature as a regulation of community life. It comes alive also when we focus on law in action as much as 'law in the books'. I first sensed that when I studied legal realism in the final LLB year. Legal education today has a responsibility to show how law can come alive through its moral meaning and its effects in building community. Lawyers, I think, have a primary responsibility to make law come alive in that way – whether in India or Britain and irrespective of cultural differences, however they are understood. It is through accepting this shared responsibility that we can best communicate with each other, recognising and transcending cultural diversity.

Name Index

Trubek, David, 147
Twining, William, 184–6

United Nations, 157
United States, 156, 296, 300, 305, 319, 321, 323, 375
United States Constitution, 188, 258–60, 263–8, 270, 273–4
United States Supreme Court, 109, 326

Van den Brink, Bert, 355
Van der Burg, Wibren, 351, 356, 359
  The Importance of Ideals, 351–61
  passim
Van der Kerchove, Michel, 125
Van Klink, Bart, 332
Vandevelde, Kenneth, 191
Varga, Csaba, 304
Verschuuren, Jonathan, 357
Vico, Giambattista, 294

Waldron, Jeremy, 348
Walzer, Michael
  Spheres of Justice, 68

Watson, Alan, 132, 290–4, 300, 302, 304, 365
Weber, Max, xix, xxiv, xxvi, 6, 7, 17, 19–21 *passim*, 23, 25, 32, 34, 39, 40, 59–60, 62, 105, 106, 110, 122, 136, 145, 149–52, 155, 159, 160, 167, 170–5, 180, 186, 187, 246, 275, 313–4, 324–8 *passim*, 331, 341, 364, 368–9
Weimar Republic, 101, 107
Westermarck, Edward, 20
Whitman, James, 156, 306, 307
Wieacker, Franz, 286, 287, 289
Wiles, Paul, 37, 38
Williams & Glyn's Bank v *Boland* (1981), 193, 200
Witteveen, Willem, 332, 334, 342, 354, 356

Yale, D. E. C., 247

Zimmermann, Reinhard, 287